Brotherhood of the Brave

From Boots to Brass, the Soldiers Who Have Shaped the US Army

Colonel Cole C. Kingseed

AUSA
ASSOCIATION OF THE UNITED STATES ARMY

STACKPOLE BOOKS
Essex, Connecticut

STACKPOLE BOOKS
An imprint of Globe Pequot Publishing Group Inc.
64 South Main Street
Essex, CT 06426
www.globepequot.com

AUSA
ASSOCIATION OF THE UNITED STATES ARMY

An AUSA Book. Published in cooperation with the Association of the United States Army.

British Library Cataloguing in Publication Information available

Library of Congress Cataloging-in-Publication Data

Names: Kingseed, Cole C. (Cole Christian), 1949– author
Title: Brotherhood of the brave : from boots to brass, the soldiers who have shaped the US Army / Colonel Cole C. Kingseed.
Description: Essex, Connecticut : Stackpole Books, [2026] | Summary: "In these colorful, insightful profiles, Colonel Cole C. Kingseed, former chief of military history at West Point, tells the stirring history of the US Army through the soldiers, from boots to brass, who have fought, led, bled, and died for their country since 1775. This book spotlights the warriors and the wars that have defined the US Army for 250 years"—Provided by publisher.
Identifiers: LCCN 2026010016 (print) | LCCN 2026010017 (ebook) | ISBN 9780811778503 paperback | ISBN 9780811778510 epub
Subjects: LCSH: United States. Army | United States—History, Military | LCGFT: Biographies
Classification: LCC U52 .K56 2026 (print) | LCC U52 (ebook)
LC record available at https://lccn.loc.gov/2026010016
LC ebook record available at https://lccn.loc.gov/2026010017

To Mary, with all my love.
Devoted wife, extraordinary mother, faithful friend.

Contents

Introduction 1

Chapter 1: Decisions Shaped Generals' Destiny 3

Chapter 2: Revolutionary Strategy 8

Chapter 3: George Washington's Indispensable Officer: Multitalented Hamilton Helped Forge Army, the Nation 13

Chapter 4: Jackson Wins with Luck, Leadership 18

Chapter 5: Mr. Polk's Commanders: Opposites in Many Ways, Taylor and Scott Found Success in Mexico 24

Chapter 6: Winfield Scott's Remarkable Lieutenants 30

Chapter 7: Generals Thrived Under Antebellum Commander 40

Chapter 8: Lincoln and the Army: A Model Civil–Military Partnership 45

Chapter 9: The Emergence of Ulysses S. Grant 53

Chapter 10: A Learned Hero: Student of War Proved Himself at Gettysburg 62

Chapter 11: Grant's Indomitable Buckeyes: Union Leaned Heavily on Leaders from Ohio 67

Chapter 12: Grant Unfiltered: Union Commander Didn't Hold Back When It Came to Other Civil War Generals 72

Chapter 13: President Wilson Selects His Commander 77

Chapter 14: The Fighting Doughboys of the American Expeditionary Forces 82

Chapter 15: Leading from the Front: Senior Commanders Under Pershing Played Key Roles in World War I 91

Chapter 16: Destined for Greatness 96

Chapter 17: No Ordinary Junior Officer: In Style and Temperament, Marshall Showed Early Promise 101

Chapter 18: Patton's Hawaiian Ordeal: Even a Legend Can Learn from His Mistakes 106

Chapter 19: Eisenhower and MacArthur: Toil, Trouble, and Turbulence in the Philippines 111

Chapter 20: The George C. Marshall Way of Leadership 116

Chapter 21: Marshall's Men 121

Chapter 22: An Uneasy Alliance: Eisenhower, Montgomery Managed Allied Victory Despite Personal Differences 130

Chapter 23: Eisenhower: The Indispensable Commander 135

Chapter 24: Ike's Three Great Decisions That Shaped World War II 143

Chapter 25: They Liked Ike: Eisenhower Was Close to a Chosen Few Soldiers 153

Chapter 26: Embracing the Media: Eisenhower Worked With, Not Against, the Press 159

Chapter 27: As Eisenhower Viewed Them 164

Chapter 28: The Extraordinary Feats of Three "Ordinary" Soldiers 170

Chapter 29: Restoring the Fighting Spirit 178

Chapter 30: A "Formidable Array of Warriors" 188

Chapter 31: World War II's Airborne Commanders: The Stuff of Instant Legend 198

Chapter 32: World War II's Triumvirate of Dual-Theater Commanders 208

Chapter 33: Army Commanders in the Pacific: Forgotten Warriors 220

Chapter 34: World War II's Army Group Commanders: Travails and Triumphs 232

Chapter 35: Marshall's Mavericks: Colorful Commanders Handpicked to Lead Army in World War II 245

Chapter 36: Class Action: West Point's 1909 Graduates Pivotal to Prosecuting World War II 251

Chapter 37: "So That They Can Understand": World War II Correspondents Informed the Homefront 256

Chapter 38: Ernie's Heroes—Correspondent Loved Frontline Troops: They Loved Him Back 261

Chapter 39: "Ties of Great Strength": Infantry Soldiers Forge Unique Kinship in Battle 266

Chapter 40: The Big Red One Loses Its Commander 270

Chapter 41: Heroism Outlasts Prejudice: The Saga of Vernon J. Baker 278

Chapter 42: Patton Pains Eisenhower: Generals Were Old Friends but Parted Ways 286

Chapter 43: The Pacific War: The US Army's Forgotten Theater of World War II 292

Chapter 44: Will the Real MacArthur Please Wade Ashore? 298

Chapter 45: What Free Men Will Do: Seventy-Five Years on, Lessons from D-Day for Today's Army 303

Chapter 46: The GI Generation: Valor Was Common Throughout the Ranks 308

Chapter 47: Gavin—"Soul of the Airborne": Young World War II General Commanded Troops' Respect 313

Chapter 48: All-American Lieutenants: The Eighty-Second Airborne in Normandy. 318

Chapter 49: Fall from Grace: The Parallel Careers of General of the Army Douglas MacArthur and Major General George B. McClellan 324

Chapter 50: Tarnished Legacies: Disgraced Generals Viewed Through Lens of History 337

Chapter 51: A Commander's Pride: World War II Pioneer Led Postal Battalion 342

Chapter 52: First Hispanic Four-Star Exemplified Warrior Spirit 347

Chapter 53: Intuitive Commanders: Successful Leaders Like Patton and Moore Anticipate Enemy Intentions 352

Chapter 54: Medal of Honor Recipients Beat Prejudice, the Enemy 357

Chapter 55: Beyond the Ia Drang Valley 362

Chapter 56: Team of Two: Moore Is Recognized for Exceptional Service 371

Chapter 57: America's Greatest Battle Captains: Who's Your Pick for Top of the Class? 375

Chapter 58: Women Played Roles in Army from the Start 380

Acknowledgments 385

Introduction

The elusive theme of this book is the subject of leadership. As Dwight D. Eisenhower once stated, "The one quality that can be developed by studious reflection and practice is the leadership of men." The study of military leadership begs several questions: Are leaders born or are they made? Do the times make the leader or does the leader shape the time? What is the role of adversity in a leader's development? Is luck the individual ingredient to accomplish a leader's goals?

Brotherhood of the Brave celebrates the American soldier-leader from the American Revolution to the present day. America's Army has been the sword and shield of the Republic for nearly 250 years. In the forefront of national defense, the US Army has never wavered in serving the nation with dedication, courage, and loyalty. On point is the American soldier whose selfless service in peace and war has fulfilled Gen. George Washington's desire that the nation possess "a respectable Army and as such will be competent to every contingency."

In the following chapters, I deal with warriors, their associations among themselves, and what inspired others to perform. I examine leaders' failures and successes in battle and the role of luck, fame, and training in determining outcomes. The articles are in chronological order by historic events, though some articles are more thematic in nature than individually focused. Others discuss the changing nature of warfare and the profession of arms.

Though I am a soldier and a historian by trade, I am a storyteller by training and inclination. If one drops the two first letters of the word "history," what remains is "story." To tell a story well, one must have a reader or listener to identify with the subject, blemishes and all. I learned from one of my mentors that when you write about soldiers, it is prudent to let them tell their own stories if possible. The principal job of a historian is to place such stories in historical context. The men and women who appear in these pages are ordinary men and women thrown into the crucible of unfathomable chaos in war. I urge the reader to concentrate on not only what happened, but also why it happened.

I write both to instruct and to entertain. As a lifelong student of military history, I examine leaders who make critical decisions under extreme stress in a martial environment. If many chapters focus on the events of World War II, it is because the conflict was so vast in its scope, so encompassing in its magnitude, and so horrific in its casualties that there is still a story to tell. Gens. George C. Marshall, Dwight D. Eisenhower, Douglas A. MacArthur, and George S. Patton appear frequently in the text because they have always intrigued me. So, too, have commanders George Washington, Robert E. Lee, and Ulysses S. Grant. The same is true concerning lesser-known leaders throughout American history as they made their significant contribution to victory or defeat.

As a former professor of history at the United States Military Academy at West Point, New York, I had the opportunity to meet so many veterans of our nation's conflicts. These warriors include Lt. Gen. Jim Gavin of the Eighty-Second Airborne Division, Col. Paul Tibbets who piloted the *Enola Gay* over Hiroshima, Japan; Lt. Col. Hal Moore of the Ia Drang Valley in the Vietnam War, and Capt. Dick Winters of *Band of Brothers* fame. The role of women in war, African Americans and other minorities in combat, and political leaders are also addressed in the following chapters.

As the title indicates, this is a book that spotlights warriors and warfare, both well-known and those who have been lost in history. This book is my tribute to the soldiers and the cause for which they willingly relinquished their youth so that future generations might enjoy the blessing of liberty. It is my sincere hope that a better understanding of their achievements will bridge the gap between their respective generations and the generation now embarking on a voyage through the twenty-first century. In a sense, the study of history and leadership is the explanation of the present. I am, of course, responsible for any errors of commission and omission.

I

Decisions Shaped Generals' Destiny

A DEFINING MOMENT IS THE POINT AT WHICH THE ESSENTIAL NATURE OR character of a person is revealed. As members of the profession of arms, military commanders frequently make critical decisions in the course of their duties. Three commanders stand out as role models for today's army. Over the course of American history, Gens. George Washington, Robert E. Lee, and Dwight D. Eisenhower all faced momentous decisions that ultimately fixed their respective places in history.

If there was an indispensable man in the formation of the United States, it is George Washington. Washington was later characterized by former Virginia Gov. Henry "Light-horse Harry" Lee (Robert's father) as "first in war, first in peace, and first in the hearts of his countrymen." The qualities of Washington's leadership that excited future President Eisenhower were his stamina and patience in adversity, first, and then "his indomitable courage, daring and capacity for self-sacrifice."

In a life of public service, the "Father of His Country" encountered incredible obstacles and challenges to ensure his country became a viable entity, but none defined Washington as a leader of character and moral courage more than his surrender of power and authority at the conclusion of the American Revolution.

With victory secured at Yorktown in 1781 and final arrangements made for the British evacuation of New York in accordance with the Preliminary Treaty of Paris signed on November 30, 1782, Washington would not remain commander in chief for even a month beyond the time all British soldiers had departed New York City on November 25, 1783.

Making arrangements to meet his officers at Fraunces Tavern in New York City on December 4, 1783, Washington raised a final toast and stated, "With a heart full of love and gratitude, I now take leave of you. I most devoutly wish that your latter days may be as prosperous and happy as your former ones have been glorious and honorable."

Having bade farewell to his officers, there was one task remaining for the general to accomplish. From Congress Washington had received his commission on June 15, 1775, and to that body he would return it. He left New York and traveled to Annapolis, Maryland, where Congress had already convened. En route, he dictated a letter on December 20, 1783, to Thomas Mifflin of Pennsylvania, the president of Congress. The reply came immediately, informing Washington that Congress would receive him in the Old Senate Chamber of the Maryland State House on December 23.

With two aides at his side and escorted by Charles Thomson, who had been secretary of Congress when Washington received his commission, Washington presented himself. Mifflin sat in front of Washington, with twenty members of Congress seated on either side of the room. The members of Congress sat silent as Mifflin announced, "Sir, the United States in Congress assembled are prepared to receive your communications."

Washington, who had commanded the Continental army since its inception, spoke slowly but clearly. "Having now finished the work assigned me, I retire from the great theatre of action; and bidding an affectionate farewell to this August body, under whose orders I have so long acted, I here offer my Commission and take my leave of all the employments of public life." Following an exchange of pleasantries, George Washington, Esq., departed the chamber and made plans to return to Mount Vernon for Christmas.

As with Washington, Lee's defining moment was off the battlefield. Having graduated from West Point in 1829, Lee dedicated his entire life to the US Army. Gen. Winfield Scott considered Lee, a hero of the Mexican–American War, the finest officer in service. Scott followed Lee's career carefully and, in October 1859, directed Lee to suppress John Brown's raid on Harpers Ferry, Virginia, now in West Virginia. When Abraham Lincoln was elected president the following year, Lee found himself increasingly involved in the darkest of American tragedies.

With seven states in secession by Lincoln's inaugural, Lee pondered his decision to cast his fate with Virginia or stand by the Union. Lee's private correspondence reveals an officer torn by conflicting emotions as he witnessed the dissolution of the Union that he had served so faithfully. As an army officer, Lee could not envision a greater calamity than the dissolution of the Union. As he wrote in January 1861, "The framers of our Constitution never exhausted so much labor, wisdom, and forbearance in its formation . . . if it was intended to be broken up . . . at will. . . . It is idle to talk of secession." But what would Virginia do?

The officers in Lee's Second US Cavalry stationed on the Texas frontier turned to their commander to declare his intention once Texas voted to secede in February 1861. Lee responded, "I shall never bear arms against the Union, but it may be necessary for me to carry a musket in defense of my native state, Virginia, in which case I shall not prove recreant to my duty." As Lee pondered his decision, he received instructions to report to Scott.

One can contemplate Lee's anguish as he met with Scott in his headquarters in Washington, DC. Scott and Lee conversed for three hours; neither officer ever revealed what they said. Did Scott offer command of the army that was being mobilized to repress the rebellion? Conflicting accounts of historians have debated this point ad infinitum. What is undeniable, however, is that Lee tendered his resignation from the US Army to Scott two days later, on April 20, 1861.

Why did Lee resign his commission? Biographer Douglas Freeman offers this explanation: "The spirit of Virginia had been alive in his heart every hour of his life. . . . He was a United States officer who loved the army and had pride in the Union, but something very deep in his heart kept him mindful that he had been a Virginian before he had been a soldier."

In his final years, Lee was frequently asked whether he harbored any regrets. In a letter to his former chief of cavalry, Lee stated, "I did only what my duty demanded. I could have taken no other course without dishonor."

In the course of a life in which he reached the pinnacle of his profession, both as a soldier and as a statesman, no decision defined Eisenhower more than the decision to launch D-Day on June 6, 1944. D-Day, the Allied invasion of Nazi-occupied northwest Europe, was the most complicated military operation in history. Due to climatic conditions, Eisenhower, now Supreme Commander of the Allied Expeditionary Force (AEF), realized there were only three days in early June 1944 when conditions were optimal to launch the invasion. If the invasion was delayed, it would be another two weeks before the AEF would sail.

Eisenhower had already postponed the invasion from June 5 when he convened his commanders and staff at his headquarters at Southwick House outside Portsmouth, England, the evening of June 4. Polling his commanders, there was no unanimity. British Gen. Bernard Law Montgomery, Eisenhower's ground forces commander, recommended proceeding, but Air Chief Marshal Sir Trafford Leigh-Mallory thought the invasion was risky, even though the meteorologist noticed a short break in the weather. Adm. Sir Bertram Ramsay informed Eisenhower that the order must be given in the next half hour if Operation Overlord was to take place on June 6.

The decision rested solely on Eisenhower. In his own words, "The mighty host was tense as a coiled spring, ready for "the moment when its energy should be released, and it would vault the English Channel." The commanders looked to Eisenhower, who weighed the decision to launch the invasion.

As he gazed at his chief, Lt. Gen. Walter Bedell Smith, Eisenhower's chief of staff, noticed the loneliness and isolation of high command. According to historian Stephen Ambrose, at 9:45 p.m. on June 4, Eisenhower said, "I am quite positive that the order must be given." Eisenhower then postponed making a formal declaration to launch the invasion and directed a final meeting the following morning for his announcement.

Six hours later, the commanders reconvened. There was still time to postpone D-Day if the weather did not improve. No additional weather predictions would be available until morning. According to Ambrose, Eisenhower queried his commanders and then said quietly but clearly, "Okay, let's go." With those words, Eisenhower fixed his place in history. In that instant, he went from one of the most powerful men in the world to the most powerless man in the world, putting the fate of Western democracy on the shoulders of the soldiers, sailors, and airmen of the AEF, whose behavior he could direct, but not control.

Adversity Reveals Character

In examining how these battle captains met their greatest challenges, the inescapable conclusion is that in times of crisis, adversity does not build character, it reveals it. For Washington, civilian control over the military establishment became the bedrock of the fledgling republic. To paraphrase Freeman, his foremost biographer, Lee's character was based in his unquestioning response to duty. To Eisenhower, difficult choices required isolation, for as he later wrote to his wife, Mamie, "Loneliness is the inescapable lot of a man holding such a job."

Little did Washington, Lee, and Eisenhower realize what destiny had in store for them.

"Decisions Shaped Generals' Destiny" was originally published in *ARMY Magazine* (February 2020).

2

Revolutionary Strategy

Washington Lost Some Battles but Won the War

Standing six feet, two inches tall, strikingly handsome, and harboring a certain profound dignity and belief in his own unshakable military destiny, Gen. George Washington was undeniably the most indispensable commander on the American side in the War of Independence. Yet history tells us that winning battles was not the key to Washington's greatness. In fact, Washington never displayed a special gift for warfare. To what, then, does one attribute Washington's ultimate success as a commander?

Nominated by Continental Congress member John Adams and appointed commander in chief of the Continental Army, Washington assumed command of the fledgling army in Cambridge, Massachusetts, on July 3, 1775. By any fair accounting, his record from then until the end of the Revolutionary War was a mixture of successes and failures.

Within a year of assuming command, Washington was successful in forcing the British to evacuate Boston. But the following year, he failed to defend New York City, lost his first pitched battle in the Battle of Long Island, and was driven from New York and New Jersey. Near the end of 1776, the American nation bordered on complete collapse.

Two small victories in New Jersey, at Trenton and Princeton (December 1776–January 1777), revitalized the patriot cause. Victory at Trenton made "a bold, resolute [Washington] even more hell-bent" on winning the war, according to Rick Atkinson in his latest book, *The British Are Coming: The War for America, Lexington to Princeton, 1775–1777*. But

British forces under command of Gen. Sir William Howe countered their previous losses during the winter of 1776–1777 by defeating Washington at the Battle of Brandywine, Pennsylvania, and capturing Philadelphia. Washington's subsequent attack at nearby Germantown failed to reverse American fortunes, and the Continental army settled into winter quarters at Valley Forge, Pennsylvania.

When France entered the war in February 1778, Washington failed to interdict the British withdrawal to New York. Three years of relative inactivity in the Hudson Highlands ushered in the final chapter of the war.

In the summer of 1781, with the aid of French ground troops and the presence of the French Navy, Washington successfully moved his army to Yorktown, Virginia, where he engineered the surrender of Gen. Charles Cornwallis and his army on October 19. That victory convinced Great Britain to end American hostilities—and the Virginia campaign concluded active military operation on Washington's front. The years 1782 and 1783 found Washington and his army encamped in the vicinity of New Windsor, New York, while he awaited the diplomatic envoys tasked to negotiate the Treaty of Paris.

In short, Washington lost far more battles than he won—but he won the last battle that assured American independence.

The Strategist

History reveals that Washington was a more adept strategist than he was a tactician. As an army commander, Washington frequently exposed his flanks to enemy attacks, as he did at Brooklyn Heights, New York, and Brandywine, suffering catastrophic defeats in the process. Having survived the New York campaign, no city, save Philadelphia, justified risking his army in pitched battle. Until his army was adequately trained by Baron Friedrich Wilhelm von Steuben at Valley Forge, the commander in chief never abandoned his defensive strategy until France deployed sufficient forces to North America to shift the balance of power in 1781. Hence Washington's reliance on the strategic defensive until he could muster sufficient resources to revert to the strategic offensive.

And Washington understood more than any of his peers that victory in the Revolutionary War largely depended on aid from France, principally the French Navy. Though intent on destroying the British forces in New

York, which Washington viewed as the greatest strategic prize of the war, he saw a strategic opportunity and acquiesced to French desires to shift the focus of the Allied war effort from New York to Virginia, where sea power could win the day.

By his own admission, Washington was a patient commander, but he was quick to seize an opportunity when the situation presented itself. "Patience," he said, "is a noble virtue, and, when rightly exercised, does not fail of its reward."

Thus, August 17, 1781, began what was one of the greatest moments in American history: Washington's decision to effect a change of base and establish a new concentration in the Chesapeake Bay area. "The victory at Yorktown," author Nathaniel Philbrick writes in *In the Hurricane's Eye: The Genius of George Washington and the Victory at Yorktown*, "was improbable at best, but it was also the result of a strategy Washington had been pursuing since the beginning of the French alliance."

Inspiring Leader

As commander in chief of the Continental Army, Washington demonstrated one of the key traits of effective leaders: He learned from his mistakes. Having been bested by Howe in 1776 and 1777, Washington refused to go toe to toe with the British Army until the odds favored the American Army. But it wasn't just his real-time ability to adapt his actions to lessons of war; it was his ability to model surety that made a difference to the revolutionary cause.

Military historian John Shy remarks that it was Washington who brought "the appearance of strength and confidence" to the American Revolutionary War effort. A Continental soldier concurred, writing, "His appearance alone gave confidence to the timid and imposed respect on the bold." In this regard, perhaps, Washington's supreme contribution to American victory was the fact that he kept the Continental Army, the backbone of the revolution, intact throughout the conflict. While the army remained in existence, the fledgling United States maintained hope of defeating the British and gaining political independence.

Washington also possessed a single-minded focus that military officers should be subordinate to civilian authority. No US Army officer, with the possible exception of Gen. George Marshall in World War II, has ever equaled Washington's effectiveness in bridging the gap between the civilian and the military in a wartime environment. With the Continental Congress wavering between bureaucratic ineptitude and radical ideology and beset by lack of support from the individual states, Washington never wavered that Congress must remain supreme.

That Congress must control the army explains why, in March 1783, Washington quashed the Newburgh Conspiracy. With victory assured on the battlefield, rebellious officers had circulated a petition suggesting the army should march to Philadelphia to address certain grievances. Washington took quick and decisive action.

First, he informed Congress; he denounced these "disorderly proceedings" and called a new meeting of the officers for March 15. At that meeting, Washington appealed to the discontented officers not to undertake steps that would "lessen the dignity and sully the glory you have hitherto maintained." As Washington opined, "We should all be considered Congress, Army & as one people, embarked in one cause, in one interest; acting on the same principle and to the same End."

So how should Washington be remembered as a general? Beyond any doubt, he was extraordinarily effective in commanding the obedience and loyalty of the men serving under him and in the halls of Congress.

Douglas Southall Freeman, Washington's foremost biographer, captures his subject's genius this way: "The essential fact of Washington's greatness was his complete dedication of himself to the duties assigned him in 1775. He had told Congress the day he accepted his command, 'I will enter upon the momentous duty and exert every power I possess in their service for the support of the glorious cause.'" That fixity of purpose characterized Washington's every movement in the deep recesses of his soul.

Though Washington agonized endlessly, he could always wage war better against Great Britain because he was not at war with himself. Simply put, another source of Washington's greatness was his self-mastery of mind and spirit. Once he mastered himself, Washington could then motivate and master his men. One of Washington's most repeated adages was "Discipline is the soul of an army." That dictum applied to Washington as well.

Not surprisingly, in April 2012, Washington was named Great Britain's greatest military foe in a contest organized by that country's National Army

Museum. Washington captured 45 percent of the final vote. Stephen Brumwell, a British-born author and specialist on eighteenth-century North America who championed Washington's cause, said Washington scored highly as an enemy on three key grounds: the immense scale of damage he inflicted on the British Army and British Empire—the most jarring defeat Britain ever suffered; his ability to not only provide inspirational battlefield leadership but also work with civilian authority whose support was critical to battlefield success; and the kind of man he was.

But here, Washington gets the final word. Reflecting on his legacy, Washington confessed amid dark days of 1776 to 1780, "You ask how I am to be rewarded for all this? There is one reward that nothing can deprive me of, and that is the consciousness of having done my duty with the strictest rectitude, and most scrupulous exactness, that if we should, ultimately, fail in the present contest, it is not owing to the want of exertion in me."

There lies Washington's true greatness.

"Revolutionary Strategy" was originally published in *ARMY Magazine* (April 2020).

3

George Washington's Indispensable Officer

Multitalented Hamilton Helped Forge Army, the Nation

The magnitude of Alexander Hamilton's feats in the short span of his remarkable career has overshadowed many facets of his life: member of the Continental Congress, principal author of the Federalist Papers and first treasury secretary. Contemporary observers tend to concentrate on Hamilton's fatal duel with Vice President Aaron Burr on July 11, 1804, but one aspect of Hamilton's extraordinary career has received scant attention—his military service as an officer in the Continental Army, precursor of the US Army.

Born on January 11, 1755, or 1757, in Nevis in the British West Indies, Hamilton immigrated to North America as a teenager and enrolled in King's College in New York City. Hamilton had always dreamed of heroism and martial glory, writing as a fourteen-year-old, "I wish there was a war."

Gaining notoriety as the author of revolutionary pamphlets in New York City, Hamilton soon parlayed his fame into a military appointment from the New York Provincial Congress. In early 1776, he received his commission as captain of an artillery company to help defend the colony. A fellow officer described the young captain as "a mere stripling, small, slender, almost delicate."

Hamilton immediately displayed an independent streak by spurning offers from general officers, including Maj. Gen. Nathanael Greene and William Alexander, Lord Stirling, to serve as their military aide.

Hamilton's baptism by fire occurred in Gen. George Washington's New York campaign in 1776. Fearless in battle, Hamilton covered the retreating Continental Army soldiers with artillery fire as they withdrew from the Hudson Highlands to the banks of the Delaware River in New Jersey. The young captain again distinguished himself during the twin battles of Trenton and Princeton, New Jersey, at which time he came to Washington's attention.

Member of the Family

Three weeks after the Battle of Princeton, in January 1777, Washington invited Hamilton to join his staff as his aide-de-camp. Though he craved battlefield distinction, Hamilton accepted Washington's offer, partly because the assignment carried with it a promotion to lieutenant colonel. From the beginning, however, Hamilton realized that postwar political glory would not go to a staff officer, but to a genuine heroic commander in the field.

As a member of Washington's "family," Hamilton served primarily as the commander in chief's personal secretary and liaison to subordinate commanders, including Maj. Gen. Horatio Gates, Maj. Gen. Charles Lee and the Marquis de Lafayette. In reality, Hamilton expanded his role from secretary to de facto chief of staff, after he reorganized Washington's headquarters and managed all Washington's personal correspondence with the Continental Congress. Even Washington's other aides quickly recognized Hamilton's organizational ability and his facility with a pen.

In one aspect, Hamilton stood alone among Washington's aides. According to Hamilton's principal biographer, Ron Chernow, Hamilton was the only member of Washington's inner circle "who felt competitive with the general or could have imagined himself running the army."

Not surprisingly, Hamilton's relationship with his commander in chief remained testy at best. Despite his young aide's brilliant performance as staff coordinator and secretary, Washington repeatedly spurned Hamilton's requests for a field command. As Washington's most capable aide, Hamilton was simply too essential to the commanding general to be transferred to a tactical command.

It was inevitable that two headstrong officers would clash. On February 16, 1781, the showdown occurred when, in Hamilton's words, "the General . . . accost[ed] me in a very angry tone." Washington stated, "Col. Hamilton . . . you have kept me waiting at the head of the stairs these ten minutes. I must tell you, sir, you treat me with disrespect." In a letter to his father-in-law Maj. Gen. Philip Schuyler, Hamilton recounted that he replied, "I am not conscious of it, sir, but since you have thought it necessary to tell me so, we part."

Martial Glory

Though Washington later apologized for his outburst of temper, the commanding general acceded to Hamilton's request for a field command. In July 1781, Washington presented Hamilton with command of a light infantry battalion. The timing was fortuitous, as Washington and his Continentals departed their New York encampment on September 7 for Virginia in the hope of destroying British Gen. Lord Charles Cornwallis and his army. Hamilton arrived at Williamsburg, and, on September 29, he joined Washington's siege lines surrounding the village of Yorktown.

Aided by French engineers, the Franco–American Army started bombarding the British entrenchments on October 9. A week later, only two British redoubts stood in the way before Washington could force Cornwallis's army to capitulate. The commanding general directed an immediate attack to capture the two redoubts, the key to the British defenses. Washington assigned a French brigade to take one redoubt and an American brigade under the command of the Marquis de Lafayette to capture Redoubt 10.

Hamilton appealed to his commander to allow him to lead the Continental brigade to seize the redoubt closest to the York River. Washington validated Hamilton's claim of seniority, giving Hamilton his last opportunity to achieve battlefield glory. Hamilton's capture of Redoubt 10 on October 14 catapulted Hamilton to legendary status as a legitimate war hero. In a sense, the Battle of Yorktown "made" Alexander Hamilton. Cornwallis surrendered on October 19, and active military operations mostly ceased until the Treaty of Paris was signed in September 1783.

Political Career

With the hostilities concluded, Hamilton returned to New York, pursued a law degree and became actively involved in the Empire State's politics. Still, service to Washington beckoned and, in the spring of 1783, Hamilton chaired a committee that outlined a detailed report to Congress that

Washington called "Sentiments on a Peace Establishment." In the report, Washington also requested a small garrison to be stationed at West Point, New York, which the future president considered the "key of America."

Hamilton's political career goes beyond the scope of this chapter, but Hamilton reemerged as a military staff officer in 1794 when President Washington suppressed the Whiskey Rebellion. The insurrection in western Pennsylvania constituted an armed protest against the excise tax on domestic distilled spirits. To quell the disorder, Washington issued a call for obedience to the law and dispatched the militias of Pennsylvania, New Jersey, Virginia, and Maryland. It fell to Hamilton to organize the force and outfit the army. Fortunately, the rebellion fizzled when the insurgents viewed the militias at its doorsteps.

Washington relinquished the presidency in 1797, and John Adams assumed the executive office. When the undeclared, so-called Quasi-War with France erupted in 1798 over improper diplomatic overtures by the final French revolutionary government, the directory, and seizure of American merchant vessels by French warships, Adams requested that his predecessor command a provisional army being organized in the event of an armed invasion by France.

Now well into his retirement at Mount Vernon in Virginia, Washington accepted Adams's invitation, provided that as commander in chief of the provisional army, he would select his most senior officers.

Because he viewed Hamilton as too ambitious, Adams attempted to persuade Washington to appoint either Maj. Gen. Henry Knox or Brig. Gen. Charles Cotesworth Pinckney as his inspector general and second in command. Washington refused to budge. Reiterating his demand that the commander in chief would select his three major generals, Washington nominated Hamilton as inspector general. Adams approved Washington's preconditions and submitted the nominations for general officers to the Senate as Washington outlined.

Why did Washington nominate Hamilton as the senior major general when Lt. Col. Hamilton was inferior in rank to Knox during the recent conflict? Despite his personal affection for Knox, "Washington did not now believe that present position should be gauged by earlier grade in an army that for full fourteen years had been inactive," Washington biographer Douglas Freeman wrote in *George Washington, Volume VII: First in Peace.*

More significant to Washington's decision was the hope that in the organization of the provisional army, "former rank will be forgot; that, among the fit and chosen characters, the only contention will be, who shall be foremost in zeal at this crisis, to serve his country in whatever situation circumstances may place him," Freeman recounted. In Washington's estimation, Hamilton was the proper man for the job.

Henceforth, Hamilton was known as General Hamilton. The remainder of 1798 saw Hamilton supervising every aspect of the provisional army. The crisis with France dissipated within two years, and the provisional army was later disbanded.

Two centuries after Hamilton's death on the dueling fields of Weehawken, New Jersey, his unbridled political ambition still clouds his true contributions to today's army. As Washington's aide-de-camp during the American Revolution, Hamilton emerged as the prototype of a modern chief of staff. By the turn of the eighteenth century, Hamilton had formulated his vision of the importance of a more professional military structure to free the country of its reliance on state militias. Such views did not come to fruition in Hamilton's lifetime, due in no small part to the national prejudice against large standing armies that characterized European monarchies.

In a series of letters and in consultation with Washington, Hamilton also advocated the establishment of a formal military academy. Such a school would develop highly trained officers specializing in military science, engineering, infantry, and cavalry tactics. "This is an object I have extremely at heart," Hamilton declared. In 1802, under President Thomas Jefferson's administration, the US Military Academy was founded at West Point.

In the final analysis, Hamilton served his country and the army best under Washington's guiding hand, first as an aide to the Continental Army's commander in chief and later as the chief financial adviser to the president of the United States. Once Washington left the scene, Hamilton's ambition frequently affected his judgment and alienated his colleagues. Still, Hamilton should be remembered as one of the army's premier advocates and visionaries as well as Washington's most indispensable officer.

"George Washington's Indispensable Officer" was originally published in *ARMY Magazine* (November 2021).

4

Jackson Wins with Luck, Leadership

FOUGHT TWO WEEKS AFTER DIPLOMATS SIGNED THE TREATY OF GHENT in Belgium on Christmas Eve 1814, Maj. Gen. Andrew Jackson's improbable victory over experienced British troops at the Battle of New Orleans on January 8, 1815, constituted the greatest American land victory of "America's Second War of Independence," the War of 1812. How could such a polyglot force of American backwoodsmen, army regulars, "freemen of color," state militia, and Jean Lafitte's Baratarian pirates defeat British regulars so decisively? A number of components contributed to the American victory, but Jackson's generalship proved the determining factor.

Jackson was born near the border of North Carolina and South Carolina in 1767. Historian Stephen E. Ambrose once described Jackson as a distinctly "American creation, a citizen soldier serving as a general officer." As a fourteen-year-old captured American soldier, Jackson refused to polish a British officer's boots, and the irate officer slashed him with his sword across the hand and forehead. Jackson's hatred of the British stemmed from that incident.

Two decades later, Jackson became a successful lawyer and prominent slaveholder, and he served in the US House of Representatives and in the Senate. In 1802, he was elected major general of the Tennessee militia. It was in this capacity that Jackson fought two successful campaigns against the Creek Native Americans in 1813 and 1814. To show its appreciation, the US War Department appointed Jackson to command the Seventh Military District, which comprised Tennessee, the Mississippi Territory and Louisiana.

Following a subsequent campaign in which he defied orders from the War Department and seized Pensacola, Florida, from the Spanish, Jackson marched to Louisiana, where he correctly predicted that the British would mount a spirited offensive to seize New Orleans. The Crescent City controlled the lower Mississippi Valley, which provided ready access to the interior of the North American continent.

The War of 1812 commenced when President James Madison, on June 18, 1812, signed the declaration of war that Congress had presented him. After two years of hostilities, the defeat of Napoleon in 1814 offered Britain an opportunity to make one final push to influence the peace negotiations. Already entrenched in Canada, Britain sought "first, to obtain command of the embouchure of the Mississippi, so as to deprive the back settlements of America of their communications with the sea." Maj. Gen. Sir Edward Pakenham, brother-in-law of the Duke of Wellington, commanded the British forces destined to participate in the Battle of New Orleans. Under his direct command were nine thousand veterans.

Spurred on by a dispatch from New Orleans's committee of public safety that informed him of the British threat to the Gulf Coast, Jackson arrived in the city on December 1, 1814. Within days, he responded decisively and issued a series of proclamations, the most significant of which read, "Major General Andrew Jackson, commanding the Seventh United States Military District, declares the city and environs of New Orleans under strict martial law."

The British initiated the fighting around New Orleans when Pakenham conducted an amphibious landing at Lake Borgne, east of New Orleans, on December 13. Ten days later, the leading elements of his army were within nine miles of the city. Maj. Gen. John Keane commanded the British advance guard that encamped on the Villere plantation, just east of the Mississippi River.

Jackson immediately sprang into action. He later wrote to Secretary of War James Monroe, "Perfectly convinced of the importance of impressing an invading enemy in the first moment of his approach with an idea of spirited resistance, I lost no time in making preparations to attack him that night." Refusing to surrender the initiative to the enemy, Jackson marched some 1,800 men toward the British encampment under cover of darkness and launched a surprise night assault against Keane's forces.

The march from New Orleans took two hours. Old Hickory initiated his attack with an artillery barrage and then ordered an infantry assault at several points of the British line. The battle lasted most of the night. Old Hickory claimed victory and reported to the War Department, "The result equaled my expectations." Falling back toward New Orleans, Jackson then constructed a strong defensive position on both sides of the Mississippi River. East of the river, Jackson's line lay behind the banks of the Rodriguez Canal. The canal bordered one side of the Chalmette plantation and ran between a low levee on the Mississippi River and a cypress swamp. With the assistance of the citizens of New Orleans, the American force strengthened the canal with a shoulder-high mud rampart strong enough to withstand concentrated cannon fire.

Pakenham arrived in front of the "Jackson Line" the day after Christmas and immediately resolved to move against the American works. On December 28, Jackson began repelling a series of probing attacks. Three days later, Pakenham inched his own line within three hundred yards of Jackson's defensive works and constructed formidable earthworks of his own. As soon as British reinforcements arrived on New Year's Day 1815, Pakenham commenced an intense artillery bombardment that had virtually no effect on the American line. The American artillerymen delivered more punishment than they received. By the time the bombardment ended, the Americans had silenced or destroyed all the British cannons. Pakenham pulled back and then prepared to assault the American positions on both sides of the river, with the main attack against Jackson's line on the Chalmette front.

Jackson correctly surmised that Pakenham planned to strike his fortifications east of the river, consisting of four thousand men, along the Rodriguez Canal. To strengthen his battle line, he constructed a small redoubt adjacent to the riverbank from right to left; Jackson employed 430 members of the Seventh Infantry Regiment, 740 Louisiana militiamen and others, five hundred members of the Kentucky military, 1,600 Tennessee militiamen, and 250 Louisiana militiamen.

On the evening of January 7, 1815, Jackson's scouts reported intense activity in Pakenham's camp, indicating an attack the next morning. While a strong British force under Col. William Thornton crossed the Mississippi to assault the American fortifications, Pakenham planned a coordinated attack against Jackson's primary position about a half mile away. The British plan called for the main body of Pakenham's army to conduct a coordinated daylight attack against the Jackson line, with Maj. Gen. Samuel Gibbs advancing on the right and Keane in a position to support the main attack. Pakenham held a reserve force commanded by Maj. Gen. John Lambert ready to exploit any success.

The battle started at dawn on January 8. Pakenham's plan disintegrated from the beginning. Heavy fog covered the plain between the combatants' lines, and Pakenham discovered that many of his troops lacked the necessary ladders to cross the ditches and scale the American rampart. With little hesitation, Pakenham ordered the attack to commence. On order, thousands of British regulars marched across the stubbled sugarcane field of battle.

As the morning sun dissipated the fog, Jackson ordered his artillery batteries to commence fire. The effect was appalling. Gibbs's column charged forward against Jackson's left and was met with devastating volley fire as rank after rank of Tennessee militia rose and fired. The British advance halted and then wavered. Within minutes, the advancing line crumbled as the survivors broke for the rear.

Pakenham attempted to stem the retreat and called for Keane's Forty-Fourth Highlander Regiment, nine hundred strong, to cross the field diagonally and support Gibbs. Pakenham was everywhere, encouraging his men while musket balls crashed into the head of the British column, leaving two hundred men killed or wounded in a single salvo. A second blast of American grapeshot followed, and Pakenham fell, mortally wounded.

Gibbs, too, was wounded, as was Keane, by the devastating fire. With no senior commander to control the action, Lambert assumed command, but his heart was no longer in the fight. With Pakenham killed and Gibbs—who later died—and Keane wounded, Lambert ordered a general retreat. Many of Jackson's commanders urged a counterattack on the British line, but Jackson refused. Assaulting British regulars by American volunteers was not a prudent course of action. Jackson deemed it better to maintain the safety of the rampart and await the enemy's next move.

The Battle of New Orleans had lasted less than two hours, but the most severe fighting had been confined to less than thirty minutes. Though the British achieved significant success west of the Mississippi River, the crushing defeat of Pakenham's main assault nullified their victory. Minor skirmishing continued in the days that followed, but the British attack on New Orleans failed to meet any of its objectives.

As soon as the guns fell silent, Jackson viewed the carnage in front of the Rodriguez Canal. As he later wrote, "After the smoke of the battle had cleared off somewhat, I saw in the distance more than five hundred Britons emerging from the heaps of their dead comrades, all over the plain, rising up." A week later, Jackson reported that the Battle of New Orleans had produced less than eighty American casualties, including thirteen killed, thirty-nine wounded, and nineteen missing. The British reported their casualties as 291 killed, 1,262 wounded, and 484 captured or missing for a total of 2,037.

Jackson's victory was due in large part to his inspirational leadership, his audacity in keeping the British off-balance, the strength of his defensive line, and his incredible luck. In the final analysis, Old Hickory had inspired the American Army to victory in the climactic battle of the War of 1812, demonstrating once again that, like a hickory branch, Jackson was thin but impossible to break.

While Jackson's victory did not influence the Treaty of Ghent, the Battle of New Orleans forced the British to abide by its terms. Moreover, the Battle of New Orleans settled the fate of Louisiana and of Florida and ended any attempt to block American expansion beyond the Mississippi River. Just as important, Jackson's victory restored American self-respect and enhanced American prestige abroad.

Washington, DC, and the country exulted in Jackson's triumph. Congress extended its gratitude "for the uniform gallantry and good conduct conspicuously displayed against the enemy . . . and thereby obtaining a most signal victory over the enemy, with a disparity of loss, on his part, unexampled in military annals." Madison concurred and directed Secretary of War James Monroe to write, "I am instructed by the President to convey to you in strong terms, his approbation of your conduct, and of that of the troops acting under you who have rendered such important services to their country."

Addressing his officers and soldiers for the final time on March 21, Jackson bade farewell and urged his army to "Go, full of honor and wreathed with laurels whose leaves shall never wither. . . . The man who slumbered ingloriously at home during your painful marches, your nights of watchfulness and your days of toil, will envy you the happiness which these recollections will afford."

And then, Andrew Jackson returned to the Hermitage outside Nashville, where destiny awaited.

"Jackson Wins with Luck, Leadership" was originally published in *ARMY Magazine* (November 2021).

5

Mr. Polk's Commanders

Opposites in Many Ways, Taylor and Scott Found Success in Mexico

If there ever was an avoidable war in American history, it surely was the Mexican–American War of 1846–1848. Although the war was conducted in other theaters, such as California and the environs of New Mexico, the principal areas of operation centered in northern and central Mexico.

Regardless of President James Polk's motives for initiating it, the conflict brought to the forefront two American commanders: Maj. Gens. Zachary Taylor and Winfield Scott. "Comparisons between these two men are actually idle, as each had a different set of circumstances facing him," military historian John Eisenhower wrote in his 1989 survey of the war, *So Far from God: The US War with Mexico, 1846–1848*.

Taylor proved more popular with the US Army as well as with the American public that flocked to Taylor's colors as he marched his Army of Occupation in the disputed territory between the Nueces River and the Rio Grande in 1846. In contrast to the self-effacing Taylor, the more pompous Army General in Chief Scott emerged from the conflict as perhaps the most capable commander the United States produced between the American Revolution and the Civil War. The conflict propelled Taylor to the American presidency in 1849. Scott, too, aspired to the nation's highest office, but he was soundly defeated in 1852 by dark horse candidate Franklin Pierce.

Yet neither commander enjoyed Polk's approval by the conclusion of hostilities.

Always protective of his political legacy, Polk, a Democrat, viewed his army commanders with suspicion. When anti-Democrat Whig Party newspapers lauded Taylor's victories at Buena Vista and Monterrey, both in Mexico, in 1846, rumors around the capital convinced Polk that Taylor was "in full chase of the presidency" as a Whig. No worse condemnation could be leveled against anyone in the mind of the incumbent president.

Taylor, who was a brevet brigadier general at the commencement of hostilities, seemed a most unlikely candidate for martial glory in the upcoming conflict between the United States and Mexico. Taylor, however, served with distinction during the War of 1812, the Black Hawk War and the Second Seminole War. In June 1845, Taylor received preparatory orders to amass two thousand troops at Fort Jessup, Louisiana, and march to Texas in the aftermath of the US annexation of the Republic of Texas. The southern border of Texas was ill-defined. Mexico considered the border as the Nueces River. The Polk administration viewed the southern border of Texas as the Rio Grande River.

On January 13, 1846, Polk dispatched Taylor to "a position on or near the east bank of the Rio del Norte [Rio Grande]." Eisenhower wrote that Taylor's advance compelled the Mexican forces to cross the Rio Grande. The first skirmish between Taylor's forces and a Mexican contingent occurred in the disputed territory on April 25, 1846. Two weeks later, Taylor scored two minor victories north of the Rio Grande at Palo Alto on May 8 and Resaca de La Palma on May 9, forcing the Mexican army to withdraw into Mexico proper. Both places are in present-day Texas.

Now that American blood was shed on American soil, Polk requested that Congress declare a state of war between the United States and Mexico. Fueled by the spirit of Manifest Destiny to extend the nation's borders to the Pacific Ocean, Polk's war resolution passed both chambers of Congress with overwhelming majorities. The president signed the declaration on May 13, 1846.

Abraham Lincoln, freshman Illinois congressional representative and vocal critic of the chief executive, later introduced eight "Spot Resolutions" to force Polk to admit that Mexico, not the United States, held jurisdiction to the actual "spot" where the war began. Lincoln's efforts proved fruitless as virtually every region of the United States hastily embraced

"Mr. Polk's War," as it was dubbed by Whig newspapers and Polk's political adversaries.

By late summer, Taylor, now a major general, advanced into northern Mexico and achieved a significant victory at Monterrey after fighting from September 21 to September 24. Taylor's exploits were heralded in the press, but Polk and Secretary of War William Marcy turned their attention to Scott's strategy to drive to the Mexican capital via the Mexican port city of Veracruz. Taylor was incensed when he received orders to confine himself to defensive operations. More disturbing to Taylor was the transfer of his best troops, particularly his regulars, to Scott.

The year 1847 dawned with Taylor's army static in northern Mexico. Defying orders from Marcy to remain in defensive positions outside of Monterrey, Taylor took matters into his own hands. Alerted that Mexican Gen. Antonio Lopez de Santa Anna planned to encircle his Army of Occupation's diminished forces at Monterrey, Taylor advanced to meet his opponent.

The subsequent clash between Santa Anna and Taylor at Buena Vista from February 22 to 23, 1847, enhanced Taylor's reputation and proved the decisive engagement of the war in the Northern Theater. Outnumbered three-to-one, Taylor inflicted a crushing defeat on his adversary. In this battle, Col. Jefferson Davis and Capt. Braxton Bragg, two future leaders of the forthcoming Southern Confederacy, distinguished themselves. The following year, Congress approved a third gold medal for Taylor for his victories.

With his victories at Monterrey and Buena Vista, Taylor emerged from the Mexican–American War as a national war hero and an attractive Whig Party candidate for the American presidency. Nicknamed "Old Rough and Ready" for his willingness to share the hardships of his soldiers, Taylor defeated Democratic Party candidate Lewis Cass of Michigan by a small majority in the election of 1848. However, sixteen months after his inauguration, Taylor died on July 9, 1850, from cholera, a bacterial infection of his small intestine.

"Old Fuss and Feathers"

Few American generals enjoyed a more stellar reputation than Scott. A general officer since March 1814 due to his gallantry at the battles of

Chippewa and Lundy's Lane in Canada, Scott assumed the office of commanding general of the US Army on July 5, 1841. Nicknamed "Old Fuss and Feathers" for his immaculate military attire and his attention to detail, Scott posed an imposing figure to all who encountered him. West Point Cadet Ulysses Grant stated that Scott was "the finest specimen of manhood my eyes had ever beheld, and the most to be envied."

No campaign in the Mexican–American War proved more decisive than Scott's campaign that culminated in the capture of Mexico City on September 1, 1847. At Veracruz, Mexico's primary port on the Gulf of Mexico, Scott conducted the first large-scale amphibious assault in American history in March 1847.

Scott then proceeded westward, following the near-identical route of Hernan Cortes, who had conquered the Aztec empire three hundred years earlier. Over the course of the next six months, Scott fought successful battles against Santa Anna at the Mexican cities of Cerro Gordo on April 18, Contreras on August 19, Churubusco on August 20, and Chapultepec on September 13 before marching triumphantly through Mexico City's main square on September 14.

According to historian K. Jack Bauer in his 1974 book *The Mexican War, 1846–1848*, "Few military leaders in American history would have attempted such an undertaking and fewer yet would have done so with an army cut off from its supply bases and reinforcements." In retrospect, it seems incomprehensible how Scott's army of less than 11,000 soldiers could repeatedly defeat far more numerous enemy forces and occupy a fortified foreign capital. Bauer related that Arthur Wellesley, First Duke of Wellington, Europe's most distinguished soldier, proclaimed "[Scott's] campaign was unsurpassed in military annals. He is the greatest living soldier."

Despite his military success in central Mexico, Scott found himself a victim of Polk's displeasure based more on Scott's political leanings than his military achievements. On recommendations from Cabinet members and from some of Scott's own officers, Polk humiliated his victorious general by convening a court of inquiry to address allegations against Scott.

In the interim, the president suspended Scott from further duties as commanding general in Mexico. The court of inquiry proved conclusive, and Scott was exonerated on July 1, 1848. No further action was taken against the victor of Mexico City, and Scott returned home to New York City.

In 1848, Congress requested that Polk order the minting of an appropriate medal in Scott's honor for his victories in central Mexico. In 1855, Scott received a brevet promotion to lieutenant general, a rank that previously had been held only by George Washington. Congress requested that Scott receive full pay and allowance retroactive to March 29, 1847, the day he received the surrender of Veracruz.

Scott retained his post of commanding general of the US Army until November 1, 1861, when he was succeeded by Maj. Gen. George McClellan. Scott split his remaining years between New York City and at the Cozzens Hotel on the grounds of the US Military Academy at West Point, New York. The old warrior succumbed to illness on May 29, 1866, and was laid to rest three days later in a quiet corner of the West Point Cemetery.

Though negotiations between American and Mexican diplomats continued following the fall of the Mexican capital, for all intents and purposes, Scott's campaign concluded large-scale operations between the belligerents. The Treaty of Guadalupe Hidalgo officially ending the war was signed on February 2, 1848.

Grant had the distinction of serving under both Taylor and Scott. In his memoirs, Grant remarked on the similarities and the different command styles between Polk's principal commanders. Taylor, Grant wrote, never wore a regulation uniform, but dressed strictly for comfort. Often ignoring his staff officers, Taylor preferred to view the battlefield through his own eyes. In issuing orders, he used a few well-chosen words to express his intent so plainly that there could be no mistaking it.

Scott proved the antithesis of Taylor in both attire and command style. He always wore all the uniform prescribed or allowed by law. Scott "was precise in language, cultivated a style peculiarly his own; was proud of his rhetoric and not averse to speak of himself in the third person," Grant remembered. Scott saw more through the eyes of his staff officers than through his own. His plans were deliberately and meticulously prepared and fully expressed in orders to subordinate commanders. The orders evidently were prepared with the view that they should be a history of the conflict, Grant recalled.

Despite their opposing characteristics, Scott and Taylor proved to be adroit commanders and brought the Mexican–American War to a successful conclusion. In summarizing the two commanders, Grant opined that Scott and Taylor were "true, patriotic and upright in all their dealings. Both were pleasant to serve under."

"Mr. Polk's Commanders: Opposites in Many Ways, Taylor and Scott Found Success in Mexico" was originally published in *ARMY Magazine* (December 2023).

6

Winfield Scott's Remarkable Lieutenants

Serving under every American president from Thomas Jefferson to Abraham Lincoln, Winfield Scott commanded soldiers in the War of 1812, the Black Hawk War, the Second Seminole War, the war with Mexico, and the American Civil War. In a career that spanned nearly five-and-a-half decades, Scott compiled an enviable record marked by battlefield success, adroit diplomacy, uncanny sagacity, and unabashed egotism. His supreme moment lay in his campaign in central Mexico during the Mexican–American War, culminating in the capture of Mexico City on September 14, 1847.

How did Scott achieve such spectacular success in a campaign that to most observers seemed destined to fail? In addition to his considerable talents of generalship, Scott attributed much of his success to a small corps of junior West Point officers, primarily engineers, who joined his "little cabinet" of military advisors. Scott's cabinet consisted of Col. Joseph G. Totten (the chief engineer for the expedition), Lt. Col. Ethan A. Hitchcock (acting inspector general), Capt. Robert E. Lee, and Scott's son-in-law, Henry Lee Scott (the commander's assistant adjutant general and chief of staff).

Totten headed the contingent from the Corps of Engineers that, in addition to Capt. Lee, included Capt. Joseph E. Johnston, lieutenants of George G. Meade, Gustavus W. Smith, George B. McClellan, and P. G. T. Beauregard. All of Totten's subordinates were officers of the highest promise, men who had stood at the very top of their respective classes at

West Point. All were destined to maintain martial immortality fifteen years later during the American Civil War.

Though Scott had served as general in chief of the US Army since July 5, 1841, then-president James K. Polk initially denied Scott active command of the first American Army that eventually would engage in hostilities with Mexico. Command of the army that Polk ordered into the disputed territory between Texas and Mexico fell to Brevet Brig. Gen. Zachary Taylor. Even before Congress officially declared war on May 12, 1846, Taylor won two swift victories at Palo Alto and Resaca de la Palma, Texas. As soon as he received word of the declaration of war, Taylor crossed the Rio Grande and invaded Mexico.

While Taylor marched, Winfield Scott—who never enjoyed cordial relations with the Polk administration—fumed. Frustrated that he was forced to remain in Washington, DC, while Taylor commanded in the field, Scott made an indiscreet comment to Secretary of War William Marcy in which he concluded that he did not "desire to place myself in the most perilous of all positions: a fire upon my rear from Washington, and a fire, in front, from the Mexicans." Polk, never a strong supporter of Scott, considered the army's highest-ranking officer insubordinate and considered his immediate relief. Only Taylor's increasing fame—gained from two additional victories at Monterrey and Buena Vista, Mexico—led Polk, ever concerned that military success might propel Taylor to seek the presidency on the opposition ticket, to agree that Scott should mount a campaign designed to capture Mexico City. It would be in this campaign that Scott's little cabinet would play a decisive role.

In November 1846, Polk formally addressed Scott and informed him that if he could trust Scott's "proper confidence in the administration," then Polk was "disposed" to assign him to the command. The ensuing campaign, the broad parameters of which the Polk administration had already decided, called for an amphibious landing to capture the port of Veracruz, followed by an expeditious overland march along the National Highway toward Mexico City, a distance of approximately 250 miles, with the express goal of capturing the Mexican capital or forcing the Mexican government to negotiate a peace treaty. Speed was essential to avoid the scourge of yellow fever so common in the coastal region.

Gathering his expedition in southern Texas, Scott embarked on ships chartered by the War Department and joined Commodore David E. Conner, who was already blockading Veracruz with his Home Squadron, in late February 1847. Conner, the senior officer of the navy in Mexican waters, had been in contact with Scott from the previous December and was all too willing to assist the army. By early March, Scott's expeditionary force was off Veracruz, with the formidable fortress of San Juan de Ulua guarding the approaches to the city from the sea. Conner had previously reconnoitered a potential landing site, and, if Scott concurred, he promised to land Scott's force directly from his naval vessels.

The following day, Scott, Conner, and their respective staffs and commanders climbed aboard the steamer *Petrita* and approached the fort of San Juan de Ulua. Venturing to within a mile-and-a-half of the fort, the party came under cannon fire. It was the first hostile fire that many, including Lee, had ever heard. One lucky shot could have sunk the small craft, killing not only Scott and Conner but also the critical members of their respective staffs, including Scott's little cabinet. Then–Second Lt. George Meade, the future victor at Gettysburg, wrote home, "one shot, hitting the vessel . . . might have been the means of breaking up the whole expedition." Not only were Meade and Lee on board, but Joseph Johnston and P. G. T. Beauregard also were. So, too, might the course of the American Civil War have been altered since Lee, Beauregard and Johnston would have become three of the first five Confederate generals elevated to the rank of full general in 1861.

On March 9, Conner landed Scott's force of nearly twelve thousand men in the largest amphibious operation in American history to date without a single fatality. In conference with his little cabinet, Scott decided to reduce the city's defense by siege rather than direct assault in order "to take the city with the least possible loss of life." To emplace his artillery, Scott turned to his engineers. Lee, Beauregard and Johnston provided excellent service, though their duties proved hazardous at times. On returning to their own lines on one occasion, Lee and Beauregard were fired on by an overanxious sentry. Both escaped injuries, although a bullet passed between Lee's arm and body, tearing his uniform.

Also active in the siege was twenty-year-old Second Lt. George B. McClellan, United States Military Academy Class of 1846, who noted that he and the other members of the topographical engineers, including Meade and Johnston, were the only engineers who provided Col. Totten, Lee's superior, with "information of value—that we had done more than all the rest." McClellan, whose ego matched Scott's, served under Lee's direction for the remainder of the siege.

Once the batteries were emplaced, the bombardment began in earnest on March 22. Five days later, Veracruz capitulated. Scott himself accepted the formal surrender of Veracruz on March 29. The capture of such an important city with minimal casualties provided Scott a firm logistical base for subsequent operations. Eight years later, Scott received a brevet promotion to the rank of lieutenant general, a rank previously held only by George Washington. Congress dated Scott's promotion retroactive to the surrender of Veracruz.

Far more important than being mentioned in dispatches was the trust that Scott's little cabinet gained as a result of the Veracruz expedition. Before Totten returned to Washington, he mentioned the services of his elite cadre of engineers. Totten cited both Lee and Johnston for having rendered "occasional aid" in staff work. Totten's high estimation of Lee merely confirmed Scott's high opinion of him. With Totten's departure, Lee became the second-ranking engineer in Scott's army and was in daily contact with the commanding general.

With his base of operations secure, Scott moved into the interior along the National Highway, the same route that Hernán Cortés had taken in 1519. The highway traversed 250 miles of road, interspersed with numerous mountain defiles, by way of Jalapa, Perote, and Puebla. The route would not be unopposed since Mexican president (and general) Antonio López de Santa Anna had recently returned from the northern battlefields where he had been repeatedly defeated by Brig. Gen. Zachary Taylor. Consolidating his political power in the capital, Santa Anna moved his approximately sixteen-thousand-man army east and set up a strong defensive position at Cerro Gordo, a pass where the highway was flanked by large hills, the largest known as El Telégrafo. El Telégrafo, 550 feet higher than the surrounding countryside, dominated Cerro Gordo, and the ground to its north was considered impassable.

In April 1847, Scott's lead elements encountered Santa Anna's formidable defenses. Beauregard conducted the initial reconnaissance and suggested that the army await Scott's arrival, which occurred on April 14. Unwilling to entrust the execution of an attack plan on the recommendation of Beauregard, Scott turned to Lee to direct the scouting. Capt. Lee advanced farther than Beauregard, and he discovered a path that led directly to the Mexican rear. At one point, Lee took refuge under a log, where Mexican soldiers came to rest. It was nightfall before Lee returned to Scott's headquarters with the news that the Americans could envelop the Mexican position.

The next day, Lee joined the lead contingent of Scott's army and guided them along the path that he had recently discovered. The battle of Cerro Gordo lasted but a few hours; in the end, the Mexican Army, with Santa Anna in the lead, fled westward. At a cost of sixty-three killed and 368 wounded from approximately 8,500 soldiers engaged, Scott had routed the principal Mexican Army. Not surprisingly, Scott attributed much of his success to Lee, who received a brevet promotion to the rank of major to date from April 18, 1847. Though he applauded all his engineers, Scott proclaimed, "I am impelled to make special mention of the services of Captain Robert E. Lee. . . . This officer, greatly distinguished at the siege of Veracruz, was again indefatigable during these operations, in reconnaissance . . . nor was he less conspicuous in planting columns to their stations under the heavy fire of the enemy."

Following a brief pause to account for the departure of many of his volunteers whose term of enlistment had expired, Scott next moved his force, now barely seven thousand soldiers, toward the valley of central Mexico. Confident of success, he made a bold move and abandoned his logistical bases in Puebla and Veracruz on June 4, effectively cutting his army off from the coast. Like Cortés before him, Scott would live off the land. On hearing of Scott's decision, the Duke of Wellington, the aged victor of Waterloo, concluded, "Scott is lost! He has been carried away by successes! He can't take the city, and he can't fall back on his base."

It would be July before Scott marched his army from Jalapa toward the Mexican capital. By now, he was scarcely ninety miles from Mexico City.

Mexico City sits in the center of a large basin of about 1,500 square miles. Three large lakes surround the city and restrict the approaches to four possible routes. Immediately south of the capital lay a large field; as was the case of El Telégrafo at Cerro Gordo, the lava flats were deemed impassable.

Entry was further limited to a number of causeways of various distances that led directly to the city's gates. The castle fortress of Chapultepec guarded the westernmost route into the city. To Lee and his engineers fell the task of devising the best approach to reach the Mexican capital.

Lee's reconnaissance revealed that the enemy had heavily fortified El Peñón, a 450-foot hill covered with artillery and commanded by Santa Anna himself. El Peñón stood astride the principal highway from Scott's position into the city. To avoid excessive casualties, Scott acted on Lee's recommendation and decided to turn the enemy by conducting a turning movement far south of the main enemy line of defense. Scott directed his army to the south and occupied the town of San Augustín. The Mexican Army lay three miles to the north at San Antonio and Churubusco. The enemy force was protected by the lava field on its west, so any attack would have to be frontal into the teeth of the enemy's defenses. Scott reorganized his army into four divisions for the final advance against Mexico City. On August 15, 1847, Scott ordered his army to advance.

Meeting little opposition, Scott reached a high ridge that lay at the base of Popocatépetl, from which he could gaze into the Valley of Mexico. Before him stood Mexico City, built on the ruins of the Aztec capital Tenochtitlan. Never one to play down the drama, according to historian John S. D. Eisenhower, Scott described the sight as "the object of all our dreams and hopes—toils and dangers—once the gorgeous seat of Montezuma. That splendid city soon shall be ours!"

Scott was determined to find an alternative approach as well as to confirm that the direct road toward Mexico City by San Antonio was as difficult as initially reported. Scott assigned this second chore to Capt. James L. Mason. Lee's reconnaissance confirmed his initial observation that given the element of surprise, infantry could advance across the lava fields before the Mexican defenders could react. That evening amongst Scott's division commanders, Lee argued vehemently for that approach.

An observer of the meeting at Scott's headquarters, Lt. Raphael Semmes, who would one day command the CSS *Alabama*, succinctly summarized the value of the most prominent member of Scott's staff: "The services of Captain Lee were invaluable to his chief. Endowed with a mind which was superior in his corps, and possessing great energy of character, he examined, counseled and advised with a judgement, tact and discretion worthy of all praise."

"His talent for topography," Semmes continued, "was peculiar, and he seemed to receive impressions intuitively which it cost other men much labor to acquire. [Capt. James L.] Mason, though a very young man, was scarcely, if at all, his inferior in this respect."

Based on Lee's reconnaissance, Scott opted for Lee's course of action and instructed him to start early the next morning with the engineer company and lay the track to move artillery. On August 19, Lee and his party moved out in accordance with Scott's orders. Lee remained in general charge of the reconnaissance; Beauregard served as his principal assistant. Second Lt. George McClellan of the engineer company was also present, as was Capt. Joseph Hooker, a future commander of the Army of the Potomac. Lee's principal biographer, Douglas Southall Freeman, speculates that perhaps here Lee saw for the first time a quiet "Mr. Jackson" who was to become the future "Stonewall" of Lee's army of Northern Virginia fifteen years later.

As the infantry followed his reconnaissance party, Lee personally accompanied the troops to a favorable position to begin the assault. Next, he personally selected a position for the batteries on the most advantageous ground to support the impending attack. That same night the senior American commander on the ground, Brig. Gen. Persifor F. Smith, of Maj. Gen. David Twiggs's division, decided to attack at first light. Lee volunteered to recross the lava field and inform Scott in order for Scott to make a demonstration on the Mexican front.

With nothing to guide him but the lightning that brightened the night sky, Lee stumbled into Scott's headquarters three miles away around 11:00 p.m. Scott immediately ordered division commander Twiggs's division into position. It was the third time Lee had negotiated the lava field, and he was at the point of human exhaustion.

The ensuing American attacks at Contreras and Churubusco proved extraordinarily successful. Twiggs cited Lee in his report: "To Captain Lee, of the engineers, I have again the pleasure of tendering my thanks for the exceedingly valuable services rendered throughout the whole of these operations." Gens. P. F. Smith, Gideon Pillow, and James Shields wholeheartedly concurred. In short, every general officer associated with the fighting at Churubusco mentioned Lee in dispatches. Scott added a final tribute when he named the officers of his staff, including his little cabinet, who deserved commendation, among them Capt. R. E. Lee "as distinguished for felicitous execution as for science and daring."

For his actions at Churubusco, Lee received a brevet promotion to lieutenant colonel as of August 20. The following year Maj. Gen. Scott stated emphatically that Lee's journeys on the nights of August 19 and 20 constituted "the greatest feat of physical and moral courage performed by any individual, in my knowledge, pending the campaign."

To Scott's surprise, the Mexican government requested an armistice the day after the battle of Churubusco. When it was evident that Santa Anna was taking advantage of the armistice to improve the defenses of the city, Scott called his officers together to consider the best way of attacking the city, including capturing the citadel of Chapultepec, its main defense. Scott charged Lee with the burden of directing the reconnaissance. Serving again as Lee's second in command was Beauregard. Scott ordered an attack on the two-hundred-foot-high citadel to commence as soon as practical. In favoring a direct assault on Chapultepec, Scott sided with Beauregard and not Lee, who favored an attack from the south.

After first dispersing a Mexican force at Molina del Rey on September 8, Scott commenced his assault on Mexico's main defenses five days later. With their reconnaissance work complete and Scott's artillery batteries in place, Lee and his engineers observed the fighting from a distance. By 9:30 a.m. of September 13, the Stars and Stripes flew over Chapultepec. When he viewed the American flag, Santa Anna reportedly exclaimed, "I believe if we were to plant our batteries in hell, the damned Yankees would take them from us."

The fall of Chapultepec signaled that the causeways that led to Mexico City's gates now lay open. Scott pushed his forces and, in hard firing, entered the city on September 13. The next day, Maj. Gen. Winfield Scott, arrayed in his finest uniform, formally rode through the Grand Plaza and took possession of Mexico City. Scott again praised Lee for his conduct at Chapultepec, and the Department of War gave Lee his third brevet, this time to the rank of colonel. Other than mopping up operations within the city itself, the fighting in Mexico was at the end.

When news of the capture of Mexico City reached Europe, the Duke of Wellington revised his earlier assessment of Maj. Gen. Scott and proclaimed that Scott's "campaign was unsurpassed in military annals. He is the greatest living soldier." The Iron Duke's praise was far more than Scott received from his own government. Fearing Scott's growing popularity with the opposing Whig Party, President Polk relieved him of his command in Mexico on February 18, 1848, and ordered him to attend a court inquiry to investigate allegations against the general in chief by some of his subordinate commanders. It was a sad ending to a brilliant campaign.

By any standards of achievement, Scott's central Mexico campaign had been remarkable. With an army of less than eleven thousand soldiers, he had defeated one exceeding thirty thousand troops defending their own capital. While sustaining fewer than 3,200 casualties, Scott had inflicted four or five times that many on his adversary. Lt. Ulysses S. Grant, a junior officer in one of Scott's divisions, believed that in the battles surrounding Mexico City, Scott's "strategy and tactics . . . were faultless."

For his part, Scott assigned credit for the campaign where he felt it was due. Historian Eisenhower recounts a dinner that Scott hosted on December 8, 1847, in honor of Brig. Gen. Twiggs, who was departing to take command at Veracruz. In attendance were Scott's senior generals and many of his brigade and regimental commanders. Also attending were three former West Point graduates actually being toasted and who were not, in general, high-ranking enough to be present. In delivering a toast to the United States Military Academy, Scott declared that but for the "science of the Military Academy . . . this army, multiplied by four, could not have entered the capital of Mexico."

In mentoring his talented subordinates, Scott had demonstrated that he was a commander of uncanny ability in recognizing talent and potential in junior officers. Of the officers who composed Scott's little cabinet and who had served on his staff, Robert E. Lee stood first and foremost in the commander's estimation. Brevetted three times for valor, Lee emerged from the conflict with lessons that he applied with great success during the American Civil War. Before departing Mexico, Lee and his fellow officers had also formed the "Aztec Club," in which Lee renewed acquaintances with many of the officers who had served under Scott. There Lee maintained close contact with Joseph Johnston, P. G. T. Beauregard, Gustavus

Smith, George McClellan, George Meade—and there he also met Ulysses S. Grant.

According to biographer Freeman, Scott's future chief of staff E. D. Keyes stated that as a result of their labors together Scott developed an "almost idolatrous fancy for Lee, whose military genius he estimated far above that of any other officer of the army." In 1858, still general in chief of the US Army, Scott referred to Lee in an official letter as "the very best soldier I ever saw in the field"—high praise indeed from a general who arguably was this nation's most talented military commander of the nineteenth century. Fifteen years later, then-general Lee and major general Scott's other talented young officers formed the nucleus of the command elite of the Union and Confederate armies that waged the Civil War.

"Winfield Scott's Remarkable Lieutenants" was originally published in *ARMY Magazine* (July 2012).

7

Generals Thrived Under Antebellum Commander

The Civil War produced a formidable array of warriors over the course of the conflict. Gens. Robert E. Lee, Ulysses S. Grant, William T. Sherman and Thomas "Stonewall" Jackson remain familiar names enshrined in America's Valhalla of military heroes, but few recognize the officer who many thought to be the finest soldier in the antebellum US Army. Gen. Winfield Scott, the commanding general of the US Army and the conqueror of Mexico City, once proclaimed Col. Albert Sidney Johnston a "godsend to the Army." Gen. Zachary Taylor, the victor at Monterrey and Buena Vista during the Mexican–American War and later US president, reported that Johnston was the "finest soldier he ever commanded."

Author Shelby Foote, in his book *The Civil War: A Narrative Part I*, notes that future Confederate President Jefferson Davis concurred with Scott and Taylor, calling Johnston "the greatest soldier, the ablest man, civil or military, Confederate or Federal, then living." Davis should have known because as secretary of war for President Franklin Pierce, he had involved himself directly in appointments, promotions and retirements of competent commanders.

So, who was Johnston and why has he been virtually forgotten by all but a few historians? Perhaps the reason lies in the fact that Johnston's Civil War career was cut dramatically short by his death at the Battle of Shiloh, Tennessee, on April 6, 1862. Due to his untimely demise, Johnston never blossomed into the martial colossus Davis believed him to be. But no one can deny that Johnston occupies a unique place in this country's military history.

Charles P. Roland, Johnston's premier biographer, posits that no other Civil War general on either side experienced such an extraordinary antebellum career. Johnston's record as a soldier was stellar. Graduating from West Point Military Academy, New York, in 1826, Johnston knew fellow West Pointers Davis, Lee, and Joseph J. Johnston well. Following graduation, Sidney Johnston performed admirably in the Black Hawk War of 1832 and in the Army of the Republic of Texas. During the Mexican–American War (1846–1848) he served as a colonel in the Texas volunteers and Taylor cited Johnston for bravery at the Battle of Monterrey.

Resigning his commission after the war, Johnston embarked on several civilian pursuits before returning to active service as paymaster for the US Army in Texas. That resulted from Johnston's association with Davis, whom Pierce had recently appointed secretary of war. Foote writes that in the thirty-five years since his graduation from West Point, Davis "contracted a severe and lifelong case of hero worship" of Johnston, who had befriended Davis at West Point.

Staff duty in the antebellum army proved tedious and by 1855, Johnston had grown disenchanted with his role as frontier paymaster. Fate again smiled on him. To cope with the Native American menace along the Texas frontier, Davis created two mounted regiments, the First and Second Cavalry. It was a forgone conclusion that command of the First Cavalry would go to Col. Edwin V. Sumner, but the Second Cavalry needed a commander and Johnston needed a regiment.

The two mounted regiments were Davis's pride and joy, and he gave Johnston the colonelcy of the Second Cavalry on March 3, 1855. The secretary of war next commissioned Lee as lieutenant colonel and assigned him as Johnston's second in command. Davis then filled Johnston's Second Cavalry with the cream of the officer corps. Following Johnston and Lee, newly commissioned Maj. William J. Hardee and George H. Thomas served next in rank.

Among the captains were Earl Van Dorn, Edmund Kirby Smith, Innis N. Palmer, and George Stoneman. John Bell Hood, Nathan G. Evans, Richard W. Johnson, Kenner Garrard, and Charles W. Field served as junior lieutenants. Each of these officers was destined to become a general officer during the Civil War.

Johnston, Lee, Hardee, Van Dorn, Hood, Smith, Evans, and Field became Confederate generals. Thomas, Stoneman, Palmer, Johnson, and Garrard earned promotions to major general in the Union army. Although criticized within some army circles that Davis filled the ranks of Johnston's regiment with old friends and acquaintances, Davis responded that "he chose men on the basis of their ability and not their seniority," according to William C. Davis in *Jefferson Davis: The Man and His Hour*.

Not surprisingly, the Second Calvary earned a reputation as "a crack regiment" even before it deployed to Texas. Johnston arrived in Louisville, Kentucky, on May 28, 1855, where he found that Lee had already partially formed the regimental headquarters. In September, Johnston moved his regimental headquarters to Jefferson Barracks, St. Louis, to complete organization and training. Orders quickly followed, directing the regiment to proceed to Texas. The primary mission of Johnston's regiment was to guard the frontier against Comanche Native Americans.

Johnston marched from Jefferson Barracks on October 27, 1855; 750 troopers strong. The march proceeded diagonally across Missouri and the northwestern corner of Arkansas, and through the present state of Oklahoma. By mid-December, Johnston crossed the Red River and entered Texas. After two-and-a-half months on the march, Johnston established regimental headquarters at abandoned Fort Mason on the banks of the Llano River on January 14, 1856.

On his arrival in Texas, Johnston directed Lee to command two squadrons of the regiment at Camp Cooper, 170 miles north of Fort Mason. At this outpost, which Lee was to call his "Texas home" for nineteen months, Lee arrived on April 9, relieving Hardee. One of Lee's first orders of business was to select a site for a new fort. On many of Lee's missions, he was accompanied by Hood, one of Lee's future division commanders at Gettysburg.

For his part, Johnston took an aggressive stand against the Native American tribes that inhabited the Texan plains. With the forces available to him, all Johnston could do was direct offensive operations against the marauding Indians. Pursue the Native Americans "to the utmost limit of your means," Johnston instructed his subordinates; treating them "with rigorous hostility" whenever they were discovered, according to Roland.

From Johnston's arrival in Texas to the turn of the decade, elements of the Second Cavalry engaged in forty small-unit actions with the Comanche. With second-in-command Lee frequently absent on court-martial duty, Johnston's line officers, including Van Dorn, Smith, Stoneman, and Hood, led the majority of these patrols. According to Robert Utley's book *Frontiersmen in Blue*, under Johnston's command, the presence of the Second Cavalry ushered in a period of tranquility, albeit brief, to the Texas frontier. Said one observer in 1856, "Our frontier has, for the last three months, engaged a quiet never heretofore known. This state of things is mainly attributable to the energetic action of the 2nd Cavalry, under the command of Col. A. S. Johnston."

Although Johnston's cavalrymen compiled an enviable combat record, his primary mission to halt Comanche attacks was destined to fail. "There is nothing in the nature of the country offering any obstacle to their movement. . . . They can come when they like, taking the risk of chastisement," the frustrated Johnston lamented, according to Roland.

Although Johnston's tenure of command of the Second Cavalry was relatively brief, he left an indelible mark on his officers. Lee and Thomas sent letters of gratitude and esteem when the War Department summoned Johnston to assume command of an expedition against the Mormon population that President James Buchanan deemed in rebellion. Johnson echoed Lee's and Thomas's accolades, writing to Johnston, "Your Regiment looks to you as its father and your reputation is the reputation of the 2nd Cavalry. . . . All would be rejoiced at [an] order sending us to you," according to Roland.

How well did the regiment's leaders fare during the upcoming Civil War? On President Davis's recommendation, the Confederate Congress appointed Johnston to full general on May 30, 1861, making him the second-ranking Confederate general of the war. Hardee achieved the rank of lieutenant general and was arguably one of the Confederacy's finest corps commanders. Smith served with distinction in the Trans-Mississippi Department and successfully repulsed the Red River Campaign led by Union Gen. Nathaniel Banks. And Hood proved to be one of the South's finest division commanders, ultimately rising to command the Army of Tennessee in the Nashville and Atlanta campaigns.

On the Union side, Thomas saved the Union Army of the Cumberland from disaster at the Battle of Chickamauga, Georgia, where he earned the sobriquet "The Rock of Chickamauga." Stoneman commanded the Army of the Potomac's cavalry corps at Chancellorsville, Virginia, and Gettysburg before being transferred to the Western Theater where he served with distinction under Sherman. Last, Palmer, Garrard, and Smith received brevet promotions to major general on March 13, 1865, for gallant and meritorious service in the field.

Secretary of War Davis may have selected the initial contingent of the Second Cavalry's leaders, but these future generals flourished under Johnston's tutelage. Due to the nature of frontier duty, Lee, Stoneman, Hood, Smith, and a host of officers developed strong personal bonds that later bore fruit on Civil War battlefields. Johnston may not have lived long enough to witness the remarkable martial success of his junior officers, but he most certainly contributed to their initial success. Small wonder why Davis viewed Johnston as the first officer of the Confederacy.

"Generals Thrived Under Antebellum Commander" was originally published in *ARMY Magazine* (December 2017).

8

Lincoln and the Army

A Model Civil–Military Partnership

HISTORY IS REPLETE WITH EXAMPLES OF CHIEF EXECUTIVES MAKING important adjustments before determining the best military team to lead the nation's armed forces in time of war. In recent months, historians have remarked on the political sagacity of President Barack Obama borrowing a page from one of his most illustrious predecessors in forming a "team of rivals" as he begins his presidency. As did Abraham Lincoln before him, President Obama has included a number of prominent political adversaries in his administration as he assumes the nation's highest-elected office in the midst of a major war. On the occasion of the bicentennial of Lincoln's birth, the current commander in chief might profit by reflecting on the challenges encountered by our sixteenth president during the Civil War, before he settled on Ulysses S. Grant to serve as the "general in chief" of the Union armies.

In his assessment of the Lincoln presidency, *Tried by War: Abraham Lincoln as Commander in Chief*, James M. McPherson states that "Abraham Lincoln was the only President in American history whose entire administration was bounded by war." From the day he took the inaugural oath until his assassination four years later, Lincoln's predominant task was to win the Civil War. Accordingly, he established policy objectives, articulated war aims and searched for a team of commanders, whose principal chore was to develop a military strategy to implement Lincoln's political objectives.

Not surprisingly, Lincoln articulated his intent to crush the armies of the newly formed Confederate States of America. In repeated messages to his army commanders, Lincoln stressed that the destruction of armies, not the capture of cities, was the surest path to winning the war. Finding the right commanders who shared this vision was a more formidable challenge. The generals best positioned to implement Lincoln's goals during the first year of the conflict were commanding general of the US Army Bvt. Lt. Gen. Winfield Scott and his immediate successor, Maj. Gen. George B. McClellan.

Scott, the aged veteran of the War of 1812 and the hero of the Mexican–American War, devised the Anaconda Plan to slowly strangle the Confederacy. Maritime strategies by their nature are long-term strategies, and, with enemy armies on the outskirts of the federal capital, Lincoln required a far quicker solution. Following the failure of Union forces at First Manassas/Bull Run in July 1861, Lincoln summoned McClellan, fresh from his victories in western Virginia, and entrusted him with command of the newly formed Army of the Potomac.

A few months later, McClellan was appointed general in chief of all Union armies. Despite constant urging from Lincoln, McClellan simply would not fight. Lincoln finally relieved McClellan of command in November 1862 because of the general's inactivity following the Battle of Antietam. Among the series of commanders of the Army of the Potomac who followed McClellan, including Maj. Gens. Ambrose Burnside, Joseph Hooker, and George Meade, Lincoln repeatedly reiterated his desire to seek a decisive engagement over Gen. Robert E. Lee's Army of Northern Virginia.

In each case, the military commanders failed to interpret Lincoln's command intent. Burnside initially moved quickly but squandered an opportunity to attack Lee before Lee was able to concentrate his entire force at Fredericksburg, Virginia. Then Burnside horribly mishandled the army in a series of ill-fated attacks against Lee's army, which was entrenched in an impregnable position.

Lincoln thought he had found a solution in Hooker, whom he appointed commanding general of the Army of the Potomac despite his personal reservations over Hooker's claim that the country needed a dictator. Lincoln wrote to Hooker, "It was not for this, but in spite of it, that I have given you the command. . . . What I now ask of you is military success. . . . I shall assist you, as far as I can. . . . Go forward and give us victories." Hooker failed badly at Chancellorsville, Virginia, in May 1863, and with Lee's army invading Pennsylvania in June, Lincoln reminded Hooker again that Lee's army, not Richmond, was the true objective. Hooker thought otherwise, and his impulsive resignation was accepted by Lincoln.

Meade followed in the commander's role and won a tactical victory at Gettysburg, but he failed to follow up his success. When Lee escaped to Virginia, Lincoln prepared a message to Meade: "My dear General, I do not believe you appreciate the magnitude of the misfortune involved in Lee's escape. He was within your easy grasp, and to have closed upon him would . . . have ended the war. . . . Your golden opportunity is gone, and I am distressed immeasurably because of it." After careful reflection, Lincoln filed the message, relieved that at least a tactical victory was better than nothing. Yet in Lincoln's mind, Meade had failed the test of command and was not the general who would prosecute the war in the manner that Lincoln intended.

As Lincoln searched for the right commander in the Eastern Theater, the most successful Union strategy was being implemented in the Mississippi River Valley and along accompanying tributaries. There, a series of commanders, most notably Ulysses S. Grant and William T. Sherman, emerged. Grant was clearly the rising star, having destroyed two Confederate armies with his capture of Fort Donelson, Tennessee, in February 1862 and Vicksburg, Mississippi, in July 1863. Though he had not met Grant, Lincoln became his staunchest ally because Grant demonstrated the tenacity that Lincoln sought. Even when Grant's tactical conduct of the 1862 battle at Shiloh, Tennessee, was called into question because the North endured excessive casualties, Lincoln stated, "I can't spare this man. He fights!" Later Lincoln would identify what Grant possessed and so many of his commanders lacked: "They [politicians and many military commanders] have no idea that the war is to be carried on and put through by hard, tough fighting—that it will hurt somebody."

Vicksburg convinced Lincoln that Grant was the type of general he needed to win the war. A week following Vicksburg's capitulation, Lincoln wrote Grant to express his "grateful acknowledgement for the almost inestimable service you have done the country." He candidly informed Grant that as president, he thought that Grant had made a serious error in his approach to Vicksburg. Lincoln continued, "I now wish to make the personal acknowledgment that you were right, and I was wrong." Lincoln had found his man.

Before he could summon Grant to Washington, DC, the Confederates won a victory at Chickamauga in northwest Georgia in September 1863, and the Union Army of the Cumberland fled to the city of Chattanooga, where they were immediately besieged. Lincoln had had enough. Reorganizing several military departments into the Military Division of the Mississippi, he placed Grant in command and authorized him to take whatever measures were necessary to remedy the situation. Grant relieved several commanders, rushed in reinforcements, and within a month routed the Confederate Army of Tennessee.

The bill restoring the grade of lieutenant general of the army, a rank previously held only by George Washington (and Winfield Scott as a brevet appointment), had been passed by Congress and became law in February 1864. Grant's nomination was sent to the Senate on March 1 and confirmed the next day. President Lincoln summoned Grant to Washington, DC, to receive his commission. On March 8, Grant arrived in the nation's capital to take command of all the Union armies. His entrance into Washington "was consistent with his image as an unpretentious man of action," according to author Doris Kearns Goodwin in *Team of Rivals*.

On arrival at Washington's historic Willard Hotel at dusk, accompanied only by his son Fred, Grant was not recognized by the desk clerk. He was initially told that nothing was available except a small room on the top floor, but once the clerk looked at the signature in the register—U. S. Grant and son, Galena, Illinois—the general's accommodations were switched. After a private dinner, Grant prepared his son for bed and strolled over to the White House to meet the commander in chief for the first time.

Grant arrived at the White House, where a large crowd had gathered for the president's weekly reception. Grant walked along modestly with the rest of the crowd toward the president. Meeting Grant for the first time, Lincoln remarked, "Why, here is Gen. Grant! Well, this is a great pleasure." After a brief exchange, Lincoln turned Grant over to Secretary of State William H. Seward to negotiate the crowd. As Goodwin describes it, the president was "delighted by the crowd's embrace of Grant, [and] he willingly ceded to the unassuming general his own customary place of honor, fully aware that the path to victory was wide enough [as a young colonel said] for the two of them to 'walk it abreast.'" After an hour, Grant returned to Lincoln, who was waiting with Secretary of War Edwin Stanton. They discussed the next day's ceremony at which Grant would formally receive his commission. Then Lincoln conferred privately with Grant to establish the general parameters of what would be the most successful civil–military partnership in American history.

According to Grant's memoirs, Lincoln stated that he had "never professed to be a military man or to know how campaigns should be conducted, and never wanted to interfere in them: but that procrastination on the part of commanders, and the pressure from the people [of] the North and Congress, which was always with him, forced him into issuing his series of 'Military Orders.' . . . [Lincoln] did not know but they were all wrong, and did know that some of them were. All [Lincoln] wanted or had ever wanted was someone who would take the responsibility and act, and call on him for all the assistance needed, pledging himself to use all the power of the government in rendering such assistance." Grant then assured Lincoln "that [he] would do the best [he] could with the means at hand and avoid as far as possible annoying him or the War Department." Grant's initial interview was over.

Grant's account of his meeting with Lincoln doesn't entirely ring true according to McPherson. Lincoln "did want to know what Grant was going to do, at least in a broad strategic sense." In April 1864, Lincoln advised Grant that as for the tactical "particulars of your plan, I neither know nor seek to know." Grant wanted to maintain his headquarters in the West, but, according to McPherson, "Lincoln made it clear that he wanted him to come east 'to see whether he cannot do something with the unfortunate Army of the Potomac.'" Two of Grant's initial decisions were to promote Sherman to command in the West and to retain Meade as commander of the Army of the Potomac. The latter was an uncomfortable arrangement, as Grant would eventually establish his field headquarters in close proximity with Meade's headquarters.

Lincoln also confessed his frustration that in the past, Union armies seemed intent on securing territorial objectives rather than focusing their efforts on the destruction of enemy armies. In addition, it seemed that the various Union armies seldom operated in concert. Lincoln had previously—and repeatedly—suggested that Buell (commander of the Union Army of the Cumberland) and Halleck (commanding general of the army), among others, devise a coordinated strategy to "move at once upon the enemy's whole line so as to bring into action our great superiority in numbers." Time and again the generals ignored him. Grant's coordinated strategy—to have the smaller armies serve a pin-down function, while the principal Union armies in the West and in the East moved simultaneously against the main Confederate armies in the field—impressed Lincoln.

Following his meeting with the president, Grant immediately conducted an inspection of his principal armies and conferred directly with his commanders, presenting his general outline for a concentrated movement of all federal armies with the expressed purpose of destroying the Confederate armies to their respective fronts. From late March 1864 to the onset of the Overland Campaign in May, Grant visited Washington, DC, once a week to confer with the secretary of war and President Lincoln.

Within a month of receiving his commission as commanding general of all Union armies, Grant issued orders to all of his commanders, outlining his general intent for the upcoming campaign. Excerpts from his orders to Sherman and to Meade, his two senior commanders, indicate that Grant fully comprehended Lincoln's military objectives.

To Sherman, Grant wrote, "It is my design, if the enemy keep quiet and allow me to take the initiative in the spring campaign, to work all parts of the Army together and somewhat towards a common center. . . . You, I propose to move against Johnston's army [Confederate Army of Tennessee], to break it up and to get into the interior of the enemy's country as far as you can, inflicting all the damage you can against their war resources. I do not propose to lay down for you a plan of campaign, but simply lay down the work it is desirable to have done and leave you free to execute it in your own way."

A similar message went to Meade: "So far as practicable, all the armies are to move together and towards one common center. . . . Sherman will move at the same time you do, or two or three days in advance, Joseph Johnston's army being his objective point, and the heart of Georgia his ultimate aim. . . . Lee's army will be your objective point. Wherever Lee goes, there you will go also."

Since Lee was the principal threat, Grant accompanied Meade's Army of the Potomac. In the campaign that followed, Grant and Meade endured fifty-five thousand casualties within six weeks, but Grant informed Lincoln that "there is to be no turning back." Later, Grant telegraphed his commander in chief: "I propose to fight it out on this line if it takes all summer." It took all summer, all autumn and all winter, but the outcome was never in doubt. With Lee pinned into the defense of Richmond, it was only a matter of time before the Union would prevail.

Lincoln never lost faith in Grant and was willing to endure political fallout as casualties mounted. On receipt of Grant's August 1864 telegram stating that Grant intended to hold Lee in the trenches of Petersburg until the latter surrendered, Lincoln wrote, "I have seen your dispatch expressing your unwillingness to break your hold where you are. Neither am I willing. Hold on with a bulldog [grip], and chew and choke, as much as possible."

On April 2, 1865, Grant broke Lee's line at Petersburg. Lee abandoned Richmond and fled west. Lincoln urged pursuit, directing Grant, "Gen. Sheridan says, 'If the thing is pressed, I think that Lee will surrender.' Let the thing be pressed." A few days later, Lee surrendered the Army of Northern Virginia at Appomattox Court House. The war was over.

In retrospect, the Lincoln–Grant partnership was the most successful command team in American history. At its foundation was a commander in chief who clearly articulated his political and military objectives and his command intent. After careful screening, often by trial and error, Lincoln discovered a general who did not always agree with the president's policies, but one who shared Lincoln's vision of how to end the war. By Grant's own admission, he had read the remarkable series of debates between Lincoln and Douglas a few years earlier, but he had by no means ever been a "Lincoln-man" in that contest. Yet Grant had always recognized the president's great ability, and he never questioned Lincoln's constitutional role as commander in chief.

Open communication between Lincoln and Grant further cemented their relationship. On conferring Grant's commission, Lincoln informed Grant that he had full confidence in Grant's abilities and that he need not know all the intricacies of Grant's strategy. Grant acknowledged that Lincoln "was willing to trust his generals in making and executing their plans," but this willingness was tempered only if those plans followed

Lincoln's intent to move rapidly and to crush the opposing armies. A review of Grant's detailed correspondence in the final year of the war reveals a commander who kept the president fully informed of all major decisions and troop movements.

Herein lay the reasons why Lincoln and Grant were so successful. Their relationship was founded on a shared strategic vision and a mutual respect for each other's abilities and constitutional roles, not political affiliation or personal ambition. Clear communication and adherence to the expressed goals of the president characterized Grant's actions throughout the war. In turn, Lincoln never wavered in his support for Grant, despite political pressure to relieve Grant from command. Those whom Lincoln did relieve were commanders who sought personal aggrandizement and those who failed to develop a coherent strategy that fulfilled the president's intent to act decisively to destroy the enemy armies.

In selecting his own defense team and in articulating his command intent in the global war against terrorism, President Obama can clearly glean lessons from how Lincoln and Grant achieved success in the most catastrophic war in American history. It took Lincoln three years to find Grant and to entrust the fate of the Union armies into his hands. Given the current international crisis in Iraq and Afghanistan, President Obama did not have that luxury of time, but he possessed one advantage that Lincoln did not—he had a proven team in place. Doubtless the current president will make adjustments, but by clearly articulating his intent and his war aims, he will have taken the initial step toward military success. By emulating President Abraham Lincoln during this nation's greatest crisis, he follows a superb role model.

"Lincoln and the Army: A Model Civil–Military Partnership" was originally published in *ARMY Magazine* (March 2009).

9

The Emergence of Ulysses S. Grant

Lt. Gen. Ulysses S. Grant emerged from the American Civil War in resplendent glory. As the victor at Fort Donelson, Vicksburg, Chattanooga, and Appomattox, Grant has long since been enshrined in the pantheon of American military commanders. Though Grant's critics claimed his victories were achieved at the price of excessive casualties, few could argue with the results Grant achieved on the battlefield. More than any other Union commander, Grant justified President Abraham Lincoln's confidence when he appointed Grant the commanding general of all Union armies in March 1864.

Could the war have been shortened had Lincoln assigned Grant command of the Army of the Potomac and ordered him to bring confederate Gen. Robert E. Lee to battle in 1863? Why did Lincoln endure a series of mediocre commanders in the Eastern Theater when Grant had already demonstrated that he was willing to fight the enemy on the very terms that the president was urging his commanders to employ? If Lincoln was so politically and militarily astute, as leading historian James McPherson claims, why did it take the president three years to appoint Grant to senior command?

No one in the US Army could possibly have imagined that Ulysses S. Grant would rise to such a prominent position during the war. Grant was appointed to the US Military Academy at West Point in 1839, but he later confessed in his personal memoirs, "A military life had no charms for me, and I had not the faintest idea of staying in the army even if I should be graduated, which I did not expect." His academic record was undistinguished, in part because Cadet Grant discovered that he "did not take hold of [his] studies with avidity [and] rarely ever read over a lesson a second time during [his] entire cadetship."

In December 1839, Congress considered a bill abolishing the Military Academy. Grant viewed these discussions as an honorable way to obtain a discharge, and he "read the debates with much interest" and "growing impatience at the delay in taking action." The resolution failed, and somehow Grant managed to graduate, in the lower half of his class. His single achievement at West Point had been to set a high-jump record on a horse that no other cadet could ride.

Initially assigned to the Fourth Infantry Regiment at Jefferson Barracks, Missouri, Grant performed well enough in the Mexican War to earn several brevet promotions. He resigned from the army in disgrace for drunkenness in 1854 and seemed unable to hold a job for any prolonged period. Thirty-nine years old and working in his father's leather goods store in Galena, Illinois, when the Civil War began, Grant immediately volunteered for service. "I feel myself competent to command a regiment, if the President, in his judgement, should see fit to entrust one to me," he informed the army's adjutant general on May 24, 1861. Because of Grant's reputation in the old army, the adjutant general did not reply. Considering Grant's past record of service in the peacetime army and his repeated failures in civilian life, few Regular Army officers would have agreed with Grant's own assessment of his martial potential. How, then, did he succeed when the war commenced? Grant owed his commission as colonel and subsequent promotion to brigadier general to the good services of Illinois Congressman Elihu B. Washburne and Governor Richard Yates, who were scraping the bottom of the barrel for officers capable of mustering the undisciplined mass of Illinois volunteers into state service. As Galena's sole West Point graduate, Grant got the job as mustering officer. Grant's own father suffered no illusion of his son's potential, telling Grant when he learned of the promotion to brigadier general, "Be careful, Ulysses, you're a general now; it's a good job, don't lose it." In the words of historian McPherson, Grant remained at best "a man of no reputation and little promise."

Grant's initial assignment found him in Missouri, a backwater theater of the conflict. When ordered to attack a Confederate regiment under the command of Col. Thomas Harris, Grant recalled, "My heart kept getting higher and higher until it felt to me as though it was in my throat. I would have given anything then to have been back in Illinois, but I had not the moral courage to halt and consider what to do; I kept right on." When his men approached the enemy's camp, Grant discovered his adversary had fled. "My heart resumed its place. It occurred to me at once that Harris had been as much afraid of me as I had been of him. This was a view of the question I had never taken before; but it was one I never forgot afterwards." Never again would Grant's conduct be marked with such trepidation and concern over his adversary's intention. Henceforth, Grant would concentrate on what he was going to do to the enemy, rather than what the enemy was going to do to him.

In September 1861, having received new orders, Grant established his headquarters in Cairo, Illinois. When he heard that Confederate troops were marching toward Paducah, Kentucky, at the mouth of the Tennessee River on the eastern shore of the Mississippi River, Grant stole a march on his opponents and occupied the town, which controlled access to the Tennessee and Cumberland Rivers. Until early November, little else happened on Grant's front, but on November 7, an aggressive Grant ignored his written orders to make a demonstration against the Confederate forces at Belmont, Missouri, a steamboat landing opposite Columbus, Kentucky, on the Mississippi River. Grant grasped an opportunity and decided on a direct, all-out attack on Belmont.

The first battle at Belmont was an engagement that some in the North criticized as wholly unnecessary and expensive in terms of casualties. Grant's critics stated that his undisciplined troops had been nearly routed looting a captured Confederate camp instead of preparing for a counterattack. When the Confederates counterattacked in force, Grant noted that his men had "cut [their] way out just as well." Grant claimed a victory, stating that all his intentions had been met and that "the victory was complete." Moreover, Grant's national troops "acquired a confidence in themselves at Belmont that did not desert them through the war," according to their proud commander.

There were notable dissenters, however. *The Chicago Tribune* printed the casualty lists, and the editor reported, "It may be said of these victims, "They have fallen, and to what end?" Nor was Maj. Gen. Henry Wager

Halleck, who had just assumed command of the Department of Missouri, impressed. In Halleck's eyes, Grant had proven himself reckless. It was not a matter of if, but when, Grant might suffer a relapse and revert to his "unsavory past." Not the least of Halleck's concerns was that he might be embarrassed by an impulsive Grant.

Now under direct command of Halleck, Grant instantly recognized that to oust the Confederates from western Kentucky, the true line of operations ran from Fort Henry on the Tennessee River through Fort Donelson on the Cumberland River, a scant eleven miles apart. Devising a plan to eliminate Fort Henry, Grant received approval, and on February 2, his expedition sailed in concert with Commodore Andrew H. Foote's transports and seven ironclad gunboats. Until the autumn of 1862, naval officers commanded the gunboats, but army officers controlled their operations. Foote's gunboats alone subdued Fort Henry before Grant's infantry arrived, prompting Grant to notify Halleck on February 6, "Fort Henry is ours. . . . I shall take and destroy Fort Donelson on the 8th."

Fort Donelson, with its garrison of around seventeen thousand defenders, proved a tougher nut to crack. After a few days' delay while he gathered reinforcements, Grant's force of approximately fifteen thousand men approached Fort Donelson on February 12. As he waited, he declared that he would "keep the ball moving as lively as possible." He quickly surrounded the Confederate stronghold. Grant ordered an immediate assault on Fort Donelson, but the Confederates successfully thwarted the attack. Grant was attending a war council with Foote when the Confederates counterattacked on February 15 in a desperate attempt to break the encirclement.

Grant returned to the action and informed one of his staff, "The one who attacks first now will be victorious, and the enemy will have to be in a hurry if he gets ahead of me." Noting that the attacking Confederates carried three days' rations in their knapsacks, Grant discerned that the defenders were trying to escape. Grant launched a vigorous counterattack that not only regained all the lost ground but also breached the Confederate entrenchments. Confederate surrender became inevitable with the collapse of their external fortifications.

The following day, Confederate Brig. Gen. Simon Buckner inquired on what terms Grant would accept the surrender of the post. Grant's somewhat "ungenerous and unchivalrous" reply—"No terms except an unconditional and immediate surrender can be accepted. I propose to move immediately upon your works . . ."—resulted in Buckner's capitulation. "Unconditional Surrender," a play on his initials U. S., made Grant the nation's newest military hero. More important, in sharp contrast to the generals in Virginia who were consistently calling for reinforcements and whose operations were marked with growing inactivity, Lincoln took notice of this fighting general and intervened periodically to protect one of the few generals who understood his desire to win the war quickly by destroying the enemy's armies.

In less than a year, Grant had gone from an unknown clerk in his father's tannery to the North's man of the hour. At Fort Donelson, Grant had captured the largest number of soldiers ever to surrender on the North American continent. Determined to take advantage of the rupture of the Confederate line in Tennessee, Grant proposed to Halleck that he immediately advance on Nashville. "I am for any move the general commanding may order," stated Grant, but Halleck, skeptical of Grant's recent success, did nothing. Nashville fell a week later to union troops under Brig. Gen. Don Carlos Buell. Grant remained where he was until Halleck prepared to move on Corinth, Mississippi, a vital railway hub.

Jealous of his subordinate's fame, Halleck attempted to take credit for Grant's twin victories as department commander, but now newly appointed Maj. Gen. Grant had clearly caught the president's eye. Grant next moved his Army of West Tennessee to Pittsburgh Landing on the Tennessee River, about twenty miles north of Corinth. Halleck directed newly promoted Maj. Gen. Buell with his troops to unite with Grant's men before moving south to Corinth. For once, the cautious Grant's instincts failed him. Believing that the Confederates were defensive-minded, he did not order his own troops to entrench. It was a critical mistake because on April 6, Gen. Albert Sidney Johnston, Confederate commanding general west of the Appalachian Mountains, launched a vigorous assault, overrunning Grant's exterior lines.

Never in American history had there been a battle like that of Pittsburg Landing. Often called the Battle of Shiloh after a log church that later served as the Confederate commander's headquarters, the battle was the bloodiest battle in American history to that time. Probably 80 percent of the Confederate combatants had never seen combat. Places like the

Hornet's Nest and the Peach Orchard became forever ingrained in the nation's memory. More than one hundred thousand men fought at Shiloh. About 25 percent became casualties. More than 3,400 soldiers died, exceeding the total of US soldiers in all previous wars.

In spite of his apparent defeat during the initial day's fighting, Grant did not panic. Rallying his men, he established a defensive line within sight of the Tennessee River and called for immediate reinforcements. Division commander William T. Sherman later remarked on Grant's iron will and his determination to attack the following morning. When Sherman reported on the first day's excessive casualties, Grant merely responded, "Lick 'em tomorrow." By midafternoon on April 7, Grant had recaptured all the lost ground and driven the Confederate Army from the field. Casualties, however, had been appalling.

Grant had won the day, but the reports of his initial unpreparedness tarnished his reputation. Halleck demanded an explanation and temporarily relieved Grant of command. Grant characteristically did nothing to respond to his critics or to appeal for political support. Ignoring the recriminations, he merely prepared for the strike toward Corinth.

Lincoln and Congressman Washburne stood firm in their support, the president stating, "I can't spare this man; he fights." Bowing to political pressure and unwilling to confront the administration in Washington, Halleck appointed Grant second-in-command that removed Grant from active operations. Grant considered resigning his commission, but Sherman urged him to stay on, thus cementing a relationship that would bear fruit on the future battlefields.

The first four months of 1862 also highlighted an important development in Grant's evolution as a combat commander. According to his memoirs, up until the battle of Shiloh, Grant believed that "the rebellion . . . would collapse suddenly and soon, if a decisive victory could be gained over [the Southern] armies. Donelson and Henry were such victories," but the Confederates had regrouped and assumed the offensive at Shiloh to make such a "gallant effort to regain what had been lost" that Grant "gave up all idea of saving the Union except complete conquest."

After Shiloh, Grant no longer pursued a policy to protect the property of the citizens whose territory was invaded. Shiloh convinced Grant that it was still humane to protect Southern civilians found in their homes, but he now intended to consume everything that could be used to support or supply Northern armies. He now considered all supplies within the reach of Confederate armies as contraband and subject to confiscation or destruction. The hard hand of war had reached the Western Theater, and Grant emerged as its most ardent advocate.

Political intrigue and the dispersion of Grant's forces to tertiary theaters marked the late spring and summer of 1862. Finally on October 25, Halleck, now in Washington as general in chief, placed Grant in command of the Department of the Tennessee. Reinforcements arrived, and by early November Grant prepared to take the initiative against his next target, Vicksburg, Mississippi. Vicksburg was important to the South because it occupied the first high ground close to the river below Memphis, and it served as a vital transportation link between the parts of the Confederacy divided by the Mississippi River. As long as the South held Vicksburg, the free navigation of the river was prevented.

Lincoln, like Grant, fully realized the city's strategic significance. Lincoln said, "Vicksburg is the key. . . . The war can never be brought to a close until that key is in our pocket." It fell to Grant to take that key. Grant's initial attempts to capture the Confederate city met with dismal failure. On December 20, 1862, a Confederate cavalry column under Maj. Gen. Earl Von Dorn destroyed Grant's secondary base of supplies at Holly Springs, thus halting his first attempt to capture Vicksburg. That same month, a federal column under Sherman was repulsed at Chickasaw Bluffs. Grant then squandered two months in late winter attempting to cut a canal through the tangled bayous to bypass the city and reduce Vicksburg's importance. That effort failed miserably, and critics questioned Grant's competence. Rumors of his drinking surfaced again, but Lincoln remained steadfast in his support.

In late March, Grant devised a daring plan. He marched his army south below Vicksburg on the western side of the Mississippi and then ordered his gunboats and transports to sail south and run the gauntlet of Confederate batteries at Vicksburg. Then-acting rear admiral David Porter's gunboats blasted their way past the city's fortifications and then transported Grant's army to the eastern shore of the Mississippi River. Now cut off from his base, Grant moved northeast in an effort to sever Vicksburg's supply lines from the east and from the south. As described in his memoirs, Grant "felt a degree of relief scarcely ever equaled since. . . . I was now in the enemy's country, with a vast river and the stronghold of Vicksburg between me and my base of supplies. But I was on dry ground on the same side of the river with the enemy."

Over the next month, Grant conducted what was arguably the most brilliant campaign of the war. He marched nearly two hundred miles, fought and won five battles (at Port Gibson, Raymond, Jackson, Champion's Hill, and Big Black) and finally surrounded Vicksburg itself. On May 19 and May 22, Grant attempted—unsuccessfully–to take the city by storm before settling on what would become a forty-seven-day siege. When Vicksburg capitulated on July 4, 1863, Grant had destroyed his second Confederate Army, capturing around thirty thousand enemy soldiers, 172 cannons, and sixty thousand rifles. The fate of the Confederacy was sealed with Vicksburg's surrender.

Five days later, Port Hudson, the last Confederate stronghold on the Mississippi River, also capitulated after a six-week siege. Lincoln proclaimed, "The Father of Waters again goes unvexed to the sea."

What traits ensured Grant's success? As Geoffrey Ward, Ric Burns, and Ken Burns observe in *The Civil War*, Grant was "methodical, dogged, and clearheaded under fire, never losing sight of his objective or what it would take to get there."

"There is one striking thing about Grant's orders," a Union general said. "No matter how hurriedly he may write them on the field, no one has ever the slightest doubt as to their meaning." He also possessed what Southern historian Shelby Foote called "four-o'-clock-in-the-morning-courage. You could wake him up at four o'clock . . . and tell him they had just turned his right flank, and he would be cool as a cucumber." Even in the direst circumstances, Grant refused to be rattled.

In addition, Grant's early mistakes as a novice commander were never forgotten. Historian Foote noted that Grant was a rarity in the war, a general who learned from his experience. And what had Grant learned? In what promised to be his first engagement, Grant learned never to second-guess his decision to attack. He gained personal confidence in his generalship at Belmont; at Forts Henry and Donelson, Grant discovered that rapid marching could keep the enemy off balance; and Shiloh taught Grant never to underestimate the enemy.

Vicksburg, however, proved to be Grant's crowning campaign. He discovered that his army could live off the country and that it was not necessary to expend considerable resources to protect lengthy lines of communications and supply. No longer confined to a set line of supply, Grant remarked that the abundance of livestock and supplies in the interior of Mississippi taught him that his army could live "twenty days with the issue of only five days' rations by the commissary." In Grant's own words, "Our loss of supplies was great at Holly Springs, but it was more than compensated for by those taken from the country and by the lesson taught." Rapid movement also confounded his enemy and kept the Confederacy's superior numbers from being brought to bear against Grant's forces.

Lincoln certainly recognized Grant's potential. Shortly after Vicksburg, the president telegraphed Grant to acknowledge the country's debt to an officer virtually unknown at the beginning of the conflict. "I do not remember that you and I have ever met personally," Lincoln wrote. "I write this now as a grateful acknowledgement for the almost inestimable service you have done the country. I wish to say a word further . . . I never had any faith, except a general hope that you knew better than I. . . . I thought you should go down the river and join [Maj. Gen. Nathaniel] Banks [at Port Hudson]; and when you turned Northward, East of the Big Black [River], I feared it was a mistake. I now wish to make the personal acknowledgement that you were right, and I was wrong."

In short, the Grant of mid-1863 emerged as a far more mature, more battle-tested commander than the Grant of 1861. By 1863, Grant had clearly mastered the intricacies of joint and independent operation deep within the enemy's territory. It would take another campaign (Chattanooga) and eight more months before Lincoln summoned Grant east to serve as general in chief of all Union armies in March 1864, but the humble man from Galena had finally arrived.

"The Emergence of Ulysses S. Grant" was originally published in *ARMY Magazine* (November 2011).

10

A Learned Hero

Student of War Proved Himself at Gettysburg

Medal of Honor recipient Joshua Lawrence Chamberlain was a genuine American hero who reached legendary status for his brilliant defense of Little Round Top during the Battle of Gettysburg.

Chamberlain began his military career as a lieutenant colonel of the Twentieth Maine Volunteer Infantry Regiment, known as the Twentieth Maine, and progressed to the rank of brigadier general, not by brevet, but by commission. Wounded six times during the Civil War, he commanded a regiment, a brigade, and a division by war's end. Immediately following the cessation of hostilities, Chamberlain received a promotion to brevet major general of volunteers.

Given his battlefield heroics during the war, one wonders: What influences shaped this remarkable leader? Since Chamberlain was a citizen-soldier who possessed no formal military training, what accounts for his tactical competence at Gettysburg, Pennsylvania; Petersburg, Virginia; and, ultimately, Five Forks, Virginia, in 1865? What lessons can be derived by current army leaders from his legacy?

A professor of languages and rhetoric at Maine's Bowdoin College, Chamberlain came from a long line of citizen-soldiers. Both his grandfather and his father served in America's wars stretching from the American Revolution to the bloodless Aroostook War of 1838–1839. In July 1862, Chamberlain offered his services to Gov. Israel Washburn Jr. of Maine; Washburn accepted and offered to make Chamberlain colonel of a newly formed regiment of volunteers. Chamberlain demurred and informed the governor that he would take a lesser role that would give him some time to learn about soldiering. "I have always been interested in military matters, and what I do not know in that line, I know how to learn," Chamberlain said. Consequently, Chamberlain joined the Twentieth Maine Volunteer Infantry Regiment as a lieutenant colonel under the immediate command of West Point graduate Col. Adelbert Ames.

As regimental commander, Ames employed much of his time educating his officers, including Chamberlain, on the finer points of battlefield tactics. Ames found his second-in-command an eager pupil. Working hard with Ames as his personal instructor in the tent they shared, Chamberlain found it "no small labor to master the evolutions of a Battalion or Brigade."

To ensure succession readiness in battle, Ames soon directed Chamberlain to conduct the drills. At Fredericksburg, Virginia, in December 1862, Chamberlain witnessed extensive action, providing him with his initial combat experience under fire.

Writing to his wife, Fannie, Chamberlain confessed, "I study—I tell you—every military work I can find." Ever the eager student, the lieutenant colonel requested Fannie send him his copy of Baron de Jomini's *The Art of War*. By supplementing Ames's tutelage with his own voracious study, Chamberlain mastered the intricacies of how best to deploy the regiment in battle formation and to execute offensive and defensive tactics.

When Ames was promoted to brigade-level command in the aftermath of the Battle of Chancellorsville, Virginia, Chamberlain assumed command of the Twentieth Maine on May 20, 1863. As regimental commander, newly promoted Col. Chamberlain quickly demonstrated that he was a leader endowed with character and also competence. On the day of his promotion, Chamberlain received 120 soldiers from the Second Maine Regiment. Their enlistment papers documented a three-year obligation they were required to honor, despite the fact that the remainder of the regiment had already returned home to Maine. Forty of the soldiers refused duty and the orders of their brigade commander. Four days later, a detail from a sister regiment delivered the mutineers to Chamberlain, since Chamberlain commanded the only Maine regiment in the Fifth Army Corps. Orders from Maj. Gen. George Meade, the corps commander, were to "make them do duty or shoot them down the moment they refused."

How to handle the mutineers? Chamberlain could never go back to Maine if he complied with Meade's orders. He arrived at a novel solution that demonstrated his true character. He assembled the reluctant soldiers and informed them that he could not treat them as "civilian guests" of his regiment, but he would treat them as soldiers should be treated. When the upcoming battle was over, he promised that he would personally "see what could be done for their claim." As a result of Chamberlain's principled stand and his compelling leadership, all but a few performed their duty at Gettysburg six weeks later.

Chamberlain again demonstrated his true character in April 1865 when Lt. Gen. Ulysses Grant personally selected him to preside over the surrender ceremonies of the infantry of the Army of Northern Virginia. Grant's orders were simply not to "humiliate the manhood" of the vanquished Confederate soldiers. Chamberlain was authorized to select his personal honor guard. He chose the Third Brigade, his former brigade after Chancellorsville, to be at his side.

Maj. Gen. John Gordon rode at the head of the Confederate column. When Gordon approached Chamberlain and his officers, a bugle sounded, and the Union line snapped to attention and delivered a marching salute, then returned his victor's salute, "honor answering honor," as Chamberlain later described it. In the spirit of President Abraham Lincoln, Chamberlain's unwillingness to rejoice over a crestfallen foe greatly contributed to national reconciliation.

Chamberlain undoubtedly demonstrated that he was a proven leader of character, but how does one account for his tactical competence at Gettysburg, where he manned the left flank of the Army of the Potomac on a spur adjacent to Little Round Top? The answer is that Chamberlain did not become a competent tactician on the second day of the battle. Much happened before the afternoon of July 2, 1863. His life experiences had prepared him for that moment, and he knew how to leverage it.

Chamberlain's specific orders from Col. Strong Vincent, his brigade commander, were "to hold his ground at all hazards." Assembling the officers of his understrength regiment, Chamberlain reiterated Vincent's orders and stressed the urgency of the situation. Typically, the commander remained cool under pressure, prompting one of his officers to remember, "Up and down the line, with a last word of encouragement or caution, walks the quiet man, whose calm exterior concealed the fire of the warrior and the heart of steel."

Chamberlain then directed one of his companies to "act as occasion might dictate, to prevent a surprise on his exposed flank and rear." Chamberlain next extended his line, by "refusing" his left wing, so that it was nearly at right angles with his right flank. At times the firing was so intense that Chamberlain later claimed, "The edge of the fight rolled backward and forward like a wave. The dead and wounded were now in our front and then in our rear."

Anticipating that enemy soldiers were gathering all their energies for a final assault against the Twentieth Maine, Chamberlain decided to "strike before we were struck by this overwhelming force in a hand-to-hand fight, which we could not probably have withstood or survive." At the moment of crisis, Chamberlain ordered, "Bayonet! Forward," and charged the surprised Confederate forces. For his "daring heroism and great tenacity in holding his position on the Little Round Top against repeated assaults and carrying the advance position on the Great Round Top," Chamberlin received the Medal of Honor from Congress in 1893.

Chamberlain's storied career is instructive for today's army leaders. First and foremost, it demonstrates the need for continuous learning. Though the army's emphasis on institutional learning has been the hallmark of the current force, Chamberlain augmented institutional learning with self-learning. He relished the opportunity to learn from seniors, peers, and subordinates. When Chamberlain's moment of truth arrived at Little Round Top, he was ready, because he had prepared himself for that moment. Throughout his life, Chamberlain had been an avid student of military history and a prolific writer, always seeking to improve his tactical and technical expertise. Even in the heat of battle, he refused to play the hand that he had been dealt. As evidenced by his leadership at Gettysburg, Chamberlain constantly sought alternate solutions—one more thing a leader could do to improve his situation, and after that, one more thing.

Last but not least, Chamberlain firmly believed that character is the foundation of leadership. Chamberlain expounded on the meaning of character when he addressed the Twentieth Maine veterans on the dedication of their monument at Gettysburg on October 3, 1889. "The lesson impressed on me as I stand here and my heart and mind traverse your faces, and the years that are gone, is that in a great, momentous struggle like this commemorated here, it is character that tells," he said. "What I mean by character is a firm and seasoned substance of soul. I mean such qualities or acquirements as intelligence, thoughtfulness, conscientiousness, right-mindedness, patience, fortitude, long-suffering, and unconquerable resolve."

Small wonder why Chamberlain's heroics in the Civil War serve as a case study for army leaders in *Field Manual 22–100: Military Leadership*. Nor is it surprising that Michael Shaara's classic *The Killer Angel*s: *A Novel of the Civil War*, featuring Chamberlain, is routinely included on the US Army chief of staff's professional reading list.

"A Learned Hero" was originally published in *ARMY Magazine* (September 2021).

11

Grant's Indomitable Buckeyes

Union Leaned Heavily on Leaders from Ohio

Within the Union high command during the American Civil War, no state contributed more to the ultimate Northern victory than Ohio. The Buckeye State proved to be a bastion of Northern military power when the Civil War engulfed the Union. An elite group of commanders—Ulysses Grant, William Tecumseh Sherman, Philip Sheridan, and James McPherson—hailed from Ohio. According to military historian John Keegan, Grant's origins may have been as significant to his generalship as his West Point education.

Over the course of the conflict, Grant and his trusted subordinates personified the restless energy that characterized Ohio's history, and its values of free enterprise rooted in personal property ownership and unflinching devotion to the republic. Though General in Chief Grant emerged as the officer who would lead the Union to victory, Grant viewed the triumvirate of Sherman, Sheridan, and McPherson as essential to the Union Cause.

Born in Lancaster, Ohio, in 1820, Sherman matriculated at the US Military Academy at West Point, New York, where he graduated sixth in his class of 1840. On detached duty in California during the Mexican–American War, Sherman was one of the few senior commanders in the Civil War who did not serve in Mexico. Like Grant, Sherman resigned his commission in the 1850s but returned to military service at the outbreak of the Civil War.

Sherman earned his first military laurels of the war to the First Battle of Bull Run, which took place on July 21, 1861. In the wake of that success, he was transferred to the Western Theater, where he commanded the District of Cairo. As commander, Sherman's role was to forward troops and supplies to then–Brig. Gen. Grant, who was leading the river expedition that captured Fort Donelson, Tennessee. Sherman's success in that capacity endeared him to Grant.

In the subsequent Shiloh campaign, Sherman commanded a division under Grant's direct command. After an initial surprise by Confederate troops at Shiloh, Tennessee, Sherman performed heroically and helped his chief form a defensive front that settled the Union line. Following the battle, Grant recommended Sherman for promotion to major general of volunteers. In the Vicksburg campaign in Mississippi, Sherman commanded a corps, and he played an instrumental role in Grant's rout of Confederate Gen. Braxton Bragg's Army of Tennessee at Chattanooga in November 1863. By the time Grant was elevated to general in chief of all Union armies in March 1864, the bond between the two Ohioans made Sherman the logical choice to succeed Grant in the vacated post of commander of the Military Division of the Mississippi.

In that capacity, Sherman led the main Western effort in Grant's campaign to destroy all Confederate armies to end the war. Sherman's force consisted of three armies totaling about one hundred thousand soldiers. Grant's instructions to Sherman were clear: to "move against Johnston's army [Army of Tennessee], to break it up and to get into the interior of the enemy's country as far as you can, inflicting all the damage you can against their war resources." Grant provided the strategic guidance, but he allowed Sherman to direct the operations of his military force.

Sherman's ensuing campaign led to the capture of Atlanta in September 1864 and facilitated President Abraham Lincoln's reelection the following November. Sherman's March to the Sea from Atlanta to Savannah, Georgia, and his Northern thrust from the Georgia coast through the Carolinas need no retelling here. By all measures, Sherman exceeded Grant's expectations. In Grant's words, "The march of Sherman's army from Atlanta to the sea and north to Goldsboro [North Carolina], while it was not accompanied with the danger that was anticipated, yet was magnificent in its results, and equally magnificent in the way it was conducted." High praise from the army's senior commander.

Sheridan was born in Albany, New York, but spent his formative years in Somerset, Ohio. Proud of his adopted state, Sheridan always considered himself an Ohioan. Unlike Sherman, who had served with Grant in the Army of the Tennessee, Sheridan earned his spurs as a division commander in Maj. Gen. George Thomas's Army of the Cumberland. Standing five feet six inches tall in his boots and weighing a scant 115 pounds, Sheridan hardly personified the warrior.

Looks were deceiving, as Sheridan possessed the exact quality that Grant desired in his subordinate commanders—a killer instinct. Most of all, Grant prized Sheridan's preparation for battle and his commanding presence in the field. Despite Grant's affinity for commanders who hailed from his Army of the Tennessee, he quickly recognized Sheridan's fighting spirit. Sheridan's division broke Bragg's siege lines at Missionary Ridge in Tennessee in November 1863. Not satisfied with the Union victory at Chattanooga, Sheridan organized a hasty pursuit of Bragg's defeated army. From then on, Sheridan could do no wrong in Grant's eyes.

Based on his assessment of Sheridan's potential, one of Grant's first decisions was to appoint Sheridan as commander of the Army of the Potomac's cavalry corps. When someone in the War Department teased the general in chief about Sheridan's diminutive size, stating, "The officer you brought on from the West is rather a little fellow to handle your cavalry," Grant responded, "You will find him big enough for the purpose before we get through with him."

And indeed, Sheridan was. In his initial raid in Richmond, Virginia, in May 1864, Sheridan soundly defeated Confederate Maj. Gen. J. E. B. Stuart's vaunted Confederate cavalry of the Army of Northern Virginia, killed its commander and returned safely to Grant's lines outside of Spotsylvania. Having proven his worth as a combat commander, Sheridan was next tapped by Grant to command the newly formed Army of the Shenandoah with instructions to follow the Confederate forces in the Shenandoah valley to the death.

Grant's instincts were justified by Sheridan's crushing defeat of Gen. Jubal Early's corps at the Third Battle of Winchester, Fisher's Hill, and Cedar Creek, all in Virginia. Sheridan laid waste to the Shenandoah Valley, depriving the Confederacy of much-needed supplies. By the time Sheridan was done, he had fulfilled Grant's wish that the valley "from Winchester up to Staunton, ninety-two miles, will have little in it for man or beast."

When news of Sheridan's victory at Cedar Creek reached Grant, he ordered a salute to his bantam cavalryman and informed Secretary of War Edwin Stanton that "I have always thought him one of the ablest of generals." In fact, Sheridan performed his task so completely that Grant summoned him to the trenches of Petersburg, Virginia, in March 1865. Sheridan promptly smashed the Confederate right wing at Five Forks, Virginia, forcing Gen. Robert E. Lee to begin his final retreat to Appomattox Court House, Virginia, a week later.

The third member of Grant's select Ohio team was Maj. Gen. McPherson, who at the time of his death near Atlanta had been elevated to command the Army of the Tennessee.

Born the son of a blacksmith near Clyde, Ohio, in 1828, McPherson secured an appointment to West Point, where he graduated first in his class in 1853. When the war began in 1861, McPherson served as aide-de-camp to Maj. Gen. Henry Halleck, Grant's immediate superior in the Mississippi Valley.

As Grant prepared to move against Fort Henry on the Tennessee River in February 1862, Halleck appointed then–Lt. Col. McPherson of the US Engineers to serve as Grant's chief engineer for the upcoming expedition. Grant biographer Ron Chernow describes McPherson as possessing an "unusually keen grasp of military affairs and a farsighted look of shrewdness in his eyes."

When Fort Donelson capitulated to Grant's army, McPherson, still an aide to Halleck, broke the news to Grant that Halleck was recommending Grant's promotion to major general. Thereafter, McPherson joined Grant's inner circle. He stood by Grant at the Shiloh campaign and commanded a brigade in what became the Army of the Tennessee in the Battle of Corinth, Mississippi.

McPherson next earned Grant's full trust and confidence in the campaign to capture Vicksburg. Now a corps commander, McPherson secured a victory at Raymond, Mississippi, on May 12, 1863, and performed extraordinarily well at Champion Hill. During the siege of Vicksburg, McPherson manned the center of Grant's line and helped negotiate the Confederate surrender on July 4. On his elevation to lieutenant general in March 1864, Grant singled out both Sherman and McPherson "as the men whom, above all others, I feel indebted for whatever I have had of success."

Not surprisingly, Grant reorganized the Union high command as he prepared to launch the climactic campaign to destroy Rebel armies in the spring of 1864. With respect to McPherson, the commanding general promoted his protege to serve as commander of the department and the Army of the Tennessee.

Sherman, too, considered McPherson a protege and assigned the Army of the Tennessee with the most hazardous missions on his drive to Atlanta from Chattanooga. McPherson constantly outmaneuvered Confederate Gen. Joseph Johnston from his defensive positions. When Confederate forces struck Sherman on July 22, McPherson immediately rode to the scene of the battle and was killed in action during the Battle of Atlanta.

The next day, Grant received the word that McPherson had been killed. Shaken by the news, Grant wrote to McPherson's grandmother, saying McPherson "formed for some time one of my military family. . . . Your bereavement is great but cannot exceed mine." In Grant's eyes, McPherson was one of the "ablest, purest, and best generals" he had. Sherman, too, was devastated by the death of his mentee. Sherman looked on McPherson as both a younger brother and logical successor. Asserted Sherman, "I expected something to happen to Grant and me; either the rebels or the newspapers would kill us both, and I looked to McPherson as the man to follow us and finish the war."

Next to Grant, no battle captains contributed more to Union victory than the Ohio triumvirate of Sherman, Sheridan, and McPherson. The trio shaped the war beyond the Appalachian Mountains during the first two years of the Civil War. Then, Sherman and Sheridan delivered the *coup de grace* to the dying Confederacy in 1865.

The three notable Buckeyes owed everything to Grant, a fellow Ohioan. It was Grant who nurtured Sherman as a division and a corps commander in the campaigns of Shiloh, Vicksburg, and Chattanooga. It was Grant who recommended Sherman to succeed him in the Western Theater, and it was Grant who appointed McPherson to command the Army of the Tennessee. And it was Grant who recommended that Sheridan command the cavalry corps of the Army of the Potomac and provided him free rein to conduct the Shenandoah campaign of 1864.

By the end of the Civil War, the Buckeye State had more than sufficient reason to be proud of its native and adoptive sons.

"Grant's Indomitable Buckeyes" was originally published in *ARMY Magazine* (May 2021).

12

Grant Unfiltered

Union Commander Didn't Hold Back When It Came to Other Civil War Generals

When President Abraham Lincoln conferred a lieutenant general commission on Ulysses Grant and appointed him general in chief of all Union armies in March 1864, Grant's first order of business was the selection of his commanders for the spring campaign.

Due to Grant's affinity for commanders who served with him in the Western Theater, Maj. Gen. William Tecumseh Sherman was the logical choice to replace Grant as commander of the Military Division of the Mississippi. The newly minted lieutenant general also demanded that Maj. Gen. Philip Sheridan be transferred to Virginia to command the Army of the Potomac's cavalry corps.

The team of Grant, Sherman, and Sheridan evolved into one of the most successful command teams in military history. But what about the other officers who led at the army and corps level in the Western Theater? How did Grant view them? And how did Grant perceive his Civil War opponents? In his memoirs, completed just a week before his death in July 1885, Grant assessed additional Union commanders as well as his principal adversaries.

Within days of receiving his commission from Lincoln, Grant journeyed to the headquarters of the Army of the Potomac to meet Maj. Gen. George Meade, its commanding general. Grant had known Meade from the Mexican–American War of 1846–1848 but had not seen him since. To Grant's surprise, Meade offered to step aside so Grant could appoint his own commander of the nation's most important army. This incident gave

Grant a more favorable opinion of Meade than did Meade's great victory at Gettysburg, Pennsylvania.

After their meeting, Grant decided to retain Meade in command, a decision he later regretted due to Meade's more deliberate approach to battle. Despite his reservations concerning Meade's caution, Grant stated that Meade was "brave and conscientious, and commanded the respect of all who knew him." On the downside, Meade "was unfortunately of a temper that would get beyond his control, at times, and make him speak to officers of high rank in the most offensive manner. . . . In spite of this defect, he was a most valuable officer and deserves a high place in the annals of his country."

Maj. Gen. Ambrose Burnside and Maj. Gen. Joseph Hooker, who served under Grant in 1863 and 1864, attracted Grant's personal attention. Burnside commanded the Army of the Potomac during the Fredericksburg, Virginia, Campaign in December 1862. He later commanded a separate corps under Grant at Petersburg, Virginia. Though he was generally liked and respected, Burnside was unsuited to command an army. As Grant explained, Burnside "knew this better than himself. He always admitted his blunders, and extenuated those of officers under him beyond what they were entitled to. It was hardly his fault that he was ever assigned to a separate command."

Like Meade and Burnside, Hooker commanded the Army of the Potomac during the Battle of Chancellorsville, Virginia, in May 1863. Lincoln regarded Hooker as a dangerous officer. When the president heard that Hooker had once stated that both the army and the government needed a dictator, Lincoln informed Hooker (when placing him at the head of the Army of the Potomac), "Of course it was not for this, but in spite of it, that I have given you the command."

Grant had seen little of Hooker during the war and was resentful that Lincoln and Secretary of War Edwin Stanton had forced Hooker on him as a subordinate commander. Grant informed Stanton that Hooker's "presence here is replete with both trouble and danger." Nor was Grant impressed with Hooker's success in securing Lookout Mountain overlooking Chattanooga, Tennessee, in November 1863. "It is all poetry," Grant wrote.

Grant singled out Maj. Gen. George Thomas's contributions to ultimate Union victory in more precise details. Thomas was never a member of Grant's inner circle, but Thomas had won the North's initial victories at Mill Springs, Kentucky, in 1862. Thomas's stand at Chickamauga, Georgia, in September 1863 saved the Army of the Cumberland from complete destruction, earning him the sobriquet "the Rock of Chickamauga." Now under Grant's direct command at Chattanooga in November 1863, Thomas captured Missionary Ridge, raising the siege of the beleaguered city. Thomas later won the war's most complete victory against Lt. Gen. John Bell Hood's Army of Tennessee at Nashville in December 1864.

In Grant's eyes, Thomas "was a man of commanding appearance, slow and deliberate in speech and action; sensible, honest and brave. He possessed valuable soldierly qualities in an eminent degree. His dispositions were deliberately made, and always good. He could not be driven from a point he was given to hold." But Grant had reservations about Thomas as a separate commander as "he was not as good, however, in pursuit as he was in action." Moreover, Grant considered ordering Thomas's removal from command until Thomas's victory at Nashville made such action moot.

At the corps level, Maj. Gen. Winfield Scott Hancock stands as the most conspicuous figure of all the general officers who did not exercise a separate command. Hancock's repulse of Pickett's Charge at Gettysburg on July 3, 1863, saw Hancock at his best. According to Grant, Hancock commanded a corps longer than any other officer, and his name was never mentioned as having committed in battle a blunder for which he was responsible.

Grant was delighted to have Hancock in command of one of the Army of the Potomac's corps when Grant initiated the Overland Campaign in Virginia beginning in May 1864. Hancock's "genial disposition made him friends, and his personal courage and his presence with his command in the thickest of the fight won for him the confidence of troops serving under him," Grant wrote.

Later political differences between the two officers led Grant to revise his opinion of Hancock. After the Democratic nomination convention in 1864 in which Hancock received a single vote, Grant said, "I have known [Hancock] for forty years. He is a weak, vain man. He is the most selfish man I know. He could never endure to have anyone else receive any credit."

What Grant implied was that Hancock had been bitten by the political bug and was more interested in pursuing a political career following the war. Political differences in 1864 aside, Hancock remained in the forefront of Union corps commanders during the war.

Another corps commander merited special praise from Grant as Grant assessed additional subordinate commanders. Alfred Terry came to Grant's attention in the later stages of the war. Terry's capture of Fort Fisher, North Carolina, in January 1865 resulted in Terry's promotion to the rank of brigadier general in the Regular Army and of major general of volunteers. Years later, President Grant appointed Terry to command the expedition against the Sioux and Northern Cheyenne tribes in 1876, culminating with the destruction of Lt. Col. George Custer's contingent of the Seventh Cavalry Regiment at the Little Bighorn in Montana.

Grant also recorded his estimate of the commanders who opposed him during the Civil War. Gen. Albert Johnston, second in seniority of the officers in Confederate service, commanded the Confederate Army at the Battle of Shiloh, Tennessee, in April 1862. Johnston became the highest-ranking general killed in the war when he fell at Shiloh. Both Confederate President Jefferson Davis and Grant expected Johnston to be the most formidable officer in Confederate service. Following Grant's victory at Shiloh, however, he revised his opinion, stating that Johnston was overrated, "vacillating and undecided in his actions."

Grant viewed Gen. Robert E. Lee, commanding general of the Army of Northern Virginia, with mixed emotions. He certainly respected Lee, but unlike other Union commanders, Grant was never intimidated by Lee. Grant saw Lee as "the acknowledged ablest general in the Confederate army," but when confronted with claims that his personal victory over Lee was simply a result of overwhelming resources, Grant claimed Lee "was of a slow, conservative, cautious nature, without imagination or humor, always the same, with grave dignity. I never could see in his achievements what justifies his reputation."

Of all the Confederate Army commanders, Grant reserved his highest accolades for Gen. Joseph Johnston, commander of the Army of Tennessee during the initial stages of the Atlanta campaign in 1864. "I think that his policy [of strategic defensive]," Grant opined, "was the best one that could have been pursued by the whole South—protract the war, which was all that was necessary to enable them to gain recognition in the end."

Hood, who succeeded Johnston as Sherman approached Atlanta, was "unquestionably a brave, gallant soldier and not destitute of ability; but unfortunately, his policy was to fight the enemy wherever he saw him, without thinking much of the consequences of defeat," Grant wrote. Hood squandered his army's fighting capability in a series of headlong attacks at Atlanta and later at the Battle of Franklin, Tennessee.

As for the Confederate cavalry, Grant stated that Lt. Gen. Nathan Bedford Forrest was "about the ablest cavalry general in the South." It was Forrest with his slashing raids who had disrupted Grant's initial assault on Vicksburg, Mississippi, by destroying the Union line of communication in December 1862. Grant concurred with Sherman's begrudging tribute that there could be no peace in western Tennessee until Forrest was dead.

In his 1988 book *Battle Cry of Freedom: The Civil War Era*, Pulitzer Prize–winning author James McPherson contends that the fate of the Confederacy was sealed once Lincoln appointed Grant general-in-chief of all the Union armies in the field. With the Union's three best generals—Grant, Sherman, and Sheridan in top commands, the days of the Confederacy appeared numbered.

With Grant in overall command, federal forces moved in concert for the first time in the war and secured Lincoln's victory. The officers who commanded these armies earned the general in chief's adulation and bequeathed a legacy of exemplary service to both the army and the nation.

"Grant Unfiltered" was originally published in *ARMY Magazine* (September 2022).

13

President Wilson Selects His Commander

Gen. John J. Pershing emerged from the Great War in resplendent glory. As the commander of the American Expeditionary Forces (AEF), Pershing had led the American forces abroad in the greatest war in history up to that time. In retrospect, the selection of Pershing to command the AEF seems a foregone conclusion. No senior officer had compiled a more distinguished combat record before the war than had Pershing, and President Theodore Roosevelt's promotion of then–Capt. Pershing to the grade of brigadier general in 1906 over the heads of approximately nine hundred senior officers seemed to confirm that destiny had marked him for senior command. Military achievements and sheer intellect alone, however, seldom dictate promotion to the most senior ranks in the army. Pershing's career demonstrates additional political and personal factors were instrumental in President Woodrow Wilson's selection of him as commander of American forces during World War I.

Pershing graduated from the US Military Academy in 1886, president of his class and the first captain of the US Corps of Cadets. Assigned to the Sixth US Cavalry on graduation from West Point, he participated in campaigns against the Apache in New Mexico and, later, the Sioux in South Dakota. A decade later, in the Spanish–American War, he served with the American force that invaded Cuba, and he received accolades from one of his superiors for his part in the assaults against the Spanish positions on Kettle Hill and San Juan Hill. Said his commander, "I have been in many fights and through the Civil War, but on my word, you were the coolest and bravest man I ever saw under fire in my life."

With the acquisition of America's global empire, Pershing next saw combat against the Lake Lanao Moros (Muslims) in the Philippines as the United States fought to subdue the insurgency in its new colony. Though only a captain, Pershing had gained national attention and as a result was a member of the first complement of army officers assigned to the newly created War Department general staff. Roosevelt informed Secretary of War Elihu Root that he intended to promote Pershing to the grade of brigadier general. Irate and impatient with an archaic military promotion system that rewarded seniority over battlefield competence, Roosevelt passed over about nine hundred senior captains and field grade officers and nominated Pershing for promotion to brigadier general in September 1906, stating, "I am sure that Pershing will make good; and that is all I have to ask of him."

The next decade added to Pershing's military laurels. Multiple tours in the Philippines and being on special assignments from the War Department monopolized his time as he neared thirty years of commissioned service. Then fate once again intervened, and Pershing was given an opportunity to perform in a position that brought him into direct contact with the senior political leaders of the Wilson administration.

When Mexican bandit Pancho Villa crossed the border and killed American citizens in Columbus, New Mexico, on the evening of March 8 and 9, 1916, war fever surged, and Wilson authorized a cross-border incursion "with the sole object of capturing Villa and preventing further raids by his band." Secretary of War Newton D. Baker named Pershing as field commander. Though the secretary of war would not normally have jumped the chain of command, Baker assigned Pershing because of his experience.

The subsequent Punitive Expedition lasted about ten months. Although Pershing never corralled Villa, his leadership of the expedition added luster to his reputation within the army and made him a national figure. Though Pershing's conduct received a certain degree of criticism from the administration's opponents, he was promoted to major general in 1916.

After German U-boats sank several unarmed merchant vessels, Wilson requested Congress on April 2, 1917, to declare war against Germany. Four days later, the president signed the war resolution, catapulting America into World War I.

The government had to immediately decide who would command the American military force. It seemed clear that in order to win the war, a large American ground force would have to be sent to Europe. Allied commissioners were already in Washington, DC, and urging the immediate deployment of an expeditionary force to the continent. Maj. Gen. Frederick Funston was the presumptive candidate to command the American forces abroad before his death in February 1917. With Funston's death, there were several legitimate candidates for the senior command, all of whom far outranked Pershing. Indeed, Pershing was the junior major general on active service. Nevertheless, age and poor health worked against these senior officers.

As the secretary of war reviewed the candidates, Baker narrowed the list to Pershing and Maj. Gen. Leonard Wood. Wood had served as the commanding officer of the Rough Riders in the Spanish–American War, had emerged as the leading spokesman of military preparedness before the United States's entry into the war, and had led and established the "Plattsburgh camps" to train potential officers in the event of war. Wood's close relationship with Roosevelt, however, was a serious negative in Baker's view because before the United States declared war, Roosevelt had publicly and vehemently condemned what he termed Wilson's lack of executive action to ready the country for a war that Roosevelt predicted was inevitable. Wood, too, had criticized Wilson's pacifism. Never a friend of Roosevelt, Wilson also distrusted Wood, who had recently criticized Roosevelt in Wilson's presence in a private conversation. Such indiscreet comments caused the president to doubt Wood's loyalty and discretion.

Pershing, on the other hand, avoided the partisan political activity and the indiscretion that characterized Wood. Not only was Pershing's distinguished combat record a rarity among other officers, but he also had more foreign service than any other general officer and had displayed matchless leadership in a variety of high-profile command assignments. In addition, though reports reached Baker that Pershing did not totally agree with Wilson's Mexican policy, Pershing scrupulously avoided any parochial or public political position in the execution of his duties. Baker could forgive personal disagreement in exchange for loyalty and obedience. In short, Baker sought an experienced general to command the AEF, not a diplomat.

Having eliminated Wood as a leading candidate to command what became the AEF, Baker settled on Pershing as the most likely commander. Other factors contributed to the selection of Pershing to command the

AEF, not the least of which was the unwavering support of his father-in-law, Sen. Francis Warren. Always quick to decipher the political machinations within Washington and with the Allied commissioners in the nation's capital, Warren quickly wired Pershing on May 3, 1917, "Wire me today whether and how much you speak, read and write French." Understanding the implications of the telegram, Pershing replied that he had spent several months in France in 1908 and "can easily reacquire the satisfactory working knowledge" of the language. A few days later, Warren sent another telegram to Pershing, implying that he should put his best foot forward and champion his own candidacy.

In addition to his father-in-law's support, Pershing played the political game well. He concealed his ambition from everyone except his closest confidants. To Robert L. Bullard, destined to command one of Pershing's armies in France, Pershing was "always a good courtier." Several days after Wilson asked Congress for a declaration of war, Pershing wrote his commander in chief, "As an officer of the Army, may I not extend to you, as Commander in Chief of the armies, my sincere congratulations upon your soul-stirring patriotic address. . . . It arouses in the breast of every soldier feelings of the deepest admiration for their leader."

A third factor influenced Pershing's selection as commander of the AEF. Throughout Pershing's career and often prompted by Warren, Pershing carefully cultivated his relationships with senior military commanders. He was not an officer whom one could serve with comfortably, but if one could put aside Pershing's aloofness and personal ambition, the future AEF commander was not a difficult subordinate. As a result, Army Chief of Staff Maj. Gen. Hugh L. Scott and most senior officers within the army championed Pershing's appointment. Maj. Gen. James F. Bell, who was Pershing's commanding officer in the Philippines, was so convinced that Baker would select Pershing that he requested an assignment under Pershing's command. Maj. Gen. Tasker H. Bliss also supported him as the best candidate.

Scott proved to be Pershing's most vocal advocate. In early May 1917, he sent Pershing a cryptic message marked "for your eye alone." As Scott informed Pershing, "Under plans under consideration is one which will require, among other troops, four infantry regiments and one artillery regiment from your department for service in France. If plans are carried out, you will be in command of the entire force." Pershing correctly construed this message to mean that these troops would form a division under his immediate command. About a week later, Pershing arrived in Washington, DC, pursuant to orders and called at once at the office of the chief of staff. Shortly after he paid his respects to Scott, Baker informed him that he would command the American division being dispatched to France.

Wilson's personal role in selecting Pershing was secondary. The president certainly was quite familiar with Pershing's reputation and was generally pleased with the outcome of the Punitive Expedition. Wilson normally delegated military promotions to his secretary of war, and Pershing's selection was no exception. It was Baker who selected him; Wilson merely approved Baker's choice. In his only meeting with Pershing before the general's departure, Wilson referred to Pershing's experience in Mexico and informed the newly designated commander that his selection was the result of their experience in having him in similar positions.

Before adjourning the meeting with Baker and Pershing, Wilson added, "General, you were chosen entirely upon your record, and I have every confidence that you will succeed. You shall have my full support." Wilson then directed Baker to formulate Pershing's formal orders and to issue his executive guidance to govern the commander's conduct on arriving in Europe.

Wilson's approval of Pershing to command the AEF proved an inspired choice. During the war, Pershing handled his increased responsibility with his usual aplomb and his customary arrogance, which alienated many Allied commanders. Nevertheless, he preserved the integrity of the AEF. He refused to be intimidated, and he was primarily responsible for insisting that the AEF fight under American command instead of being broken up as piecemeal replacements for British and French forces. How instrumental was the AEF in winning the war? Historians differ, but there is little doubt that Gen. John J. Pershing proved the right officer to command the American force. In 1919, a grateful Congress concurred, elevating Pershing to the rank of general of the armies.

"President Wilson Selects His Commander" was originally published in *ARMY Magazine* (May 2014).

14

The Fighting Doughboys of the American Expeditionary Forces

In assessing the reasons for the Allied victory during World War I, American Expeditionary Forces (AEF) commander Gen. John J. (Black Jack) Pershing noted that "upon the young commanders of platoons, companies and battalions fell the heaviest burden." Deeds of daring, to use Pershing's phrase, were legion during the war, and there were many whose heroic services had been recognized over the course of the war. In his memoirs, however, Pershing mentioned only three soldiers whose battlefield exploits he deemed particularly extraordinary and representative of the fighting spirit of the AEF.

Best typifying the spirit of the rank and file of the AEF were a reserve officer, a draftee from the mountains of northern Tennessee, and a Regular Army man. Of the more than 2 million soldiers who composed the American Expeditionary Forces over the course of the war, Pershing singled out Maj. Charles W. Whittlesey, who refused to surrender the "Lost Battalion" of the Seventy-Seventh Division; CPL Alvin C. York of the Eighty-Second Division, who single-handedly killed twenty-five enemy soldiers and captured 132 Germans; and Lt. Samuel Woodfill from the Fifth Division, who personally attacked a series of German machine-gun nests near Cunel, France, and killed the crews of each in turn until reduced to the necessity of assaulting the last detachment with a pick, dispatching them all. All three soldiers fought in the Meuse–Argonne offensive that began the last week of September 1918 and continued until the armistice on November 11.

Few legends from the Great War have endured as long as the story of the Lost Battalion. In reality, Maj. Charles W. Whittlesey's First Battalion of the 308th Infantry, Seventy-Seventh Division, was never lost, nor was the Lost Battalion a single battalion. What became known as the Lost Battalion was actually seven companies from two separate infantry battalions and two machine-gun sections from the 306th Machine Gun Battalion. From October 2, 1918, until the surrounded doughboys were relieved a week later, Whittlesey was the senior commissioned officer of the besieged defenders. Capt. George G. McMurtry, an old Rough Rider, commanded Whittlesey's sister battalion from the same regiment.

Whittlesey lacked the military presence of a Pershing or a Woodfill. A "slender bespectacled New Englander, a man of manners, a practicing lawyer in New York" is how doughboy historian Laurence Stallings describes him in the book *The Doughboys: The Story of the AEF*. Not a professional soldier, Whittlesey had earned his commission through one of the Plattsburgh, New York, camps designed in the American preparedness movements in 1916. His previous wartime experiences had been unremarkable.

By October 1, 1918, Whittlesey's First Battalion positioned itself on the front line within the Argonne Forest, under orders to continue the attack the following morning toward Charlevaux Mill, with McMurtry's Second Battalion in direct support. Due to the attrition during the previous week's combat, the fighting strength of the combined battalions was less than seven hundred. To their front was a deep ravine that separated the left flank companies from the main body.

At precisely 0630 hours, Whittlesey plunged forward under the cover of an intense artillery bombardment. The assault across the corps front failed immediately, but by early afternoon on October 2, the division commander renewed the attack. Whittlesey somehow discovered a gap in the enemy defense and penetrated the German line to a half mile. McMurtry's Second Battalion was hot on his heels. Casualties, however, had reduced their combined strength to approximately 550 men.

Awaiting reinforcements, Whittlesey assumed direct command of the survivors and relayed his position to battalion headquarters. Alone in the Argonne since his flanking elements had failed to match his advance, Whittlesey established a defensive posture and waited for the inevitable German counterattack. He did not have to wait long.

By midafternoon, the Germans had recovered from their initial surprise and began penetrating Whittlesey's perimeter. Whittlesey dispatched two of his eight carrier pigeons to the division commander, requesting resupply of ammunition and giving his approximate position. Maj. Gen. Robert Alexander, commanding the Seventy-Seventh Division, ordered a rescue attack on October 3, but the relief effort failed due to heavy fog and determined German resistance that reduced the assaulting Americans by 50 percent. Whittlesey was now hopelessly surrounded with little expectation of relief. By the end of the day, he had lost 222 men, eighty-two of them killed.

October 5 proved to be the worst day of the battle. Friendly artillery descended on Whittlesey's troops and wiped out one platoon. Now subject to enemy artillery and mortar fire, Whittlesey released two more carrier pigeons in an attempt to halt the fratricide. McMurtry was badly wounded, and the Lost Battalion was under repeated infantry and hand grenade assault. To make matters worse, aerial resupply was totally ineffective. The next day produced no relief as the Lost Battalion again held their position by the skin of their teeth.

On October 7, nine soldiers from McMurtry's battalion attempted to escape the encirclement, only to be killed or captured by the enemy. Later that afternoon, one of the prisoners, PVT Lowell R. Hollingshead, under protest, delivered a surrender demand from the German commander to Whittlesey. The letter read in part, "The suffering of your wounded men can be heard over here in the German lines, and we are appealing to your humane sentiments to stop. A white flag shown by one of your men will tell us that you agree with these conditions." Whittlesey treated the surrender demand with utter contempt and sent no reply. Hearing nothing from the Americans except cries of profanity, the Germans attacked the Lost Battalion with increased intensity.

Down to their last rounds of ammunition and dying from thirst, Whittlesey's Lost Battalion repelled the final German assault. That same afternoon, an American battalion from the 307th Infantry Regiment finally reached Whittlesey's beleaguered troops and provided rations, medical supplies and ammunition. Whittlesey waited until the afternoon of October 8 to withdraw his troops. By that time, the Lost Battalion had captured the imagination of the American high command. Gen. Alexander himself visited Whittlesey in the Argonne and congratulated him on his spirited defense. Only 194 of the original 554 doughboys who started the attack on October 2 stood unwounded.

The army promoted Whittlesey to lieutenant colonel following the relief of the Lost Battalion and pulled him from the front line. On December 5, Whittlesey was honorably discharged from active service. The next day he was awarded the Medal of Honor. A civilian once again, Whittlesey returned to his law profession where he served as an associate for a prestigious law firm from 1919 to 1920, but he never adjusted to civilian life—always haunted by the death that he had witnessed in the Argonne Forest. Whittlesey later committed suicide when he jumped from a ship en route to Havana on November 26, 1921.

About the time that the Lost Battalion was finally rescued, acting corporal Alvin York of Pall Mall, Tennessee, experienced his personal rendezvous with destiny; he was later promoted to the rank of sergeant. York was the unlikeliest of heroes. Drafted in November 1917, this Tennessee mountaineer proved a natural hunter whose marksmanship was already legendary. On receipt of his draft notice, York immediately submitted his paperwork as a conscientious objector, but the district board rejected his request. Twenty-nine years old when the United States entered the war, York was assigned to First Platoon, Company G, 328th Infantry Regiment, Eighty-Second Infantry (All-American) Division. Commanding York's company was Capt. E. C. B. Danforth, an officer whom York came to admire.

Not that far from where the Lost Battalion was rescued, York's company moved forward to the vicinity of the village of Chatel-Chéhéry, France, near the edge of the Argonne along the Aire River. On October 8, Company G moved forward without artillery support. Instantly the company encountered stiff enemy resistance, and the attack stalled. At that point, Danforth decided to send a small detachment of men from the 1st Platoon around the left flank of the company line. Corp. Bernard Early commanded the platoon-size detachment, with York commanding one of three infantry squads. Within minutes, Early's force ran into heavy machine-gun fire and was reduced to seventeen men.

Moving through the dense undergrowth, the doughboys came across two German stretcher bearers who fled as soon as they saw the American platoon. Early followed and soon stumbled on an encampment of twenty-five German soldiers, whom they promptly captured. As Early rounded up the prisoners, a German officer hollered a command, and two concealed machine guns started firing on the Americans. Early fell with five bullets in his body. Six doughboys died instantly, and another two were wounded in addition to Early, leaving York and seven others unharmed.

Now the senior noncommissioned officer, York seized command. Leaving the remnants of his command, he crawled to a position where he could draw a bead on the enemy machine-gun nests. "In order to sight me or swing their machine guns at me," he later explained, "the Germans had to show their heads above the trenches." Every time a gunner appeared, York picked him off, emptying three clips of ammunition in the process. Just then, a German officer with six men with fixed bayonets charged York from twenty-five yards away. York promptly killed each with a carefully aimed shot, starting with the rear soldier and working his way forward.

Having disposed of the enemy to his immediate front, York led the prisoners to the rear. En route to the American lines, he encountered several additional machine-gun positions and directed that his senior prisoner order them to surrender, too. With a single exception, the Germans descended the hill and surrendered to York. One of the enemy soldiers tested York and tossed a grenade at his captors. York immediately shot him through the heart. The remainder of the prisoners got the message and marched off to captivity.

By this time, York had captured more than one hundred enemy soldiers, and he was afraid that his detachment would be fired on by his own artillery. How many enemy dead he had left on the ridge was anyone's guess. Fortunately, a relief squad sent to aid CPL Early met York as he neared American lines. Reporting to the battalion adjutant, York relinquished more than 130 prisoners. He left at least twenty-five enemy dead on the battlefield. When Gen. George B. Duncan, newly assigned commander of the All-American Division, later asked York how many he thought he had hit, York replied, "General, I would hate to think I missed any of them shots; they were all at pretty close range—50 to 60 yards."

Not surprisingly, Pershing judged York the outstanding civilian soldier of the AEF. Allied Supreme Commander Gen. Ferdinand Foch concurred and awarded York the Croix de Guerre with palm, adding, "What you did was the accomplishment by any private soldier of all the armies of Europe." As for Alvin York, he stated in 1926 that he had rather it be said that he gave his life toward aiding his fellow man than to be remembered as a warrior who had capitalized on his fame as a fighter.

As remarkable as were York's achievements in the Argonne, in Pershing's estimation they were second to those of acting Capt. Samuel Woodfill, an ex-sergeant from the old army. To Pershing, Woodfill was the outstanding figure in the AEF, America's "doughboy of doughboys." Born in Indiana in 1883, Woodfill joined the army at the time of the Philippine Insurrection and then reenlisted for the first of four hitches with the Third Infantry Regiment in Alaska, where he became the only American soldier to outshoot the Royal Canadian Mounted Police. From the Arctic, Woodfill was transferred to the Mexican border in 1916 during the crisis following Pancho Villa's raid on Columbus, New Mexico.

Wearing six hash marks on his sleeve by the time Congress declared war on Germany in April 1917, Sergeant Woodfill accepted an appointment as a reserve lieutenant, one of the many battle-hardened noncommissioned officers (NCOs) to join the commissioned ranks. It was a smooth transition. As Woodfill later stated to reporter Lowell Thomas, the NCO Corps "had been as good as captains for years because during the frequent absences of their company commanders they had run the outfit."

Now with Company M, Sixtieth Regiment, Fifth (Red Diamond) Division, Woodfill barely survived the Saint-Mihiel Offensive in September 1918 and then moved his company to a railroad line east of Cunel in the Argonne Forest. Woodfill's battalion was scheduled to attack on October 14, 1918, but a day earlier, Woodfill's commander directed him to conduct a combat reconnaissance to identify the enemy's main line of resistance within the Bois de la Pultiere, several hundred yards to their front.

No sooner had they crossed the line of departure when Woodfill's company encountered several machine-gun nests that inflicted horrific casualties on Woodfill's lead platoons. The enemy fire seemed to be coming from three directions. One gun was to Woodfill's right in the abandoned stable, another was to his front, and the third was from the church tower in a little village, about 250 yards to Woodfill's left. Unable to maneuver his command, Woodfill directed his company to remain in position as he crawled forward to ascertain the location of the first machine gun. Working his way around the flank of the machine-gun nest, Woodfill fired four carefully aimed shots, killing four members of the machine-gun crew as each attempted to sight the gun. The remaining German soldier attempted to escape, but another shot from Woodfill's Springfield brought him down as well. Woodfill then moved forward to examine the position. As he approached the gun, a German officer sprang toward Woodfill. Woodfill and the officer fought hand-to-hand until Woodfill subdued his opponent and killed him with his pistol.

As Woodfill's company resumed their advance, a second machine gun opened fire on them. With his company dispersed throughout the woods, control was virtually impossible. Woodfill described the ensuing action as "every man for himself." The enemy was in a shallow dugout, with the head and shoulders of the gunner in plain sight. With a five-cartridge clip, Woodfill dispatched him and several other enemy soldiers with carefully aimed shots.

Continuing his advance, a third machine gun opened fire on the assaulting Americans. Crawling on his stomach to get closer to the enemy, Woodfill located the enemy position in the woods on the edge of a trench that ran back into the enemy lines. Though his eyes were burning with mustard gas, he picked off five men with a single clip of ammunition. Running forward to inspect the machine-gun nests, Woodfill discovered another German soldier whom he promptly dispatched with his Colt automatic.

For once Woodfill let his guard down, thinking he had wiped out the entire machine-gun nest. Before he could respond to noise from the side, a German soldier rushed Woodfill from behind around a run in the trench, rifle in hand. Woodfill pulled the trigger, but his Colt jammed. Grabbing a long-handled pickax stuck into the side of the trench, Woodfill crashed the pick down on the enemy's head. He then wheeled just in time to miss a bullet in the back from one of the wounded Germans. With another blow of the pick, Woodfill finished him off as well. Within the span of a few hours, Woodfill had captured three machine guns and killed more than eleven Germans.

Now well within the enemy lines and under intense fire, Woodfill requested reinforcements from his battalion commander who instructed him to return to their former position. When he reported to the command post, Woodfill's battalion commander asked him what he had been doing to the Germans. "I got a few," Woodfill responded. "Yeah, I know you did," the commander responded. In his memoirs, Woodfill described his action as "a frontiersman stalks machine gun."

The armistice found Woodfill recuperating in a hospital, suffering from pneumonia resulting from repeated gassings during the Argonne offensive. Within weeks Woodfill received orders to Chaumont, France, Pershing's headquarters, where he received his Medal of Honor from Pershing himself. Among the sixteen other recipients was Capt. McMurtry from the Lost Battalion.

Fate would finally bring Whittlesey, York, and Woodfill together three years later when Congress authorized the burial of an unidentified American soldier from World War I in the plaza of the new Memorial Amphitheater at Arlington National Cemetery. A War Department committee reviewed three thousand wartime citations and narrowed the search for pallbearers to one hundred soldiers for Army Chief of Staff Pershing to review. Without hesitation, the "Iron Commander" selected York, Whittlesey and Woodfill. President Warren G. Harding presided over the interment ceremony on November 11, 1921. Also in attendance were former presidents William Howard Taft and Woodrow Wilson.

The interment was the first and only time that Whittlesey, York, and Woodfill stood together. Two weeks after the ceremony, Whittlesey booked passage on the SS *Toloa*, a steamship bound for Havana, Cuba. Prior to coming aboard, he had put his affairs in order and paid next month's rent in advance. On November 24, Whittlesey walked to the rail and jumped overboard. When Woodfill heard of Whittlesey's death, he guessed that those four days in the Argonne Forest must have put too heavy a strain on the former commander of the Lost Battalion.

York returned to Tennessee following the war and worked a farm given to him by the state of Tennessee in recognition of his wartime heroics. He later established an agricultural institute in the Valley of the Three Forks of the Wolf and enjoyed a brief resurgence of fame when Hollywood beckoned in 1941 to tell the story of his life, with Gary Cooper portraying the soft-spoken York. The subsequent years proved difficult for York. As *Life* magazine described York in a special issue in 1997, "This exemplar of the American fighting man died in 1964, all but forgotten" by the nation he had served so well.

Following the war, Woodfill reverted to his NCO status to preserve the tenure of his service, since as a reserve officer, he would have lost his military benefits. That reduction in rank seemed appropriate, stated historian Stallings, because Woodfill served as "the eternal sergeant of Black Jack's esteem." Woodfill died alone on his farm in 1951 and was buried at Arlington National Cemetery, not far from the Iron Commander himself.

It has been four score and twelve years since the guns fell silent along the Meuse River and in the Argonne Forest. Why write of Whittlesey, York. and Woodfill now? The Great War, more than the Spanish–American War, ushered the United States onto the world stage, and that awesome projection of military power was borne on the backs of the American doughboys who fought in France in 1918. Gen. Douglas MacArthur, himself one of the most highly decorated commanders from that conflict, said it best in his final address to the US Corps of Cadets: "His [the American soldier's] name and fame are the birthright of every American citizen. . . . From one end of the world to the other, he has drained deep the chalice of courage." Representing the 2 million soldiers of the AEF, Charles Whittlesey, Alvin York, and Samuel Woodfill most certainly would agree.

"The Fighting Doughboys of the American Expeditionary Forces" was originally published in *ARMY Magazine* (November 2010).

15

Leading from the Front

Senior Commanders Under Pershing Played Key Roles in World War I

In the aftermath of the festivities surrounding the centennial of the Great War, the doughboys of the American Expeditionary Forces have virtually vanished from our national consciousness. And despite the fact that nearly 2 million American ground forces served in France, few of their countrymen can identify the senior field commanders of World War I. Gen. John Pershing commanded the American Expeditionary Forces (AEF), but who led the field armies that contributed to victory for the Allied and associated powers?

American combat operations in World War I were confined to a seven-month period between May and November 1918. Until the AEF embarked on the second phase of the Meuse–Argonne Offensive, Pershing wore dual hats: commanding general, AEF, and commanding general, First US Army. He also assured that subordinate commanders, division commanders and above met his personal standards of appearance and deportment. Many a good officer failed the intense scrutiny of Pershing's steely-eyed gaze when he reported to Pershing's headquarters at Chaumont, France.

On July 24, 1918, Pershing issued orders creating the First Army. Before then, the AEF had fought in corps and divisions. On July 31, Pershing issued General Order No. 1 assuming command of his army. The activation of First Army ensured that American forces would operate as an autonomous entity alongside the British and French armies on the Western Front. The Meuse–Argonne Offensive became the AEF's greatest battlefield effort of World War I. The four-seven-day attack in the heart of the

Hindenburg Line, beginning September 26 and lasting until November 11, 1918, was conducted in three phases. Some 1.2 million AEF troops were engaged, though probably no more than four hundred thousand were in action at any one time.

Despite Pershing's insistence on "open warfare"—to avoid embracing the trench warfare mentality and to reestablish maneuvering on the battlefield—frontal attacks by the AEF remained unsophisticated. Casualties mounted as First Army prepared to assault the most heavily defended German line of resistance. When Allied commander in chief Marshal Ferdinand Foch expressed his displeasure that "the [American] advance through the Argonne had presented undeniable difficulties to the American staffs," Pershing temporarily suspended his offensive on October 11.

The halt allowed Pershing to consider his options for renewal of First Army's attack and to revise the command structure of the AEF. Now that the AEF had grown in size and complexity, the scale of military operations proved too difficult for a single commander to function as both a tactician and a member of the Allied High Command. Stepping away from battlefield coordination, however, proved a hard decision for the "Iron Commander." By mid-October, however, Pershing reluctantly stepped aside from active battlefield coordination and assumed the role of an army group commander. As army group commander, Pershing possessed equal status with British Field Marshal Douglas Haig of Great Britain and Gen. Henri-Philippe Petain of France, answerable only to Foch.

Pershing relinquished command of First Army to newly promoted Lt. Gen. Hunter Liggett. He next activated Second US Army under the command of Lt. Gen. Robert Lee Bullard. Liggett and Bullard successfully conducted AEF's field operations until the cessation of hostilities on November 11, 1918. At three years older than AEF commander Pershing, Liggett was a West Point graduate who had fought on the Western frontier against Native American tribes, in the Spanish–American War, and in the Philippines. The president of the Army War College before World War I, Liggett had compiled a distinguished combat record before the war.

In March 1917, Liggett, now commanding the Forty-First Division, deployed the division to France. He assumed command of I Corps on January 15, 1918, and prepared the corps for battle. Somewhat portly and with a ferocious appetite, Liggett had not made a favorable impression with Pershing due to his increasing waistline. Yet Liggett was a soldier's soldier and a tactical genius. Ever cognizant that Pershing disapproved of his physical appearance, Liggett reportedly told him, "There is no fat above my collar."

Following activation of I Corps, Liggett exercised general command of the American divisions that recently arrived in France. He performed exceedingly well in the spring and summer campaigns in central France. Having already gained Pershing's confidence, Liggett's corps not only participated in the Second Battle of the Marne but also played a pivotal role in the reduction of the Saint-Mihiel salient in mid-September 1918, the AEF's first all-American offensive.

Liggett's assumption of command of First Army on October 16 assured the "undivided attention of a master tactician, a man not concerned with politics and broader issues," according to John Eisenhower in his book *Yanks: The Epic Story of the American Army in World War I.* Similar to that of Maj. Gen. George Meade's relationship with Lt. Gen. Ulysses Grant during the Civil War, Liggett's role as the single army commander proved awkward in the second phase of the Meuse–Argonne Offensive. Even though Pershing had officially relinquished command of First Army to Liggett, the Iron Commander repeatedly interposed his "suggestions" to Liggett.

That said, First Army successfully pierced the Hindenburg Line and succeeded in cutting the Sedan-Mézières railroad, the object of the offensive. On November 10, a small contingent of Liggett's forces actually crossed the Meuse River but was unable to establish a strong lodgment. Liggett intended to advance the following day when the guns fell silent.

In the war's final campaign, command of the Second Army rested on Bullard's shoulders. Much like Pershing and Liggett, Bullard had earned his combat spurs for frontier service and in the Philippines. More important, he established a deep personal relationship with Pershing that predated the Great War. Said Bullard's principal biographer, Allan Millett, "Few officers ever got close to Pershing, and few tried. Yet many served him well, and Robert Lee Bullard was one of them."

When Bullard arrived in France in 1917, he received the unenviable task of creating the AEF school system that Pershing deemed critical in creating an independent American Army. Due to his success in developing the infantry schools in the Gondrecourt area, Bullard was the logical successor to command the First Infantry Division once the AEF chief relieved the former division commander in December 1917. In that capacity, Bullard earned accolades for winning the Battle of Cantigny in May 1918, America's initial battle in World War I. After seven months of command of the Big Red One, Bullard was promoted to command III Corps. As corps commander, Bullard led his forces in the Aisne–Marne Campaign in July 1918. Despite excessive casualties, Pershing deemed Bullard's generalship highly successful.

Bullard's principal task as a corps commander in the Meuse–Argonne Offensive was to penetrate German defenses in the Argonne Forest, "formidable terrain made more lethal by German fortifications named the *Kriemhilde Stellung*," according to Millett. Progress was slow and casualties were excessively high. On October 11, Bullard discovered that Pershing had reassigned him to command the newly activated Second Army. The next day, Bullard learned that his chief expected him to prepare Second Army for a major offensive on both sides of the Moselle River in the direction of Metz, France. Bullard realized the activation of Second Army was a result of the obvious broadening of the width and depth of German defensive positions.

In the final stages of the Meuse–Argonne Offensive, Second Army would play a limited role in the final assault of the Hindenburg Line. Liggett's First Army comprised the main attack; Bullard's Second Army played a supporting role. Bullard's specific orders were "to execute local operations sufficiently vigorous to reconnoiter the enemy and to develop whatever partial success may be obtained," Foch wrote in *The Memoirs of Marshal Foch*. In the week before the armistice, Bullard conducted a series of limited raids and prepared a major offensive toward Metz. Bullard's assault was scheduled for November 11 when Pershing informed him that Germany had accepted the Allied conditions for a ceasefire. For Bullard, the war was over.

So why have Liggett and Bullard been forgotten? More so than the Korean War, the American experience in World War I remains "the Forgotten War." Most historians view the Great War as a mere precursor to World War II. Equally significant is the fact that in the euphoria that accompanied the termination of hostilities, Pershing's name shone far more brightly than that of his subordinate commanders. By December 7, 1941, the senior commanders of the AEF, all of whom were about Pershing's age, were too old to serve in World War II. Indeed, the AEF commander in chief outlived Liggett and Bullard; Pershing passed away in 1948.

In the interwar period, the army-level commanders of World War I yielded to the company and field grade officers who matured into the general officers of World War II. Future commanders and staff officers such as George Marshall, George Patton Jr., and Douglas MacArthur all served as junior officers under Liggett and Bullard. Foch, not always Pershing's strongest advocate, provided the ultimate compliment to the officers and soldiers of the Allied armies. Said Foch to his national commanders, "You have full right to be proud, for you have crowned your standards with immortal glory, and won the gratitude of posterity."

To his credit, Pershing realized the laurels of victory should crown the head of his subordinate commanders as well. "To the higher commanders and their staff," Pershing wrote, "great credit is due for the successful performance of an exceptionally complicated and arduous task." Pershing's glowing accolades became Liggett's and Bullard's reward and their final tribute.

More than a century after the end of the Great War, we honor Liggett and Bullard for their dedicated service and applaud their sacrifices in "the war to end all wars." They merit more widespread recognition.

"Leading from the Front: Senior Commanders Under Pershing Played Key Roles in WWI" was originally published in *ARMY Magazine* (November 2020).

16

Destined for Greatness

Between World War I and World War II, the US Army maintained the Fifteenth Infantry Regiment in China. The regiment's mission focused on "safeguarding the lives and property of American diplomats, missionaries, and business entrepreneurs," according to author Eric Larrabee in his 1987 book, *Commander in Chief: Franklin Delano Roosevelt, His Lieutenants, and Their War*.

The regiment was sent to China after the Boxer Rebellion, a violent uprising against foreigners that occurred in 1900. Six national governments, including the United States, had quickly dispatched troops to quell the unrest. Service in the Fifteenth Infantry Regiment offered distinct contrasts to service in America, not the least of which was the regiment's original mission to protect the legation staff in Peking, now known as Beijing. Regimental headquarters located in the city of Tientsin, the principal port and business center of northern China, attracted a special breed of commissioned and noncommissioned officers.

These elite soldiers became widely known throughout the peacetime army as the "old China hands." Between 1925 and 1930, twenty-five officers stationed at Tientsin, also known as Tianjin, later served as general war officers in World War II and Korea. Among the old China hands were George Marshall, Joseph Stilwell, and Matthew Ridgway, all destined for higher station in the upcoming global conflict.

To what degree did their collective experiences in the Fifteenth Infantry Regiment pave the way for their future successes? Is the old China hands association more myth than reality?

Marshall's introduction to China occurred in 1914, when he took leave from his regiment stationed in the Philippines and toured the Manchurian battlefields of the Russo–Japanese War. Newly promoted to the rank of lieutenant colonel, Marshall returned to China in August 1924 as executive officer of the Fifteenth Infantry Regiment. As regimental executive officer, Marshall assisted Col. W. K. Naylor, who commanded the Fifth. Together, they developed strategic plans to keep competing factions within the Chinese government outside of the restrictive zone surrounding Tientsin. Holding the railroad and providing a robust regimental defense were paramount.

As Naylor described them, Marshall's daily duties included "inspection of a four-mile outpost line established three miles south of the [Tientsin] compound, and patrolling a little for my own information." When Naylor was relieved of command in 1926, Marshall assumed command of the regiment until a new commanding officer arrived. Marshall's final efficiency report before departing the regiment came from Brig. Gen. William Connor, head of the US Army Forces in China. Connor rated Marshall superior in every category, describing him as "one of the best officers in the Army."

Marshall's experience in China proved instructive in formulating his most lasting contribution to the officer corps of the interwar US Army. After five months in Tientsin, he wrote, "I find the officers are highly developed in the tactical handling or functioning of weapons, in target practice, in bayonet combat, but when it comes to simple tactical problems, the actual duties of troop leading procedures, they all fall far below the standards they set in other matters."

Observing one field exercise in China, Marshall found an officer, who Marshall discovered stood first in his class at the Infantry School, faced with the problem of enveloping the flank of a hostile force. Despite his classroom prowess, the officer seemed incapable of drafting an order in a timely manner. That experience spurred Marshall to "get my hands" on Fort Benning, Georgia, the home of the infantry, where he embarked on an ambitious program to revamp the instruction and techniques of the Infantry School.

Marshall later served as assistant commandant of the Infantry School, where he developed a generation of future general officers. In 1939, President Franklin Roosevelt selected Marshall as army chief of staff.

Following his retirement from the army staff in November 1945, Marshall reluctantly answered President Harry Truman's request to serve as US special envoy to China. He had come full circle from his days as a fledgling lieutenant when he initially arrived in mainland China.

Of all the officers who served in the Fifteenth Infantry Regiment following World War I, none understood the Chinese mind better than Maj. Stilwell. Stilwell was already a recognized old China hand long before Marshall arrived in 1924. Stilwell had been to China in 1911 and had witnessed the revolution against the Manchu dynasty that made China a republic. At the conclusion of the Great War, the army dispatched Stilwell to Peking as a language officer, serving from 1920 to 1923. There, Stilwell immersed himself in Chinese culture to a degree virtually unknown by Westerners.

Returning to China in 1926, Stilwell, now a battalion commander, renewed his acquaintance with Marshall, often serving as interpreter for the regimental executive officer. Stilwell and Marshall had first met in 1918 when Stilwell was an intelligence officer who helped plan the Saint-Mihiel Offensive of World War I. Though their tours of duty in China overlapped for only eight months, it was "long enough for what had been mere acquaintance to blossom into a bond of mutual respect," historian Barbara Tuchman wrote in her 1970 book, *Stilwell and the American Experience in China, 1911–1945*. Working in such close proximity with Marshall, Stilwell developed a healthy respect for Marshall that he seldom afforded a senior officer.

Stilwell departed China in 1929 to report to the Infantry School is in the US as head of the Tactical Section, reporting directly to Assistant Commandant Marshall. Marshall's selection of Stilwell to head the section proved to be an inspired choice and cemented the mutual admiration between the two officers. Indeed, Marshall had held the position open for Stilwell because he clearly understood that his fellow old China hand shared his belief that short, simple orders were best.

Marshall never forgot Stilwell's performance in Tientsin and at Fort Benning. In the devastating aftermath of Pearl Harbor, the army chief of staff selected Stilwell to serve as the overall American representative to China as chief of staff to Nationalist government leader Chiang Kai-shek. In a February 1942 memorandum to Stilwell, Marshall spelled out

Stilwell's multifunctional role: commanding general of US Army Forces in the China–Burma–India Theater, chief of staff to the supreme commander of the China Theater, supervisor of lend-lease, and US representative on any Allied war council. Stilwell served in those positions until he was relieved of duty in a dispute with Chiang in 1944. The following year, Marshall assigned Stilwell to command Tenth US Army in the wake of the death of its commanding general on Okinawa, Japan.

In his memoir, Ridgway dedicates but six paragraphs to his service with the Fifteenth Infantry Regiment. According to Ridgway, service in the regiment provided him the rare opportunity and the high privilege to serve with Marshall, then commanding the regiment. Among Capt. Ridgway's principal tasks were to conduct a series of alerts when the regiment went to man the outer defenses around Tientsin.

When a Chinese force of twelve thousand men, soldiers of a local warlord, were reported to be marching toward the restricted zone in 1926, Ridgway selected two soldiers to observe the force. Much to his relief, the Chinese contingent skirted the restricted zone, and Ridgway returned to headquarters.

That evening, Ridgway reported his observations to Marshall. Marshall merely nodded. It was, in Ridgway's words, "a routine contact." Brief as that encounter was, Ridgway stated that Marshall's later friendship and faith in a fellow old China hand had a profound effect on his own career. Marshall's and Ridgway's paths converged again at Fort Benning when Ridgway attended the Infantry Advanced Course and Marshall served as assistant commandant. Ridgway later accompanied Marshall on several tours of South America. In 1939, the future commander of the Eighty-Second Airborne Division received orders to report to the War Plans Division in Washington, DC, where he served on the War Department's general staff. Service on the general staff provided Ridgway with nearly daily contact with Marshall, now army chief of staff.

As with Dwight Eisenhower, Ridgway had been denied combat service during World War I. Anxious to avoid a recurrence of stateside duty following America's entry into World War II, Ridgway repeatedly bombarded Col. Walter Bedell Smith, Marshall's staff secretary, for transfer to the line. Finally, one day when Ridgway stuck his head in Smith's office and asked, "Any word?" Smith looked up from his desk.

"Yes," Smith said. "This morning General Marshall said, and I quote, 'Tell Ridgway I'm tired of seeing him hanging around out there every time my door opens. When I have something for him, I'll send for him.'"

Service in Tientsin during the mid-1920s with the Fifteenth Infantry Regiment had been ideal, but far removed from the field army that Marshall, Stilwell, and Ridgway preferred. As stated by Tuchman, the regiment served "under the rather paradoxical injunction to avoid conflict, imposed by American policy which was concerned not merely to keep out of trouble but also to avoid inhibiting Chinese national development." If challenged, all the regiment could do was bluff. As a result, the regiment was militarily incapable of executing its wartime mission. Faced with a difficult assignment, inadequate firepower and, intense political restrictions, regimental officers bonded in a spirit of camaraderie not generally witnessed in stateside posts.

Marshall, Stilwell, and Ridgway were no exception to the rule. The close association of the old China hands continued far beyond their respective tours of duty in Tientsin. Although Stilwell's and Ridgway's time with Marshall was limited in 1926, they made favorable impressions on the future army chief of staff that bore fruit on the future battlefields of World War II.

"Destined for Greatness" was originally published in *ARMY Magazine* (December 2021).

17

No Ordinary Junior Officer

In Style and Temperament, Marshall Showed Early Promise

During a military and civilian career that spanned a half-century, General of the Army George C. Marshall served with highest distinction as US Army chief of staff, secretary of state, and secretary of defense, and was a two-time recipient of *Time* magazine's "Man of the Year," for both 1943 and 1947. Long before World War II thrust him on the national stage, however, Marshall had compiled an enviable record of achievement as one of America's most celebrated junior military officers. By examining Marshall's efficiency reports prior to World War I, one might conclude that Marshall was destined for greatness.

Marshall arrived at the Virginia Military Institute in 1897 and graduated in 1901 as First Captain of the Corps of Cadets. On Marshall's graduation, VMI Superintendent Scott Shipp described him this way: "He is of fine physique and soldier-like appearance . . . with natural powers of command and control." Reflecting on his cadet years four decades later, Marshall stated, "This institution gave me not only a standard for my daily conduct among men, but it also endowed me with a military heritage of honor and self-sacrifice."

Marshall immediately applied for a commission in the Regular Army. He signed his commission on February 3, 1902, at which time Second Lt. Marshall received his initial assignment to the Thirtieth Infantry Regiment in the Philippines. Marshall's initial efficiency reports with the regiment reveal an officer whose abilities were characterized as average with respect to performance, but whose general conduct and bearing were "excellent."

As with the majority of second lieutenants, Marshall's company commander noted that he "should be entrusted with important duties and is qualified for his current position."

Two years later, Marshall served at Fort Reno in the Oklahoma Territory, where for the first time his post commander noted that he demonstrated marked ability for detail on the general staff. According to Maj. W. R. Abercrombie of the Thirtieth Infantry Regiment, Marshall was "a first-class all-around officer. In the event of war, he is best suited for duty as a quartermaster and adjutant."

As a result of his performance, in the spring of 1906, Marshall was offered an opportunity to attend Infantry and Cavalry School at Fort Leavenworth, Kansas. He immediately accepted. Commanding the Leavenworth schools was Brig. Gen. J. Franklin Bell, who insisted that regimental commanders send their most qualified officers to attend the initial course.

Under normal conditions, Marshall would not have been eligible to attend the Leavenworth schools. In 1906, newly promoted Army Chief of Staff Bell directed that henceforth, only officers in the rank of captain would attend the course. Marshall got in just under the wire. Plagued by self-doubt, he later confessed, "I wondered what was going to become of me without any preparation of any kind."

It was at Fort Leavenworth where Marshall hit his stride. Working harder than ever in his life, Marshall graduated first in his class. Reviewing Marshall's academic report, Brig. Gen. Charles B. Hall, commandant of service schools, characterized the young lieutenant as "an exceptionally bright, capable young officer of much promise." In 1907, the Infantry and Cavalry School was renamed the Army School of the Line. Only half the graduates were eligible for the second-year course at the Army Staff College. Marshall had applied himself so diligently that he was one of the officers selected for an additional year at Fort Leavenworth. By the time the class graduated in 1908, Marshall had repeated his earlier performance and graduated first in his class.

Maj. J. F. Morrison, acting commandant of the Army Service Schools, wrote Marshall's efficiency report, in which he stated that in the event of war, Marshall was best suited for line or general staff because he "possessed one of the best minds I know. He is mentally very mature for his years—a most promising officer." Reflecting on his experience at the Army Staff College in 1908, First Lt. Marshall noted, "My reading of course was pretty helpful, as was my study of past operations. I learned how to digest them. . . . My habits of thought were being trained. While . . . I learned little I could use . . . I learned how to learn. . . . I began to develop along more stable lines."

Marshall remained at Fort Leavenworth for another two years as an engineering and military art instructor. In that time, he developed strong relationships with officers destined to serve in senior positions during World War I. In the summer between academic years, Marshall served with highest distinction as an instructor with the Pennsylvania National Guard.

In 1910, Marshall completed his four years at Fort Leavenworth and was eligible for duty in the line. Nominally assigned as commander of Company D of the Twenty-Fourth Infantry Regiment, Marshall found himself gainfully employed in division-size maneuvers and in the activities of the Department of War's Division of Militia Affairs. When Congress passed legislation allowing the president to detail army officers for regular tours of duty with the National Guard as instructors, Gov. Eben S. Draper of Massachusetts requested the War Department assign Marshall to his jurisdiction.

Not surprisingly, Marshall excelled as an instructor, but he was anxious to return to the line. In 1913, he arrived at Fort McKinley on the Philippine Islands for duty with the Thirteenth Infantry Regiment. According to Marshall's principal biographer, Forrest C. Pogue, "Fort McKinley was tailor-made for an ambitious young staff officer in training, and particularly for Marshall," who found himself once more under the eye and wing of Bell, now commanding general of the Department of War's Philippine Department. Though Marshall commanded a company, he remained on detachment with the staff for the first six months and did not command his unit for a single day.

Within his first months on the islands, Marshall was assigned as adjutant to the "White Force," scheduled to simulate an invasion of Luzon in Bell's maneuvers of January 1914. The White Force was to act as the invader that, having landed at Batangas, about 115 kilometers from Manila, would attack and capture the Philippine capital. The "Batangas maneuvers" proved a watershed event in Marshall's career.

Commanding the White Force was Col. William C. Butler, an aged commander on the brink of retirement, whom Marshall described as "a courtly gentleman, a very nice fellow," but thoroughly incompetent. On the eve of the maneuvers, Capt. Jens Bugge, a close friend of Marshall and one of Marshall's former students at Fort Leavenworth, was designated as the detachment's chief of staff. Just as the maneuvers were set to begin on January 22, 1914, Bugge became violently ill. Though junior in rank, Marshall received orders to replace him, making him de facto commander of the White Force.

Future general of the army (and later general of the air force) Henry H. "Hap" Arnold observed Marshall during the maneuvers. "Under the shade of a bamboo clump lay a young lieutenant with a map spread before him. It developed that he was dictating the Order for the attack that was to break through the defenders' line. I told my wife I had met a man who was going to be Chief of Staff of the Army some day."

Later, the chief umpire of the White Force reported to Bell that the exercise had been "a severe task which [Marshall] carried out successfully and for which he deserves great credit."

Marshall had reason to be proud of his performance. In a March 21, 1914, letter to his brother, Marshall wrote, "I had an opportunity that rarely ever comes to a colonel and has never been heard of before being given to anyone below that rank, except General [John J.] Pershing. . . . I had absolute command and control of the Detachment, appointed even the adjutant and aides. The Colonel was ignored and not even consulted." Marshall's exploits were clearly recognized by his superiors.

Having read the after-action reports of the Batangas exercises, Marshall's company commander, Capt. Ezekiel J. Williams, passed on the glowing accolades from Bell's office. Williams stated that his lieutenant would "be an excellent brigade adjutant, division chief of staff, assistant chief of staff, or in command of troops." Williams continued, "This officer, for his years of service, age, and rank, is one of the most completely equipped for military service it has been my lot to observe." Williams later stated that "should the exigencies of the service place him in exalted command, I would be glad to serve under him." Brig. Gen. Hunter

Liggett, new commanding general of the Philippine Department, echoed Williams's assessment and detailed Marshall as his aide-de-camp.

Marshall returned to the United States once his foreign service was completed. In 1916, Maj. Gen. Bell, now commanding the Department of War's Western Department, assessed Marshall's performance duty. Bell said Marshall is "an officer of very exceptional ability where military art is concerned. . . . In the event of war, he is especially well qualified to perform duty of Chief of Staff for corps or army, or to command same."

On October 13, 1916, Marshall received his promotion to captain. When Congress declared war against Germany on April 6, 1917, Bell assumed command of the Department of War's reorganized Department of the East. Two months later, on June 3, Bell urged Maj. Gen. William L. Sibert, newly designated commanding general of the First Division, to appoint Marshall as a general staff officer for immediate service abroad.

Marshall sailed for France in 1917 as a captain on the staff of the commanding general of the First Division. Within a year, he was promoted to full colonel and had attracted the attention of Pershing, commander of the American Expeditionary Forces. In assigning Marshall as his aide-de-camp, Pershing recognized what so many previous commanders had acknowledged: In style and temperament, Marshall was no ordinary officer.

"No Ordinary Junior Officer: In Style and Temperament, Marshall Showed Early Promise" was originally published in *ARMY Magazine* (August 2019).

18

Patton's Hawaiian Ordeal

Even a Legend Can Learn from His Mistakes

Long before Gen. George S. Patton Jr. achieved international recognition as one of World War II's most celebrated heroes, he had compiled an enviable military record. A recipient of the Distinguished Service Cross for gallantry in action and the Distinguished Service Medal for distinction in a post of high responsibility during World War I, Patton emerged as one of the US Army's most vocal proponents of armored warfare. Less well-known was Patton's tour of duty with the Hawaiian Division, where his promising career was nearly sidetracked when he was relieved from duty as the division's operations officer.

Then-major Patton arrived in Hawaii in March 1925. Detailed to Schofield Barracks, he was appointed acting G-1 (personnel officer) and G-2 (intelligence officer) of the Hawaiian Division. Patton's transfer to Hawaii was fortunate for an officer interested in training regiments, brigades and a division for war. In the continental United States, the army was dispersed in small detachments. As in the Philippines and Panama, however, Schofield Barracks could accommodate a sizable number of troops. Patton arrived in time to view the Grand Joint Army and Navy Exercises in April 1925. He found much that he disliked in the annual maneuvers, but he earned the commendation of Lt. Col. J. B. Murphy, who served as an official observer of the annual exercises. Stated Murphy, "His tactical judgment is superior, he is well balanced, and he is a quick and enthusiastic worker." Murphy continued, stating that in his opinion Patton "would be an excellent commander of combat troops during war."

In November 1926, Patton was reassigned to G-3 (operations officer), a post he had long sought because its functions were more akin to his peacetime interests of training and preparing troops for combat. As G-3, he served as the division commander's advisor on tactical matters and often spoke in the name of the commander to subordinate commanders. As was his custom, the outspoken Patton made his presence felt immediately.

The Twenty-Second Brigade of the Hawaiian Division held an exercise on how to conduct the advance guard, but Patton felt the demonstration was substandard and minced no words in his written critique to the brigade commander. He informed the brigade commander that the purpose of an advance guard "is the infliction of death wounds and destruction on the enemy troops with a view to establish both physical and moral ascendency over them. The gaining of ground in such a combat is simply an incident, not an object. . . . All exercises should be conducted with this idea in view." Patton compounded his error and instructed all brigade, regimental and separate unit commanders to correct certain derelictions in military bearing among officers and men.

Rather than submitting his report to the division commander for his signature, Patton signed the report himself. It was an example of his lapses of military protocol. The brigade commander found Patton's remarks utterly tactless, and he complained to the division commander. For a staff officer to "correct" a brigade commander was not only ill conceived but also a violation of military protocol. Within months of assuming the G-3 post, Patton found himself the object of scorn from several senior tactical commanders.

Patton also offered his views on reducing the number of troops engaged in supply and administrative details in order to retain the maximum number of soldiers involved with military training. He then suggested an innovative training program to study how a division could gain protection against low-flying airplanes. Patton's plan contradicted a War Department board that mandated that ground troops disperse once they were spotted by planes. Patton opined that passive defense was no solution. To determine the efficacy of his own theory that a more proactive defense was more suitable, he proposed an exercise to determine whether his idea was indeed practical. Maj. Gen. William R. Smith, the Hawaiian Division commander, issued a letter prepared by Patton on the subject and ordered a demonstration.

In May 1927, the effectiveness of Patton's notion was tested. Observing the exercise by the direction of the division commander, Patton wrote a scathing critique of the results. Having learned his lesson, he submitted his comments to Smith, who directed his adjutant to sign the paper and sent it to the brigade commander. In his critique, Patton noted that the officers in the battalion that had taken part in the exercise had failed on a number of critical points, not the least of which was that they had failed to use every available weapon to engage the enemy and had failed to coordinate fires. "As a result of these defects," Patton wrote, "the impression was inescapable that the officers and men had not grasped the spirit of the proposed regulations."

For tactical commanders who prided themselves on their leadership and their units' war readiness, these were strong words from a relatively young staff officer. Though Smith signed Patton's report, it was common knowledge that the author of the critique was not Smith, but Patton. As muttering among senior officers against Patton escalated, Smith removed Patton from the G-3 position and appointed him G-2. Smith stated his reason for transferring Patton to his intelligence officer was that he "was too positive in his thinking and too outspoken."

Patton confided his resentment in a letter to his wife, Beatrice: "Gen S. [Smith] must think he was wrong as he had had both Floyd and Capt. Coffey tell me that it was only dire necessity which made him relieve me as G-3. Of course, he is either a fool or a liar, probably both." His demotion reminded him of his reduction from second to sixth corporal at West Point for being "too d— military."

Though his reassignment to the G-2 post was disguised as routine, Patton remained embittered. In the judgment of Carlo D'Este, Patton's foremost biographer, Patton "had been thinking and acting more like the World War I colonel he had once been than a relatively junior major. Patton's yen for a war was inconsistent with the politics of peacetime soldiering." What was clearly evident was simply that Patton's abrasive nature and his denunciation of errors committed by superior officers had earned him one antagonist too many. Fifteen years later, these traits would reappear on the battlefields of Europe, but during the campaign in Western Europe, Patton seemed content to confine his impatience with senior officers to his personal diary.

Stung by his relief, Patton rededicated his efforts on the study of amphibious warfare and leadership in combat. In his 1927 lecture, "Why Men Fight," Patton posited that superiority in leadership was hereditary and argued that the United States was hindered in finding leaders because of its "mono-class system." "In this country," he said, "we start our search handicapped by the absence of potential leaders' consequent upon our lack of civilian class distinction." As another example, his paper "Drills for Fighting" presented the outlook of a mature and thoughtful professional officer.

In another lecture, "Tanks Past and Future," he told his audience he had "devised an American system of tank employment, which, though far from perfect, had worked satisfactorily. It was an error to have tanks precede the infantry against weak trenches." "In future," Patton opined, "it will be better to have the tanks follow the infantry over the front . . . and then deploy ahead for the passage through the delaying area."

Despite his chagrin over being relieved of duty, Patton applied for an extension of his tour with the Hawaiian Division. His motives requesting an extension to stay at Schofield Barracks are unclear. The War Department promptly denied his request and ordered him to be transferred to the Office of the Chief of Cavalry in Washington, DC, in May 1928. The Chief of Cavalry implied that Patton had been selected to serve in his office because "mechanization looms very large in the War Department today, and your past experiences will serve you in this."

Reflecting on Patton's tour with the Hawaiian Division, Martin Blumenson wrote, "Patton's three years in Hawaii were a pleasant social interlude and a sobering professional experience." D'Este concurs, stating that while in Hawaii, Patton wrote about the war he knew, understood and discerned as few others did. Patton's social life had never been better, his writing was prolific, and eventually his bitterness at being relieved was partially mitigated by the glowing endorsement of Maj. Gen. Fox Conner, the new commander of the Hawaiian Division. Conner wrote, "I have known him for fifteen years, in both peace and war. I know of no one whom I would prefer to have as a subordinate officer."

About a decade later, Patton returned to Hawaii for a second tour of duty, once again drawing a reprimand from Maj. Gen. Hugh A. Drum, the Hawaiian Department commander, this time for unsportsmanlike conduct during the Inter-Island Polo Championship of 1936. Again, Patton survived the encounter with his commanding general. Drum and Patton put aside their differences and, as with Conner, Patton earned high marks from his commanding officer. Drum wrote, "Heretofore I have noted on this officer's Efficiency Report a weakness in 'Tact.' In the last year he has overcome this weakness in a satisfactory manner." Perhaps lost on Patton was the realization that he had matured tremendously but without losing the ruthless drive that characterized his leadership in World War II.

"Patton's Hawaiian Ordeal: Even a Legend Can Learn from His Mistakes" was originally published in *ARMY Magazine* (April 2015).

19

Eisenhower and MacArthur

Toil, Trouble, and Turbulence in the Philippines

In Dwight D. Eisenhower's own words, Army Chief of Staff Gen. Douglas MacArthur was "a forceful—some thought an overpowering—individual, blessed with a fast and facile mind, interested in both the military and political side of our government." Eisenhower served closely with MacArthur for seven years. Those years were extremely important in Eisenhower's career, for during that period he obtained experience in the ways of the highest levels of government.

What began as a cordial relationship between MacArthur and his senior assistant gradually degenerated during the Philippine years when Lt. Col. Eisenhower served as MacArthur's chief of staff in Manila. What happened to drive these two future World War II leaders apart? The traditional rivalries between theater commanders in wartime are well known; the deterioration of the relationship between MacArthur and Eisenhower is not.

The relationship between the two men began when MacArthur became army chief of staff in 1930. At the time, Eisenhower served as assistant executive, Office of the Assistant Secretary of War. He held this position until February 20, 1933, when he was reassigned as special assistant to MacArthur. Though MacArthur knew that Eisenhower preferred troop duty, in January 1932, the latter wrote his father-in-law, John S. Doud, informing him that MacArthur had wanted him to remain in his present job. Eisenhower later recalled that MacArthur "was very nice to me—and after all I know of no greater compliment the bosses can give you than I want you hanging around."

Of MacArthur, Eisenhower wrote, "Fifty-two years old. Essentially a romantic figure. . . . Very appreciative of good work, positive in his convictions—a genius at giving concise and clear instructions. . . . Placed a letter of commendation on my record—and has assured me that as long as he stays in the Army, I am one of the people earmarked for his 'gang.'" Eisenhower took particular delight in the army chief's endorsement of his own capabilities, but little could he have known that the next seven years with MacArthur would prove exasperating for both men.

Working for MacArthur had its perks, including glowing efficiency reports by the army chief of staff, but Eisenhower never relished his role as a member of the Washington, DC bureaucracy. Years later, he told his son, "I always resented the years I spent as a slave in the War Department," yet when the opportunity to leave MacArthur presented itself, he demurred. MacArthur's tenure as army chief of staff terminated in 1935, and he contemplated his next assignment. Just a year earlier, Congress had passed the Tydings–McDuffie Act, granting the Philippine commonwealth status as a prelude to complete independence, which would come in 1946. Elections had not yet been held in the archipelago, but the overwhelming favorite to win the presidency was Manuel Quezon. In late 1934, Quezon requested President Franklin D. Roosevelt to dispatch MacArthur to Manila to head the US military mission.

MacArthur's first priority was to select his personal staff, and he wanted Eisenhower as his senior aide. According to Eisenhower, "General MacArthur lowered the boom on me, so to speak. . . . I was in no position to argue with the Chief of Staff." Contrary to his later claims that MacArthur had lowered the boom, Eisenhower was pleased by his transfer to the Philippines because he thought it would be a wonderful professional opportunity. His decision did not sit well with his wife Mamie, who confided to a friend, "Ike is ruined. He has gone off to the Philippines with that man MacArthur."

The Military Mission landed in Manila on October 26, 1935. Eisenhower's principal responsibility was the development of the Philippine Defense Plan. The Philippine years proved so frustrating to Eisenhower that he dedicated a short ten pages in his personal memoirs, *At Ease: Stories*

I Tell to Friends, to his service with MacArthur in the Philippines. Once in Manila, he began questioning his decision to accompany MacArthur. When Quezon conferred the title of field marshal on MacArthur on August 24, 1936, Eisenhower thought the whole occasion "rather fantastic" and tried to persuade MacArthur to refuse the title. Years later, he discovered that the title was not Quezon's idea; rather, it was that of the general himself. Eisenhower voiced his frustration with his boss's penchant for surrounding himself with yes-men. In his mind, such an attitude was hardly surprising, since he thought the general was "raised in the conception of Douglas MacArthur superiority."

After several months, Eisenhower confessed, "I've remained on this job, not because of the Gen.—but in spite of him. . . . I'm at a crossroad. If the Marshal [MacArthur] is to persist in his arbitrary methods, and is going to make things as unpleasant, if not impossible, . . . then I'm for home." Reflecting on the two years with MacArthur since the former army chief of staff arrived in Manila, Eisenhower recalled, "We have been beset on all sides by difficulties arising from personal ambition, personal glorification, personal selfishness."

The year 1938 proved to be the most stressful and most demanding year of Eisenhower's service in the Philippines. It was then that an incident took place that weakened his relationship with MacArthur. In January 1938, the general thought that it would be good for Filipino morale if the people could see their army in Manila. The culmination of the large demonstration of strength would be a big parade. Unfortunately, MacArthur had not discussed the planned troop movement with Quezon. When an irritated Quezon questioned MacArthur, the general blamed his zealous lieutenants for proceeding with the plans despite the fact that he had in fact ordered Eisenhower to set up the parade.

MacArthur returned to his headquarters and was exceedingly unhappy with his entire staff. He claimed that he had never meant for the staff to proceed with preparations for the parade; he had only wanted them to investigate it quietly. Incensed that MacArthur was questioning his integrity, Eisenhower exploded. "General, all you're saying is that I'm a liar, and I am not a liar, and so I'd like to go back to the United States right away." Putting his arm around Eisenhower's shoulder, MacArthur backtracked and said, "It's fun to see that Dutch temper take you over. It's just a misunderstanding, and let's let it go at that."

For Eisenhower, however, the die was cast. If MacArthur possessed a low tolerance for perceived affront to his own integrity, so did his senior aide. Writing thirty years after their heated exchange, Eisenhower claimed, "This misunderstanding caused considerable resentment, and never again were we on the same warm and cordial terms." Nor did either man attempt to mend matters with the other.

When Eisenhower was visiting the United States to garner support for the Philippine army, MacArthur replaced him with Maj. Richard K. Sutherland. When Eisenhower landed at Manila on November 5, 1938, he confided in his diary that he "found a vastly different situation, so far as it affects me and my work." Recalling MacArthur's resentment of Eisenhower's popularity with the Filipinos in general and his intimacy with Malacañang Palace, the seat of the Philippine government, Eisenhower stated that while he was stateside, MacArthur removed him completely in official affairs from Malacañang. MacArthur also rearranged the office force so that Eisenhower was "no longer his [chief of staff]. But only another staff officer."

Eisenhower continued, "Why the man should so patently exhibit a jealousy of a subordinate is beyond me. . . . Of course, he has accomplished one thing he wanted to do, that is, make certain that I'd get out as soon as I decently can." Consequently, he applied to transfer to the United States, and on May 27, 1939, the War Department assigned Eisenhower to the Fifteenth Infantry Regiment at Fort Lewis, Washington. On December 13, 1939, the Eisenhower family departed Manila. MacArthur, outwardly cordial, was happy to see him go.

Unbeknownst to Eisenhower, his return to the United States proved extremely beneficial. No longer associated with MacArthur's falling star in the Philippines, he moved quickly to reestablish himself in the array of officers in Army Chief of Staff George C. Marshall's orbit. Within two years, Eisenhower was summoned to Washington, DC, in the aftermath of the debacle at Pearl Harbor.

In the final analysis, it is difficult to affix blame for the deterioration of the MacArthur–Eisenhower relationship during the 1930s. That the two spirited officers would eventually clash seemed inevitable. Undoubtedly, both MacArthur and Eisenhower profited from their relationship—MacArthur from the service of a brilliant staff officer and Eisenhower, as he later said, from "the administrative experience gained under General MacArthur," which helped prepare him for "the great responsibilities of the war period."

In later years, both men tended to smooth over their differences, and eventually they buried the hatchet. As MacArthur's eightieth birthday approached on January 26, 1960, Eisenhower wrote a letter to his former boss in which he stated that the event "brings to all our people a renewed feeling of gratitude for your dedicated services to our common country." Shortly thereafter, MacArthur traveled to Washington, DC, for a brief, emotional reunion that was also their final parting.

MacArthur died on April 5, 1964; Eisenhower followed five years later on March 28, 1969. The two men formed an uneasy, albeit unequal, partnership during the years in which they served together. Better to remember the more cordial days in the War Department than to recall the Philippine years when their on-and-off animosity poisoned their relationship and neither officer seemed to make much effort to realize what the other was going through.

"Eisenhower and MacArthur: Toil, Trouble, and Turbulence in the Philippines" was originally published in *ARMY Magazine* (January 2015).

20

The George C. Marshall Way of Leadership

With the possible exception of George Washington, Gen. George C. Marshall Jr. arguably remains the most distinguished officer to wear the uniform of the US Army. In a military-diplomatic career that spanned a half-century and three wars, Marshall not only inspired a generation of World War II leaders but also proved to be the quintessential selfless servant.

Not surprisingly, Marshall experienced numerous defining moments during his extraordinary career, those moments when a leader's decisions or actions alter one's career and perhaps even destiny. What was the secret of Marshall's success? What lessons did he bequeath to future army leaders?

Perhaps his initial defining moment occurred when then-lieutenant Marshall was stationed at Fort McKinley in the Philippines in 1913. In the words of biographer Forrest C. Pogue, Marshall was "soon engaged on the project that, through a combination of accident, talent, and extraordinary devotion of energy, was to make his fame." Assigned as adjutant to the "White Force" and scheduled to simulate an invasion of Luzon, Marshall later noted that Maj. Gen. J. Franklin Bell, the commanding officer of the Philippine Department, had decided to relieve the White Force commander, Col. William C. Butler, because of incompetence.

When Marshall's immediate boss, Capt. Jens Bugge, suddenly became ill and had to be evacuated, adjutant Marshall was designated to replace Bugge as acting chief of staff, making him de facto commander of the White Force. In Marshall's own words, "I had the advantage of being a first lieutenant with the largest force of troops in the Philippines, which I could command in a very extensive maneuver campaign." The maneuver's chief umpire, Col. James B. Erwin, informed Bell that the exercise "was by far the best that he had ever attended."

Also impressed was Lt. Henry H. "Hap" Arnold, who would be chief of the Army Air Forces in World War II. Arnold was in Batangas during the exercises and recorded a memorable picture of Marshall lying on his back in a bamboo clump, glancing at a map and dictating the precise orders of an attack that was eventually to break through the defending forces' line. Arnold was so moved that he wrote his wife and informed her that he had just seen a future chief of staff in action.

Three years later during World War I, Marshall served as operations officer for the First Division on the Western Front. When Gen. John J. Pershing, the American Expeditionary Forces commanding general, questioned the tactical competence of division commander Maj. Gen. William L. Sibert, rumors around AEF headquarters were rampant that Pershing was seeking grounds to relieve Sibert.

The critical day occurred on October 3, 1917, when Pershing and his staff arrived at Gondrecourt to witness a demonstration by Maj. Theodore Roosevelt Jr.'s battalion that Marshall had arranged on short notice. Pershing asked Sibert to conduct a critique. Pershing was not pleased with Sibert's critique and then "just gave everybody hell." In Marshall's view, Pershing "was very severe with General Sibert . . . in front of all the officers. Among other things, he said that we didn't show any signs of much training; we had not justified the time we had had here . . . [Pershing] didn't give General Sibert a chance to talk at all."

Stung by Pershing's rebuke, then-captain Marshall cast aside military decorum. As Pershing turned away, Marshall, "mad all over," put his hand on the general's arm. "General Pershing, there's something to be said here, and I think I should say it because I've been here longest," Marshall said, according to his biographer.

Pershing halted. "What have you got to say?"

According to Benjamin F. Caffey, Marshall's assistant in the Operations Section during 1918, when Marshall became angry, he tended to talk rather rapidly and "overwhelm his opponent by a torrent of fact." In this case, Marshall himself later recalled that he had "forgotten all that I said, but I had a rather inspired moment." Those officers who witnessed Marshall's outburst were "horrified," but Pershing remained calm and walked away, saying, "You must appreciate the troubles we have."

Marshall, aware he had violated military protocol by speaking to the general in such an abrupt manner, upped the ante when he replied, "Yes, General, but we have them every day . . . and we have to solve every one of them by night." Years later, Marshall reflected on this exchange and said that though he never regretted his actions, he learned a valuable lesson about the need to control his temper.

Marshall's willingness to confront Pershing in spite of the potential consequences to his own career advancement marked him as an officer of character and moral courage. With this instance, no retribution came. On the contrary, whenever Pershing visited the division thereafter, the AEF commander would often take Marshall aside to determine the combat efficiency of the First Division. In 1918, Pershing appointed Marshall to serve as a key member of his operations staff.

One of a leader's primary responsibilities is to train other leaders. Nowhere was that more evident than during Marshall's tenure as assistant commandant of the Infantry School at Fort Benning, Georgia. In this role, Marshall also served as head of the academic department. Marshall viewed the assignment as a way to make a mark not only on the Infantry School itself but also on the US Army as a whole.

His initial task was to improve the quality of instruction. By simplifying the instruction and concentrating on writing clear and concise field orders, Marshall engineered what has been called an almost complete revamping of the instruction and technique. During his five years at Benning, "Marshall's Men" who were either students or on the faculty included future generals Dwight D. Eisenhower, Omar Bradley, J. Lawton Collins, Matthew Ridgway, Joseph Stilwell, James van Fleet, and Jacob Devers.

As assistant commandant, Marshall encouraged free and open discussion and unorthodox solutions to tactical problems. He did not neglect logistics and supply. Marshall himself believed that the faculty of the Infantry School during his last three years on station "was composed of the most brilliant, interesting, and thoroughly competent collection of men I have ever been associated with."

Brig. Gen. Marshall was serving as deputy chief of staff when he was summoned to a high-level White House meeting on November 14, 1938.

Along with senior officials from the departments of war and treasury, Marshall sat stoically to hear President Franklin D. Roosevelt outline his plans to build ten thousand airplanes. Military expenditures dictated that such an increase of air power would be at the expense of the War Department's manpower need and munitions required by the airships.

Marshall noted that as the president made his arguments, "There was a great difference of opinion" about how the buildup would be financed and the planes utilized. In Marshall's own words, Roosevelt "did the major portion of the talking," and "most of the others agreed with him entirely [and] had very little to say and were very soothing." Then the president "finally came around to me," Marshall recalled. "I remember he called me 'George.' So, he turned to me at the end of this general outlining . . . and said, 'Don't you think so, George?'"

"I replied, 'I am sorry, Mr. President, but I don't agree with that at all.' I remember that ended the conference. The President gave me a . . . startled look and when I went out, they all bade me goodbye and said that my tour in Washington was over."

This was the first time Marshall placed himself in direct opposition to Roosevelt, but it would hardly be the last. To Roosevelt's credit, he did not hold Marshall's outspokenness against him. On the contrary, Roosevelt informed Marshall on April 23, 1939, that although Secretary of War Harry Woodring had yet to be informed, Roosevelt was nominating Marshall to be chief of staff of the army on Gen. Malin Craig's official retirement, scheduled for August 31, 1939.

Perhaps due to his opposition to the president over the rearmament issue, Marshall graciously thanked Roosevelt and said how honored he was to receive the appointment but that he wanted the right to say what he thought and that it might often be unpleasant. When Marshall asked whether that would be all right, Roosevelt said, "Yes."

Not missing a beat, Marshall said, "You said yes pleasantly, but it may be unpleasant." When Roosevelt indicated that this was why he had selected Marshall, the newly designated chief of staff said, "I feel deeply honored, sir, and I will give you the best I have."

Marshall's appointment as chief of staff fulfilled a lifelong ambition, but the posting he most coveted was that of supreme commander of the Allied Expeditionary Force destined to invade Europe on D-Day. As late as December 2, 1943, Marshall believed Roosevelt would assign him this role.

The choice of commander to lead the cross-channel invasion was essentially between Marshall and Eisenhower. Roosevelt had previously hinted that the position should go to Marshall but following the Tehran Conference in Iran in November 1943, the president expressed second thoughts. Landing in Cairo to meet Eisenhower on December 4, Roosevelt sent his personal adviser, Harry Hopkins, to feel out the chief of staff about his preference. Always the selfless servant, Marshall refused to advocate for his own candidacy. He merely endeavored to make it clear that he would go along wholeheartedly with whatever decision the president made.

The next day, Roosevelt summoned Marshall to his villa and asked him his preference, but Marshall refused to express it. Such a decision was "too great for any personal feelings to be considered. I did not discuss the pros and cons of the matter." As Marshall later recalled, the president ended their conversation with, "I feel I could not sleep at night with you out of the country." Roosevelt then named Eisenhower as supreme commander.

The following day, Marshall drafted a telegram to Russia's Josef Stalin, informing him of Roosevelt's decision. As a true mark of Marshall's character, the chief of staff recovered the draft from the message center and scribbled across the bottom, "Dear Eisenhower: I thought you might like to have this as a memento. It was written very hurriedly by me as the final meeting broke up yesterday, the President signing it immediately. G.C.M."

Marshall's legacy to the US Army can be summarized best in a 1944 letter he wrote to an elementary school class that had asked about his thoughts on leader development. Marshall wrote that character was the most important factor in selecting general officers and that character involved "integrity, unselfish and devoted purpose, a sturdiness of bearing when everything goes wrong and all are critical, and a willingness to sacrifice self in the interest of the common good."

Striving to be a leader of character, competence, and moral courage—that was how Marshall led his life. That truly was "the Marshall way."

"The George C. Marshall Way of Leadership" was originally published in *ARMY Magazine* (February 2017).

21

Marshall's Men

EVEN BEFORE THE GUNS FELL SILENT IN EUROPE ON V-E DAY, BRITISH Prime Minister Winston Churchill labeled US Army Chief of Staff Gen. George C. Marshall as the true "organizer of victory." The army that Marshall inherited in 1939 stood seventeenth in the world, ahead of Bulgaria and just behind Portugal. Marshall's success in building the US Army from a token force of fewer than 174,000 officers and enlisted men to more than 8.25 million soldiers by 1945 contributed mightily to Allied victory in the greatest war of the twentieth century.

In the fifty years since his death, Marshall has been so glorified in the annals of history that it is difficult to objectively assess the general many consider the greatest American soldier since George Washington. Though Marshall's achievements as chief of staff remain legendary, perhaps his greatest triumph lay in his uncanny ability to identify and develop commanders who displayed "aggressive and determined leadership" in the conduct of their duties.

Marshall served two years as deputy chief of staff before taking the oath of office as army chief of staff on September 1, 1939, the day Hitler invaded Poland and World War II began. "My day of induction into office was momentous," he wrote a colleague, "with the starting of what appears to be a world war." At the time, the US Army was top-heavy with an inordinate number of senior generals and colonels whom Marshall considered to have long outlived their usefulness.

In Marshall's eyes, the major impediment to creating a more modern military force was that the US Army had no elimination process. When officers were passed over for promotion, they continued on at their current rank, creating a drag on the whole military system. The army had an accumulation of colonels who were already in their sixties. Many of these officers either presided over promotion boards or had developed a cadre of younger officers whom they infected with their pessimism.

As Marshall informed Forrest Pogue, his principal postwar biographer, military officers changed considerably at certain points during their careers. Around age forty-six or forty-seven, subtle changes in an officer's distinctive characteristics as a leader became evident. By their early fifties, changes were more frequent, and by age sixty, very frequent. When senior officers neared mandatory retirement in their mid-sixties, very few were usable. Simply put, as the older senior officers aged, "greater was the rarity of finding a man who had retained his previous characteristics of command, control, and organization and administration."

What the army needed most, in Marshall's opinion, were more youthful commanders who could withstand the rigors of extended field combat. Drawing from his own experience in France in 1918, Marshall noted, "Leadership in the field depends to an important extent on one's legs and stomach and nervous system, and on one's ability to withstand hardships and lack of sleep and still be disposed energetically and aggressively to command men, to dominate men on the battlefield." He continued: "Only a man of positive characteristics of leadership, with the physical stamina that goes with it, can function under those conditions."

Consequently, with the full support of Secretary of War Henry L. Stimson, the chief of staff was instrumental in fostering congressional legislation that established a board of officers to remove the unfit and that authorized the secretary of war to carry out its recommendations. Thus, Marshall was able to place on the retired list hundreds of officers whom he believed were already "retired on active duty." This was the same bill that allowed Marshall to recommend promotion of officers such as Dwight D. (Ike) Eisenhower, Mark W. Clark, and George S. Patton over the heads of literally hundreds of officers far senior in grade.

Having solved the retention problem, Marshall next moved to find the best officers to command the division, corps, and army units destined for war. In his desk, he maintained a list of colonels, lieutenant colonels, and majors whom he knew or were recommended by others in whom he had great confidence. The names were scrawled in Marshall's famed "black book," along with the names of officers whom Marshall intended never to promote. On the book's pages were the names of virtually every corps and army commander in the upcoming war.

As usual, Marshall drew heavily on his own experience, particularly the five years he had spent at Fort Benning, Georgia, as assistant commandant of the Infantry School. As assistant commandant, Marshall was head of the Academic Department. During his tenure at Fort Benning, some two hundred future general officers of World War II (and after) were either students or teachers there.

Heading the Tactical Section at Fort Benning was an "old China hand," Lt. Col. Joseph (Vinegar Joe) Stilwell. Convinced that Stilwell was the right man for the job, Marshall had held the tactics section open for a year until Stilwell arrived at the Home of the Infantry. Stilwell totally revised tactical instruction; from then on, he could do little wrong in Marshall's eyes. A leader of enormous prejudices, Stilwell was brilliant, but difficult. Later Stilwell commanded American forces in the China–Burma–India (CBI) Theater, but his chief problem was his tactlessness. On station in China in World War II, Stilwell repeatedly referred to Chiang Kai-shek as "Peanut," though he claimed to Marshall that he was only indiscreet with his personal staff. Chastised by the army chief, Stilwell discovered that he couldn't control his staff from communicating his indiscretions to others. Ultimately, Stilwell was relieved of command in the CBI, more for political reasons than military failure. Because Stilwell was a fighter, however, Marshall subsequently appointed him commander of Tenth US Army when its commander, Lt. Gen. Simon Bolivar Buckner, was killed in action on Okinawa, Japan.

Marshall's choice to lead the Second Section (logistics, supply, training, and signal communication) was Lt. Col. Morrison C. Stayer. For the Weapons Section, Marshall selected Maj. Omar N. Bradley. Later, Bradley would be the first member of his West Point class to wear the stars of a brigadier general in the Regular Army. To lead the Fourth Section, in charge of history and publications, Marshall found another friend from China days, Maj. E. Forrest Harding.

Marshall later confessed that he had also wanted Eisenhower as an instructor at Fort Benning. Marshall had initially met Ike outside Gen. John J. Pershing's office, where Eisenhower had been detailed to assist Pershing on the Battle Monuments Commission. Harding and Stayer were destined to serve as major generals in World War II; Stilwell's, Bradley's and Eisenhower's careers need little amplification here.

Two other officers who caught Marshall's eye prior to the war were George S. Patton and Terry de la Mesa Allen. Marshall had known both men well from World War I. Neither met Marshall's normal criteria for senior command, but the chief of staff made exceptions in their cases. Marshall felt strongly, according to Pogue, that "Patton's love of violence, his needless profanity and obscenity, and his gaudy showmanship were all serious defects in a commander." Yet he saw behind Patton's "adolescent caperings the skill of a professional, who added to years of training a natural talent for fighting and the ability to make men go beyond the limits of what they believed themselves capable of doing in battle." More than once during World War II, Marshall and his protégé, Eisenhower, saved the eccentric Patton from himself.

As with Patton, Marshall displayed a fondness for Allen, future commanding general of Marshall's World War I division, the First Infantry Division. A member of Marshall's instructional staff at Fort Benning, Allen was a fighter by nature, a trait that made him indispensable in battle but won him few friends in peacetime. Unfortunately, Allen displayed "a weakness as a disciplinarian and as a team player." After Patton relieved Allen of his command in Sicily, at the request of Bradley, Allen returned to the United States and was given another divisional command.

Working in the staff secretariat of the secretary general staff at the beginning of World War II were several additional Marshall protégés, including Omar Bradley, Mark Clark, Matthew B. Ridgway, Maxwell D. Taylor, J. Lawton Collins, and Walter Bedell Smith. All were destined to hold senior command and staff positions in the war. Indeed, Marshall held up Bradley's promotion to corps command four times until Bradley straightened out the Twenty-Eighth Division. Once Bradley accomplished that task, Marshall sent him to join his classmate Eisenhower in North Africa. Shortly after he arrived in theater, Eisenhower assigned Bradley to command II Corps while Patton planned the invasion of Sicily.

More than any other officer whose name entered Marshall's black book, Eisenhower constituted the preeminent "Marshall man." Marshall had been gathering information on Ike for years. Maj. Gen. Fox Conner, who headed Pershing's operations division in World War I, thought well of him. So did Pershing. As Pogue notes, another of Marshall's close acquaintances from the Great War, Maj. Ben F. Caffey, stationed in Manila, had written the deputy chief of staff in 1939 from the Philippines: "LTC D. D. Eisenhower, Infantry, familiarly known as Ike, has been an especially brilliant member of the [Douglas MacArthur] mission. He is 'going places,' or I miss my guess." Small wonder that Marshall summoned Eisenhower to Washington in the immediate aftermath of Pearl Harbor.

Working for Marshall in the War Department was not always easy, as Eisenhower discovered when he reported for duty in the War Plans Division in December 1941. Ike quickly learned not to expect lavish praise. The best you could hope for, Ike recorded in his journal, was, "You are not doing so badly so far." But because Eisenhower performed so well, Marshall rewarded him with a more important job.

Even if an officer made it into Marshall's black book, there was no guarantee he would remain. "I'm going to put these men to the severest tests which I can devise in time of peace," Marshall confessed. "I'm going to start shifting them into jobs of greater responsibility than those they hold now. Then I'm going to change them, suddenly, without warning, to jobs even more burdensome and difficult. . . . Those who stand up under the punishment will be pushed ahead. Those who fail are out at the first sign of faltering."

For every officer who met Marshall's stringent standards, many more fell by the wayside. To understand why, one only needs to review Secretary of War Stimson's personal assessment of Marshall. On January 31, 1942, Stimson told Marshall that he had found that public figures fit into two classes: "first, those who are thinking primarily of what they can do for the job which they hold, and second, those who are thinking primarily of what the job can do for them." Marshall was "at the very top of my list of those I would place in the first category. . . . You are one of the most selfless public officials that I have ever known."

Not surprisingly, those officers who vigorously advocated their personal advancement had no place in Marshall's Army. Take the case of Lt. Gen.

Hugh Drum, who had been one of Marshall's principal rivals for the position of chief of staff. Initially advanced by Stimson to head the "China Mission," Drum made it known that he preferred not to languish in the backwater of the war in a far-off theater. Tempers flared when Drum made his preferences known to Marshall, who told Drum in no uncertain terms that in the present crisis every officer was expected to serve without regard to personal ambition.

As soon as Drum departed the office, Marshall conferred with the secretary of war and recommended that Drum not be favorably considered for the China Mission. Consequently, Marshall nominated his personal choice, Stilwell, for the command, and Stilwell received the assignment. (Drum never saw active field service in World War II.) Not particularly happy with the decision, Stilwell replied, "I'll go where I'm sent." This was precisely the selflessness that the army chief expected.

Even Patton, one of Marshall's oldest friends, discovered that his close relationship with the army chief of staff only went so far. As Marshall recollected to Pogue, one of Patton's colonels had written some "sharp criticisms of the War Department, wholly unjustifiable." Marshall knew Patton had encouraged the colonel to do so. Later, when Marshall toured the battlefront, Patton asked Marshall to promote the colonel. Marshall refused the request.

When Patton pressed the matter over dinner, Marshall told him, "This is not the time to bring this up. This is a social gathering, not a business meeting. I am speaking now as the chief of staff to Gen. Patton and not to my friend, Gen. Patton. You have encouraged the colonel in his attacks, and you have destroyed him. I will not promote him. Never mention it to me again." Patton prudently dropped the issue.

Nor was Patton the only senior commander with whom Marshall had occasional trouble. MacArthur was a special case. Having already served five years as chief of staff from 1930 to 1935, MacArthur remained convinced that Marshall and his deputy, Eisenhower, had scuttled his Philippine command in early 1942 by not rushing supplies and reinforcements to his beleaguered soldiers on Bataan. Marshall did all within his power to relieve the starving force, but considering the logistical constraints placed on the army during the first months of the war, it was an impossible task. Yet it was Marshall who wrote the recommendation for MacArthur's Medal of Honor.

While some members of the War Department's staff seemed reluctant to get tough with senior officers in the field, a referral of the matter to the chief of staff usually settled the issue. Marshall wrote to some, stating exactly what he thought, and indicated that this was the last time he intended to get personally involved in the matter.

Such was the case with Lt. Gen. Walter Krueger, the commander of Sixth Army. Of all the senior generals "of the line" at the time Marshall became chief of staff, only Krueger received army-level command during World War II. Krueger often proved "difficult unless he got his way," Marshall reminisced. Krueger didn't want any National Guard troops assigned to his command. Marshall told him he would have to take his share, and that was final. Marshall then directed that all copies of this type of correspondence be destroyed.

In contrast to his dealings with MacArthur, Marshall appeared almost paternal in his response to Eisenhower's requests for the European Theater. "You list your final desires, and so far as I can see now, they will be approved," Marshall informed the newly appointed Supreme Commander in early 1944. Here again, Marshall's support had its limits. For the upcoming invasion of France, Ike requested all the proven commanders who had distinguished themselves in North Africa and Sicily. Eisenhower particularly desired Maj. Gen. Lucian K. Truscott Jr., who had commanded the Third Infantry Division in Sicily. Marshal drew the line, informing Ike that the Mediterranean Theater required seasoned commanders as well. He gave Eisenhower most, but not all, of the officers he had requested

Given the manner in which he weeded out many high-ranking officers, Marshall enjoyed his share of detractors. Those officers placed on the retired list were especially critical. Equally bitter, notes historian Eric Larrabee, were the wives of those officers, often long acquainted with Marshall, whom he refused to promote or place in positions of command. "[Marshall] was once our dear friend," one wife wrote to Pogue, "but he ruined my husband." Other observers criticized the chief for creating an old-boy network, where only those who had incurred Marshall's favor during the Fort Benning years were destined to command troops in combat.

Some accused Marshall of forcibly retiring "the brains of the Army," referring to his reliance on youth.

Others, writes Pogue, claimed that Marshall "didn't always pick good men, that he formed quick impressions, made snap judgments and sometimes serious mistakes." Col. James A. Van Fleet, Ike and Bradley's classmate from West Point, is a case in point. Van Fleet was an excellent officer whose promotion Marshall delayed, confusing him with another officer whose name sounded similar and who wasn't as good. When the mix-up was straightened out, Van Fleet moved up fast. He was an exception to the rule, however. By any standard of excellence, Marshall was right far more times than he was wrong in his assessment of commanders.

By his own admission, Marshall's most serious mistake lay in the mobilization of African American units. In retrospect, Marshall felt that he should have kept the mobilization camps in the northern sections of the country. Instead, he moved these men and their units into the South, where they encountered prejudices "utterly beyond our control." Such prejudices "violently excited the blacks from the North who were unaccustomed to such matters of segregation as they found in the South, particularly in the very small towns." It was one of Marshall's few misjudgments.

Ever attuned to history's judgment, Marshall remained reluctant to comment on the efficiency of officers whom he had personally selected for senior wartime command. "I am not going to do this," he told Pogue. "I think if anything like this got into the book [Pogue's four-volume biography of Marshall] in any way . . . all the attention would go to that and all the acrimonious debate would go to that, and nothing to the really important part of the text. I don't think it would be quite fair because the officer would have no chance to answer it at all."

In the final analysis, Marshall's control over the promotion and retirement of Regular Army officers created a body of commanders and staff officers who led the US Army to victory in the most devastating conflict in history. Collectively, this cadre of officers constituted the most formidable array of warriors in our nation's history. More than any other officer, Marshall modernized the American Army.

Eisenhower, who proved to be Marshall's most able subordinate, gets the final word. Writing to Marshall on the eve of the termination of the European war, Eisenhower cabled, "I think you should make a visit here at the earliest possible moment while we are conducting a general offensive. You would be proud of the Army you have produced. . . . You would be struck by the 'veteran' quality of the whole organization. . . . You could see, in visible form, the fruits of much of your work over the past five years."

"Marshall's Men" was originally published in *ARMY Magazine* (December 2009).

22

An Uneasy Alliance

Eisenhower, Montgomery Managed Allied Victory Despite Personal Differences

At best, coalition commanders make strange bedfellows. Gen. Dwight Eisenhower, Supreme Allied Commander of the Allied Expeditionary Force during World War II, and British Field Marshal Bernard Law Montgomery, commander of the war's Twenty-First Army Group, could not have been more different in temperament.

While Montgomery was flamboyant and temperamental, Eisenhower was reserved and more calculating. Throughout the European war, they endured a less-than-cordial relationship that needlessly prolonged the conflict, some historians say.

To Eisenhower's son John Eisenhower, Montgomery proved the heaviest cross his father bore during the European war. When asked how difficult it was for the Supreme Allied Commander to command Montgomery and Gen. George Patton Jr., two of the conflict's most dynamic generals, John Eisenhower, later US ambassador to Belgium, responded, "You are only half right; compared to Monty, Patton was no problem at all."

Annoyed from the Start

Eisenhower's initial meeting with Montgomery occurred in the late spring of 1942, when Army Chief of Staff Gen. George Marshall directed Eisenhower and Maj. Gen. Mark Clark to fly to England to ascertain the state of preparedness of American forces in the United Kingdom. According to Clark, Montgomery seemed irked at having to take time from his other duties to brief two unknown American generals. During the briefing, Eisenhower lit a cigarette. Montgomery brusquely said he did not permit smoking in his headquarters. Only Eisenhower's "beet-red face betrayed his annoyance," according to military historian and biographer Carlo D'Este in his book *Eisenhower: A Soldier's Life*.

Even though Montgomery served as one of Eisenhower's army commanders in North Africa, Sicily, and Italy, the two were able to settle their personal differences during that time. In December 1943, President Franklin Roosevelt selected Eisenhower as Supreme Allied Commander for the invasion of northwest Europe, code-named Operation Overlord.

While he considered Montgomery a difficult subordinate, Eisenhower admired Montgomery's tactical acumen and held no reservations when British Prime Minister Winston Churchill chose Montgomery as the senior British commander for the upcoming invasion.

Having worked closely with Montgomery in the Mediterranean Theater, Eisenhower assigned Montgomery as the land forces commander for D-Day and the ensuing campaign in Normandy, France. In the spirit of Allied solidarity, Eisenhower also appointed British officers as his deputy commander and the chiefs of the naval and air forces for Overlord.

Following D-Day, which occurred on June 6, 1944, Montgomery's cautious approach and his penchant for what he called "tidying up the battlefield" frequently caused dissension within the Allied high command. The ultimate victory in Normandy was due in large part to tenacious fighting by the Allied air and ground forces, logistical superiority and Montgomery's adept handling of the battlefield.

Still, differences remained between Eisenhower and Montgomery. The two senior Allied commanders remained poles apart when it came to the conduct of war. According to Montgomery, "[Eisenhower's] creed appeared to me to be that there must be aggressive action on the part of everyone at all times. My military doctrine was based on unbalancing the enemy while keeping well-balanced myself. . . . I had learnt [the doctrine of balance] in the battle fighting since 1940, and I knew from experience how it helped to save men's lives."

On September 1, 1944, Eisenhower assumed command of the land battle and relegated Montgomery to army group command, a level that placed Montgomery on par with Lt. Gen. Omar Bradley, commander of the Twelfth US Army Group. To assuage Montgomery's pride, Churchill elevated Montgomery to field marshal status. To soothe Montgomery's fragile ego, Eisenhower approved Montgomery's scheme to launch Operation Market Garden in September 1944, a disastrous attempt to bridge the Lower Rhine River at the Dutch town of Arnhem.

Eisenhower's support of Montgomery did not play well in American circles because shifting Allied logistical allocations to Montgomery's Twenty-First Army Group from Bradley's army group temporarily halted then-lieutenant-general Patton's thrust eastward to the Rhine. Told to assume the defensive from Nancy in eastern France to Luxembourg, the fuming Patton wrote in his personal diary, "Monty will not take orders. So, we have to . . . Monty does what he pleases, and Ike says 'yes, sir.'"

Patton's reservations aside, Eisenhower reallocated logistical support to Montgomery in part to achieve an equality of contribution between the British and the Americans. In retrospect, Eisenhower clearly understood what Montgomery meant to British national pride. In short, Eisenhower's decision was political more than military.

Eisenhower's broad-front strategy, vis-à-vis Montgomery's single thrust into Germany, demonstrated the complexities of leadership within an allied coalition. Both Eisenhower's and Montgomery's strategies possessed merits, but Eisenhower demonstrated his prerogative as Supreme Allied Commander to ensure that the British and Americans would win the war in tandem—no single general, no national army, would win the war. Victory was going to be an Allied victory, with the British and Americans playing an equal part. Eisenhower firmly believed that triumph in Europe must be shared, especially given the expanding American dominance in men and materiel.

This equitable recognition cut no ice with Montgomery, who informed British Field Marshal Alan Brooke, chief of the imperial general staff, that Eisenhower's "ignorance as to how to run a war is absolute and complete." Brooke added his personal assessment of Eisenhower in his wartime diary, writing, "Ike knows nothing about strategy and is quite unsuited to the post of supreme commander."

Matters reached a predictable climax when Montgomery challenged Eisenhower's authority during the Battle of the Bulge. Germany's Ardennes Offensive began on December 16, 1944, quickly penetrating the American front line in the Ardennes Forest. Eisenhower met with both

Bradley and Montgomery within the first weeks of the campaign. When Eisenhower met Montgomery on December 28 during a lull in the battle, the scene was set for a showdown.

Eisenhower urged an immediate attack on the German salient, but Montgomery hesitated. Eisenhower assumed that Montgomery agreed to attack on January 1, but Montgomery's offensive did not commence that day or the following day. True to form, Montgomery overplayed his hand. Cabling Eisenhower, Montgomery resurrected his notion that he be placed in operational control of all Allied ground forces to allow the Supreme Allied Commander to manage the political machinations of the alliance.

Eisenhower immediately called Montgomery's bluff and informed his subordinate, "I assure you that in this matter I can go no further. . . . I have planned" to advance on a broad front and he, Eisenhower, would serve as the single ground commander, not Montgomery.

To ensure Montgomery understood that the issue of a single ground commander was now closed, Eisenhower informed Montgomery that he no longer would tolerate any debate on the subject. If Montgomery persisted, Eisenhower would "present our differences to the [combined chief of staff]."

Montgomery continued his theatrics until Maj. Gen. Freddie de Guingand, his chief of staff, discreetly informed his boss that the Americans intended to nominate Gen. Harold Alexander, the Allied commander in chief in the Mediterranean Theater, to replace Montgomery if the differences between the two senior commanders persisted. Montgomery belatedly apologized to Eisenhower.

Rather than let matters rest, Montgomery held a news conference on January 7, 1945, during which he claimed full credit for halting the German Ardennes Offensive and denigrated the American contribution to the Allied victory. The British press, specifically the *Tabloid Daily Mail*, wrote a headline that said, "Montgomery Foresaw Attack, Acted 'On Own' to' Save Day."

Much of the American anger that followed centered on Montgomery's jingoistic and self-serving assessment of the Battle of the Bulge. This time, Eisenhower let the matter pass and focused on the true objective of resuming the advance into the heartland of Germany and winning the war. Still, the tension between Eisenhower and Montgomery lingered until V-E Day, May 8, 1945.

The rancor between the two commanders manifested itself long after the war and continued until Eisenhower's death in 1969. When the retired field marshal visited President Eisenhower in Gettysburg, Pennsylvania, in May 1957, even Eisenhower could not have forecast Montgomery's tactlessness before the reporters who accompanied the two wartime commanders during a tour of the battlefield. At one point, Montgomery voiced his contention that both Gen. Robert E. Lee and Maj. Gen. George Meade should have been relieved of their respective Gettysburg commands.

Also, though ostensibly speaking to Eisenhower, Montgomery often raised his voice so the reporters could hear, a tactic Eisenhower so abhorred that he began to walk away from Montgomery. Eisenhower later recalled, "I was resentful of his obvious purpose, and his lack of good taste and I merely replied, 'Listen, Monty, I live here. I have nothing to say about the matter.'" A year later, Montgomery published his memoir, originally titled *The Sparks Fly Upward*, in which he was critical of Eisenhower as Supreme Allied Commander.

In an April 1959 interview with American correspondents Edward Murrow and Charles Collingwood, Montgomery declared, "One of the mysteries of the war was why Eisenhower had failed to understand the battle plan in Normandy—and that by failing to concentrate the Allied armies thereafter, [Eisenhower] had prolonged the war and invited the American debacle in the Ardennes."

Eisenhower exploded. Other than a transatlantic TV discussion via satellite a decade later, Eisenhower never addressed another word to the field marshal for the remainder of his life. Even Montgomery's foremost biographer, Nigel Hamilton, admitted that "their relationship, never easy, was at an end, and once again Monty had no one to blame but himself."

That said, both Eisenhower and Montgomery proved to be an indispensable team in defeating Adolf Hitler in the campaign in northwest Europe. They should be remembered not for their disparate personalities and operational differences but because they became the principal catalysts of victory over Nazi Germany.

"An Uneasy Alliance: Eisenhower, Montgomery Managed Allied Victory Despite Personal Differences" was originally published in *ARMY Magazine* (February 2022).

23

Eisenhower

The Indispensable Commander

SIXTY-FOUR YEARS AFTER HIS GREATEST MILITARY VICTORY, GEN. Dwight D. (Ike) Eisenhower remains a popular subject of biography. Two recent studies have portrayed the Supreme Commander, Allied Expeditionary Force, as a quintessential rags-to-riches American hero. Both biographers have awarded Ike high marks for character but have said little about his direct contribution during the climactic battle of the Western Front during World War II.

The Eisenhower who commanded the Allied Expeditionary Force in the spring of 1944, was a far more mature battle captain than the untested commander who led the invasion force that landed in North Africa in November 1942. In the Mediterranean Theater, British chief of the Imperial General Staff Gen. Alan Brooke attempted "to push [Ike] into the stratosphere and rarefied atmosphere of a Supreme Commander, where he would be free to devote his time to the political and interallied problems, whilst we inserted . . . our own commanders to deal with the military situations." Though many senior British officers remained skeptical of Ike's operational ability during the campaigns in the Mediterranean, Eisenhower proved to be the indispensable factor in the Allied victory on D-Day.

Nowhere was Eisenhower's evolution as a coalition commander more evident than in the six months that preceded the Allied invasion of northwest Europe. During that crucial period, Ike made a series of critical decisions that greatly enhanced the chances of success for the impending invasion. These actions addressed the full range of joint/combined operations, including ordering major revisions to the initial invasion plan, selecting key subordinates and demonstrating a clear comprehension of the intricacies of conducting coalition warfare.

Eisenhower arrived in London on January 15, 1944, to prepare and to mount the cross-channel invasion, code named Operation Overlord. Having received his appointment as Supreme Commander directly from President Franklin D. Roosevelt following the second anniversary of the Japanese attack on Pearl Harbor, Ike immediately examined the invasion plan and found it lacking in scope and in the number of divisions allocated to the initial attack. Together with the land forces commander, British Gen. Bernard Law (Monty) Montgomery, Ike directed that additional forces be assigned to the invasion force and that the geographic scope of the invasion area be vastly expanded to include a sixty-mile stretch of the Normandy coast.

The next area in which Eisenhower made significant impact on the invasion was in his selection of subordinates. Determined that the solidarity of the Anglo-American coalition remain paramount, Ike continued the structure of Allied headquarters that had proved successful in the Mediterranean where his principal air, land and sea commanders were British officers. Each of the three subordinate service chiefs, however, had been selected long before Eisenhower's arrival in England. Though Montgomery was not his primary choice for land forces commander, Ike deferred to Prime Minister Winston Churchill, who championed Monty's cause. The selections of Air Chief Marshal Trafford Leigh-Mallory to command all tactical air assets assigned to Overlord and Adm. Bertram Ramsay to exercise overall control of Operation Neptune, the code name allocated to the naval dimension of the invasion, were far less controversial.

Against then–Lt. Gen. Omar Bradley's objections, Eisenhower went out on a limb and resuscitated the career of then–Lt. Gen. George S. Patton Jr. Bradley, destined to command the American First Army on D-Day, preferred that Patton not play a conspicuous role in the upcoming invasion. In both North Africa and Sicily, Bradley had served under Patton. Now the tables had been turned as Eisenhower had designated Bradley as the senior American ground commander for D-Day. When and if Patton arrived in theater, he would command an army under Bradley, who would move up to command an army group. Meanwhile, Patton remained in limbo in Sicily because of an incident in which he slapped a hospitalized soldier the preceding summer.

Only in early 1944 did Ike summon Patton to England. It did not take Patton long before he again embarrassed Eisenhower and Army Chief of Staff Gen. George C. Marshall. On April 25, Patton addressed a small assembly at Knutsford, a pleasant town in northwestern England. Instead of confining his remarks to the real purpose of the event, Patton opined that it was "the evident destiny of the British and Americans, and of course the Russians, to rule the [postwar] world."

For Eisenhower, this was almost the final straw. Ike informed Marshall that he was becoming "exceedingly weary of Patton's habit of getting everybody into hot water through the immature character of his public actions and statements." Marshall left Patton's fate in Eisenhower's hands but cautioned Ike that "the decision is exclusively yours. . . . Do not consider [the] War Department position in the matter. Consider only Overlord. . . . Everything else is of minor importance." Eisenhower decided to keep him on board, but not before he issued a sharp rebuke to Patton, who once again promised to refrain from his outrageous behavior.

Patton would serve a valuable purpose on D-Day, just not in the manner that the flamboyant general desired. Patton's major contribution to D-Day was in command of a fictitious army group presumably to land at the Pas-de-Calais. He would later command Third (US) Army, but only after the lodgment area had been firmly established. Meanwhile, Eisenhower promised Marshall that "the volatile, offensive-minded Patton would always serve under the more even-handed Bradley."

With respect to the other American commanders, Ike placed his personal stamp of approval on every division commander and higher. According to one recent biography, his "criterion was unambiguous: No officer was selected whom he did not know personally. . . . Numerous West Point classmates, along with veterans of the North African and Italian campaigns, were among those tapped to fill the roster of jobs." Eisenhower's usual pattern was to discuss each prospective officer with Bradley and his own chief of staff, then–Lt. Gen. Walter Bedell Smith. In every case, one of the three officers knew the designee well. Ike then sent a written request to Marshall. This procedure produced the desired effect. Eisenhower and

Bradley felt comfortable with the vast majority of commanders with whom they had served in the Mediterranean.

In the end, Marshall did not assign Eisenhower every officer he requested, but the army chief of staff ensured that Ike had the tools at hand to make D-Day successful. To assist Eisenhower in the planning and preparation for the invasion, Marshall assigned a number of officers who had served conspicuously in the Pacific Theater, such as Maj. Gen. Charles (Pete) Corlett, to Eisenhower's headquarters. Corlett had established his reputation by seizing Kwajalein Island in the Marshall archipelago. Gen. Marshall offered Corlett's services to Eisenhower, whom he hoped would benefit from Corlett's amphibious experience.

The army chief would be sorely disappointed. Corlett was not a member of Eisenhower's "Mediterranean clique." Ike reluctantly accepted Corlett in order not to alienate Marshall, but Eisenhower was not pleased with the arrangement. Once in England, Corlett found himself to be the proverbial outsider, "an interloper from the Pacific, a son-of-a-bitch from out of town." He soon discovered that the officers surrounding Ike's headquarters considered anything that had occurred in the Pacific strictly "bush-league stuff" and that no one was interested in his thorough knowledge of amphibious methods.

Nor were Bradley and Patton impressed. By Bradley's own admission, Corlett, whom he had known from his cadet days, was not one of his favorite officers. As for Patton, Corlett was strictly ".32-caliber," only slightly better than the Supreme Commander's assessment of then–Lt. Gen. Jacob Devers, another Marshall protégé, whom Ike persuaded his chief to send to the Mediterranean Theater to avoid Devers playing a conspicuous role in the upcoming invasion. Yet had Corlett's recommendations concerning the inadequate ammunition allocations and the lack of amphibious tractors to support the initial assault been accepted, undoubtedly fewer American lives would have been lost.

Another area in which Ike left his imprint on the upcoming invasion was his utilization of air assets in support of Overlord. Contrary to popular belief, Eisenhower did not threaten to resign if strategic air forces were not placed in his immediate command for D-Day. That issue had already been decided during operations in the Mediterranean Theater. The more important issue was where the strategic or long-range bombers ought to concentrate their attacks preceding D-Day. Eisenhower remained insistent that the heavy bombers ought to attack the railroad network in France, the low countries and western Germany (the Transport Plan). British Air Chief Marshal Arthur (Bomber) Harris and American then–Lt. Gen. Carl Spaatz preferred continuing the aerial assault on Germany's industrial capacity (Operation Pointblank).

According to Eisenhower's aide, Churchill had taken the position that either the Royal Air Force (RAF) Bomber Command should be independent of the Supreme Commander's control but work in conjunction with Ike and his forces or only a part of the Bomber Command should be under Ike's control. Eisenhower sought to clarify "the exact pattern of command" of the air resources. In the end, Ike prevailed because he would not budge. As he reported to Marshall, Ike said that the British were trying to make him change his mind, but "I have stuck to my guns because there is no other way in which this tremendous air force can help us."

The solution was muddled but ultimately clear. Eisenhower's deputy commander, Air Chief Marshal Arthur Tedder, would now supervise all air operations for Overlord. Eisenhower as "a direct agent of the Combined Chiefs of Staff [CCS] for the execution of Overlord" and British Air Chief Marshal Charles Portal, chief of the Air Staff and the CCS executive for Pointblank, were to approve the air program developed for Overlord. Then, the "responsibility for supervision of air operations out of England of all the forces engaged in the program, including US Strategic and British Bomber Command . . . should pass through the Supreme Commander."

The next dimension in which a more mature Eisenhower emerged was his willingness to empower his subordinates. In that capacity, he lent the full weight of his office to give Montgomery complete support in the latter's adverse assessment of the original assault plan. According to that plan, the Allied assault would consist of three divisions attacking on a relatively narrow front. Montgomery insisted that a five-division assault, supported by three airborne divisions, across a much wider front was necessary. Ike not only supported Monty but also postponed the invasion until early June to allow extra time to assemble the additional landing craft and logistical support.

The utilization of airborne resources posed a particular problem. From the initial planning stage, Montgomery and Bradley had insisted on using airborne divisions to secure the flanks of the landing force. In the American zone behind Utah Beach on the Cherbourg (Cotentin) Peninsula, Bradley and his senior airborne advisor, then–Brig. Gen. James Gavin, stoutly agreed to the inclusion of two airborne divisions to block German reinforcements from disrupting the invasion. Over the objections of Leigh-Mallory, Ike approved the request.

On the eve of the invasion, however, Leigh-Mallory again raised the old question concerning the wisdom of airborne operations into the Cotentin Peninsula. Leigh-Mallory was quite sincere in protesting what he termed "the futile slaughter" of two fine divisions. A combination of unsuitable landing ground and expected resistance constituted an undue hazard for the airborne soldiers, who would be vulnerable until the amphibious forces moved inland. Leigh-Mallory anticipated casualties reaching 70 percent in the glider units.

Ike consulted Bradley to refute Leigh-Mallory's concerns. It was risky, of course, stated Bradley, but the American commander insisted that the success of the Utah Beach landing was predicated on the seizure of the exits behind it by the airborne forces—no airborne drop, no Utah beach. That was enough for Eisenhower. If Bradley felt the airborne divisions were crucial to Utah's success, so be it. Retiring to his tent to "sweat out the decision," Ike announced the attack was to go as planned.

Two other factors characterized Ike's maturation as a commander on the eve of the invasion: the willingness to make critical decisions on less-than-perfect information and the acceptance of accountability and responsibility for the decisions that he made.

Weather and meteorological data dictated that the invasion must occur between June 5 and 7 or the next possible period in mid-June. In Eisenhower's own words, he felt that "the only remaining great decision to be faced before D-Day was that of fixing, definitely, the day and hour of the assault." It was at Southwick House that Ike made the decision he was born to make.

Following a one-day postponement due to severe weather conditions in the English Channel, the senior commanders met again to discuss the feasibility of designating June 6, 1944, as D-Day. Meeting on the evening of June 4, Ike polled his subordinates. Group Capt. (Dr.) John Stagg, a civilian meteorologist on loan to the RAF, predicted a temporary slackening in the inclement weather on the morning of June 6.

Then it was the commanders' turn. Monty recommended proceeding with the invasion. Leigh-Mallory, who feared excessive casualties among the airborne troops, remained pessimistic. Ramsay opined that if the invasion was to go forward, an order had to be given now. Ike weighed all the alternatives and said, "I am quite positive we must give the order. I don't like it, but there it is. . . . I don't see how we can do anything else."

The Allied commanders in chief convened one last time at 4:15 a.m. on Monday, June 5, for a final update. Again, Ike polled his commanders and received an optimistic assessment from Stagg. The decision to designate Tuesday, June 6 as D-Day now rested on the shoulders of the Supreme Commander. After final careful consideration and deep reflection, Eisenhower announced his decision: "Okay, we'll go." With three words, Ike launched the largest amphibious invasion in history. There could be no turning back now.

In his highly favorable treatment of his grandfather, historian David Eisenhower notes that "many have narrated this decision—few have evaluated it." Friedrich Ruge, Field Marshal Erwin Rommel's naval adviser that evening, later reflected that Eisenhower had made the decision on insufficient intelligence without having to clear the decision with higher headquarters. The responsibility lay solely on the shoulders of the Supreme Commander. Montgomery, never a strong Eisenhower supporter, noted that "Eisenhower was in good form and made his decision quickly."

Now that he had made the decision, Eisenhower held himself personally accountable for the success or failure of the invasion. He returned to his trailer and penned a note in his own hand. Temporarily placing the note in his tunic, he later gave it to his naval aide. The message read, "Our landings in the Cherbourg-Havre area have failed to gain a satisfactory foothold, and I have withdrawn the troops. My decision to attack at this time and place was based upon the best information available. The troops, the air and the Navy did all that bravery and devotion to duty could do. If any blame or fault attaches to the attempt, it is mine alone." Eisenhower initially dated the message July 5, rather than June 5.

Before North Africa, Sicily, and Italy, Eisenhower had written a similar message. No attempt was made to escape responsibility and accountability in the event that the invasion failed. No greater testament to the Supreme Commander's character exists than this simple message that he kept in his wallet ready for reference.

D-Day, of course, was a great success and the pinnacle of Eisenhower's storied career. By evening, nearly 156,000 Allied soldiers were firmly in place along the Normandy coast. German counterattacks had failed to dislodge the assault force. To his dying day, Eisenhower took greater pride in the Allied success on June 6, 1944, than he did in any single achievement during his presidency.

Returning to Normandy on the twentieth anniversary of D-Day, Eisenhower paid an emotional visit to Omaha Beach, where 2,500 Americans had fallen. Sitting on the wall of the American cemetery overlooking the once-bloodstained beach, Ike reflected on the sacrifice of the Allied soldiers, sailors, and airmen, so many of whom had given their last full measure of devotion. In an effort to put their sacrifice into perspective, Eisenhower paid them the ultimate tribute: "These men came here—British and our allies, and Americans—to storm these beaches for one purpose only, not to gain anything for ourselves, not to fulfill any ambitions that America had for conquest, but just to preserve freedom."

It seemed a fitting epitaph from the commander who himself had done so much to ensure the success of D-Day.

"Eisenhower: The Indispensable Commander" was originally published in *ARMY Magazine* (June 2008).

24

Ike's Three Great Decisions That Shaped World War II

In the seventy years since the United States embarked on World War II, the reputations of many senior field commanders have ebbed and flowed. None has withstood the judgment of history more so than that of Gen. Dwight D. (Ike) Eisenhower, Supreme Commander of the Allied Expeditionary Force. Over the course of the European war, Eisenhower made numerous critical decisions involving the selection of subordinates, military strategy, and the cohesion of the Western Alliance, but three controversial decisions stand out and mark Ike as a great commander: the decision to launch D-Day, the broad-front strategy and the redirection of Allied forces from Berlin toward the Southern Redoubt in April 1945. Ike's three critical decisions as Supreme Commander not only dictated the course of the war in northwest Europe but also laid the foundation for the postwar world.

Two years from the day when Japan attacked Pearl Harbor, President Franklin Roosevelt informed Eisenhower that he was to command the Allied Expeditionary Force. Though the president had considered Army Chief of Staff Gen. George Marshall for the appointment, Roosevelt felt he could not spare Marshall from Washington, DC. Consequently, he appointed Eisenhower, whom he considered "the best politician among the military men. He is a natural leader who can convince other men to follow him, and this is what we need in his position more than any other quality." Ike proved an inspired choice.

On February 12, 1944, Eisenhower received the formal directive from the Combined Chiefs of Staff (CCS): "You are hereby designated as Supreme Allied Commander of the forces placed under your orders for operations for liberation of Europe from Germans. . . . You will enter the continent of Europe and, in conjunction with the other United Nations, undertake operations aimed at the heart of Germany and the destruction of her armed forces." This mission statement formed the foundation of Ike's wartime strategy as he organized Supreme Headquarters Allied Expeditionary Force (SHAEF). Given complete latitude by the CCS, Eisenhower defined operations aimed at the "industrial heart" of Germany, the Ruhr, and the Saar, concluding that such operations would lead to the destruction of the German armed forces because the Germans would defend the industrial heart with maximum forces available.

Though the British provided the details of D-Day and the proposed site of the landings, only the Supreme Commander could make the fateful decision to launch the invasion. On June 1, Ike transferred SHAEF (Advance) to Southwick House, Adm. Bertram H. Ramsay's headquarters north of Portsmouth. Weather and meteorological data dictated that the invasion must occur between June 5 and 7 or the next possible period in mid-June. In Eisenhower's own words, he felt that the only remaining great decision to be faced before D-Day "was that of fixing, definitely, the day and hour of the assault." It was at Southwick House that Ike made the decision that he was born to make.

Following a one-day postponement due to severe weather conditions in the English Channel, the senior Allied commanders met to discuss the feasibility of designating June 6, 1944, as D-Day. Meeting on the evening of June 4, Ike sought recommendations from his principal subordinates. First up was Group Captain James M. Stagg, the chief meteorological officer for Operation Overlord, who predicted a temporary slackening in the inclement weather on the morning of June 6.

Then it was the commanders' turn. Field Marshal Bernard Montgomery, commanding the ground forces, recommended proceeding with the invasion. Air Chief Marshal Trafford Leigh-Mallory, who feared excessive casualties among the airborne troops, remained pessimistic. Ramsey opined that if the invasion were to go forward on June 6, an order had to be given immediately. Ike weighed all the alternatives and said, "I am quite positive we must give the order. I don't like it, but there it is. . . . I don't see how we can do anything else."

The Allied commanders convened one last time at 4:15 a.m. on Monday, June 5, for a final update. Again, Ike polled his commanders and again he received an optimistic assessment from Stagg. The decision to designate Tuesday, June 6, as D-Day now rested on the shoulders of the Supreme Commander. After final careful consideration and deep reflection, Eisenhower announced his decision: "Okay, we'll go."

With those three words, Ike launched the largest amphibious invasion in history and took the initial steps on the road to Berlin. There could now be no turning back. Having witnessed the lead-up to Ike's decision, his chief of staff, Walter Bedell Smith, later recalled being struck by "the isolation and loneliness of high command." Historian Carlo D'Este said more eloquently in *Eisenhower: A Soldier's Life*, "June 5 was a supreme test of [Ike's] generalship and his ability to keep his nerve under the most trying circumstance he would ever face as a commander. There would be other crises ahead, but none approached the magnitude of D-Day."

By late summer, the Normandy campaign was successfully concluded with the liberation of Paris. As the Allied armies moved north through the Pas de Calais and into Belgium and then east toward the German border, the size of Ike's forces and the extent of the Allied front dictated that Eisenhower "take direct control of the land forces operating on the Continent." In his report to the CCS, Ike stated that the "change in the command set-up was necessary . . . due to the diverging lines of operation and the need for having a commander on each of the main fronts capable of handling, with a reasonable degree of independence, the day-to-day operation in each sector."

Consequently, Ike established his operational headquarters on the Continent and Montgomery's responsibility for arranging the coordination between his Twenty-First Army Group and Lt. Gen. Omar N. Bradley's forces terminated. Montgomery's command was now designated the Northern Group of Armies, while Bradley assumed command of the Twelfth, or Central, Group of Armies. Soon to come under Eisenhower's command was the Southern Group of Armies under command of Lt. Gen. Jacob L. Devers, whose armies had landed in southern France in late summer. Another significant change occurred on August 8 when all British and

American airborne forces were consolidated and placed under the single command of Lt. Gen. Lewis Brereton to form the First Allied Airborne Army. This force now constituted SHAEF's strategic reserve.

Ike's decision to advance on a broad front, versus a narrow thrust, toward the heartland of Germany was entirely consistent with his belief that victory in Europe would be achieved by an Allied effort rather than a British or American one. This decision proved one of the most controversial of the war and brought the Supreme Commander considerable criticism from Montgomery and Chief of the Imperial General Staff Field Marshal Alan Brooke. Throughout the campaign in northwest Europe, both Montgomery and Brooke remained contemptuous of Ike's tactical and strategic abilities. Not surprisingly, the change in the direction of the land campaign did not sit well with Montgomery, who had previously served as land forces commander.

According to the Supreme Commander's grandson, David Eisenhower, Eisenhower's long-range thinking emphasized two cardinal points. After securing ports sufficient to supply the Allied Expeditionary Force, all Germans were to be cleared from areas west of the Rhine before an invasion of Germany. A lesser objective of closing the Rhine in its entirety would be to overrun the Saar basin and to seize the Siegfried Line defenses west of the river behind which the Germans could concentrate at will strong counterattacks. Another would be to "preposition Allied forces for two or more major thrusts across the river, which would enable the Allies to isolate the Ruhr while establishing a wide front for the final advance into Germany and link up with the Red Army." To achieve this, command unity would be paramount to Ike's overall strategy as the Allied force advanced along a broad front.

To compensate for Montgomery's perceived "demotion," Prime Minister Winston Churchill promoted Monty to the rank of field marshal. Chagrined that he now directed but a single army group, Montgomery argued vehemently that the Allied advance be directed along a single thrust by his Twenty-First Army Group, but Ike disagreed. After V-E Day, Monty wrote, had we "run the show properly, the war could have been finished by Christmas 1944. The blame for this must rest with the Americans," or, specifically, Eisenhower.

To assuage Monty's hurt feelings and to determine whether the Germans could succeed in establishing renewed and effective resistance, Ike approved Operation Market Garden, Monty's abortive attempt to bridge the Lower Rhine and advance into Germany in September 1944. To support Monty's armored thrust to capture several bridges throughout Holland, Eisenhower deployed First Allied Airborne Army. The ensuing operation—poorly planned and even more poorly executed—ended in disaster.

Why had Ike approved it and committed SHAEF's strategic reserve? Quite simply, Eisenhower knew what the war meant to the British, and he felt that he had to give Monty an opportunity to validate his strategic assumptions. Moreover, he sought to keep British prestige high in light of the growing preponderance of American industrial and military might. Market Garden was one of the few times when the Supreme Commander approved a strategy on purely nationalistic grounds.

The decision to support Monty's plan hardly constituted Ike's finest hour. With the commitment of SHAEF's strategic reserve, the Allied advance soon ground to a halt in mid-September 1944. Commenting on the logistical problems now plaguing Eisenhower's advance, historian Cornelius Ryan remarked, "The Germans were losing faster than the Allies could win." Antwerp, the only Belgian port large enough to support the Allied advance, was not completely secured until November. In short, logistical problems, coupled with an increasingly tenacious enemy defense, led to a reassessment of Allied strategy.

Historians continue to debate whether Eisenhower squandered the opportunity to end the war in the autumn of 1944. Both sides of the debate fall basically along national lines, but with Market Garden a failure, Eisenhower returned to his original strategy and ordered a general advance along a broad front—Monty in the north, Bradley in the center and Devers in the south. Ike's decision precipitated a crisis in the Allied High Command. Montgomery pleaded for the priority of supplies, but Ike cabled his subordinate, "We must immediately exploit our success by promptly breaching the Siegfried Line, crossing the Rhine on a wide front and seizing the Saar and the Ruhr." Later Eisenhower added, "I see no reason to change this [broad-front advance] conception."

Was the broad-front strategy the right choice? Historians' opinions differ on its efficacy, as did those of the primary combatants—seventy years of postmortem have done little to settle the issue. Montgomery repeatedly claimed that with proper resources, he could have bridged the Rhine and taken Berlin before Christmas had the Supreme Commander approved an advance of forty divisions under Monty's direct command. Bradley and Third Army commander George S. Patton confined their criticisms of Ike to their respective diaries, Patton stating that "Ike was more British than the British." "Oh, God, for John J. Pershing," lamented Patton, remembering Pershing's refusal to amalgamate American divisions into French and British commands during the Great War. Ike was in charge, however, and he maintained the broad-front advance.

What is undeniable is that Ike's broad-front strategy maintained consistent pressure on Germany's western frontier, but it also contributed to the initial defeat of American forces in the Ardennes region of Belgium when Hitler launched his last major offensive in the west on December 16, 1944. David Eisenhower, a prominent historian in his own right, states that the broad-front strategy left the Germans with no real alternative but to select the unpromising Ardennes sector for their December offensive. When it was spent, the Allies found themselves well poised for the Rhine crossings that would go forward almost effortlessly in March. But that was all in the future.

In the days following the German assault, Bradley dismissed the enemy offensive as merely spoiling attacks and discounted the severity of Hitler's great gamble. Ike took a different view when the true scope of the offensive was revealed. Alerting the 82nd and 101st Airborne Divisions, he rushed them to the area around Saint-Vith and Bastogne. Gathering his American commanders together on December 19, Ike admonished them in no uncertain terms that "the present situation is to be regarded as one of opportunity . . . and not of disaster. There will be only cheerful faces at this conference table."

Eisenhower next directed Patton to prepare an offensive to penetrate the German advance from the south. What followed was Patton's most brilliant campaign as he raced to Bastogne, relieving the beleaguered garrison on December 26. In the interim, Ike ceded control of Bradley's First US Army under Courtney Hodges to Montgomery for the upcoming battle. The move severely strained the Supreme Commander's relationship with Bradley, but the reallocation of military forces made perfect military sense as Bradley seemed incapable of directing those forces split by the German advance. By mid-January 1945, the German attack was spent and the "bulge" flattened. The cost, however, had been severe.

Again, Montgomery raised the scepter of a single overall ground forces commander. This time Ike had had enough. Infuriated that Montgomery had informed the press that unless he be given "full operational direction, control, and coordination for a northern advance, otherwise there would be another failure," Ike prepared a communiqué to the Combined Chiefs of Staff, informing them that he and Monty could no longer work together as a team. Belatedly, Montgomery realized that he had overplayed his hand and drafted an "eyes only" message to Eisenhower, promising that Ike would hear no more of the subject.

Ike's last great decision in the war centered on the Allied advance into the German heartland. As outlined in his final report to the CCS, Eisenhower envisaged operations for 1945 would now fall into three phases: "first, the destruction of the enemy forces west of the Rhine and closing to that river; second, the seizure of bridgeheads over the Rhine from which to develop operations into Germany; and third, the destruction of the remaining enemy east of the Rhine and the advance into the heart of the Reich." This purpose had guided all his actions since early 1944. In mid-March, led by Hodges's First US Army, the Western Allies established a secure bridgehead over the Rhine. Montgomery and Patton bridged the last natural barrier into Germany a week later.

The Wehrmacht defended the Ruhr industrial region with all its might, but by April, resistance totally collapsed. German prisoners were being rounded up at a rate of five thousand a day. The final count in the Ruhr was 317,000, including twenty-four generals and an admiral. Once the process of eliminating the enemy forces in the Ruhr had reached a stage when they no longer presented any potential threat to Allied security, Ike laid out his strategy for a thrust deeper into Germany. All that remained was the end game. In developing his strategy, the Supreme Commander had to decide whether to accelerate his advance and attempt to seize the German capital or redirect Allied forces elsewhere.

Should Eisenhower attempt to beat the Russians to Berlin? Many in the Allied camp thought so, including the British prime minister. Churchill favored a direct advance toward the German capital, but in Ike's eyes, the city was a "prestige objective" that lacked military significance. Ike remained intent on the destruction of enemy forces wherever they were. Moreover, Bradley estimated that such a drive would result in more than one hundred thousand casualties for an objective that would be handed over to the Russians in accordance with the Yalta Accords. Russian casualties were actually three times Bradley's estimate. Left unsaid was that American military strength was needed for the final assault on Japan as soon as the European war was successfully concluded.

By April 11, advancing units of Bradley's armies had reached the Elbe at Magdeburg. Berlin was still more than fifty miles away. In light of the military situation, Eisenhower wrote off Berlin and redirected American forces south to destroy the National Redoubt, Germany's last major stronghold in the Bavarian Alps. The reports of a Nazi stronghold proved illusory, but only in hindsight. As Stephen Ambrose so artfully articulated Eisenhower's thinking, "In March 1945 . . . [Roosevelt's] policy was to defeat Germany, redeploy to the Pacific . . . and get along with the Russians. Eisenhower did not question the policy; he did do his best to carry it out."

Ike's decision about the importance of capturing Berlin differed considerably from those of the British. On April 1, Churchill went over Eisenhower's head and appealed directly to Roosevelt. When Montgomery protested the removal of Lt. Gen. William Simpson's Ninth US Army from his command, thus denying him the resources to take Berlin, even if the Supreme Commander had so approved such a thrust, Ike declared, "That place [Berlin] has become, so far as I am concerned, nothing but a geographical location, and I have never been interested in these. My purpose is to destroy the enemy's forces and his powers to resist."

Was it the right decision? Churchill chided Ike and the American chiefs of staff as being neophytes in the complex world of power politics. Eisenhower stood firm. "I am the first to admit that a war is waged in pursuance of political aims, and if the Combined Chiefs of Staff should decide that the Allied effort to take Berlin outweighs purely military considerations in this theater, I would cheerfully readjust my plans and my thinking so as to carry out such an operation," Ike later added. The CCS did not even discuss Eisenhower's cable and left the decision to the Supreme Commander. That settled the matter. There would be no advance to Berlin.

Could Eisenhower have actually captured the German capital? The jury is still out. Historian Ambrose remains skeptical, stating that Eisenhower's critics assume that the Russian timing would have been the same even if Simpson's Ninth Army had pushed on for Berlin. Simpson had nearly fifty thousand veteran troops poised to strike, but Stalin had more than 1 million ready to go. And though Eisenhower seldom responded to his critics who damned him for not striking directly toward the German capital, as a presidential candidate in 1952, Ike stated that none of his detractors had offered to "go out and choose the 10 thousand mothers whose sons would have been killed capturing 'a worthless objective.'"

Field Marshal Montgomery and Gen. Patton vehemently disagreed with Eisenhower's decision. Montgomery argued pointedly, "The Americans could not understand that it was of little avail to win the war strategically if we lost it politically." In his postwar memoirs, Monty continued to state his case that Ike had made a grave error in not advancing toward Berlin, "Because of this curious viewpoint we suffered accordingly from V-E Day onward and are still so suffering, it became obvious to me in the autumn of 1944 [that] we were going to 'muck it up,' I reckon we did."

Patton, too, came straight to the point. In responding to Ike's strategy of avoiding a costly battle in Berlin in order to maintain the pressure on other fronts and to dedicate overwhelming resources to care for thousands of German displaced persons and Allied prisoners of war, Patton said, "Ike, I don't see how you figure that out. We had better take Berlin, and quick!"

"Well, who would want it?" Ike asked.

Patton rested his arm on the Supreme Commander's shoulder and said, "I think history will answer that question for you."

On May 2, Berlin fell to the Russians. Eisenhower, in turn, sought to protect his flanks. SHAEF G-2 had accepted Nazi propaganda at face value that Germany was preparing the impenetrable Alpine Redoubt for a final defensive stand. As Supreme Commander, Ike could hardly dismiss such a report. While preparing for a safe junction with Soviet armies along the Elbe, Eisenhower directed Bradley to redirect his advance toward Bavaria and the elimination of the mythical redoubt. By the end of April, Eisenhower's armies had captured Bavaria and stood on the Czech frontier.

Ike subsequently approved an advance across the border but denied Patton the opportunity to capture Prague. As with Berlin, Prague remained a political, not military, objective in the Supreme Commander's eyes.

On May 5, German resistance across the entire front came to a speedy end. Ike now turned his attention toward securing the unconditional surrender of Nazi Germany in accordance with Roosevelt's unilateral proclamation at Casablanca in January 1943. Two days later, Ike accepted the unconditional surrender of Nazi Germany, informing the Combined Chiefs of Staff that "the mission of this Allied force was fulfilled at 0241 local time, May 7, 1945."

In retrospect, many of Ike's decisions remain controversial, but Roosevelt historian Eric Larrabee credits Eisenhower with ensuring that American armies stood forth at the close of the war in proportion to their numbers and their contribution to the fighting. What Eisenhower had accomplished was the fulfillment of Roosevelt's desire that the United States would not withdraw from Europe into the isolation and non-interventionism that characterized the aftermath of World War I. In the figure of Dwight D. Eisenhower, the United States was in Europe to stay, and "on this rock would be built the Truman Doctrine, the Marshall Plan, the North Atlantic Treaty Organization, and the world we have lived in since."

The verdict of history wholeheartedly concurs.

"Ike's Three Great Decisions" was originally published in *ARMY Magazine* (August 2011).

25

They Liked Ike

Eisenhower Was Close to a Chosen Few Soldiers

One of Gen. Dwight D. Eisenhower's biographers described the future US president as "handsome, gregarious, fun loving, and vain." Sentimentality, the biographer said, was a trait Eisenhower eschewed. Throughout his life, Eisenhower rarely displayed his true feelings to his family or associates. In a public career that spanned a half-century, however, Eisenhower made notable exceptions to his rule. Three comrades in arms stand out: Gen. Leonard T. "Gee" Gerow, Lt. Col. James Basevi "Jimmy" Ord, and Gen. George S. Patton Jr.

Leonard T. "Gee' Gerow"

By Eisenhower's account, Gerow was his best friend during the interwar years. A graduate of the Virginia Military Institute, Gerow was two years older than Eisenhower. Their association dated to 1915, when both were second lieutenants stationed at Fort Sam Houston on the outskirts of San Antonio with the Nineteenth Infantry Regiment.

Second lieutenants are a clannish group, and it was not surprising that Eisenhower and Gerow developed a friendship that would take them from Fort Sam Houston to Fort Leavenworth, Kansas, in the 1920s and to the War Department in the 1930s to the outset of World War II.

Unlike Eisenhower, Gerow saw service in France in World War I while Eisenhower commanded Camp Colt, a training camp for tankers near Gettysburg, Pennsylvania. Their paths converged again at Fort Leavenworth, when both officers entered the Command and General Staff

School in 1925. There, Eisenhower and Gerow became off-duty study companions. Since Eisenhower's quarters at Otis Hall were more accommodating than Gerow's, Eisenhower established "a model command post" where the two students covered the walls with maps and discussed the afternoon's problem sessions.

The arrangements paid off handsomely, with Eisenhower graduating number one in his class. Gerow was not far behind. The night after graduation, Eisenhower and Gerow hosted a celebratory party at a downtown Kansas City, Missouri hotel. The party ended the following morning after Eisenhower sang some of his best-loved songs, his favorite being "Abdul the Bulbul Amir."

Three years later, Eisenhower and Gerow served together again, this time in Washington, DC, where they worked closely with Assistant Secretary of War Frederick Payne. Both Eisenhower and his wife, Mamie, thoroughly enjoyed renewing their friendship with the Gerows, a relationship that was cut short when Kathryn Gerow died at age forty-six on June 17, 1935.

Before her passing, Eisenhower confided in his diary his personal assessment of the officers with whom he worked. Of Gerow, Eisenhower stated, "I know of no job in the Army, either in peace or war that he could not perform brilliantly . . . I have no language sufficiently forceful to describe his efficiency and general worth."

While Eisenhower toiled with Gen. Douglas MacArthur in the Philippines from 1935 to 1939, he maintained frequent contact with his close friend, who was now executive officer of the War Plans Division, of the War Department general staff.

Things moved fast in Washington in those days, and when the Japanese attacked Pearl Harbor, Army Chief of Staff Gen. George C. Marshall directed Eisenhower to report to Brig. Gen. Gerow for "emergency duty." Marshall could not have made a more inspired choice. Eisenhower was familiar with the Philippine defenses and an expert in industrial mobilization. When Marshall reorganized the War Department staff, he selected Eisenhower as head of the War Plans Division, replacing Gerow, who Marshall felt had become "stale from overwork."

With Eisenhower on the scene, Marshall assigned Gerow to command the 29th Infantry Division. When Eisenhower became Supreme

Commander of the Allied Expeditionary Force, he tapped Maj. Gen. Gerow as his V Corps commander for the Omaha Beach assignment. Later, Eisenhower recommended Gerow be promoted and made commander of the Fifteenth Army.

Eisenhower and Gerow had come a long way since Fort Sam Houston in 1915.

James Basevi "Jimmy" Ord

Eisenhower had befriended another future officer before his active-duty service began. The West Point class of 1915 is known as "The Class the Stars Fell On" because fifty-nine of its 164 graduates reached general officer rank. One cadet who did not reach that exalted plateau was Ord, the grandson of one of Gen. Ulysses S. Grant's corps commanders. However, the 1915 West Point yearbook had labeled Ord "a much-appreciated acquisition wherever he may go and will never be lacking in friends or companions."

Following graduation, Ord served with distinction in the Punitive Expedition of 1916 while Eisenhower remained at Fort Sam Houston. A decade later, fate brought the classmates back together while Eisenhower was attending the Army War College at Fort McNair in Washington, DC, along with Gerow. Since many of Eisenhower's fellow students and some general staff officers lived in the Wyoming Apartments in downtown Washington, Mamie reopened "Club Eisenhower." Gerow was there and so was Ord.

In 1935, both Eisenhower and Ord worked for Army Chief of Staff MacArthur. When MacArthur's tour of duty as chief of staff was finished, he accepted an offer from President Manuel Quezon of the Philippines to be his military adviser. MacArthur requested that Eisenhower serve as his assistant military adviser and later as his chief of staff. MacArthur offered to have Eisenhower select an officer to be his assistant. Eisenhower chose Ord, and his friend enthusiastically accepted.

Eisenhower and Ord's primary duty was to develop the Philippine Defense Plan. Working for MacArthur proved a mixed blessing for the two men, and they came to resent their boss's erratic behavior and egotism. Misery loves company, and by the late 1930s, the once warm and close relationship between Eisenhower and MacArthur had deteriorated.

Consequently, Eisenhower relied heavily on Ord to maintain his sanity and composure.

With Ord, Eisenhower could be himself. One biographer described Ord as "jovial, roly-poly, intelligent, and brave." Moreover, Ord was fluent in Spanish and was a skilled organizer and superb staff officer. Together, Eisenhower and Ord developed a defense plan that was doomed to failure due to financial constraints. Happily, both were promoted to lieutenant colonel on July 1, 1936.

As was his custom, Eisenhower confined his frustration to his diary. "I'm ready to go. No one seems to realize how much energy and slavery Jim and I put into this d— job."

The straw that broke the camel's back occurred in January 1938 when MacArthur instructed his two staff officers to prepare a budget that included funds for a massive parade through the streets of Manila. When Quezon asked MacArthur who had authorized such an expenditure, MacArthur blamed Eisenhower and Ord.

The year 1938 brought additional frustration to Eisenhower and Ord. To alleviate the frustration and anxiety, Eisenhower had decided to obtain a pilot's license. Ord followed suit. As part of the defense plan, the duo decided to train Philippine pilots to fly light aircrafts, more for reconnaissance and supply than for combat. Several weeks later, on January 30, with Eisenhower ill and confined to a hospital bed, Ord died in a freak airplane accident.

Ord's death left a tremendous void in Eisenhower's life. Eisenhower later described Ord as "the most brilliant officer, of his time, in the American Army" and said he "felt as close to him as even to my own brothers." Eisenhower personally arranged for Ord's funeral with full military orders.

Without Ord, the zest in Eisenhower's life disappeared. Though Lt. Col. Richard K. Sutherland took Ord's place in the office, Eisenhower confessed that as a companion and comrade, no one could fill the void left by Ord's death. Had Ord survived, there is little doubt he would have occupied a special place in Eisenhower's World War II command.

George S. Patton Jr.

During his second tour of duty at Camp Meade, Maryland, in 1919, Eisenhower met Patton, who became a lifelong friend. From the beginning,

Eisenhower knew Patton was special. Indeed, he dedicated a chapter of his reminiscences to "Colonel George Patton."

Patton and Eisenhower were part of a group of young officers who believed tanks were ill-served as infantry support weapons. Fresh from the battlefields of Europe, Patton remained convinced that tanks could break into the enemy's defensive positions and then exploit their success. Over the next one and a half years, the duo expanded their theories and began writing articles, Eisenhower for the infantry, Patton for the cavalry. Their respective branch chiefs thought such theories were dangerous and inconsistent with army doctrine. One effect of their rebukes was to bring Eisenhower and Patton even closer.

Before they parted company in 1920, Patton introduced his friend to then–Brig. Gen. Fox Conner, who was the mentor Eisenhower later described as "the one more or less invisible figure to whom I owe an incalculable debt." It was Conner who secured Eisenhower the opportunity to attend the Command and General Staff School at Fort Leavenworth in 1925.

Patton, who had graduated a year earlier, provided his class notes to Eisenhower. And Patton was one of the first officers to congratulate Eisenhower when Eisenhower finished number one in his class. Patton was convinced his notes were the prerequisite for his friend's success. Immediately after Eisenhower graduated, he received a congratulatory telegram from Patton stating, "It shows that Leavenworth is a good school if a HE man can come out one."

After Eisenhower graduated from Fort Leavenworth in 1926, Eisenhower's and Patton's paths diverged. Six years later, however, they were back in Washington, Eisenhower as an assistant military adviser to Army Chief of Staff MacArthur, Patton as the regimental executive officer of the Third Cavalry. Both officers witnessed the Bonus Army of 1932, when some fifteen thousand unemployed World War I veterans marched on Washington to demand millions of dollars in bonuses the government had promised them. The army evicted the veterans; one was killed, and several were wounded. The affair brought great discredit to the army.

It was not until the eve of World War II that Eisenhower and Patton renewed their association beyond casual correspondence. Each played significant roles in the War Department's General Headquarters Maneuvers of September 1941. As chief of staff of brevet Lt. Gen. Walter Krueger's Third Army, Eisenhower helped devise the winning strategy for Third Army's victory against brevet-Lt. Gen. Ben Lear's Second Army. Patton's Second Armored Division was the featured attraction, and Patton demonstrated his emphasis on audacity, mobility, and firepower.

The maneuvers not only tested doctrine and tactics but also, to Marshall's expectations, identified the service's most promising leaders. Both Eisenhower and Patton emerged as shining stars. Two months after Eisenhower received his first star, Japan attacked Pearl Harbor. One week later, Marshall summoned Eisenhower to Washington to serve on Gerow's staff. The following month, Patton assumed command of First Armored Corps. The rest, they say, is history.

Eisenhower emerged from World War II in glory. At the conclusion of the European war, he received an invitation to speak at London's Guildhall on June 12, 1945. In perhaps the most poignant section of his address, Eisenhower stated, "Humility must always be the portion of any man who receives acclaim earned in blood of his followers and sacrifices of his friends."

Though Eisenhower was referring to the Allied Expeditionary Force, he was also paying tribute and acknowledging his personal gratitude to three dear friends: Gerow, Ord, and Patton.

"They Liked Ike" was originally published in *ARMY Magazine* (December 2019).

26

Embracing the Media

Eisenhower Worked With, Not Against, the Press

In the highly charged environment in which the US Army frequently finds itself, friction between senior officers and reporters can foster resentment over the age-old controversy concerning the public's right to know and the need for military secrecy. No commander addressed this question more adroitly than Gen. Dwight Eisenhower during World War II.

After a quarter-century in which he served principally as a staff officer, Eisenhower burst onto the national scene during the War Department's General Headquarters (GHQ) Maneuvers of 1941. These peacetime war games introduced a number of military officers to the public, but then–colonel Eisenhower was the most noteworthy. As chief of staff of Lt. Gen. Walter Krueger's Third US Army, Eisenhower later wrote, "My tent turned into something of a cracker-barrel corner where everyone in our army seemed to come for a serious discussion, a laugh, or a gripe."

Among the visitors were senior members of the press who Eisenhower cultivated with his engaging personality. In his widely syndicated newspaper column, Drew Pearson paid the unheralded staff officer the ultimate compliment, writing that Eisenhower "conceived and directed the strategy that routed the Second Army," which acted as Third Army's adversary during the war games. Krueger's chief of staff "has a steel-trap mind plus unusual physical vigor."

Shortly thereafter, Eisenhower embarked on a meteoric trajectory that propelled him to Supreme Allied Commander, Allied Expeditionary Force, in December 1943. Following the maneuvers, Army Chief of Staff Gen. George Marshall promoted Eisenhower to general officer and subsequently assigned him to command the North Africa Theater.

Burgeoning Public Relations

Until World War II, senior army officials paid scant attention to the role of public relations. Marshall remedied this oversight by creating the Bureau of Public Relations within the War Department. Its purpose was to explain the army's mission, purposes, means, and needs. As Marshall's protege, Eisenhower was keenly aware of the necessity of informing the American public of the army's requirements.

Later, Eisenhower stated that cynics described public relations as a "maternity gown designed to hide the true figure of fact. Undoubtedly, as abused by those who cover up or mislead, public relations can be stigmatized as mere propaganda or outright mendacity. Properly practiced, however, some form of it is necessary in a republic where the citizens must know the truth."

Despite being well-versed in public relations, Eisenhower initially struggled over the most effective manner to balance military secrecy with his civic duty to keep the American public informed concerning their soldiers at war. A case in point: When reporters informed Eisenhower that Lt. George Patton Jr. had slapped two enlisted soldiers in hospitals in Sicily, Eisenhower did not immediately grasp the full implications of Patton's acts because, Eisenhower said, "Patton is indispensable to the war effort—one of the guarantors of our victory."

Eisenhower initially sought to kill the story by informing reporters that he had personally delivered a strong reprimand to Patton and ordered Patton to apologize to the soldiers. However, by mid-November 1943, Pearson "sensationalized" the story on his weekly syndicated radio program, according to military historian Carlo D'Este in his book *Patton: A Genius for War*.

Only Eisenhower's steadfast support of Patton kept the Seventh US Army commander in theater and saved him for the upcoming campaign in northwest Europe. But Eisenhower had learned a hard lesson about cultivating relationships with reporters.

Reporters were scrupulously careful—when they understood—not to compromise security. When secrecy had to be tightly observed, more than once, Eisenhower later stated, "I found that I could take correspondents into my confidence, telling them the full story of what was planned, and asking them to say or write nothing until the need for secrecy had ended."

Of greater concern for Eisenhower was the period during which combat operations were halted and correspondents tended to speculate on future operations. Knowing that the enemy read those reports and columns, many of which proved accurate, Eisenhower's novel solution was drastic. A week before Operation Husky—the invasion of Sicily in July 1943—he held a news conference and revealed the broad outline of the campaign.

Why did Eisenhower opt for full disclosure? Though he later wrote that this experiment in public relations was not one that he cared to repeat, Eisenhower placed on every reporter in the theater a feeling of the same responsibility that he and his associates bore.

From that moment onward, until after the attack was launched, nothing speculative came out of the theater, and no representative of the press attempted to send out anything that could possibly be valuable to the enemy. After Husky was completed, many correspondents informed Eisenhower of the fear they felt that they might be guilty of even inadvertent relation of the secret.

Eisenhower did not replicate that decision with respect to Operation Overlord, the invasion of northwest Europe, due to the necessity of maintaining total secrecy concerning the timing and location of D-Day. But three months later, Brig. Gen. Everett Hughes, an old friend, visited Eisenhower. Hughes described a gathering of friends who joined him in tackling Eisenhower "about the growing public relations problem—the need to play up the American side of the battle in France," professor and Eisenhower grandson David Eisenhower wrote in *Eisenhower at War 1943 to 1945*. Dwight Eisenhower explained to Hughes that American leadership had to be "low key" if things were to work after the war in Europe.

Eisenhower possessed strong beliefs about press censorship in wartime. In his view, military security was the only rationale for press censorship. Reporters should be encouraged, rather than discouraged, to mention numerical designation of military units and the name of their commander, such as Patton's Third Army, when those units and commanders had previously been identified by the enemy.

It must be remembered, Eisenhower noted, "that censorship denies to the fighting soldier the immediate opportunity to see that his services and exploits are recognized and appreciated. The soldier likes to read about his unit and about his local commander. . . . The freest possible flow of news is not only in keeping with our traditions, but also the best way to keep the public accurately informed and working in support of the war effort. The saving of lives and military success are normally the only sound reasons for interference."

Real News

Not surprisingly, Eisenhower held firm beliefs that every soldier in the war had the right to hope that all people may have the advantages of a free press and the free exchange of information throughout the world. In reviving the military supported newspaper *Stars and Stripes*, Eisenhower hoped to create a facility that would be beneficial to the war effort. Its specific objective was to make factual news readily available to American fighting men in the European Theater.

When rumors reached Eisenhower to the effect that the staff of *Stars and Stripes* felt they had been subjected to unwarranted pressure by officers who apparently sought to dictate the newspaper's policy, Eisenhower intervened. In a letter to Brig. Gen. Oscar Nathaniel Solbert, chief of Special and Information Services in the European Theater, Eisenhower reminded Solbert, "I want to make it clear that no officer or official in the Theater is authorized to issue instructions to the paper, except through you, and then only if acting for me in any official capacity."

Eisenhower added a cautionary note to the editor of the publication, writing, "The paper must not, under any circumstances, become a propaganda sheet for exposition of any person's particular views and convictions, including mine and those of the editorial staff. . . . The only censorship and restrictions applicable to the paper are those that are imposed upon all other publications for reasons of security." In Eisenhower's opinion, *Stars and Stripes* should be a free, decent newspaper, run by soldiers, for soldiers.

Valued Partner

As Supreme Commander, Eisenhower avoided any hint of self-promotion and insisted on complete credit to his subordinate commanders and staff. In a letter to his brother Edgar, Eisenhower explained his rationale: "To the extent possible in a position such as mine, I have constantly shunned the headlines. This has not been entirely due to a sense of modesty, but because of the nature of an Allied Command. Any 'glory grabbing' on the part of the top man would quickly wreck an institution such as this. Happily, the official requirement has coincided exactly with my personal desire."

Throughout his war years and his presidency, Eisenhower viewed the press not as the enemy of the people but as a valuable partner in maintaining a vibrant democracy. Eisenhower treated reporters with the same dignity that he treated his soldiers. Consequently, his relations with the press remained frank and cordial. And the traffic information was two-way: in Eisenhower's mind, the press reflected far better than a military staff could the reactions of civilians at home and even of troops in combat.

Herein lies the lesson for today's army leaders.

"Embracing the Media: Eisenhower Worked with, Not Against, the Press" was originally published in *ARMY Magazine* (February 2021).

27

As Eisenhower Viewed Them

As the European war approached its dramatic conclusion, Gen. Dwight D. Eisenhower, Supreme Commander Allied Expeditionary Force, prepared a list of thirty-eight outstanding general officers, arranged roughly according to the value of the services the officers had rendered during the war. Eisenhower's list was a result of his meeting in Marseilles in late January 1945 with Army Chief of Staff Gen. George C. Marshall. At that meeting, Marshall expressed his embarrassment that the US Navy had nominated a number of flag grade officers to four-star rank while the army had far fewer general officers at the four-star level.

In addition to performance, Eisenhower considered the officers' qualifications for future usefulness. Some officers occupied two levels of command, such as Lt. Gen. Mark W. Clark, who served as US Fifth Army commander before being elevated to command Fifteenth Army Group in Italy. Position and opportunity inescapably played a certain part in determining his priorities, noted Eisenhower, but where a corps commander had performed *magnificently* as opposed to an army commander's good performance—then the former was rated higher.

Eisenhower's list reflected a composite view of his personal conclusions as well as those of Lt. Gen. Walter Bedell Smith, his chief of staff, and Lt. Gen. Omar N. Bradley, Twelfth Army Group commander. Bradley compiled his order of merit list at Eisenhower's request in December 1944, about two weeks before the Battle of the Bulge. In a subsequent cable to Marshall, Eisenhower said he did not know whether such an assessment would have any value to the army chief of staff, but he would be glad to provide Marshall a copy.

Eisenhower ranked Bradley first; his outstanding characteristics included "quiet but magnetic leader; able, rounded field commander; determined and resourceful; modest." Since the campaign in Sicily, Bradley had emerged as Eisenhower's most trusted adviser and commander. With Gen. George S. Patton Jr. in temporary exile following the slapping incidents, Eisenhower had selected Bradley as the senior American commander for the upcoming invasion of Western Europe. In Eisenhower's opinion, Bradley remained the officer whose tactical and strategic judgment he considered "almost unimpeachable."

Of the army-level commanders, Eisenhower passed over longtime friend Clark as well as Lt. Gen. Alexander M. "Sandy" Patch (Seventh Army), Lt. Gen. Courtney H. Hodges (First Army), and Lt. Gen. William H. Simpson (Ninth Army), selecting Patton (Third Army) as the outstanding army commander of the war. Eisenhower labeled Patton a "dashing fighter, shrewd and courageous." Long before he assumed command of the Allied Expeditionary Force, Eisenhower urgently requested Patton as one of his army commanders for Operation Overlord. In April 1945, Eisenhower nominated Patton to four-star rank before any other army-level commander.

Eisenhower and Patton had been friends since 1919, when they served at Camp Meade, Maryland. When Eisenhower recommended Patton for promotion to permanent major general, he cited Patton's combat performance to date. Patton's "job of rehabilitating the Second Corps in Tunisia was quickly and magnificently done." His "leadership of the Seventh Army [in Sicily] was close to the best of our classic examples." Still, Eisenhower noted that Patton would never be advanced beyond army-level command and would be most useful in an exclusively American theater rather than in an Allied one.

Bradley, who served under Patton's command in Sicily and later became his boss in northwest Europe, disagreed with Eisenhower's assessment. In Bradley's estimation, Patton ranked third behind Hodges and Lt. Gen. Lucian King Truscott as army-level commanders. Had it been left up to Bradley, he would not have included Patton in the campaign in northwest Europe.

Martin Blumenson, Patton's premier biographer, opines that Bradley was jealous of his Third Army commander. In his posthumously published autobiography, *A General's Life*, Bradley directed his venom against Patton. Bradley posits that only Patton's untimely death prevented him from becoming "a boring parody of himself—a decrepit, bitter, pitiful figure, unwittingly debasing the legend." Of course, Bradley never expressed this opinion when Patton spearheaded the breakout from Normandy, or when Patton's northward advance raised the Siege of Bastogne in December 1944.

Second to Patton as an army commander, Eisenhower placed Truscott, whom he deemed an "experienced, balanced fighter; energetic; inspires confidence." Truscott had impressed Eisenhower as commander of the Third Infantry Division in Sicily. As with Patton, Eisenhower requested Truscott's service on D-Day, but Marshall refused to leave the Mediterranean Theater devoid of all the top field commanders. In February 1944, Truscott assumed command of VI Corps following the debacle at Anzio. Later, Truscott's VI Corps participated in the landings in Southern France as part of Operation Anvil on August 15, 1944. Truscott was promoted to lieutenant general in September 1944, succeeding Clark as commanding general of Fifth Army in Italy.

Patch, another one of the war's dual-theater commanders, assumed command of the Seventh US Army in March 1944 and landed in Southern France in August 1944 as part of Operation Anvil (known later as Operation Dragoon). In Eisenhower's estimation, Patch had demonstrated he was a "cool fighter, balanced, energetic." Overshadowed by Patton, whom he succeeded as Seventh Army commander, Patch may well have been the most underrated army-level commander of World War II. Comparing Patton to other field army commanders in March 1945, Eisenhower wrote that "it would be difficult indeed to choose between him, Hodges and Simpson for army command, while Patch is little, if any, behind the others." Prior to stepping down as army chief of staff, Marshall compiled a list for promotion to the permanent grade of brigadier general. He rated Patch first.

Surprisingly, Eisenhower placed Gen. Leonard T. Gerow ahead of Gen. J. Lawton Collins as the finest corps-level commander in the European Theater. Gerow's elevated status reflected Eisenhower's personal preferences and prejudices. Eisenhower and Gerow had been friends since Eisenhower's first assignment at Fort Sam Houston, Texas, in 1915. They were later classmates at Fort Leavenworth, Kansas, in 1925, with Eisenhower edging Gerow, who commanded V Corps at Omaha Beach on D-Day, was a "good fighter, balanced, calm, excellent planner, always optimistic, selfless, a leader." Eisenhower promoted Gerow to command US Fifteenth Army in January 1945.

In contrast to his boss, Bradley selected Collins, another one of the war's dual-theater commanders, as the premier corps commander in theater. Eisenhower, too, was impressed with Collins's performance, stating that the VII Corps commander was a "particularly fine commanding general in battle."

Eisenhower also cited Maj. Gen. Matthew B. Ridgway as one of his top three corps-level commanders. Ridgway commanded the Eighty-Second Airborne Division in Normandy and assumed command of the XVIII Airborne Corps in August 1944. Two months before V-E Day, Eisenhower labeled Ridgway "one of the finest soldiers this war has produced."

Not limiting himself with frontline commanders, Eisenhower placed his own chief of staff, Smith, as the top staff officer in theater even though Smith had been serving as Marshall's secretary of the general staff. Throughout the campaign in northwest Europe, Smith superbly fulfilled the role of Eisenhower's "hatchet man," allowing Eisenhower to concentrate on more critical matters. Indispensable to the Supreme Commander, Smith earned accolades as "outstanding as Chief of Staff of Superior Headquarters. Firm, loyal, highly intelligent."

Other staff officers who merited Eisenhower's praise included Maj. Gen. Harold Roe "Pinky" Bull, assistant chief of staff at Supreme Headquarters Allied Expeditionary Force, and Maj. Gen. Alfred M. Gruenther, Clark's chief of staff in Italy. Eisenhower listed Bull's outstanding qualifications as "good judgement, careful, energetic," but as much as he appreciated Bull's operational acumen, Eisenhower admired Gruenther more. Eisenhower listed Gruenther's chief characteristics as "brainy, energetic and loyal." Gruenther would go on to succeed Eisenhower as the Supreme Commander of NATO and was Eisenhower's first recommendation to succeed him as the Republican Party nominee for president of the United States.

Topping the list of air commanders was Lt. Gen. Carl A. "Tooey" Spaatz, whom Eisenhower described as "experienced and able . . . loyal and cooperative; modest and selfless." Spaatz commanded the US Strategic Air Force in Europe. Eisenhower rated his senior airman on par with Bradley in his communique to Marshall. Additional Army Air Force commanders who ranked high on Eisenhower's order of merit were Lt. Gen. Jimmy Doolittle ("dashing, learns rapidly, enthusiastic") and Lt. Gen. Ira C. Eaker, who served in the Mediterranean ("cooperative, firm, experienced").

In Eisenhower's opinion, Lt. Gen. Clarence R. Huebner of the First Infantry Division was the finest division commander in theater. Huebner assumed command of the Big Red One in the wake of Maj. Gen. Terry de la Mesa Allen's relief following the campaign in Sicily. Huebner commanded the division with distinction at Omaha Beach and remained in command until January 1945, when he succeeded Gerow as commander of V Corps.

Rounding out Eisenhower's top three division commanders were Maj. Gens. Ernest N. Harmon and James A. Van Fleet. Harmon had compiled an enviable record with the Second Armored Division and later, the First Armored Division in the Mediterranean Theater of Operations. After the war, Harmon led the US Constabulary in Europe and then became deputy commander of Army Ground Forces from 1947 until his retirement the following year. Eisenhower described Huebner, Harmon, and Van Fleet as "outstanding divisional leaders; experienced fighters."

The only general officer for whom Eisenhower had harsh words was Lt. Gen. Jacob L. Devers, commander of Sixth Army Group. Eisenhower and Devers never liked each other; Eisenhower, Bradley, and Smith did not consider Devers part of their inner circle. Eisenhower ranked Devers No. twenty-four of thirty-eight officers, adding that Devers "had not produced among the seniors of the American organization that feeling of trust and confidence that is so necessary to continued success."

What Marshall did with Eisenhower's list is unknown, but Eisenhower repeatedly used his order of merit to recommend promotions and postwar assignments. By the war's end, Eisenhower suggested the army chief visit the European Theater to see the army he had produced. In addition to the "veteran' quality of the whole organization," Eisenhower said, Marshall "would be amazed at the high average of ability in the [Supreme

Headquarters Allied Expeditionary Force]'s higher command team. These Army Group, Army, Corps, and Division commanders comprised a team that could scarcely be improved upon."

"As Eisenhower Viewed Them" was originally published in *ARMY Magazine* (August 2015).

28

The Extraordinary Feats of Three "Ordinary" Soldiers

In his notes on combat experience during the Tunisian and African campaigns, Maj. Gen. E. N. Harmon observed that men will follow a good leader practically anywhere and under any conditions of battle. Therefore, placing the right men in positions of leadership is the most important safeguard for success in battle that a commander can have.

Addressing the veterans on the fiftieth anniversary of D-Day, President Bill Clinton spoke not of Eisenhower, Bradley, Patton or Ridgway, but of men like Len Lomell, Joe Dawson, Lyle Bouck Jr., and the countless, often nameless, thousands who fought to preserve democracy a half-century ago. Citing an essay by William Brown, the president acknowledged that in their youth, these men and their peers saved the world. No other generation can make that claim.

Today, the veterans of World War II are but footnotes in the history of this century's greatest struggle; in a larger sense, however, they represent perhaps the most remarkable generation of fighting men and women this country has ever produced. Before their memory fades from our consciousness, it is fitting to reflect on their achievements. The stories of three soldiers help us remember the patriotism, heroism and sacrifices of the many who answered freedom's call.

On June 6, 1944, First Sgt. Len Lomell was the acting platoon leader of Company D, Second Ranger Battalion. According to Omar Bradley, the Rangers' mission was the most dangerous and difficult task of D-Day—to land under fire at the face of the one-hundred-foot cliffs of Pointe du Hoc, scale the heights, and destroy a battery of 155-millimeter (mm) coastal guns to prevent the enemy from shelling the invasion beaches and ships at sea.

Born in Brooklyn, New York, in 1920, Lomell entered military service on June 13, 1942, at Fort Dix, New Jersey. Seeking additional adventure, he was one of the first volunteers to join the Rangers since their activation on April 1, 1943. Fourteen months later, Lomell was one of nearly two hundred men from D, E, and F Companies who landed on the ten-meter-wide beach at the base of Pointe du Hoc. No sooner had he landed than Lomell sustained his first wound, a bullet through his right side.

Ignoring the pain and grave risk, Lomell quickly led his platoon up the cliff and systematically began destroying German machine-gun nests through fire and maneuver. He continued his courageous assault through two enemy lines of resistance to the rear of the German position. To the Rangers' surprise, the 155-mm battery was nowhere to be seen. The only "guns" that occupied the casemates were telephone poles. Tracks leading inward indicated that the battery had displaced somewhere toward the interior.

Reaching the coastal road, Lomell and his fellow Rangers immediately established roadblocks and began patrolling. Having scaled a hundred-foot cliff and fought across two hundred meters of heavily defended ground, Lomell's company was reduced to only twenty-two men from the initial contingent of seventy Rangers. Leaving the survivors of his platoon along the road, Lomell took SSgt. Jack E. Kuhn, acting platoon sergeant, to search for the missing battery.

About 250 meters inland, Lomell and Kuhn discovered the guns hidden in an apple orchard. They were set up in battery firing position with ammunition at the ready. To Lomell's amazement, the closest Germans, approximately seventy-five men, were one hundred yards away, having withdrawn because of the initial bombardment. It appeared to Lomell and Kuhn that the Germans were checking equipment and preparing to return to the firing position.

Realizing that thousands of American lives were at stake if the battery remained intact, Lomell sensed a fleeting opportunity. Directing Kuhn to cover him and armed with two thermite grenades, Lomell destroyed the traversing and recoil mechanisms of the two nearest guns. He then bashed the sights of the third gun with the stock of his rifle. Not satisfied with this partial success, Lomell sprinted back to the highway. Collecting all the thermite grenades from his platoon, he returned and disabled the remaining guns. Within ninety minutes of landing, Lomell and his Rangers had accomplished their mission.

For its remarkable achievement on D-Day, the Second Ranger Battalion received the Presidential Unit Citation. In addition, First Sgt. Lomell earned the Distinguished Service Cross (DSC) for his extraordinary heroism. Len Lomell went on to become battalion sergeant major and on October 7, 1944, became the first Second Ranger Battalion ranger to receive a battlefield commission. Wounded three times, he was honorably discharged from the army on the last day of 1945.

Ten kilometers east of Pointe du Hoc, a similar drama was being played out on Omaha Beach. By the time Company G, Sixteenth Infantry Regiment, First Infantry Division reached shore, the initial assault waves of the fabled Big Red One had succumbed to the withering fire of German machine guns and indirect fire. Company G was under the command of Capt. Joe Dawson, the gangly thirty-one-year-old son of a Baptist preacher from Waco, Texas.

Landing under heavy fire, Dawson found total chaos as men and material were literally choking the seawall at the water's edge. He knew that unless he could galvanize his men into action, they would be cut to shreds on the beach. Dawson moved rapidly to the front. Blowing a gap in the concertina wire at the foot of the bluffs, he began the dangerous ascent. Midway up the slope he met Lt. John Spaulding with the remnants of his own platoon. Directing Spaulding to cover his advance, Dawson proceeded toward the summit.

Nearing the crest, he tossed two grenades and eliminated a German machine-gun position that was creating havoc on the beach below. Without waiting for reinforcements at the top of the bluff, Dawson and his men pressed on until they had silenced the remaining German positions. No one had penetrated the enemy defenses until this moment.

Dawson attributed his success on D-Day to poor German marksmanship and the fortunate ability to control his command both in landing together and in maneuvering up the bluff together as a fighting unit. Once his men reached the summit, they were able to engage the enemy directly with small-arms fire, which forced the Germans to cease the concentrated small-arms, machine-gun, and mortar fire with which they were sweeping the beach below. Gen. Eisenhower presented Dawson with the Distinguished Service Cross for his dynamic leadership at Omaha Beach.

What Company G accomplished on D-Day, however, was merely one episode in a long war, according to Dawson who reflected on his career fifty years later. The worst combat he encountered during the war occurred outside Aachen in October 1944. Aachen was the first German city to be captured by the Allies and the former capital of Charlemagne's empire. As such, it held a special significance for Adolf Hitler that transcended its strictly military value.

In early September, Courtney Hodge's First US Army had penetrated the Siegfried Line, encircled Aachen and prepared to meet the expected German counterattacks. The brunt of numerous counterattacks was borne by Company G, reinforced and still under the command of Joe Dawson. Moving into position, Dawson established his defense east of Aachen along an 838-foot-high ridge running approximately four hundred yards.

Two days later, on September 16, the Germans attacked in battalion strength. The intensity of the attack carried the enemy into the American defense, but the GIs held. Following two weeks of intense artillery bombardment, the Germans attacked again on October 4. The result was the same—more than 350 enemy casualties littered the battlefield, "a figure unprecedented in the division's history" according to the First Division's operations officer.

For thirty-nine days and nights, Dawson's men held the ridge. At times the front lines were no farther than fifty feet apart. More than once, Dawson called in protective artillery fire within ten yards of his own command post. Often the combat was hand to hand, and at times it seemed that the American defenders could not hold another minute. On October 15, a final regimental attack collapsed in the face of Dawson's artillery and infantry fire.

How did they hold in the face of overwhelming enemy numbers? The answer lies in Dawson's own words: courage and determination. Speaking to war correspondent Gordon Fraser after five weeks in the line, the beleaguered commander reflected on the loneliness of leaders who must make the crucial decisions in war. "How do you think I feel when I tell them there is no coming off the hill? They come in and say . . . 'I can't stand it any longer. I can't. I can't'. . . and I take them by the shirt and say . . . 'you will . . . you will . . . you've got to stand it in spite of yourself,' and what do they do? They go back up there and die." For thirty-nine days in the fall of 1944, the men of Company G fought and died in their foxholes along what entered First Infantry Division lore as "Dawson's Ridge."

But by battle's end, Aachen remained secure. For its role in the defense of the first German city to be captured, Dawson's Company G, like Lomell's Rangers, earned the Presidential Unit Citation. Gen. Eisenhower also nominated the Big Red One to receive the Distinguished Unit Citation, stating that the fighting around Aachen was the outstanding operation of the First Infantry Division in the European Theater. All that stood against German success was what Dawson termed "just one lousy little old G.I. company"—one lousy company and the indomitable spirit of its commander.

Two months after Dawson's heroic stand, the intelligence and reconnaissance platoon of the Ninety-Ninth Infantry Division's 394th Infantry Regiment moved into a quiet sector of the Ardennes front. The platoon leader was First Lt. Lyle J. Bouck Jr., an experienced officer one day shy of his twenty-first birthday. Bouck had enlisted in the Thirty-Fifth Infantry Division (National Guard) in 1938 at the age of fourteen to earn one dollar a day per drill each week and to attend summer camp so he could eat three square meals a day. After graduating from Officer Candidate School in 1941, he volunteered for combat duty in 1944.

What made the intelligence and reconnaissance platoon unique was that Bouck and Maj. Robert Kriz, the regimental S-2, had selected every member of the platoon. Kriz and Bouck wanted men who were intelligent, expert riflemen, and comfortable with the outdoor life. At twenty, Bouck was the second youngest member of the platoon.

On December 10, Kriz briefed Bouck on a new mission. His orders were to occupy a prepared defensive position being evacuated by a unit from the Fourth Infantry Division. Bouck was to improve the position, and act as the eyes and ears of the regiment on the adjacent divisional and corps boundary. In addition, Bouck was to maintain contact with a tank destroyer unit located in the small village of Lanzerath barely one hundred meters to their front. Bouck's position afforded his platoon a perfect observation post from which to look into German territory.

It seemed to many that the war would soon be over. As American GIs dreamed of returning home, the Germans were planning a massive counterattack to regain the initiative in the west. Unknown to Bouck, Lanzerath lay astride Gen. Sepp Dietrich's Sixth Panzer Army's counterattack axis.

Under Bouck's supervision, the platoon hastily improved its position. At the urging of Kriz and with help from a friend at ordnance, Bouck also assembled an array of weapons that included four carbines, one Browning automatic rifle, one light machine gun and a .50 caliber machine gun mounted on a jeep in a dug-in position. The platoon's firepower sounded like a "battalion in the attack demonstration at Fort Benning," noted Bouck a half century later. Heavy snow fell on December 13 and 15, camouflaging the platoon's extensive defensive network.

On December 16, Hitler unleashed the Ardennes Offensive. A tremendous artillery barrage fell on Bouck's forward positions, but the intelligence and reconnaissance platoon suffered no casualties. As the tank destroyer unit evacuated Lanzerath, Bouck and a small reconnaissance team edged forward into a better observation position. What they saw startled them. A German column was assembling for an attack, but the enemy seemed oblivious to the precise location of Bouck's men.

Shortly after dawn, the German infantry approached, having been alerted to Bouck's position by one of the town's inhabitants. Fortunately for the Americans, the German Third Parachute Division's Ninth Regiment was inexperienced and conducted its assault without supporting fires. Bouck's pleas for artillery support also went unheeded, but within minutes the snow in front of the platoon had turned red with the blood of German dead and dying. Miraculously, not a single American was killed, although several sustained minor wounds.

Reporting the action to regiment, Bouck received the following orders: "Hold at all costs." And hold they did—against two more determined enemy attacks. By midafternoon, however, Bouck's men were running low on ammunition, and fatigue was setting in. Despite repeated calls for reinforcements, no relief arrived. Bouck estimated that more than four hundred enemy lay in the snow before him. The ground was so thick with enemy dead that it was virtually impossible to see the snow beneath them. Still Bouck refused to withdraw, acting on his last orders.

As darkness fell, another German attack supported by two assault guns edged forward. This time the enemy was more successful. Infiltrating the American position, the enemy eliminated foxhole after foxhole. Finally, wounded and with his ammunition exhausted, Bouck and the remainder of the platoon were captured. Taken to Lanzerath as darkness descended, Bouck whimsically noted that it was his twenty-first birthday.

How had a single platoon of American soldiers been able to withstand such vigorous assaults by German paratroopers? Bouck credited his selection of terrain, the high quality of the men in his platoon, the corresponding inexperience of his German adversaries, and the platoon's constant and intense training on the fundamentals of combat. He might have added his own inspirational leadership.

Of the eighteen members of the platoon, two were killed in action, and the remainder wounded or captured. Somewhat belatedly, the platoon received a Presidential Unit Citation, and Bouck, like Lomell and Dawson, won the Distinguished Service Cross. In addition to the cross awarded to Bouck, the platoon earned three Distinguished Service Crosses, five Silver Stars, and ten Bronze Stars with V devices, thus becoming the most heavily decorated platoon for a single action in World War II. The soldiers had earned the distinction. Bouck and his platoon had inflicted nearly five hundred casualties on the enemy and, more important, had delayed German attack for a full day.

In Retrospect

How did the American Army succeed against the Germans? The answer lies, in large measure, in the leadership of junior officers and NCOs. Without them and countless others, there surely would have been none of the great victories that we typically attribute to our most revered general officers. We still applaud their efforts and marvel at their achievements. Collectively, they answered their country's call not for personal glory, but because there was a war to be won and no one but them to win it.

The challenges the army's small unit leaders faced in World War II were daunting. It was not easy ordering men to scale Pointe du hoc, fight from a foxhole for thirty-nine days on Dawson's ridge or face overwhelming odds in the snow around Lanzerath. What distinguished Lomell, Dawson, and Bouck? Why were they so successful?

Again, we turn to the first man to reach the summit of the bluffs overlooking Omaha Beach for the answer. When his men looked to him for leadership, Dawson said he "had to answer those guys because I wear the bars. I've got the responsibility." Although Dawson later recalled that he was unsure whether he had what it took to do the job, he, Lomell, and Bouck fulfilled their responsibilities to their country and their soldiers in a most distinguished manner. For this, we take time to cherish the memory of their actions.

"The Extraordinary Feats of Three 'Ordinary' Soldiers" was originally published in *Army Magazine* (January 1996).

29

Restoring the Fighting Spirit

In his memoirs of the Korean War, Gen. Matthew B. Ridgway noted that every soldier learns in time that war is a lonely business. All a commander's study, all his training, all his drill anticipates the moment when abruptly the responsibility rests solely on him to decide whether to stand or pull back, or to order an attack that will expose thousands of men to sudden death.

No officer encountered a greater challenge than Gen. Ridgway when he assumed command of Eighth Army in Korea in December 1950. After Chinese intervention, the Eighth Army suffered a catastrophic defeat, and pessimism permeated the ranks. What was needed before the army could return to the offensive, said Gen. Ridgway, was the restoration of fighting spirit. Eighth Army required pride in itself, confidence in its leadership and faith in its mission.

Three commanders in World War II faced similar challenges. Lt. Gen. Robert L. Eichelberger, Maj. Gen. E. N. Harmon, and Lt. Gen. Lucian K. Truscott Jr. each received an urgent summons from the theater commander to restore a defeated army's fighting spirit. Each succeeded in reversing his army's fortunes.

Robert L. Eichelberger did not fit the popular image of a combat commander. A classmate of George S. Patton Jr. at West Point, Gen. Eichelberger served on the Mexican border in 1916 and later earned the Distinguished Service Medal and the Distinguished Service Cross for duty as the operations and intelligence officer for the American Expeditionary

Force in Siberia. He then served as secretary, War Department general staff, for both Douglas MacArthur and Malin Craig before receiving an appointment as superintendent of the US Military Academy in 1940.

Fifty-five years old when Japan attacked Pearl Harbor, Gen. Eichelberger requested combat duty and received command of the Seventy-Seventh Division, a National Guard unit from New England and the metropolitan New York area. His superlative performance caught the attention of Gen. George C. Marshall, the Army Chief of Staff. Gen. Eichelberger assumed command of I Corps, a stateside training unit, in June 1942. Shortly thereafter, he and his staff received orders to report to General MacArthur, then serving as commanding Gen. of the Southwest Pacific Area.

By midsummer 1942, Japanese ground forces were once again on the march in the Southwest Pacific. On July 21, they landed a large task force on the Papuan Peninsula at the lower end of the island of New Guinea. Seeking to anchor their southern boundary, the Japanese resolved to take Port Moresby, the capital of Papua.

Gen. MacArthur quickly decided to defend Australia by seizing the initiative in New Guinea. On October 1, General Headquarters issued the first comprehensive plan to destroy the Japanese Buna-Gona beachhead on the northern Papuan coast. Unfortunately, the combined American–Australian offensive was poorly planned and even more poorly executed. By November, a tenacious Japanese defense had halted the Allied offensive in its tracks.

Summoning Gen. Eichelberger to his headquarters at Port Moresby on November 30, Gen. MacArthur ordered him to go to New Guinea and seize Buna. There was no mistaking the seriousness that Gen. MacArthur attached to the mission. "Bob," he informed Gen. Eichelberger, "I'm putting you in command at Buna . . . remove all officers who won't fight . . . put sergeants in charge of battalions and corporals in charge of companies—anyone who will fight. Time is of the essence." He then added, "I want you to take Buna, or not come back alive. And that goes for your chief of staff too." Within hours, Gen. Eichelberger joined the Thirty-Second Division at Buna.

What he found at Buna would have disheartened a weaker commander. The Thirty-Second Division was tired, riddled with malaria and demoralized. There was little evidence of discipline. In one company, every soldier was running a fever. To evacuate all the troops would have invited disaster. Gen. Eichelberger decided to fight.

A thorough reconnaissance of the front lines by vehicle and by foot convinced him that many of the commanders had not been to the forward positions. Nor were commanders familiar with Japanese dispositions as there had been no night patrolling. Inspired leadership based on a genuine concern for the welfare of the soldiers was lacking.

Gen. Eichelberger made an immediate inspection at the front lines. Though the two wings of his force were only three miles apart, it took seven hours to walk from one flank to the other. Stopping all fighting, the general took two days to unscramble the units and establish an orderly chain of command. His message was clear: although jungle fighting is generally done at the small unit level, soldiers do best when they understand where they are going and why.

After assessing the tactical situation, Gen. Eichelberger began his transformation of the Thirty-Second Division. His first priority was to improve morale. Two imperatives were necessary: reorganization of the troops and immediate improvement of supply. For the first time in weeks, troops received hot meals. To Gen. Eichelberger, hot food and full stomachs were elemental as morale builders and well worth the hazard of a sniper's bullet.

Next, he ensured that leaders were in positions of leadership. Replacing many commanders, including the division commander, with members of his staff, Gen. Eichelberger selected officers who were aggressive and eager to engage the enemy.

With morale on the upswing and failed tactical leaders replaced, Gen. Eichelberger focused the division on the enemy. On December 5, he ordered a general offensive. By nightfall the advance was negligible, but the following day, the Americans continued the attack. Gen. Eichelberger established his forward command post within 125 yards of the front. The effect of his presence was electric. In his report to Gen. MacArthur, the I Corps commander stated, "The number of our troops who tried to avoid combat today could be numbered on your fingers."

Knowing the importance of soldiers seeing their commanders in the field, Gen. Eichelberger always wore his silver stars on his collar. His activities during a normal day, according to one account, "could well be classified as interference, but were, as a practical matter, assurances of maximum effort . . . his three stars were in evidence . . . that the high command was taking a very personal interest in the fight." At one point an enemy soldier fired at the general's command group from a range of fifteen yards before a hail of bullets killed the sniper.

Over the next month, the American forces inched forward. Command inspections, better rations, constant reconnaissance, and improved medical care rapidly transformed the Thirty-Second. Together with a platoon of light tanks, Gen. Eichelberger continued the advance on December 18. Progress was slow but steady.

By January 2, 1943, organized resistance at Buna Mission had ceased. It was a "grand day," as Gen. Eichelberger described in a letter to his wife. By his own accord, he had been luckier than most officers, having suffered no wounds or illness. He was the only American general in the combat zone not to become a casualty. Over the course of the campaign, he had lost thirty pounds. Yet the general had galvanized his task force and achieved the first significant land victory against the Japanese.

Why were the Americans successful? Gen. Eichelberger noted that in battle the margin between victory and defeat was often narrow. Under the pressures of combat, officers and men alike tended to forget that the enemy was hard pressed too. Sometimes just plain stubbornness wins the battle that awareness and wisdom might have lost. At Buna, Japanese morale cracked before the Americans' did.

Gen. Eichelberger failed to mention his own contributions to victory. The Thirty-Second Division, which had performed so poorly in November, was the same division that won in December. The difference was Gen. Eichelberger and then restoration of the division's fighting pride.

For his inspirational leadership, the general received an oak leaf cluster to add to his Distinguished Service Cross for extraordinary heroism in action and for displaying extraordinary courage, marked efficiency and precise execution of operations during the Papuan campaign.

Half a world away, in the desert of North Africa, another commander received a telegram to report to Gen. Dwight D. Eisenhower at Allied Force Headquarters in the wake of a crushing defeat at Kasserine Pass. Casualties at Kasserine were high as Field Marshal Erwin Rommel's audacious attack caught American forces unprepared for their first full-scale combat in the African Theater.

Moreover, Gen. Eisenhower was less than satisfied with the performance of Maj. Gen. Lloyd R. Fredendall, commander of the US II Corps. To complicate matters, Gen. Fredendall was hardly on speaking terms with Orlando Ward, his principal subordinate and the commander of the First Armored Division. In fact, Gen. Fredendall had requested Ward's immediate replacement.

Receiving Gen. Eisenhower's cable was Ernest N. Harmon (US Military Academy, 1917), commander of the Second Armored Division. Gen. Eisenhower considered Maj. Gen. Harmon the best armored division commander in the army. On February 20, 1943, Ike ordered Gen. Harmon to report "for limited field duty." Arriving in Algiers, Gen. Harmon discovered his mission was to first "restore the situation [at Kasserine], then report direct to Eisenhower whether he should relieve Ward or Fredendall." Officially he was to serve as Gen. Fredendall's deputy corps commander.

Within a day, Gen. Harmon was en route to Gen. Fredendall's headquarters, having absolutely no knowledge of the alignment of American troops, the disposition of British and French troops in the area or the actual tactical situation. When Gen. Harmon and his aide finally reached the II Corps command post, Gen. Fredendall relinquished command of the battle to him on the spot. According to Lucian Truscott, then in command of Ike's advance command post, Gen. Fredendall handed Gen. Harmon an envelope saying, "Here it is. The party is yours." Placing Gen. Harmon in command of the "battle in progress," Gen. Fredendall then summarized the tactical situation.

As soon as Gen. Harmon arrived, the telephone rang and Gen. Fredendall began arguing with the caller about the arrival of thirty-three tanks. Gen. Harmon confirmed he was in command and ordered that the tanks be brought forward immediately. Wasting no time on amenities, he then commandeered a half-track and went forward to confer with Ward and Brig. Gen. Cameron G. Nicholson, commanders of the First Armored Division and the British Sixth Armored Division respectively.

According to Gen. Harmon's memoirs, he had already decided on a course of operations by the time he reached the division headquarters. His decision was simple: he was confronted with a situation in which American troops had fled in the face of the enemy. First order of business was to halt the flight, turn the men around, then recapture the lost ground. Gen. Harmon's first order was succinct, "We are going to hold today and counterattack tomorrow. Nobody goes back from here."

Next, he countermanded the orders of Gen. Sir Kenneth Anderson, the British commander of Allied troops in the Tunisian Theater. Anderson had wanted to move an artillery brigade from the Ninth Division north from the area of operations, but Gen. Harmon needed the support for his counterattack. Taking full responsibility for his action, Gen. Harmon reasoned that if the attack failed, no one would care.

Convinced his division commanders understood his intent, Gen. Harmon then reconnoitered the terrain for his attack. At the same time, he inspected the artillery batteries and disposed the tanks that had arrived in midmorning. After reporting his plan to Gen. Fredendall, Gen. Harmon then got some rest.

In midafternoon, February 23, the Allies launched a heavy attack to secure Kasserine Pass. German resistance was minimal; Rommel had withdrawn under cover of darkness. Allied infantry and armor moved forward with artillery support. Two days later, German troops were back where they had started at the beginning of their own offensive on February 14.

By any measure of achievement, Gen. Harmon had performed miracles during his short tenure at the front. The transformation on the Kasserine front from the debacle of mid-February to the time Gen. Harmon's attack drove the Germans to the east was almost unbelievable. True, Rommel had already ordered a withdrawal, but American commanders had no way of knowing that.

What was more important was that the Allied army in Tunisia, and the American II Corps in particular, gained confidence they sorely needed. Never again would an American corps perform as poorly in combat as II Corps did at Kasserine Pass. And Earnest Harmon deserved much of the credit for that transformation.

Like Gen. Eichelberger, Gen. Harmon produced order from the chaos of battle. In short order, he replaced defeatism with optimism. His willingness to take responsibility in the face of adversity and possible insubordination restored the fighting spirit. Within twenty-four hours of his arrival,

American troops had resumed the offensive. Within two days, they had recaptured Kasserine.

As a postscript, Gen. Fredendall dispatched Gen. Harmon back to Algiers as soon as the outcome of the offensive was decided. Reporting to Gen. Eisenhower, Gen. Harmon gave his chief a candid appraisal of both Fredendall and Ward. Ward was fine for a while; Fredendall must go.

Ike then offered Gen. Harmon command of II Corps, but he respectfully declined, stating that ethically he could not recommend the relief of a superior officer and then take his command. Recommending that George Patton get the job, Gen. Harmon returned to Morocco and his Second Armored Division.

For his service in Tunisia, Gen. Harmon received a Legion of Merit. In a letter to Gen. Eisenhower, he respectfully requested a personal note reflecting the way Ike felt he had handled the special mission during that critical period in late February. Gen. Eisenhower replied, a month later, stating how impressed he had been with Gen. Harmon's "calmness, courage, and leadership . . . during the final stages of the German Advance." He then added that Harmon had "demonstrated that kind of leadership that we need in the prosecution of this war. I am truly grateful to you."

Unfortunately, there was yet another tragedy in the Mediterranean Theater before the war was over. On January 22, 1944, Anglo-American forces under the command of Maj. Gen. John P. Lucas stormed ashore at Anzio. Resistance was light, Gen. Lucas's VI Corps having surprised the Germans. The VI Corps was actually seventy miles north of the Allied soldiers who were facing the strongly fortified German Gustav Line.

Gen. Lucas's mission was deliberately vague: "to seize and secure a beachhead and to advance on the Alban Hills." Whether Gen. Lucas was to move toward the Alban Hills and sever the main line of communication to the south or move to the Alban Hills was left to the general's discretion. The reason for the vagueness was to keep VI Corps flexible and not commit it to any single course of action.

Gen. Lucas secured the beachhead, then awaited reinforcements and supplies before moving inland. By that time, Field Marshal Albert Kesselring, German commander in Italy, had seized the initiative from Gen. Lucas and counterattacked with every unit at his disposal. Within a week of the landing, the Anglo-American force was under siege.

In one of the more controversial decisions of the war, Lt. Gen. Mark W. Clark, Fifth Army commander, then relieved Gen. Lucas without prejudice on February 22. Whether Gen. Clark's actions were justified is beyond the scope of this chapter. He was obviously dissatisfied with the state of affairs at that time, which found the Allied force under constant bombardment. Although he denied he had lost confidence in the VI Corps commander, Clark clearly had done so. Moreover, he reasoned that Gen. Lucas had lost confidence in himself.

To replace a commander whom he deemed tentative and "worn out," Clark selected Maj. Gen. Lucian K. Truscott Jr., former commanding general of the Third Infantry Division and Gen. Lucas's deputy commander at the time. In twenty-six years in the army, Gen. Truscott had earned a reputation as an aggressive cavalryman in the mold of Gen. J. E. B. (Jeb) Stuart.

A veteran of North Africa and Sicily, Gen. Truscott had more than once crossed swords with Patton and was one of the few commanders who dared stand toe-to-toe with him. Which commander was more feared or more vulgar in speech was a subject of speculation among the soldiers of the Third Division and Patton's Seventh Army.

Gen. Truscott's philosophy in battle reflected a competitive nature that demanded victory at all costs. He once told his son, "You fight wars to win! Every good commander has to have some sonofabitch in him. If he doesn't, he isn't a good commander. . . . It's as simple as that. No sonofabitch, no commander."

The immediate problem confronting Gen. Truscott was the restoration of confidence in VI Corps. After assessing the situation, he was fully aware of how close the beachhead had come to disaster. The narrow escape indicated that corps headquarters had never been positive and confident in either planning or directing operations.

In addition, there was a lack of understanding between British and American commanders and staffs. Frequent German artillery and air attacks caused Allied morale to deteriorate further. Gen. Truscott's initial impression was that lower echelons of command entertained the feeling that "corps" and "army" were unduly concerned for their own safety.

The journal of Gen. Truscott's aide described the flurry of activity that characterized the new commander's first day on the job. Calling together his subordinate commanders, the general supervised his first full-scale air meeting to lay groundwork for further support development. He then discussed subsequent operations with his ground commanders and ordered realignment of beachhead defenses.

Whereas Gen. Lucas commanded from the safety of his command post, Gen. Truscott ventured to the front lines. Commanding from the rear, not that there was any rear area at Anzio, was anathema to Gen. Truscott. Touring his old division and the Forty-Fifth Infantry Division along the front lines, Gen. Truscott then conducted a late afternoon staff meeting and coordinated for logistical and anti-parachute defense. It was a full day, but Gen. Truscott had produced a noticeable change on his first day in command.

The appearance of the commanding general quickly galvanized the beleaguered defenders of the beachhead. For the first time in a month, a feeling of optimism permeated the command. Unlike Buna and Kasserine, however, there would be no short-term reversal of fortune at Anzio. German strength was too great, and geography favored the enemy. Still, a subtle transformation in the unit's fighting spirit was under way.

Other changes quickly followed. Gen. Truscott removed staff officers from underground shelters. He organized and developed anti-aircraft defenses and counter battery fires. When told that his unorthodox proposal was not the technique employed by the Artillery School, Gen. Truscott responded, "Well, general, I don't give a damn what the Artillery School teaches. I want this problem solved and I want it solved right now. I have suggested a possible solution. You have until dark tonight to find a better one."

Within a week of assuming command, Gen. Truscott had revitalized VI Corps. When the Germans launched their last-ditch effort to eradicate the beachhead on February 29, they were met by determined resistance. Gen. Truscott's counterpreparation fires, coupled with intense air and artillery support and well-conceived counterattacks, halted the German advance.

The worst was over. The beachhead would survive. Though it would take months to mount sufficient combat power to conduct a full-scale offensive and to link up with Fifth Army, Lucian K. Truscott Jr. had saved the day.

Four months following his successful rehabilitation of VI Corps, Gen. Truscott conducted the breakout offensive that drove the German Army from Rome. Transferred to France, he participated in Operation Dragoon and subsequently assumed command of Fifth Army in Italy in December 1944. After the war, he succeeded his old mentor Patton as commanding general of Third Army in Bavaria.

In assessing Eichelberger, Harmon, and Truscott, several common elements of leadership are evident. Each commander made an immediate assessment at once. Placing key leaders in positions of leadership, they then focused their troops on the enemy and the mission, and away from thoughts of self-preservation. They directed all their thoughts and actions at improving the morale and fighting spirit of the troops.

At Buna, Kasserine, and Anzio, they clearly understood that the ability of a unit to fight had more to do with its frame of mind. Psychological strength, more than numerical strength or physical capability, was the key to success.

Restoring the fighting spirit to a defeated army is perhaps the most difficult task a commander must undertake. Eichelberger, Harmon, and Truscott not only accomplished this task but also did so in the face of tenacious foes. In the process, they bequeathed a legacy of combat leadership to future generations.

"Restoring the Fighting Spirit" was originally published in *ARMY Magazine* (March 1996).

30

A "Formidable Array of Warriors"

In a statement before the Seventy-Ninth Congress, Britain's wartime leader, Winston Churchill, remarked that he had witnessed the creation of America's mighty army, which had emerged victorious in every theater against the most resolute enemies. To create great armies was one thing, noted the prime minister; to lead them into battle and to handle them effectively was quite another.

Four of the officers with whom Churchill was most familiar were the commanding generals of the armies that made up Lt. Gen. Omar N. Bradley's Twelfth Army Group. Under the field armies were twelve corps, forty-eight divisions, and more than 1.3 million soldiers by V-E Day. This constituted the largest purely American force in history. Leading Gen. Bradley's armies was a distinguished quartet of warriors—Lt. Gen. Courtney H. Hodges, George S. Patton Jr., William H. Simpson, and, in the war's final months, Leonard T. Gerow. They shouldered the principal burden at the operational level of war against the German Wehrmacht in the bitter fighting in northwest Europe.

Lt. Gen. Courtney H. Hodges had served with distinction on Gen. John J. Pershing's Punitive Expedition into Mexico, and he commanded both a battalion and a regiment in World War I, earning a Distinguished Service Cross. Like all the army commanders in World War II, Gen. Hodges owed his rise to prominence to his association with Gen. George C. Marshall, army chief of staff, with whom Hodges had served on the Infantry Board in the early 1930s. Gen. Hodges later became commandant of the Infantry School, preceding Gen. Bradley in that position, and in May 1941, Marshall appointed Hodges chief of infantry.

Gen. Hodges assumed command of the Third Army in the United States before his deployment to England in 1944, where he served as Bradley's deputy commander for the upcoming invasion of Europe. According to the Overlord plan, Gen. Bradley would command the First Army until sufficient forces were available to activate a second American Army, at which time he would move up to command the Twelfth Army Group and his deputy would take the reins of the First Army.

Gen. Bradley used Gen. Hodges to train the fresh divisions arriving in England so he could concentrate on inspections and operational planning. Similarly, Gen. Hodges delegated many of the day-to-day operations to his chief of staff, Maj. Gen. William B. Kean Jr., whom contemporary observers believed to be the real brains of the First Army.

Gen. Hodges served as Gen. Bradley's understudy until July 27, when, in the midst of the COBRA breakthrough, Gen. Bradley ordered him to keep close track of the three corps on the First Army's left flank. Gen. Hodges's subsequent performance in Normandy was steady, if uninspired. His First Army bore the brunt of Adolf Hitler's gamble to sever the American lines at Mortain. The destruction of the bulk of the German armor in the Falaise pocket was facilitated in no small part by Gen. Hodges's ability to hold the western side of the pocket until Field Marshal Sir Bernard L. Montgomery and Gen. Bradley joined forces in mid-August.

In the advance toward Germany, Gen. Hodges once again proved himself steady, although he never achieved the public acclaim accorded Gen. Patton. At best, the First Army's operations reflected Gen. Hodges's background. An infantryman by trade, he thought it "safer, sounder, and, in the end, quicker to keep smashing ahead" than to risk all in a campaign of maneuver. This perspective was more reminiscent of infantry operations during Lt. Gen. Ulysses S. Grant's Wilderness Campaign and Gen. Pershing's offensives in World War I than it was of an age in which mechanization and motorization had restored mobility to the battlefield. Not surprisingly, the First Army suffered heavy casualties in the advance toward Germany's western frontier, particularly in the fighting in the Hurtgen Forest.

Nor was the Battle of the Bulge Gen. Hodges's finest hour. His faulty troop dispositions and poor intelligence reports contributed to the disaster in the Ardennes. At times he appeared dazed, never grasping the full impact of the size and speed of the enemy advance. He lost control of the battle, and had it not been for his transfer to Field Marshall Montgomery's Twenty-First Army Group and the injection of Gen. Matthew B. Ridgway's XVIII Corps into the breach, the disaster might have reached catastrophic proportions. What saved the First Army was the inspired leadership at the corps, division, and regimental levels, coupled with the indomitable spirit of its soldiers.

Still, the First Army was first to breach the Rhine at Remagen, and Gen. Hodges performed magnificently in the subsequent operations aimed at eliminating the Ruhr pocket. Both Gen. Eisenhower and Gen. Bradley rated Gen. Hodges as the most capable all-around army commander in the European Theater. To Gen. Eisenhower, Gen. Hodges was the "spearhead and the scintillating star" of the final advance into Germany. As to Gen. Hodges's overall value, the Supreme Commander reminded Gen. Marshall that it was the First Army, not Gen. Patton's Third, that had been given "the most difficult [task], but one that had been brilliantly and speedily executed, often against much resistance."

Gen. Bradley concurred, stating that of all his principal subordinates, Gen. Hodges required the least supervision. Ranking his commanders at war's end, he rated Hodges highly. In Gen. Bradley's eyes, Gen. Hodges was a "general's general, blending dexterity and common sense to produce a magnificently balanced command."

In sharp contrast to the methodical Hodges stood the mercurial George S. Patton Jr. Gen. Patton actually commanded the Seventh Army in Sicily and the Third Army in France and Germany. Like Hodges, Patton had attracted Marshall's attention in World War I and during the years before World War II. A 1909 graduate of the US Military Academy, he also served on the Punitive Expedition, gaining national acclaim for his heroism in a highly publicized engagement with Pancho Villa's band of raiders. While in France with the American Expeditionary Forces, then–Col. Patton, commander of a tank brigade, earned the Distinguished Service Cross for valor during the Meuse–Argonne Offensive.

His exploits between the wars need little enumeration here. By the time of the Texas–Louisiana maneuvers of September 1941, in which he commanded the Second Armored Division, Gen. Patton had fashioned an image of a hard-driving, "hell-bent for leather" cavalryman. Already a legend within the army, he appeared on the cover of *Life* magazine, which heralded the leadership of the most visible proponent of the army's armored force. Underneath the stern countenance that graced America's favorite periodical was the ultimate warrior. Gen. Patton, more than any of his contemporaries, dedicated his entire life to the study of his profession, and when the war tocsin sounded, he responded.

Both Gens. Marshall and Eisenhower remained ambivalent toward the eccentric Patton. Both admired the manner in which he had rehabilitated II Corps in Tunisia in the wake of the Kasserine debacle. In Sicily, Gen. Patton commanded the Seventh Army brilliantly, traversing the island, first to Palermo, then beating Field Marshal Montgomery to Messina. Gen. Eisenhower characterized his Sicilian campaign as a "model of swift conquest which would be studied by future classes in the staff college in Leavenworth." In the process, Gen. Patton earned the grudging respect of our British allies and demonstrated that American forces were every bit their equal.

Yet it was in Sicily that Gen. Patton demonstrated the irrationality and imbalance that more than once caused Marshall and Eisenhower to question his utility. Gen. Marshall was hardly alone in his assessment that Gen. Patton's "love of violence, his needless profanity and obscenity, and his gaudy showmanship were all serious defects in a commander." Gen. Eisenhower agreed and, like his chief, abhorred those unfortunate personal traits in Patton that caused him "some most uncomfortable days."

On the positive side, Gen. Eisenhower characterized Gen. Patton as a truly aggressive commander "whose troops [would] not be stopped by ordinary obstacles." Recommending his Seventh Army commander for promotion to permanent major general, Gen. Eisenhower remarked that Patton was more suited to operations in an exclusively American theater and not in an Allied one.

Gen. Patton's relationship with Gen. Bradley, who had been his subordinate in both North Africa and Sicily, has attracted its share of attention in postwar literature, but Gen. Patton was a dutiful subordinate once he assumed command of the Third Army in August 1944. Though he privately railed against what he considered Gen. Bradley's timidity and lack of strategic vision, he remained extraordinarily cooperative, confining his frustrations to the privacy of his diary. Gen. Patton alone of the senior American commanders, understood that the destruction of German armed forces, not the gaining of territory, was the guiding principle of war. Still, when Gen. Bradley ordered a halt to his northward thrust at Argentan, Gen. Patton complied, knowing full well that a golden opportunity to shorten—even end—the war was passing.

Patton's supreme moment was not in Normandy, but on the German border. When Hitler launched his last great offensive in the Ardennes on December 16, 1944, Gen. Eisenhower called on Gen. Patton and his Third Army to halt the German offensive. Within three days, Patton turned his army ninety degrees, from the east to the north, and relieved the surrounded garrison at Bastogne. His performance in disengaging three divisions and shifting then to a major offensive in another direction was simply masterful. No other commander could have moved as quickly and assuredly.

Like all military commanders, Patton attracted his share of criticism. Gen. Eisenhower noted that Gen. Patton tended to become pessimistic and discouraged when he became bogged down in the close-in fighting in the Moselle. In such instances the Third Army commander needed a great deal of moral patting on the back. Despite Gen. Eisenhower's postwar recollections, however, it was Gen. Patton on whom he repeatedly relied when disaster loomed. And it was Gen. Patton whom Gen. Eisenhower rated as his most valuable army commander, calling him a "dashing fighter, shrewd, and courageous." It is not surprising that Gen. Patton was the Allied general most feared by the Germans.

Two decades after the war, Eisenhower remembered his friend as a "genius in pursuit [and] a natural in exploiting the weaknesses of the Nazi forces" on a fluid battlefield. This had been true in Sicily, in the dash from Normandy to Metz, and again when the Third Army traversed the Rhine in March 1945. At war's end Patton's forward columns had crossed the Austrian and Czechoslovakian frontiers. By Patton's own reckoning, the Third Army had inflicted 1,486,700 casualties on the enemy, while suffering 136,865 of its own. Third Army had also captured more prisoners of war than any other army—more than 1 million. He had indeed earned his pay.

Rounding out Gen. Bradley's Twelfth Army Group in the fall of 1944 was Gen. William H. Simpson's Ninth Army. A classmate of Gen. Patton and the youngest member of his class, Gen. Simpson had served with Pershing in the Philippines and had commanded an infantry company in "BlackJack's" Punitive Expedition. At age thirty, he was already chief of staff of the Thirty-Third Division in World War I, where he was repeatedly cited for bravery. His interwar service was similar to that of most of his contemporaries, including a variety of school, command, instructor, and staff assignments. By September 1943, Simpson was a lieutenant general and commander of the Fourth Army in the southern United States.

The Fourth Army, redesignated first the Eighth and then the Ninth Army, landed in Europe on August 27, 1944, and became operational in Brittany. Gen. Eisenhower was not averse to having Gen. Simpson in theater, but he remarked to Gen. Marshall that he believed some of Gen. Bradley's corps commanders had demonstrated the capacity for leadership and for handling large formations and were thus better suited to taking over a new army command than was an officer who had not actually demonstrated that ability. Gen. Marshall remained firm, for he was convinced of the necessity of assuring that generals who trained large armies in the United States would not be denied opportunities to command in combat. In the campaign ahead, Gen. Simpson would more than once prove his mettle.

Following the surrender of Brest in September, Gen. Bradley positioned Gen. Simpson on the far left of his advance, between Hodges's First Army and Montgomery's British front in Holland. His purpose was twofold: the Ninth Army was less experienced and could be more easily spared than the veteran First or Third, and, according to his memoirs, Gen. Bradley anticipated that Montgomery would eventually wangle a US Army from Gen. Eisenhower to strengthen his British Army Group. In the subsequent advance to the Roer River, Gen. Simpson performed well, earning what historian Russell Weigley claims was "Bradley's affections as the army he could count on simply to go about its business."

Gen. Simpson's cool leadership during the Ardennes battles was particularly admirable. Realizing that a team effort was critical in halting the

German advance, Gen. Hodges rushed his Seventh Armored Division to bolster Maj. Gen. Troy Middleton's VIII Corps at Saint-Vith. He then reconfigured his tactical dispositions to strengthen the northern shoulder of the "bulge." Of all the army commanders, it was Gen. Simpson's thinking that seemed closest to Gen. Eisenhower's assessment of the scope and intensity of the German offensive. By the tenth day of the offensive, seven of Gen. Simpson's divisions were heavily engaged in the First Army's sector.

From the Roer River to the Rhine River, Gen. Simpson found himself under the operational control of Field Marshal Montgomery, which he accepted with his customary acquiescence. Transferred to the Twenty-First Army Group in the midst of the Ardennes battle, Simpson seemed to work well with Montgomery. Following a brilliant campaign culminating in the Roer River crossings in February and March 1945, he demanded and received a more autonomous role in crossing the Rhine as part of Montgomery's Operation Plunder. In the initial directive for the river crossing, Montgomery had assigned command of the operation to Miles Dempsey's British Second Army, relegating Ninth Army's participation to a single corps. Simpson protested and Montgomery relented. Issuing a new directive, Montgomery assigned a portion of the crossing to the Ninth Army.

Gen. Simpson's Ninth Army returned to Gen. Bradley's control on April 4, and by the middle of April elements of the Ninth and First Armies had effectively closed the Ruhr pocket, capturing 317,000 Germans in the process. His rapid advance to the Elbe, reminiscent of Patton's dash across France the preceding summer, made him the first Allied commander to reach the river and meet the Russians. Gen. Simpson was prepared to move toward Berlin when he was halted by orders from the supreme commander. Whether Gen. Simpson could have traversed the final fifty miles and captured Berlin remains a subject of speculation today.

Of Gen. Simpson's contributions to the Allied victory there can be little doubt. "If Simpson ever made a mistake as an Army commander," stated Gen. Eisenhower, "it never came to my attention. Alert, intelligent, and professionally capable, he was the type of leader that American soldiers deserve." What endeared Simpson to Eisenhower and Bradley was the quiet and balanced style through which he exercised command. Unlike the temperamental Hodges and the outspoken Patton, Simpson remained "uncommonly normal" and caused neither the supreme commander nor Gen. Bradley any problems.

Maj. Gen. Leonard T. "Gee" Gerow commanded the fourth army in Gen. Bradley's Twelfth Army Group. Like the Army Chief of Staff Gen. Gerow was a graduate of the Virginia Military Institute. He knew Eisenhower and Bradley well. Gerow finished the infantry advanced course at Fort Benning, Georgia, first to Bradley's second. A lifelong friend of the supreme commander, Gerow and Eisenhower were classmates at the Command and General Staff School in 1925. Gerow graduated second in his class, several hundredths of a point behind Eisenhower. Later, Gerow was Eisenhower's predecessor at the war plans division in the War Department in 1941. When Marshall assigned Gerow to command the Twenty-Ninth Division, Eisenhower replaced Gerow as Marshall's principal operational planner. Not surprisingly, both Marshall and Eisenhower maintained a high regard for Gerow's abilities.

When D-Day approached, Gen. Eisenhower tagged Gen. Gerow to command one of the two American assault corps. Gen. Gerow, now the V Corps commander, led the assault on Omaha Beach. His performance in the subsequent fighting in the bocage was sufficient to merit Gen. Eisenhower's consideration for promotion to army level command in late August. Gen. Eisenhower told Gen. Marshall in mid-September that Gerow was "doing beautifully." Only the rapid advance of Lt. Gen. Jacob L. Devers's Sixth Army Group up the Rhone Valley and the diversion of several American divisions to that sector postponed Gen. Gerow's promotion to army command.

Following the Normandy breakout, V Corps remained in the forefront of Gen. Hodges's First Army. The Fourth Infantry Division and Jacques Leclerc's Second French Armored Division liberated Paris under Gen. Gerow's corps control. From the French capital, Gen. Gerow renewed V Corps's assault beyond the Seine. By the eve of Montgomery's abortive Market Garden offensive, Gerow was already positioned along Germany's West Wall. There, starved for ammunition and fearful that he had reached the culminating point of his advance, he halted. With little encouragement and no significant support from Gen. Hodges, Gen. Gerow had little recourse.

For the next three months, V Corps conducted the same close-in fighting that characterized Gen. Hodges's campaigning. Casualties mounted as Gen. Gerow bore the brunt of the second battle of the Hurtgen Forest in mid-November. When the Germans launched their offensive on December 16, Gen. Gerow, now a seasoned corps commander, was one of the first to realize that the thrust was not a mere local counterattack. Retracting his lines on his own initiative, Gen. Gerow prepared to meet the onslaught. Concentrating all available artillery pieces and reinforced with elements from Maj. Gen. J. Lawton Collins's VII Corps, Gen. Gerow held the Elsenborn Ridge and stymied the Germans' attempts to exploit their initial success. It was a commendable performance.

In anticipation of the prolonged campaign east of the Rhine, Gen. Bradley soon formed a Fourth American Army. Gerow received promotion to lieutenant general on January 1, 1945, and assumed command of the Fifteenth Army on January 16.

So swiftly did the enemy resistance crumble west of the Rhine, however, that Gen. Bradley abandoned plans for commitment of Gen. Gerow's army in the line and ordered it to hold the west bank of the river as a "semi-occupational army."

In addition, the Fifteenth Army assumed responsibility for containing the enemy forces continuing to resist in Lorient and Saint-Nazaire, France. Gen. Gerow's chief contribution then became staging and equipping units newly arrived from the United States, a rather inglorious end to his combat service. Yet, in Gen. Eisenhower's assessment, Gen. Gerow was the best corps commander in the theater, a "good fighter, balanced, calm, optimistic, [and a] selfless leader." Gen. Gerow also earned high marks from Gen. Bradley, who rated him just below Gen. Patton and Gen. Collins in overall effectiveness.

In the final analysis, the American armies that fought in the European Theater were led by able, dedicated commanders. Bradley's Army group was no exception.

Despite the historiographical trend to attack the quality of the American leadership and the effectiveness of the US Army in Europe, on the whole the successes of Gen. Bradley's Army commanders far outweighed their failures. In one of his final communiques to Gen. Marshall,

Gen. Eisenhower noted that these commanders, along with Gen. Bradley, "make up a team that could scarcely be improved upon."

That each made operational and tactical errors is indisputable, but, on the whole, Hodges, Patton, Simpson, and Gerow commanded armies with distinction. When called on, Gen. Bradley's commanders, with minor exceptions, met the challenge of combat and constituted an integral component of what one historian has called the most formidable array of warriors this country has ever produced.

"A 'Formidable Array of Warriors'" was originally published in *ARMY Magazine* (May 1996).

31

World War II's Airborne Commanders

The Stuff of Instant Legend

In his essay on generalship, British theorist J. F. C. Fuller noted that the three pillars of generalship are courage, creative intelligence, and physical fitness—the attributes of youth rather than middle age. Lt. Gen. George S. Patton Jr. expressed similar sentiments about the need for competent, aggressive commanders. According to Gen. Patton, wars might be fought with weapons, but they are won by soldiers. It is the spirit of the men who follow and the men who lead that produces victory.

Nowhere were the physical and mental demands of leadership more evident than in the American airborne units and the officers who commanded these elite organizations in World War II. With the introduction of a new type of warfare, airborne commands placed a greater premium on youth, vigor, and imagination than on experience.

Gen. Matthew B. Ridgway, Lt. Gen. James M. Gavin, Gen. Maxwell D. Taylor, Maj. Gen. William N. (Bud) Miley, and Maj. Gen. Joseph M. Swing personified the tenacity, the spirit, and singleness of purpose required to command elite divisions in combat. Collectively, they embodied the essence of military professionalism during this century's greatest conflict.

American paratroopers, past and present, owe a special debt to Gen. Ridgway, arguably the finest combat officer this nation has produced. A 1917 graduate of the US Military Academy, Ridgway was instrumental in the development of American parachute and glider units during the war. His proteges read like a "Who's Who" of airborne operations—virtually every airborne divisional and regimental commander served with Ridgway in some capacity. Miley, Gavin, and Swift all served as assistant division commanders (ADCs) and Gen. Taylor was chief of staff to Gen. Ridgway in the Eighty-Second Airborne Division.

At the beginning of the war, Gen. Ridgway, an ADC under Maj. Gen. Omar N. Bradley, took command of the Eighty-Second Infantry Division and converted it into an airborne division. His knowledge of airborne tactics, to say nothing of the configuration of an airborne division, was nil. Gen. Ridgway characteristically developed a rigorous training program that within months produced what he termed "twelve thousand hardy characters who weren't afraid to jump, or duck in over tree tops and hedges to crash in a rocky field in a glider."

In May 1943, Gen. Ridgway deployed his division to Africa in preparation for the upcoming invasion of Sicily, which proved to be a sobering test for the Eighty-Second and its tactics. Gen. Gavin's 505th Parachute Infantry Regiment made a widely scattered drop on July 10, and elements of Col. Reuben Tucker's 504th fell victim to friendly fire the following evening.

Twenty-three troop transports were shot down by American naval and coastal fire. The American parachute regiments suffered eighty-two dead (including Brig. Gen. Charles L. Keerans, the ADC), 131 wounded, and sixteen missing. Gen. Dwight D. Eisenhower demanded an immediate inquiry and halted all subsequent airborne operations.

Going ashore by amphibious landing craft on D-Day, Gen. Ridgway did his best to restore order. So far advanced was his command post (CP) that Gen. Patton allegedly chided him, stating, "that damn Ridgway has got his CP up where his outposts ought to be." Gen. Ridgway considered this rebuke to be a compliment, coming from Gen. Patton.

The effectiveness of the Eighty-Second in Sicily was best summed up by Gen. Kurt Student, Germany's foremost authority on airborne operations. Gen. Student recalled in 1945 that "the Allied airborne operation in Sicily was decisive . . . had not the airborne forces blocked the Hermann Göring Division from reaching the beachhead, that division would have driven the initial amphibious forces back into the sea."

Although Sicily was Gen. Ridgway's first test in commanding a division in combat, it was hardly his last. His rapid deployment of the division to Italy in September 1943 probably saved Lt. Gen. Mark W. Clark's invading force from disaster. On June 6, 1944, Gen. Ridgway jumped with the Eighty-Second into Normandy. Thirty-three days later, on July 8, Ridgway and the Eighty-Second were relieved of combat duties. In the interim they had, according to historian Clay Blair, become the stuff of instant legend.

Under Gen. Ridgway's personal leadership, the division had established a remarkable record of combat performance. Col. Ralph P. Eaton, the division chief of staff, noted with justifiable pride that the Eighty-Second had earned the reputation of being "a pack of jackals; the toughest, most resourceful and bloodthirsty infantry in the ETO [European Theater of Operations]."

But the cost had been high. After a month of continuous combat, Gen. Ridgway's paratroopers had suffered 46 percent casualties, including 1,282 dead and 2,373 wounded severely enough to require evacuation.

For his part, Gen. Ridgway also earned the praise of his superiors. Gen. Bradley expressed his personal appreciation for a magnificent job and Maj. Gen. J. Lawton Collins awarded him the Distinguished Service Cross. The highest accolades came from Gen. Eisenhower, who promoted Gen. Ridgway to command of the XVIII (US) Corps, consisting of the Eighty-Second, 101st, and the newly arrived Seventeenth Airborne Divisions.

Over the course of the remainder of the war, twenty-two divisions served under Gen. Ridgway's direct command at one time or another. In addition to the American airborne divisions, they included some of the most valiant outfits in the Allied service—the US First Infantry Division and the Third Armored Division, and the British Sixth Airborne, the Commando Brigade, and the Sixth Guard's Armored Brigade.

When Gen. Ridgway was promoted to corps command, then–Brig. Gen. James M. (Slim Jim) Gavin, Ridgway's hand-picked successor, assumed command of the Eighty-Second Airborne. Like his mentor, Gen. Gavin had earned his combat spurs in the Mediterranean. Spearheading the Allied invasion of Sicily, Gen. Gavin's 505th Regimental Combat Team conducted the first mass combat drop in American history. Although widely dispersed, Gen. Gavin's men performed heroically, delaying the Hermann Göring Division from conducting a concentrated counterattack against Gen. Patton's Seventh Army.

According to historian Blair, Gavin's own defense of Biazza Ridge was one of the finest, most dogged displays of leadership during World War II. Although British commanders downplayed the contributions of the Eighty-Second, the American consensus was that Gen. Gavin had made a significant impact on the operation. Gen. Ridgway awarded him the Distinguished Service Cross.

Following distinguished service in Italy, Gavin was appointed brigadier general in September and assistant division commander on October 10, 1943. It was in this capacity that Gen. Gavin, serving as commander of Task Force A, made up of the 505th, 507th, and 508th Parachute Infantry Regiments, jumped into Normandy. Having been instrumental in the development of the airborne plan, Gen. Gavin distinguished himself at the Merderet River crossings west of Ste-Mere Eglise. His personal leadership was nothing short of inspirational and confirmed his potential for division-level command.

On August 16, Gen. Gavin took command of the Eighty-Second Airborne Division. Promotion quickly followed, making him, at thirty-seven, the youngest division commander since George Custer in the Civil War. Gen. Ridgway heartily endorsed Gen. Gavin's promotion despite his subordinate's junior rank. Gavin had been a brigadier general for only nine months, but had proved to be, in Gen. Ridgway's words, "a proved battle leader of the highest type."

Within a month of his elevation to division command, Gavin made his fourth combat jump, leading his proud division in Operation Market Garden, Field Marshal Sir Bernard L. Montgomery's aborted attempt to seize crossing sites across the Rhine at Arnhem. The mission assigned to the Eighty-Second Airborne was to seize a series of bridges from Nijmegen to Grave, in the center of the Allied axis of advance. On September 17, 1944, Gen. Gavin led 7,250 parachutists into Holland with the bridges at Nijmegen as the primary objectives.

Despite initial success, Gen. Gavin's paratroopers soon ran into intense German resistance. September 20 rivaled the most difficult hours of the Eighty-Second Airborne Division in Normandy. Gen. Gavin himself called it a day unprecedented in the division's combat history. Under heavy counterattack by two German combat teams, Gen. Gavin positioned himself where the decisive fighting was taking place. To historian Blair, Gen. Gavin was "a one-man fire brigade."

Issuing orders under fire, Gen. Gavin conducted a personal reconnaissance and made appropriate alterations to his plan. He ordered several counterattacks and supervised a river crossing under fire. By evening, all designated bridges were in the Eighty-Second's hands. Gen. Sir Miles Dempsey, British Second Army commander, called Gen. Gavin's men "the greatest division in the world." Although Operation Market Garden had failed, Gen. Gavin's performance had been commendable.

Nor were airborne operations Gen. Gavin's only contribution to the Allied victory. When the Germans burst through the Ardennes in December, Gen. Gavin's Eighty-Second was once again rushed into the breach. Gen. Gavin, temporarily in command of XVIII Corps until Gen. Ridgway arrived from England, ordered the 101st Airborne Division to Bastogne and his own Eighty-Second to the northern shoulder of the German offensive.

Once Gen. Ridgway arrived, Gen. Gavin reverted to command of his own division and again performed magnificently. The Eighty-Second was in continuous contact with the enemy until January 9, when it was relieved by the Seventy-Fifth Infantry Division. Gen. Gavin's frontline leadership had more than once been the critical factor in holding the thin line of American paratroopers.

Gen. Gavin remained in command of the veteran Eighty-Second Airborne until the end of the war. Subsequent fighting in breaching the Siegfried Line and the Hurtgen Forest, which he likened to something from the lower levels of Dante's Inferno, only added to his battle laurels. The spring of 1945 heralded preparations for an airborne assault on Berlin in which the Eighty-Second planned to land south of Tempelhof airfield. When the attack was cancelled, Gen. Gavin led his division across the Elbe River at Bleckede, Germany, and on May 2, he received the surrender of the German Twenty-First Army Group commanded by Gen. Kurt von Tippelskirch, totaling 150,000 prisoners. For Gen. Gavin and the Eighty-Second Airborne Division, the war in Europe was over.

Gen. Gavin was hardly the only Ridgway protege who earned his spurs in combat. Like Ridgway and Gavin, Gen. Maxwell D. Taylor was a veteran of the Eighty-Second, having served as chief of staff from 1942 to 1943. Arriving in North Africa in March 1943, then–Brig. Gen. Taylor served as the commander of division artillery during the invasion of Sicily.

He also briefly served as assistant division commander following Brig. Gen. Charles L. Keerans Jr.'s untimely demise as a result of fratricide.

Gen. Taylor's performance so impressed Gen. Ridgway that he was given responsibility for planning the airborne portion of the subsequent invasion of Italy. A highly successful covert reconnaissance mission to Rome to determine the feasibility of airborne operations in the vicinity of the Italian capital raised Gen. Taylor's stock in the estimation of the Allied High Command.

Not surprisingly, when Maj. Gen. William C. Lee, commanding general of the 101st Airborne Division, suffered a heart attack in February 1944, Eisenhower and Bradley selected Gen. Taylor for the job. His appointment was not particularly welcomed by the staff of the 101st because he was viewed as an "outsider," having never served with the division, and his combat experience was limited. In the months ahead, however, Gen. Taylor proved his mettle.

On D-Day, Gen. Taylor's mission was to seize and hold the four causeways spanning the marshes behind Utah Beach and then occupy the line of the Douve River to shield the southern flank of the VII Corps. Gen. Taylor's drop, not quite as dispersed as Gen. Ridgway's, resulted in the early capture of the objectives, although casualties mounted throughout the day. Stubborn German resistance hindered the capture of Carentan until June 14, a full week later than the overly optimistic D-Day prediction.

Casualties in Normandy, however, had been severe—nearly 4,670, including the ADC, Brig. Gen. Donald F. Pratt, the senior airborne commander killed on D-Day. Yet the division had endured its baptism by fire and Gen. Taylor had justified Gen. Bradley's confidence, earning the Distinguished Service Cross in the process.

Redeployed to England, Gen. Taylor prepared the 101st for its next operation. On September 17, Taylor conducted the division's second combat jump, which involved 6,695 paratroopers as part of Market Garden. His specific objectives included the bridge at Zon over the Wilhelmina Canal, to be followed by an attack to clear Eindhoven. Although the initial landing was successful, the Germans succeeded in destroying the Zon bridge, delaying the capture of Eindhoven until the following day. The British armored column, harassed in its own right, finally passed through Gen. Taylor's position on D+2, a full twenty-four hours behind schedule.

Gen. Taylor likened the operations of the 101st in defending its sector of the Eindhoven–Arnhem highway to the operations of the US Cavalry in defending the railroads as they pushed westward through Indian country. In the end, the 101st performed well in a lost cause—the British First Airborne Division was virtually destroyed at Arnhem.

In early December, Gen. Taylor was ordered to Washington to represent the XVIII Corps in discussions regarding changes in the organization and equipment of the airborne divisions. While in Washington, Gen. Taylor learned of the German attack in the Ardennes and the plight of the 101st Airborne Division at Bastogne, which was under the temporary command of Brig. Gen. Anthony C. McAuliffe. The 101st's defense of Bastogne quickly passed into legend and needs little account here. The attitude of the individual soldier in America's airborne units was summed up on the first day of the battle: "They've got us surrounded, the poor bastards!"

According to Gen. Taylor, the two great disappointments of the war were the canceled airborne assault on Rome and his own absence during the first ten days of the battle of Bastogne. His chagrin, however, was tempered by his pride in the division's accomplishment. From Gen. McAuliffe's defiant refusal to surrender to Gen. Taylor's return on December 27, the division had written the brightest page in the "Screaming Eagles'" proud history. On March 15, Gen. Eisenhower presented the unit the first Presidential Unit citation ever awarded to an entire division for gallantry in action.

By Gen. Taylor's own admission, the remainder of the war was anticlimactic for the 101st Airborne division. V-E Day found Gen. Taylor's veterans occupying Berchtesgaden, Adolf Hitler's Alpine retreat. There they captured Field Marshal Albert Kesselring. Initially earmarked to join General of the Army Douglas MacArthur in the Pacific for the final offensive against Japan, Gen. Taylor was in France when news of V-J Day reached his headquarters. On August 22, he took leave of the 101st Airborne, bidding an affectionate farewell to a division that he had led from Normandy to Berchtesgaden.

Less well known than the commanders of the Eighty-Second and 101st Airborne divisions were Maj. Gen. William N. (Bud) Miley and Maj. Gen. Joseph M. Swing, commanders of the Seventeenth Airborne and Eleventh Airborne divisions, respectively. Gen. Miley, a US Military Academy graduate in the class of 1918, commanded the 501st Parachute Battalion in

October 1940. The 501st developed the parachute infantry techniques that were later characteristic of the army's most successful airborne operations.

Promoted to ADC of Gen. Ridgway's Eighty-Second Airborne, Gen. Miley assisted his commander in the transformation of the Eighty-Second from an infantry to an airborne division. Shortly thereafter, he received command of the Seventeenth Airborne, activating his command on April 15, 1943. Deploying to Europe in the autumn of 1944, Gen. Miley joined Gens. Gavin and Taylor as divisional commanders when Gen. Ridgway activated XVIII Corps. His initial test of combat came on January 4, 1945, when the Seventeenth Airborne Division participated in Maj. Gen. Troy H. Middleton's VIII Corps attack to destroy the "Bulge."

The results were not surprising. With inadequate artillery support and dense fog, Gen. Miley ran into a buzz saw. Determined German attacks soon pushed him back to his starting point, but he regrouped and attacked again three days later, this time with three regiments abreast. The outcome was similar, with Gen. Miley suffering what he himself called "terrific" casualties. For a time, Gen. Patton contemplated relieving Gen. Miley but reconsidered. Still, the Third Army commander was not pleased at Gen. Miley's handling of the division, stating that "the 17th Airborne . . . got a very bloody nose."

Another attack on January 13 proved far more successful. By the time the Germans were eradicated in the Bulge, Gen. Miley had matured as a combat commander. Gen. Patton also noticed the improvement in Gen. Miley, stating that the airborne commander had "finally found himself and had done well." Gen. Miley and the Seventeenth Airborne had successfully passed their "trial by combat."

Two months later, the Seventeenth passed yet another test. As part of the final airborne operation of the war in Europe, Gen. Miley and the Seventeenth Airborne joined the Thirteenth Airborne and British Sixth Airborne Division in Operation Varsity, Field Marshal Montgomery's much-ballyhooed crossing of the Rhine.

Varsity commenced on March 24, 1945. It was a massive undertaking, with the American airborne armada consisting of 4964 plus 4613 equal 9577 men, of whom 4,964 were parachutists and 4,613 deployed by glider. Heavy smoke obscured the landing zones, resulting in the dropping of Gen. Miley's division more than one mile from the intended drop zones. An unusually high number of C-46 Commando aircraft, which were not equipped with self-sealing fuel tanks, burst into flames en route to the drop zones.

Once on the ground Gen. Miley moved rapidly to consolidate his dispersed units. Although historians will long debate the merits of Operation Varsity—Gen. Bradley considered it yet another example of Montgomery's penchant for "overkill"—Gen. Miley was pleased with his unit's performance. By the end of D-Day, at a cost of 159 killed and 522 wounded, the Seventeenth had accomplished all of its objectives, capturing more than 2,800 Germans. Varsity proved to be the Seventeenth's only combat jump. For the remainder of the war in Europe, Miley remained in Supreme Headquarters, Allied Expeditionary Force reserve, performing occupation duty.

On the other side of the world, Gen. Joseph M. Swing's Eleventh Airborne Division deployed to the Southwest Pacific Theater in May 1944 but was never used as a division in the airborne role for which it was conceived because of the shortage of troop-carrier planes and gliders. Gen. Swing was a US Military Academy classmate of Eisenhower and Bradley, and a former division artillery commander under Gen. Ridgway in the Eighty-Second. Gen. Swing served as Gen. Eisenhower's airborne advisor during the early stages of the Mediterranean campaign. Perhaps his most notable service before deployment to the Philippines was as the leader of the "Swing Board," a special War Department board formed in the wake of the Sicily debacle to determine policy on the mission and the scope of airborne programs and operations.

In February 1943, Gen. Swing activated the Eleventh Airborne Division. For the next year he prepared the division for combat, overseeing every aspect of its training. Committed to combat on the island of Leyte in the Philippines in October 1944, the Eleventh Airborne Division was the only airborne division that saw combat in the Pacific war. The subsequent fighting on Luzon toughened the division and earned Gen. Swing a reputation as one of America's premier divisional commanders.

February 1945 also witnessed elements of the Eleventh Airborne participating in some of the most dangerous exploits in the unit's history. In mid-February, Col. George Jones, the commander of the 503rd Regimental Combat Team, recaptured Corregidor in what was arguably the most difficult combat jump in World War II. While Gen. Swing and the remainder of the division pierced the Japanese Genko Line outside Manila, B

Company of 511th Parachute Infantry Regiment, commanded by Lt. Gen. John M. Ringler, joined the division's Provisional Reconnaissance Platoon in the liberation of 2,147 Allied civilians and prisoners of war interned at Los Banos camp on February 23.

Only the rapid collapse of Japanese resistance in the wake of Hiroshima and Nagasaki prevented Gen. Swing from spearheading the final invasion of Japan. To the surprise of no one in the Eleventh Airborne Division, Gen. Swing was in the first aircraft that landed at Atsugi Airfield near Yokohama on August 30 to begin the occupation of Japan. He immediately took charge of the air base and later met Gen. MacArthur, whom President Harry S. Truman had designated to receive the formal Japanese surrender.

A Fifth Airborne Division, the Thirteenth, commanded by Maj. Gen. George W. Griner, and later by Maj. Gen. Elbridge G. Chapman Jr., was activated on August 13, 1943, and deployed to Europe in the final stages of the war, although it saw no combat as a divisional entity and was frequently called on to furnish replacements for the Seventeenth, Eighty-Second and 101st divisions. At war's end, Gen. Chapman's Thirteenth Airborne Division was on standby near Auxerre, France, for possible airborne operations. Like Gen. Taylor's 101st Airborne Division, the Thirteenth was destined for Japan when the war ended.

In the final analysis, America's airborne commanders were a special breed of warriors. Dedicated professionals, they had matured in the interwar army, taking full advantage of the army's emphasis on institutionalized education. Ambitious and tough as steel, all relished their role in the pioneering effort of conducting airborne operations. Unaccustomed to leadership from the rear, each preferred to command from the forward echelons.

Gen. Gavin summed up what was required of airborne commanders in describing Gen. Ridgway in Sicily: "Lots of courage, he was right up front every minute. Hard as flint and full of intensity . . . sometimes it seemed as though it was a personal thing: Ridgway versus the Wehrmacht."

Not surprisingly, the commanding generals of America's elite divisions bequeathed a legacy of combat leadership that endures to the present day.

"WWII's Airborne Commanders—'The Stuff of Instant Legend'" was originally published in *ARMY Magazine* (July 1996).

32

World War II's Triumvirate of Dual-Theater Commanders

Gen. George C. Marshall viewed the selection of officers for high command as one of his most complicated and important duties as army chief of staff. Of the senior officers he selected for corps- and army-level command, only a few served with distinction in both the Pacific and the European Theaters of Operations. Heading the list of dual-theater commanders were Alexander M. Patch, J. Lawton Collins, and Charles H. Corlett.

Each member of this triumvirate graduated from the US Military Academy. None of their academic performances gave the slightest indication of the fame they would later achieve as combat commanders. Collins achieved the highest academic honors of the three, graduating Thirty-Fifth in the class of 1917, the same class that produced Mark Clark and Matthew Ridgway. Patch and Corlett ranked in the bottom third of the class of 1913.

Both Corlett and Patch served with the American Expeditionary Forces (AEF) in France in 1918. Then Capt. Patch commanded a battalion in the First Infantry Division during the Meuse–Argonne Offensive, while Corlett was the chief signal officer's executive officer in Gen. John J. Pershing's AEF. (Because of the nature of his assignment, Corlett did not serve in direct combat.) Collins remained stateside, but on promotion to captain in 1919 he deployed to Europe as a member of the Army of Occupation. All three men were also products of the Leavenworth system and the Army War College during the interwar period, and Collins was a graduate of the Army Industrial College as well.

By the eve of World War II, the three commanders were rising stars in an officer corps that Gen. Marshall was rapidly preparing for war. Each had demonstrated the vital qualifications of leadership, force, and vigor that Gen. Marshall demanded in his general officers. Collectively, Gens. Patch, Collins, and Corlett were exceptionally prepared for the challenge of high-level command. It was no surprise that the chief of staff summoned each for combat duty when the war tocsin sounded in the immediate aftermath of Pearl Harbor.

Patch was the first to receive the call. Four months before the Japanese attack, he was relieved of his duties as a regimental commander in the Ninth Infantry Division and placed in command of the Infantry Replacement Training Center at Camp Croft, South Carolina. In January 1942, then–Maj. Gen. Patch assumed command of Task Force 6814, responsible for the defense of New Caledonia and neighboring islands in the South Pacific. In cooperation with the military forces of the United Nations, Gen. Patch's mission was to hold New Caledonia against attack.

At a time when Japanese forces were advancing southward at an alarming rate, New Caledonia was critical in maintaining the logistical lifeline to Australia. In addition to his operational challenges, Gen. Patch became closely involved in improving relations with the French colonials. For his efforts in resolving problems arising from the delicate political situation, he received the Distinguished Service Medal. In May 1942, Gen. Patch assumed command of the Americal Division (Twenty-Third Infantry Division), a designation combining the words "America" and "Caledonia."

In October, Gen. Patch deployed elements of the Americal to Guadalcanal to reinforce troops led by Marine Gen. Alexander A. Vandegrift, who was engaged in a desperate struggle to seize the island. On November 19, Gen. Patch himself was on the scene, often operating within one hundred yards of the front lines. In accordance with original plans, he relieved Gen. Vandegrift in a simple ceremony on December 9. Gen. Patch had become the senior ground commander. Adm. William F. (Bull) Halsey Jr. immediately directed Gen. Patch to "eliminate all Japanese forces on Guadalcanal."

From December to February, intense fighting flared on Guadalcanal. Following a minor tactical setback, Gen. Patch, commanding XIV Corps, launched a series of offensives that culminated in the total destruction of

Japanese forces on the island. On February 9, he cabled Adm. Halsey: "Total and complete defeat of Japanese forces on Guadalcanal effected today. . . . Am happy to report . . . Tokyo Express no longer has terminus on Guadalcanal."

Adm. Halsey's candid response was typical: "When I sent a Patch to act as tailor for Guadalcanal, I did not expect him to remove the enemy's pants and sew it on so quickly."

Suffering from recurring bouts of malaria and pneumonia, Gen. Patch returned to the United States and took command of a training corps at Fort Lewis, Washington. Needing recuperation, he instead found himself in the center of a controversy when a reporter hinted that the general had leaked the fact that naval code breakers had broken the secret Japanese code that resulted in the death of Adm. Isoroku Yamamoto. An exchange of telegrams with Gen. Marshall resulted in some discomfort for Gen. Patch, but he soon found himself once again in a combat theater of operations.

As one of the few commanders with previous combat experience at both the division and the corps level, Gen. Patch should not have been surprised when, on March 1, 1944, he received command of the US Seventh Army—the army that Lt. Gen. George S. Patton Jr. had commanded so magnificently in Sicily. Gen. Patch's mission was to prepare his unit for the invasion of southern France. Code-named Anvil (and later changed to Dragoon in early July), the invasion of the Rhone Valley received Gen. Patch's full attention in the spring and summer of 1944. To the Seventh Army commander's immense relief, his knowledge of amphibious war in the Pacific gave him instant credibility among the Allied Mediterranean leadership.

Spearheaded by Maj. Gen. Lucian K. Truscott's VI Corps, Seventh Army attacked on August 15 and met with immediate success. Ever cognizant of the importance of Allied harmony as a result of his interaction with the French administration of New Caledonia, then–Lt. Gen. Patch insisted that French Gen. Jean-Marie de Lattre de Tassigny's Army B participate in the capture of the key ports of Toulon and Marseilles. The French captured both cities by August 28.

As the French consolidated the ports, Gen. Patch sent Gen. Truscott north to link up with elements of Gen. Patton's Third Army. Gen. Truscott's movement was nothing short of miraculous, confirming his reputation as one of the best fighting generals in the war. Months ahead of schedule, Seventh Army joined forces with Maj. Gen. Wade H. Haislip's XV Corps of Patton's Third Army on September 10 and 11. On September 15, Gen. Patch relinquished operational control of Dragoon forces to Lt. Gen. Jacob L. Devers, the newly activated commander of the US Sixth Army Group.

By any measure, Gen. Patch had performed superbly. The Allies captured fifty-seven thousand German prisoners in the first two weeks of the campaign alone, at a loss of only four thousand French, and twenty-seven hundred American casualties. Almost equally low casualty rates followed Dragoon all the way up the Rhone Valley. Most important, the Mediterranean ports provided the logistical support that was crucial in maintaining Gen. Eisenhower's drive to the West Wall.

Gen. Patch's finest hour, however, lay ahead. As Gen. Devers directed his army group east, Gen. Patch's Seventh Army was the first Allied force to reach the Rhine on October 19. Led by Lt. Gen. Philippe Leclerc's Second French Armored Division, Seventh Army captured Strasbourg on November 23. A month later, the Germans counterattacked in the Ardennes and Gen. Patch was forced to halt his advance and defend the portion of the line vacated by Gen. Patton, whom Lt. Gen. Omar N. Bradley ordered to smash the southern shoulder of the Bulge.

Fortunately for the Allies, Ultra intercepts warned that the Germans were also planning for a limited offensive against Gen. Devers's Sixth Army Group. Intelligence indicated the Germans would attack between January 1 and 3. The attack, code-named Nordwind, began on New Year's Eve. The subsequent fighting in the Vosges Mountains produced some of the most intense combat of the war. By late January, Gen. Patch had halted the German offensive, destroying a large portion of the German Nineteenth Army in the process. On February 11, Gen. Patch received the Croix de Guerre with Palm and the Legion of Honor, Degree of Commander, from Charles de Gaulle for his leadership in stopping the German drive.

For the remainder of the war, Gen. Patch performed with characteristic vigor. On March 15, Seventh Army resumed the offensive aimed at piercing the Siegfried Line and securing the Saar-Palatinate region. Three days later, the German defenses collapsed. On March 26, Gen. Patch was across the Rhine. Three weeks later, Nuremberg fell, followed by the liberation of

Dachau on April 29. In May, Gen. Eisenhower issued a special order in which he said, "The whole Allied Expeditionary Force congratulates the Seventh Army on the seizure of Munich, the cradle of the Nazi beast."

V-E Day found Gen. Patch in the vicinity of Augsburg, in southern Bavaria. Three days earlier, Seventh Army had received the unconditional surrender of the remnants of the German Nineteenth Army. The same day, Gen. Patch, along with Gens. Devers and Haislip, received the surrender of German Army Group G, thus ending combat operations on the Seventh Army's front. For Gen. Patch, the war was over.

A warrior to the end, Gen. Patch died on November 21, a victim of the pneumonia that had plagued him throughout the war. Gen. Eisenhower, then the army chief of staff, eulogized his old friend, calling him a "soldier's soldier." His leadership in battle, both in the Pacific and in Europe, had contributed immeasurably to the defeat of his enemies. Gen. Eisenhower noted that Gen. Patch's most outstanding achievement in Europe was his brilliant leadership of the Seventh Army. In his assessment of army-level commanders, Gen. Eisenhower rated Gen. Patch third only to Gens. Patton and Truscott. As a commander of Allied forces, Gen. Patch was unsurpassed.

Like Gen. Patch, Gen. Collins served with distinction in the Pacific and Europe and commanded a division at Guadalcanal. Following a tour in the Philippines in the 1930s, Collins was on temporary duty with the secretariat of the general staff in Gen. Marshall's office during the early days of the European war. Detailed as chief of staff of VII Corps in January 1941, then–Col. Collins earned a reputation as a superb officer during the corps's large-scale maneuvers in the summer and autumn of 1941. At the outset of the Pacific War, Col. Collins was chief of staff to the commander of the Hawaiian Department, Lt. Gen. Delos C. Emmons.

While coordinating the ground defenses of Oahu, Collins received his first star on February 14, 1942. Two months later, he assumed command of the Twenty-Fifth Division and immediately began preparing the division for combat. He did not have to wait long. In October, Gen. Collins received orders to report to Gen. Douglas MacArthur's Southwest Pacific Theater. Diverted en route to Australia, Gen. Collins reported to Adm. Halsey in New Caledonia on December 10, 1942, in preparation to relieve the First Marine Division on Guadalcanal.

Assigned to Gen. Patch, Gen. Collins received the mission of relieving one of America's regiments without delay and, on completion of this relief, to seize and hold a line approximately three thousand yards to the west, in preparation for a coordinated attack to eliminate the Japanese forces on Guadalcanal. On January 10, Gen. Collins launched his first attack. Despite increasing casualties, the division's initial assault was successful. In the process, Gen. Collins received the sobriquet of "Lightning Joe," a derivative of "lightning," the telephone code of division headquarters.

On January 22, Gen. Patch launched XIV Corps in a final assault to eliminate Japanese resistance. Again Gen. Collins provided the main effort of the corps, enveloping the enemy's southern flank. Forsaking the policy in which officers in the South Pacific did not wear their insignia of rank for fear of attracting snipers, Collins wore his two stars on his collar. His inspiration was instrumental in the American victory. Gen. Patch cited the Twenty-Fifth ("Tropic Lightning") Division for its rapid advance and skillful maneuver in breaking the enemy's power to offer further effective defense.

Subsequent fighting in New Georgia added luster to Collins's rising star. While on leave in Washington in December 1943, he paid a call on Gen. Marshall, who queried him on the operations in the Pacific. Unbeknownst to Collins, Eisenhower was negotiating with Marshall concerning the identity of the assault corps commanders for Operation Overlord. Above all, Eisenhower needed an experienced combat commander to lead the amphibious assault. Though he preferred Truscott, Eisenhower gladly settled on Collins when Truscott's presence was required at Anzio. Consequently, Collins received command of VII Corps on February 12. At age forty-seven, he was the youngest corps commander in active service.

Gen. Collins commanded VII Corps for the remainder of the war in Europe, and the corps's performance was legendary. In preparation for D-Day, Gen. Collins drilled his men in the lessons he had learned in conducting amphibious operations in the South Pacific. Landing on Utah Beach, VII Corps soon joined the paratroopers of the Eighty-Second and 101st Airborne Divisions. Ashore himself on D+1, Gen. Collins directed the efforts to sever the Cotentin Peninsula and to isolate Cherbourg. After rapidly expanding the bridgehead, he captured the crucial port on June 27, 1944.

As elements of VII Corps mopped up Cherbourg, Gen. Collins prepared to lead the main assault of Operation Cobra, Gen. Bradley's plan to break the stalemate in Normandy. Again, the VII Corps commander performed brilliantly, transforming Gen. Bradley's breakthrough to a breakout. It was Gen. Collins, instinctively surmising that the German defenses were on the verge of collapse, who committed the armor divisions that swept to Coutances, France. As one historian correctly noted, it was Gen. Collins who carried the ball in Normandy. And it was he who blunted the German counterattack at Mortain, thus enabling the Allies to close the Falaise pocket.

In the advance across France and Belgium, Gen. Collins again was in the vanguard of Lt. Gen. Courtney H. Hodges's First Army. By September 5, VII Corps was on the Meuse. Liege fell on September 7. Following a temporary halt because of gasoline shortages, Gen. Collins plunged ahead, attacking Aachen and the dense Hurtgen Forest about ten miles to the south. The Germans in Aachen surrendered on October 19. The Hurtgen Forest was a tougher nut to crack.

In retrospect, Gen. Collins called the Aachen–Hurtgen campaign the toughest, most costly of the VII Corps's operations in Europe. Though he naturally defended his corps's actions in the campaign, Gen. Collins failed to display the imagination that had characterized his previous battles in the campaign in Normandy and subsequent drive to the German border. It is true that the forested terrain did not provide many opportunities for maneuver, but VII Corps's operations resulted in attrition that needlessly bloodied frontline divisions and resulted in unnecessary casualties. Gen. Collins did not clear the forest until December 9.

Within three weeks, he was thrown into the line to stem the German offensive in the Ardennes. Defending a portion of the northern shoulder, VII Corps again performed admirably. On January 3, 1945, Gen. Collins resumed the offensive with the Second and Third Armored Divisions in the lead. Attacking until January 22, when it was pinched from the line by the convergence of Gen. Ridgway's XVIII Airborne and Gen. Patton's III, VII Corps achieved all their objectives.

Long known as Gen. Bradley's "fair-haired boy," Gen. Collins also attracted the growing admiration of the Supreme Commander. As early as January 1945, Gen. Eisenhower wrote Gen. Marshall that the Battle of the Bulge only added to the excellent reputation Gen. Collins enjoyed at Supreme Headquarters, Allied Expeditionary Force (SHAEF). Gen. Eisenhower often noted that Gen. Collins was one of the finest officers in his command and that if vacancies ever occurred in army command, he would be immediately selected. Of the corps commanders in the AEF, only Gen. Collins was acceptable to the Supreme Commander to fill the impending vacancy of SHAEF's operations officer.

In the war's waning months, Gen. Collins led VII Corps across the Roer to the Ruhr. In Cologne, VII Corps captured its 140,000th prisoner since D-Day. Crossing the Rhine on March 14, Gen. Collins formed the northern flank of Gen. Bradley's thrust east of the river. Again Gen. Collins played a critical role in the destruction of a German army. Encircling the Ruhr pocket from the south, VII Corps joined Lt. Gen. William H. Simpson's Ninth Army on April 1, surrounding more than 325,000 Germans. Shortly thereafter, Gen. Eisenhower formally recommended Collins for promotion to lieutenant general, which he received on April 16.

Gen. Eisenhower's recommendation was based on Gen. Collins's performance from Normandy to the German frontier. The VII Corps commander had repeatedly demonstrated that he was a master of tactics and a dynamic leader. Faced with difficult tactical situations, Gen. Collins had never once failed to conduct his battles to the entire satisfaction of his army and army group commanders. In overall ability, Gen. Eisenhower rated the VII Corps commander second only to Lt. Gen. Leonard T. (Gee) Gerow, whom he had elevated to command the Fifteenth Army. Gen. Bradley concurred, rating Gen. Collins as his best corps commander during the campaign in northwest Europe.

In the war's final month, Gen. Collins completed another encirclement in the Harz Mountains pocket. In the process, VII Corps collected another eighty thousand prisoners. In May, Gen. Collins went to Torgau, where he personally met the lead elements of the Soviet Army on the Elbe. Thus ended Gen. Collins's combat experience in World War II. Directed to join Gen. MacArthur for the final invasion of Japan, Gen. Collins was in California when news of events in Hiroshima and Nagasaki signaled the end of hostilities.

Pete Corlett was also an aggressive and well-respected corps commander. He acquired expertise in amphibious warfare in the Gulf of Alaska and the Shelikof Strait, where he served as commander of Fort Greeley, Alaska, before the war. A superb trainer, he examined every aspect of amphibious operations, concentrating on indirect fire support for assaulting units, combat loads for individual soldiers, and command and control between ship and shore. For him, Kodiak Island and the Aleutians, with their perilous tides and rugged terrain, were the natural training grounds for amphibious warfare.

Following his capture of Kiska from the Japanese, Corlett found himself promoted to commander of the Seventh Infantry Division. His mission from Adm. Chester W. Nimitz was to capture Kwajalein Island in the Marshall archipelago. Improving on the amphibious techniques used so successfully in the Aleutians, Corlett attacked on January 30, 1944.

Kwajalein fell a week later, at a cost of 372 killed and 1,600 wounded. Japanese losses were more than twenty times Corlett's casualties. He earned the Naval Distinguished Service Medal and the Silver Star for gallantry in an operation that Gen. Marshall said approached perfection. Unfortunately, the rigors of Pacific combat exacerbated Gen. Corlett's lifelong struggle with pneumonia.

Gen. Marshall thought that Gen. Corlett's knowledge of amphibious operations might be useful to the Overlord planners, so he dispatched him to Europe in March 1944. There, Gen. Corlett found that his combat experience in the Pacific was of little interest to the SHAEF planners. Gen. Patton, no stranger to amphibious operations, was equally skeptical. In his diary, Gen. Patton noted that Gen. Eisenhower had sent for a general "who had captured a Pacific Island in a 'nearly perfect' maneuver." He then added sarcastically that Gen. Corlett did not have to fight until after he got ashore. Upset that the Supreme Commander had drawn on his own reservoir of knowledge concerning amphibious warfare, Gen. Patton stated that Gen. Eisenhower tended to underrate all Americans who served under him and overrate Americans, obviously including Gen. Corlett, who had served elsewhere.

The advanced state of planning for the invasion of Normandy resulted in Gen. Eisenhower assigning Gen. Corlett command of XIX Corps, one of the follow-up corps. Hurt that neither Gen. Eisenhower nor Gen. Bradley ever mentioned his record in the Pacific, Gen. Corlett recommended alterations in the fire support plan and voiced his concern about the low ammunition allocation of the assaulting corps. To his chagrin, his ideas were brushed off, giving Gen. Corlett the impression that senior SHAEF officials regarded the Pacific theater as "bush-league stuff, meriting no consideration." What Gen. Corlett did bring to the European Theater was knowledge of commanding large units in combat.

On June 12, however, XIX Corps moved into the line and immediately made an impact. It was Gen. Corlett's corps that finally captured Saint-Lô on July 18 through 19, making Gen. Collins's subsequent breakout a possibility. Protecting Gen. Collins's exposed flank as Cobra became a reality, Gen. Corlett blocked German counterattacks to reestablish a defensive line across the Cotentin Peninsula. On August 31, Gen. Eisenhower wrote Gen. Marshall, informing the chief of staff that Gen. Corlett was capable of handling an army.

Gen. Hodges, First US Army commander and Gen. Corlett's immediate superior, did not agree. Although Corlett's corps was one of the first Allied forces to enter Belgium, Gen. Hodges remained extremely critical of what he termed Corlett's "snail pace" as First Army attempted to close the Aachen gap. Dissatisfied at Gen. Corlett's progress against the fortifications of the Siegfried Line, Gen. Hodges demanded speed. On more than one occasion he and Gen. Corlett had heated exchanges. Under terrific pressure and sustaining inordinate casualties, Gen. Corlett finally closed the gap with Gen. Collins on October 17. The action came too late to save Gen. Corlett, however.

On October 18, on Gen. Hodges's recommendation, Gen. Bradley relieved Gen. Corlett, "without prejudice and without reflection of his ability as a commander." Gen. Corlett's final meeting with Gen. Hodges was short but courteous. There was no love lost between the two commanders.

The official explanation for his dismissal was Gen. Corlett's declining health. (In the relief order, Gen. Bradley noted that Gen. Corlett was not in good health and that he had shown signs of being tired.) Gen. Eisenhower cabled Gen. Marshall on October 20, telling him that he was sending Gen. Corlett home for a physical checkup and rest. Placing Gen. Corlett on sixty days detached service, Gen. Eisenhower requested that he return to theater as soon as the War Department determined he was fit for duty. For Gen. Corlett, however, the war in Europe was over.

Too professional a soldier to complain about what he obviously considered a severe injustice, Gen. Corlett bore his disappointment well. In January 1945, Gen. Marshall rewarded him with command of XXXVI Corps and again ordered him to the Pacific. Before he could deploy, the European war intervened, and the divisions designated for XXXVI Corps were dispatched to Europe in the wake of the Ardennes Offensive. Consequently, XXXVI Corps reverted to a training headquarters with no active units assigned. When V-J Day arrived, Gen. Corlett was preparing divisions returning from Europe for deployment to the Pacific. He never saw combat again.

In assessing Gen. Corlett's performance as a corps commander, Gen. Bradley ranked him at number twenty among active commanders in theater. Gen. Corlett failed to make Gen. Eisenhower's list of the top thirty-eight officers. Did Gen. Corlett receive a raw deal from Gens. Bradley and Hodges? It is hard to say. By his own admission he was tired, rundown, and perhaps sick. Moreover, his temper was short, and he found himself at odds with his commander. As the Supreme Commander remarked to his chief of the operations division in December 1944, some officers did not realize they were momentarily exhausted. Gen. Corlett fell into this category.

His relief in no way detracted from an extraordinary career. Since 1941, he had been in positions of great responsibility. Gen. Corlett had organized the army base at Kodiak and been in temporary command of the Alaskan Department during the naval battle at Attu and during the intensive bombing and reconnaissance of Kiska, and organized, planned, and commanded the expedition that seized Kwajalein. He had commanded the XIX Corps through France, Belgium, Holland, and into Germany. And at war's end, Gen. Corlett stood ready to command an expedition to seize the Kuril Islands and then participate in the assault on the Japanese home islands.

In retrospect, Gens. Patch, Collins, and Corlett formed a unique triumvirate of commanders. Viewed by some officers as interlopers from the Pacific, they overcame prejudices and met the challenges of dual-theater command. Far more important than their expertise in conducting amphibious operations was their experience directing divisions and corps, which each brought from the Pacific to the European Theater. It was the combat experience gained on Guadalcanal, Kwajalein, Kiska, and New Georgia that contributed most to Allied success in the campaigns in France and Germany.

Of the three, Gen. Collins ranked highest in the estimation of Gens. Marshall, Eisenhower, and Bradley. Gen. Collins may well have been the best corps-level commander of the war. Gen. Patch also demonstrated superb leadership skills. His direction of Seventh Army rivaled that of the more flamboyant Gen. Patton and exceeded that of Gens. Hodges and Simpson in the Supreme Commander's estimation.

As for Gen. Corlett, he never overcame the impression that he was an "outsider from the other theater." Still, he performed with distinction at the corps level and was the only member of the trio who commanded a combat corps in both the Pacific and the European Theaters. Along with Gens. Patch and Collins, Gen. Corlett made significant but largely unrecognized contributions to the Allied victory.

"World War II's Triumvirate of Dual-Theater Commanders" was originally published in *ARMY Magazine* (September 1996).

33

Army Commanders in the Pacific

Forgotten Warriors

To a majority of Americans, World War II in the Pacific is perceived as primarily a naval war. Images of battleships ablaze in Pearl Harbor, the great carrier battles at Midway and the flag raising on Mount Suribachi have all but eclipsed the mighty contribution of the US Army. All these years after Gen. Douglas MacArthur received the Japanese surrender aboard the USS *Missouri*, few but veterans and historians recall the heroic efforts of the army's frontline commanders.

Over the course of the war, the United States employed three armies and twenty-one divisions in the Pacific Theater, excluding the units serving in the China–Burma–India Theater, as opposed to forty divisions in Europe by the fall of 1944. The preponderance of troops had deployed to the Pacific in 1942. Once the army committed troops to the Mediterranean Theater and the buildup for the cross-channel attack, not one new division was deployed to the Pacific after September 1944.

Who led the American forces who served so gallantly in the jungles of New Guinea, the Philippines, and Okinawa? Aside from MacArthur, Robert L. Eichelberger, and Joseph W. (Vinegar Joe) Stilwell, who else commanded the US Army in the Southwest and Central Pacific? Three commanders in particular—Jonathan M. Wainwright, Walter Krueger, and Simon B. Buckner Jr.—served with highest distinction during operations in the Pacific.

Largely forgotten after the fall of Bataan and Corregidor, Wainwright spent the remainder of the war in a prisoner of war camp. Krueger, the most successful of the three, commanded the Sixth Army in the campaigns "from down under to Nippon" (the title he gave his memoirs of the Pacific war). Buckner, who commanded the Tenth Army and whose father was a well-recognized hero of the Confederacy, was killed in action. Although each encountered a different fate, all three contributed mightily to the Allied victory.

Gen. Wainwright was near the end of an illustrious military career when he boarded the US Army transport *Grant* in September 1940, en route to the Philippines. A 1906 graduate of the US Military Academy, Wainwright, like MacArthur, earned the distinction of being selected first captain of the Corps of Cadets.

Following a career in the cavalry, Wainwright was returning to the islands where he first experienced combat against the Moros in 1909. He commanded the Philippine Division, which contained, in addition to a large contingent of Filipino troops, the largest American Army unit in the islands.

As the United States and Japan moved to the precipice of war, Wainwright, having become MacArthur's senior field commander, assumed command of the North Luzon Force, which consisted of four infantry (Philippine Army) divisions and one cavalry regiment. One of the divisions (the Seventy-First) could be committed only on the authority of MacArthur. Wainwright's orders were to protect airfields and prevent hostile landings in his area. MacArthur's plan called for "no withdrawal from beach positions."

Following the near annihilation of MacArthur's air force on Clark Field on the opening day of the war, Wainwright prepared for the inevitable invasion. By his own admission, inadequate time to prepare his force had left the untrained and ill-equipped Philippine army units with the North Luzon Force doomed even before they encountered the invading Japanese force. Following initial landings on December 10, 1941, in northern Luzon, the Japanese struck in force at Lingayen Gulf in the gray dawn of December 22. The transports conveyed the Japanese Fourteenth Army commanded by Lt. Gen. Masaharu Homma. Philippine resistance was light as many frontline units deserted their beach defenses. Homma's troops quickly forced Wainwright to withdraw to stronger defensive lines across the central Luzon plain.

One day after the Lingayen Gulf landings, Gen. MacArthur issued War Plan Orange-3, a contingency plan that called for a withdrawal to the Bataan Peninsula and the evacuation of Manila. Wainwright's mission was crucial—he was to conduct a delaying action on successive lines to the final defensive position on Bataan.

Of the five defensive lines, only the last was to be organized for a protracted defense. Wainwright supervised the operation with characteristic efficiency and soon MacArthur's force was united on the Bataan Peninsula. Unfortunately, MacArthur had not accumulated adequate supplies on Bataan to withstand a protracted siege if immediate reinforcements were not received from American bases in the Pacific.

The defense of Bataan officially began on January 7, 1942. On that day Wainwright took command of the western sector of the Bataan Defense Force, which became I Philippine Corps, consisting of three Philippine army divisions and miscellaneous troops—about twenty-five thousand soldiers in all. With most of the Japanese effort directed against the eastern defenses of the peninsula, Gen. Wainwright conducted a series of limited counterattacks but was forced to give ground. His personal leadership galvanized his soldiers on more than one occasion. By late January, however, the limited depth of Bataan precluded further withdrawal.

After President Franklin D. Roosevelt ordered MacArthur to Australia to prepare for the Allied counteroffensive, Wainwright assumed command of the Luzon force, in March 1942. Though Gen. MacArthur intended to retain command in the Philippines from his base in Australia, Gen. George C. Marshall had other ideas. Nominating Wainwright for promotion to lieutenant general "because of the confidence I have in your leadership and in the superb gallantry of the devoted band of American and Filipino soldiers under your command," Gen. Marshall prepared a communiqué for the president's signature that appointed Wainwright commander of all US forces in the Philippines.

Transferring his headquarters to Corregidor, Gen. Wainwright directed the defense of Bataan. Command of the Luzon Force was assigned to Maj. Gen. Edward P. King Jr., an artillerist who had served as Gen. MacArthur's principal fire support officer since the outbreak of war. For the next four weeks, the line successfully resisted Japanese penetration and envelopment efforts. In savage fighting, the Bataan force eliminated numerous pockets of enemy resistance and annihilated several amphibious task forces. On the verge of starvation and running dangerously low on supplies and ammunition, the US forces refused to capitulate. In the process, the "battling bastards of Bataan" inspired a nation.

On March 28, Gen. Homma launched a major offensive but was repelled. Three days later he attacked again but was again beaten by what Gen. Wainwright called "the bayonets of malarial men with not enough food in their bellies to sustain a dog." On April 9, Gen. King, unable to sustain organized resistance and without the approval of Gen. Wainwright, surrendered.

With the fall of Bataan, Gen. Wainwright's days on Corregidor were numbered. Under direct artillery fire, the garrison on the island began a twenty-seven-day battle for survival. Refusing to fire on the tip of Bataan for fear of hitting his captured men, Gen. Wainwright prepared for the inevitable. On May 4, the tempo of the shelling increased significantly. On the following morning, Japanese forces landed on Corregidor. With no antitank guns, the garrison fought in vain to withstand the combined arms assault. On May 6, 1942, Gen. Wainwright, with "profound regret and with continued pride in his gallant troops," went to meet the Japanese commander.

Forced to surrender all American and Filipino troops in the Philippine archipelago, Gen. Wainwright spent the remainder of the war in a series of prison camps. Gen. Marshall sought to award him the Medal of Honor for his spirited defense of the Philippines, but Gen. MacArthur intervened, stating that it "would be a grave injustice to a number of other general officers of practically equally responsible positions who . . . exhibited powers of leadership and inspiration to a degree greatly superior to that of General Wainwright." It was Gen. MacArthur at his vindictive worst, having ignored the fact that he had received the Medal of Honor under similar circumstances. Gen. Marshall quietly shelved the nomination, but he planned to resubmit it at a more opportune time.

In his memoirs, Gen. Wainwright described his first day of captivity as "the beginning of hell." Haunted for the remainder of the war for surrendering his command and unsure of whether his name had been sullied by his action, Wainwright endured unspeakable mental and physical hardships. A prisoner for three years, he was moved from Formosa to Kyūshū, then to Korea, and finally to Manchuria. Not until August 16, 1945, did Wainwright discover the war was over. He had endured nearly 1,200 days of captivity.

Arrangements were hastily made to have Gen. Wainwright witness the formal surrender of the Empire of Japan aboard the USS *Missouri*. On August 31, 1945, his plane landed at Yokohama, and he was quickly ushered in to see his former commander. Grasping Gen. Wainwright's hand, Gen. MacArthur, for once in his life, was speechless. He noted later that "the emotion registered on that gaunt face still haunts me." All Gen. Wainwright asked of his chief was command of a corps, the same command that he had exercised in 1942.

To his great satisfaction, Gen. Wainwright occupied the position of honor behind the Supreme Commander during the ceremony, and he received one of the pens used by Gen. MacArthur to sign the instrument of surrender. On September 10, Gen. Wainwright received the ultimate tribute for a soldier. In a public ceremony at the White House, President Harry S Truman awarded him the Medal of Honor. Neither Gen. Marshall nor the nation had forgotten.

Gen. Krueger, like Gen. Wainwright, served under Gen. MacArthur with gallantry and determined leadership. A sixty-one-year-old career soldier at the outbreak of the war, Krueger first joined the army as a private during the Spanish–American War. Commissioned in 1901, he was a product of the army's institutional emphasis on professional education. A graduate of the Army War College and the Naval War College, Krueger commanded various infantry units in his career, including the Sixth Infantry Regiment, Sixteenth Infantry Brigade and Second Infantry Division. He also commanded VIII Corps before assuming command of Third Army in 1941. During the Texas–Louisiana maneuvers of September 1941, Krueger's Third Army performed superbly, largely because of the organizational brilliance of its chief of staff, then–Col. Dwight D. Eisenhower. Of the forty-two division, corps, and army commanders who participated in the maneuvers, only eleven went on to significant combat commands in World War II. Of these, only Krueger and George S. Patton Jr. led field armies in combat.

Gen. Marshall's decision to keep Gen. Kreuger spoke well of Krueger's potential for wartime leadership. Long determined to avoid sending American soldiers into combat under general officers too old to command troops in battle under the terrific pressures of modern warfare, Gen. Marshall decided to place the army's fate in the hands of leaders who could stand up to "the severest tests which he could devise in time of peace." Of all the senior generals (corps and army commanders) "of the line" at the time Gen. Marshall became chief of staff, only one—Gen. Krueger—was given command of US troops in battle.

On January 12, 1943, Krueger received a radiogram informing him that the commander in chief of the Southwest Pacific Area had requested the immediate transfer of Gen. Krueger and Third Army Headquarters to the Pacific. Gen. MacArthur was particularly anxious to work with Gen. Krueger, who had been chief of his war plans divisions during Gen. MacArthur's tenure as army chief of staff. Moreover, Gen. Krueger had been intimately involved in developing amphibious doctrine and was the army's foremost expert in joint operations.

Though Gen. MacArthur's request for the transfer of Third Army was turned down, Gen. Krueger received orders to organize and activate the headquarters of a new army, which he did in January 1943.

Gen. Krueger and the forward elements of his newly designated Sixth Army arrived in Brisbane, Australia, in February 1943. To circumvent American forces serving under an Allied land forces commander who was Australian, Gen. MacArthur created an independent tactical organization known as Escalator Force (later called Alamo Force) to conduct operations. As in the Philippines, MacArthur formulated all strategic plans, issued directives designating the operations and commanders, and provided the resources to conduct them, but he did not prescribe the tactical measures or methods to be employed. This was Gen. Krueger's responsibility.

In the ensuing campaign, Gen. MacArthur and the Third Fleet commander, Adm. William F. (Bull) Halsey Jr., launched a series of strikes to follow up Allied success in New Guinea and the Solomons. The ultimate prize was the Japanese stronghold at Rabaul on the island of New Britain. The immediate objective was the seizure of airfields along the New Guinea and Solomon coasts from which to whittle down the enemy's strength and provide air cover for future Allied assaults. Gen. Krueger seized the Woodlark and Kiriwina Islands, followed by a series of amphibious assaults on New Britain. Subsequent directives from the combined chiefs of staff directed Gen. MacArthur to neutralize rather than capture Rabaul.

During the ensuing campaign, dubbed Operation Cartwheel, Gen. Krueger superbly orchestrated a series of amphibious landings that demonstrated his expertise in conducting joint operations.

To complete the encirclement of Rabaul in February 1944, Gens. MacArthur and Krueger next turned to the Admiralty Islands in the Bismarck Archipelago. Again Gen. Krueger's efforts were successful. By mid-1944, Gen. Krueger had ten American divisions under his command as he continued his advance up the coast of Dutch New Guinea. The substantial increase and the complexity of operations in the Southwest Pacific Area led Gen. MacArthur to activate the Eighth Army under the command of Gen. Eichelberger. At the same time, Gen. MacArthur formally dissolved Alamo Force, thus casting aside the thinly veiled disguise that Gen. Krueger's Sixth Army had worn for two years.

Krueger became the linchpin of Gen. MacArthur's greatest campaign, the reconquest of the Philippines. As overall commander of ground troops, Gen. Krueger commanded the forces in what Gen. MacArthur labeled the crucial battle of the war in the Pacific. On Krueger's shoulders rested the fate of the Philippines and the future of the war against Japan. On October 20, 1944, A-Day (in the Pacific, commanders used designations other than D-Day to indicate the date for launching a major operation), Sixth Army battled ashore. While the greatest naval battle in history raged in Leyte Gulf, Gen. Krueger's force secured the beachhead and moved inland. By December 26, Gen. MacArthur reported the Leyte–Samar campaign closed except for minor mopping-up. Unfortunately, it took Gen. Eichelberger's veterans months to eliminate several "minor" pockets of staunch Japanese resistance. In the interim, Gen. Krueger secured Mindoro, an island across the narrow Verde Island Passage from Luzon.

Relinquishing control of all troops, duties and missions in the Mindoro area to Eighth Army on January 1, 1945, Gen. Krueger prepared for the final assault on Luzon. The major combat units initially available to Sixth Army for the Luzon campaign were the I Corps (commanded by Maj. Gen. Innis P. Swift), XIV Corps (commanded by Maj. Gen. Oscar W. Griswold), the 158th Infantry Regimental Combat Team, Thirteenth Armored Group, and two infantry divisions in reserve (the Twenty-Fifth Infantry Division and the Eleventh Airborne Division). The initial combat strength of Sixth Army, excluding the Eleventh Airborne Division, was

152,447. Other units joined the troop list when the full extent of Japanese forces was finally realized.

Landings on Luzon began on January 9, 1945. Initial opposition was light but steadily stiffened as Gen. Krueger's forces advanced down the central Luzon plain. All the while, Gen. MacArthur exerted enormous pressure on Gen. Krueger to accelerate Sixth Army's advance to recapture the Philippine capital as quickly as possible. According to MacArthur biographer D. Clayton James, Gen. Krueger ranked next to Lt. Gen. Richard K. Sutherland, Gen. MacArthur's chief of staff, as the officer who most frequently felt the wrath of the Old Man.

Gen. Krueger secured Manila on February 27, but desperate fighting continued on Luzon long after that. By June 30, Sixth Army controlled most of the island, but an estimated twenty-five thousand Japanese troops remained in the mountains. The following day, Gen. Eichelberger's Eighth Army assumed responsibility for operations on Luzon and for clearing the remaining islands. Gen. MacArthur declared the Philippine Islands secure on July 4, 1945, but the cost had been high. Battle casualties numbered 8,140 killed, 29,557 wounded, and 157 missing. Noncombat casualties were proportionately higher. In turn, Gen. Krueger and his men killed 173,563 and wounded 7,297 of their adversaries while engaging and defeating the largest Japanese Army encountered in the Pacific war.

Though MacArthur at times found Krueger less than enterprising and even timid, he had reason to be pleased with his senior army commander. Even at the height of his dissatisfaction with Krueger's progress, MacArthur recognized the Sixth Army commander's distinguished record by nominating him for promotion to four stars in February 1945. Krueger received his promotion on March 5, well ahead of Gen. Bradley and other European Theater commanders. It was a fitting tribute to a great soldier.

The Luzon campaign terminated Gen. Krueger's combat service. Entrusted by Gen. MacArthur to command American ground forces for Operation Olympic—the initial invasion of Kyūshū in November—Gen. Krueger was ecstatic when Japan accepted the Potsdam ultimatum on August 14, 1945. His remaining days in the Pacific were confined to occupation duty in Kyūshū and western Honshu. On December 31, 1945, Sixth Army relinquished its occupation duties to Eighth Army and redeployed to the United States.

Unlike Gens. Wainwright and Krueger, Simon B. Buckner Jr. never served in the Southwest Pacific Theater. His opportunity to command a field army occurred in support of Adm. Chester W. Nimitz's Central Pacific drive. His tragic death at the moment of victory denied him his place in the pantheon of American military heroes.

Born on July 18, 1886, Buckner spent two years at the Virginia Military Institute before receiving his appointment to the US Military Academy in 1904. He graduated four years later and selected Infantry as his brand of service. Exemplary service in Panama and the Philippines, coupled with a distinguished record as a trainer and educator, led to his appointment as commandant of cadets at the US Military Academy in 1933. His future adversary on Okinawa, Lt. Gen. Mitsuru Ushijima, held a similar post at the Japanese Imperial Military Academy.

The years before the war saw Buckner in a variety of training and inspection tours. He became a colonel in 1937 and attained the rank of brigadier general on September 1, 1940. From 1940 to 1944, Gen. Buckner was the senior army officer serving in the Alaskan Defense Command (later redesignated the Alaskan Department) at Fort Richardson, Alaska. Promoted to major general on the eve of war, Buckner played an instrumental role in the recovery of Attu in the Aleutians in May 1943 and was cited for "exceptionally distinguished and meritorious service."

Transferred to the Central Pacific Area in June 1944 after being promoted to lieutenant general, Buckner formally assumed command of Tenth Army in September. The remainder of the year found him training the force that would participate in Operation Iceberg, the code name for the invasion of Okinawa. His training program was later recognized by the presentation of the Navy Department's Distinguished Service Medal. Gen. Buckner's Tenth Army was made up of seven combat-experienced divisions in two combat corps, the all-Marine III Amphibious Corps of three divisions under Maj. Gen. Roy S. Geiger and the XXIV Army Corps of four divisions under Maj. Gen. John R. Hodge. Tenth Army included a total of 183,000 assault troops and 115,000 technical and logistical troops. Although Tenth Army had not previously directed combat operations, its corps and divisions had been combat-tested before the invasion of Okinawa.

American forces landed in Okinawa on Easter Sunday, April 1, 1945. Overall command of the invasion rested on Adm. Raymond A. Spruance; Gen. Buckner commanded the ground forces. With virtually no opposition, Tenth Army moved inland. Correspondent Ernie Pyle, covering a Marine regiment, noted the invasion beach was so calm, "there wasn't a dead or wounded man in our sector." The Marines quickly eliminated resistance on the northern part of Okinawa, and the area was declared secured by April 20. The situation in the south was far different. There, Gen. Ushijima had constructed a series of strong concentric defensive lines, centered on the ancient castle town of Shuri in the south-central portion of the island.

As casualties mounted, both on the ground and in the fleet, Gen. Buckner pushed steadily onward until he encountered the heavily fortified Shuri Line. Gen. Buckner's progress typified his personal approach to war—slow and methodical. Admirals Nimitz and Spruance, who were suffering heavy casualties to kamikaze raids, urged Gen. Buckner to speed up his advance, but he reminded his naval superiors that the land campaign was his responsibility. Preferring to attack deliberately with massive firepower rather than risk yet another amphibious assault, Gen. Buckner eschewed any suggestion of conducting an "end run" to outflank the Shuri Line. There would be no Anzio on Okinawa.

It was not until mid-May that Tenth Army captured Maeda Ridge and Sugar Loaf Hill and renewed its advance. On May 27, Gen. Buckner ordered his III Amphibious and XXIV Army Corps to maintain unrelenting pressure on the enemy. Shuri Castle was captured on the last day of May as Gen. Ushijima withdrew to a final offensive line. Gen. Buckner assured correspondents, "It's all over now but cleaning up pockets of resistance." For Gen. Buckner and Tenth Army, this would prove to be a colossal overstatement.

As the Americans advanced south from the Shuri Line, combat on Okinawa took its cruelest form. According to historian Allan R. Millett, "Every hill became a battleground of flying grenades and raking machine gun fire." To clear caves, the attackers used what Gen. Buckner described as his "blowtorch and corkscrew" method. Tank-infantry teams drilled holes in cave roofs and then used phosphorus grenades to ignite gasoline or napalm poured through the holes.

By mid-June it was only a matter of time for the American advance to complete the destruction of Ushijima's Thirty-Second Army. In the process Tenth Army lost its commander.

On June 18, Gen. Buckner visited the forward observation post of the Eighth Marine Regiment, Second Marine Division. Shortly after 1300 hours, a Japanese artillery observer spotted Buckner's party and launched a five-gun barrage. A round exploded overhead, sending shrapnel and a piece of coral into Gen. Buckner's chest. He was dead in ten minutes. No other member of his party suffered a scratch. Gen. Geiger assumed temporary command of Tenth Army until Gen. Marshall dispatched Gen. Stilwell on June 23.

Okinawa was the only Pacific campaign that took the lives of both opposing commanding officers. With Americans closing in on his headquarters, Gen. Ushijima committed ritual seppuku on June 22. Okinawa was declared secured on June 22, 1945, after eighty-three days of battle. Total American battle casualties were enormous, including 12,520 dead or missing and 36,631 wounded. Of the total, Tenth Army endured 4,582 killed, ninety-three missing, and 18,099 wounded. Gen. Ushijima's tenacious and spirited defense, with a force far larger than planners had anticipated, resulted in America's greatest number of casualties in the Pacific war.

Not surprisingly, Gen. Buckner attracted a great deal of criticism for his cautious tactics. Even Gen. MacArthur, quick to compare Operation Iceberg's high casualty figures with his own "moderate" totals for the entire Southwest Pacific Area from Melbourne to Tokyo, joined a chorus of Marine generals and Navy admirals in stating that the commanders on Okinawa had unnecessarily "sacrificed thousands of American soldiers." What Gen. MacArthur failed to appreciate was that Okinawa was the first battle in the Pacific in which a single American Army opposed a Japanese Army commanded by a defensive genius willing to sacrifice his entire force to forestall the impending invasion of the Japanese homeland. Stung by Gen. MacArthur's remarks, Adm. Nimitz supported his ground commander and refused to join the "Buckner-bashing" fray. Adm. Spruance, on the other hand, doubted "if the Army's slow, methodical method of fighting really saved any lives in the long run."

Monday-morning quarterbacking always produced brilliant and innovative tactics, but it seems inconceivable that Gen. Buckner, with complete air and sea superiority, opted for repeated frontal assaults when less costly options, such as secondary landings to envelop the Japanese defenses, were available. Had Buckner survived Okinawa, it is doubtful that Gen. MacArthur would have kept him in command for the forthcoming invasion of Japan. In Gen. MacArthur's eyes, Gen. Buckner was too heavily influenced by Adm. Nimitz, and MacArthur preferred his own man to command one of his armies.

On reflection, Gens. Wainwright, Krueger, and Buckner made contributions to victory that have been largely forgotten amidst the carnage of the Pacific war. Gen. Wainwright functioned best at the division and corps levels, where he was free to execute the quick, bold strokes that were the hallmark of the cavalry. As for Gen. Krueger's performance, Gen. MacArthur delivered the ultimate accolade. In *Reminiscences*, MacArthur wrote, "I do not believe that the annals of American history have shown him superior as an Army commander. Swift and sure in attack, tenacious and determined in defense, modest and restrained in victory—I do not know what he would have been in defeat, because he was never defeated."

Gen. Buckner's achievement is best reflected in the citation of his Distinguished Service Cross (posthumous), which states, "The outstanding leadership, tactical genius and personal courage of Gen. Buckner thoroughly inspired his command and culminated in final victory in Okinawa." It seems a fitting epitaph.

Collectively, Gens. Wainwright, Krueger, and Buckner inspired the nation and led the army to victory across the broad expanse of the Pacific, through the impenetrable jungles of the Philippines and over the fissured surface of Okinawa. History has not accorded them due credit for their achievements. Future generations will do well to include this trio of warriors in the Valhalla of military heroes.

"Army Commanders in the Pacific—Forgotten Warriors" was originally published in *ARMY Magazine* (November 1996).

34

World War II's Army Group Commanders

Travails and Triumphs

To conduct war in the European and Mediterranean theaters, the US Army adopted a unique organization based on the British model of an army group. The essential task of the army group commander was to coordinate the operations of two or more armies. Supreme Allied Commander Gen. Dwight D. Eisenhower, initially uncomfortable with such an organization, later viewed the arrangement as necessary to coordinate the actions of Allied armies that had increased in manpower and logistical resources to such an extent that they were beyond the capabilities of command and control of a single headquarters Though army group headquarters flourished in Europe, there was no such organization in the Pacific, where Gen. Douglas MacArthur preferred to control personally the actions of his respective armies.

In the final two years of the war, three American officers served as army group commanders. Along with British Field Marshal Sir Bernard L. Montgomery, who commanded the Twenty-First Army Group, Lt. Gens. Omar N. Bradley and Jacob L. Devers were Gen. Eisenhower's principal subordinates in the campaigns in France and Germany. The third member of this illustrious trio, Lt. Gen. Mark W. Clark, served in Italy under British Field Marshal Sir Harold Alexander. Having earned his reputation primarily as commander of Fifth Army, Gen. Clark found himself elevated to army group command only in the final six months of the war in the Mediterranean.

Foremost among the army group commanders was Bradley, commander of the Twelfth Army Group. At war's end, Bradley commanded the largest single American ground force in history, 1.5 million men in four armies. Yet many years after V-E Day, the verdict concerning the merits of Bradley's generalship remains debatable. Was Bradley the "GI's general," whom Ernie Pyle discovered in Sicily and whom Eisenhower proclaimed was "preeminent among the commanders of major battle in this war"? Or are two recent Patton biographers closer to the mark in speculating that had Bradley's and Patton's roles been reversed in northwest Europe, Germany would have never survived the catastrophic defeat in Normandy, and the war might have ended in autumn 1944?

Gen. Bradley's rise to the upper echelons of US Army command in Europe was not without merit. A classmate of Eisenhower at the US Military Academy, Bradley missed combat in World War I. An infantryman, Bradley attracted the attention of Marshall while the latter served as the assistant commandant of the Infantry School in 1930. As chief of the weapons section, Bradley made a favorable impression and entered Marshall's famed "black book," from which he chose many World War II commanders. A decade later, Marshall, then the deputy chief of staff, selected then–Lt. Col. Bradley to serve as a member of his personal secretariat.

Bradley's star continued to rise when, in February 1941, he became the first member of the US Military Academy class of 1915 to become a brigadier general. While performing his duties as commandant of the Infantry School at Fort Benning, Georgia, Bradley remained under the tutelage of Gen. Marshall. After commanding two stateside infantry divisions in rapid succession, Bradley received orders to join Gen. Eisenhower in North Africa.

Rushed to Eisenhower's headquarters in the wake of the Kasserine disaster, Bradley served as Gen. Eisenhower's "eyes and ears." When Lt. Gen. George S. Patton Jr. took command of US II Corps in March, he asked for Bradley as his deputy commander. Refining his knowledge of the art of war under Patton's guidance, Bradley took command in April, when Patton left to concentrate on planning for the invasion of Sicily. Under Gen. Bradley, II Corps captured Bizerte, and in the subsequent Sicilian campaign he again commanded II Corps with success. In the process,

Bradley confirmed Eisenhower's opinion that he was "the best-rounded combat leader in our service." More important, Bradley had demonstrated what Eisenhower termed a fine capacity for leadership and a thorough understanding of the requirements of battle.

Gen. Bradley received the coveted appointment to go to England and prepare the American forces for the Normandy invasion. Since the job involved activating, forming and organizing not only an army headquarters but also an army group, the officer Gen. Eisenhower selected would play the dominant role in the impending invasion. There was much to commend Gen. Bradley. He had demonstrated a talent for manipulating units in tightly contested fighting in the mountainous terrain of central Sicily, and he had never caused Gen. Eisenhower to worry. The campaign confirmed that Bradley had matured as a highly competent commander.

Not surprisingly, Gen. Bradley was the officer entrusted with commanding the American Army that stormed ashore at Omaha and Utah Beaches on D-Day. In the opening stages of the campaign, Gen. Bradley again demonstrated the cool leadership that had led to his selection as commander of the First US Army. Yet it was in Normandy that Bradley first attracted a fair amount of criticism for his orchestration of the battle. Bogged down in the bocage that prevented his army from employing the maximum range of weapons and mobility at its disposal, Gen. Bradley boldly conceived and executed Operation Cobra in late July. Spearheaded by Maj. Gen. Joseph L. (Lightning Joe) Collins's VII Corps, Cobra led to an unparalleled opportunity to destroy the German Army in France.

With the front burst wide open by Gen. Collins's advance and with Gen. Patton's Third Army newly activated, Gen. Bradley, commander of Twelfth Army Group, failed to close the Falaise–Argentan gap. Though Bradley later accepted full responsibility stating that he preferred "a solid shoulder at Argentan to the possibility of a broken neck at Falaise," he had the resources at hand to close the gap, and he did not. His error led to the escape of an estimated fifty thousand German troops and, more important, a substantial number of officers and headquarters that would reform to fight another day.

How could this have happened? The answer reflects Gen. Bradley's personal approach to war. As an infantryman, Bradley tended to concentrate on the close-in battle. He was best in planning the lodgment of the

Normandy beachhead and in mustering his force for a breakthrough at Saint-Lô. Given the fluidity of combat once the restrictions of mobility were removed, he was out of his element. While Gen. Patton, with his background as an armored commander, viewed battle as a series of movements over a number of map sheets, Gen. Bradley saw only grid squares. To paraphrase the Carthaginian Hamilcar Barca when he described Hannibal after the Battle of Cannae, Bradley knew how to gain a victory, but not how to use it.

In the subsequent drive to the West Wall, Gen. Bradley again proved his mettle. Not until the Germans attacked unexpectedly in the Ardennes in mid-December did criticism of Gen. Bradley's handling of the front reappear. This time it was Gen. Eisenhower who first grasped the severity and the extent of the German penetration and cautioned Gen. Bradley to send two armored divisions to reinforce Troy H. Middleton's struggling VIII Corps.

For his part, Gen. Bradley grossly misjudged the enemy's intention. Personally stung by talk of unpreparedness, a shocked Bradley reluctantly concurred with Eisenhower's transfer of Lt. Gen. Courtney H. Hodges's First Army and Lt. Gen. William H. Simpson's Ninth Army to Field Marshal Montgomery's Twenty-First Army Group to facilitate command and control of both sides of the "Bulge." With only Gen. Patton's Third Army at his disposal, Gen. Bradley later concluded that his acquiescence was one of his biggest mistakes of the war. The subsequent elimination of the Ardennes pocket by Montgomery and Patton only solidified Bradley's growing frustration with working alongside egotistical allies and difficult subordinates.

Understanding the humiliation Bradley perceived as a result of the loss of his armies to Montgomery at the height of the German counterattack, the Supreme Commander cabled Marshall in mid-January, writing that Bradley's record of solid accomplishment from the time he arrived in theater in February 1943 warranted favorable consideration for promotion to general. As for the near disaster in the Ardennes, Eisenhower noted that the real answer lay in the leadership exhibited by the commander in meeting unexpected problems. In this regard, Bradley had handled himself admirably after the initial offensive.

Bradley's management of the Twelfth Army Group's crossing of the Rhine also reflected well on him. He was quick to reinforce the Remagen bridgehead and relieved another corps commander whom he believed acted too cautiously in expanding the bridgehead. Bradley had acted forcefully and, along with Eisenhower, developed a strategy that led initially to the encirclement and destruction of German forces in the Ruhr and then to the final advance to the Elbe. It was Bradley's defining moment in the war.

By the close of the war in Europe, Bradley was undeniably Eisenhower's top lieutenant and his most indispensable subordinate. Eisenhower described Bradley as a "quiet but magnetic leader; able, rounded field commander; determined and resourceful; modest." Though latter-day historians would question Bradley's tactical competence, Eisenhower had no doubts. Eisenhower considered Bradley his most trusted adviser and most competent commander. In a final letter before Bradley left Europe to take up his new position as administrator of Veterans Affairs, Eisenhower conveyed his personal gratitude to Bradley for his leadership and forcefulness and for the professional capacity that made him one of America's great leaders and soldiers.

Like Bradley, Mark Clark was one of Eisenhower's friends and confidants. With the possible exception of Patton, Clark was Eisenhower's closest friend before the war. The war only served to strengthen the professional and personal bond that existed largely because Eisenhower owed much of his prewar success to his association with the officer whom Winston Churchill later dubbed the "American Eagle."

Born in Madison Barracks, New York, on May 1, 1896, Clark followed Devers and Bradley to the US Military Academy. Graduating in April 1917, Clark served with distinction with the Eleventh Infantry Regiment of the Fifth Division in France during World War I. While in temporary command of a battalion, Clark was seriously wounded near the Vosges Mountains, but he recovered sufficiently to join the General Staff Headquarters, First American Army. In that capacity, he participated in the Saint-Mihiel and Meuse–Argonne Offensives, but fame and glory eluded the ambitious young officer.

The interwar army found Clark attending the service schools that prepared talented officers for the responsibilities of wartime command. On graduation from the Army War College in 1937, Clark received his break.

Assigned to the General Staff Corps with duty with the Third Infantry Division at Fort Lewis, Washington, Clark immediately earned the reputation of being one of the army's premier trainers. At Fort Lewis, Clark also attracted the attention of George C. Marshall, who commanded the Division's Fifth Brigade at nearby Vancouver Barracks. Clark's evaluation of Marshall's performance in a mock exercise cemented the future chief of staff's favorable impression of Clark. Subsequent exercises organized by Clark also met Marshall's approval, and it became only a matter of time before Marshall, as deputy chief of staff, would summon Clark to Washington.

The call came soon enough, and Clark joined General Headquarters, US Army, as an operational planner and Brig. Gen. Lesley J. McNair's principal assistant. As he had with Bradley, Marshall recommended Clark for immediate promotion to brigadier general in July 1941, thereby skipping the grade of colonel. The 1941 Texas–Louisiana maneuvers justified Marshall's confidence in Clark's potential for senior command. It was also on Clark's recommendation that Marshall ordered Brig. Gen. Eisenhower to the War Plans Division in the aftermath of the Pearl Harbor disaster. Henceforth, the names of Eisenhower and Clark would be irrevocably linked. When Marshall later assigned Eisenhower command of the European Theater of Operations, US Army, he simultaneously appointed Clark commander of II Corps, the principal invading force for Operation Torch.

As the date for the invasion of North Africa approached, Clark, having become Eisenhower's deputy commander in chief and principal planner for Operation Torch, made a highly publicized, dangerous reconnaissance to Africa to arrange details for the proposed landings. His mission was a success, as were subsequent amphibious assaults on November 8, 1942. In Eisenhower's opinion, Clark had clearly demonstrated his potential for army-level command, but Clark's penchant for self-promotion antagonized many of his colleagues, who doubted the wisdom of appointing Clark as Eisenhower's deputy.

In early December Marshall designated Clark commanding general of Fifth Army, the first American Army to be activated in the European Theater. Although Patton was reportedly angered over Clark's receiving the coveted assignment, it was a logical choice. Clark was, in Eisenhower's words, the "best trainer, organizer, and planner I have ever met," and Fifth Army was essentially a training headquarters in early 1943. Despite being torn between loyalty for his two friends, Eisenhower heartily endorsed Marshall's decision.

In accepting command of Fifth Army, Clark may have missed a golden opportunity to command the American Army that would participate in the cross-channel invasion. Still, a "bird in the hand" was too attractive to release. In assessing the ambitious Clark, Eisenhower noted, "The title of Army commander was too attractive" and Clark had "begged and pleaded" for it "for some time." Clark's foremost biographer had argued that had Clark accepted the job of American advisor to Churchill instead of commander of Fifth Army, he might have been in the right place at the right time to have received the most coveted ground assignment of the war—command of the American invasion force in Normandy.

In September 1943, Clark and Fifth Army launched Operation Avalanche, the invasion of the Italian mainland. The enemy outnumbered Clark's initial assault force, which consisted of the British X Corps and US VI Corps. Determined German resistance left the American corps "badly bruised," and at the height of the battle Clark contemplated withdrawing his force. Only American firepower, coupled with timely reinforcement from Maj. Gen. Matthew B. Ridgway's Eighty-Second Airborne Division, prevented disaster. Clark's courageous leadership stiffened Anglo-American resolve, and he was instrumental in the final defeat of the German force.

Clark found the succeeding winter campaign equally frustrating. Not only did the British commander of Fifteenth Army Group downplay Clark's Fifth Army, but Hitler's decision to defend south of Rome also resulted in a war in which terrain played the dominant role in delaying the Allied advance. Naples fell on October 1, 1943, but progress was slow. Determined to reach Rome as expeditiously as possible, Clark's army slogged northward against a series of heavily defended lines.

January 1944 was a bad month for Mark Clark. His forward elements had inched northward until they encountered entrenched German divisions behind the Rapido River. In one of the more controversial decisions of the campaign, Clark ordered Maj. Gen. Fred L. Walker's Thirty-Sixth Infantry Division to cross the Rapido in an effort to ease the pressure from

Maj. Gen. John P. Lucas's forthcoming landing at Anzio, scheduled for January 22, 1944. It was an unmitigated disaster, with the division losing almost 1,700 men. Clark accepted initial blame, directing his frustration at Walker.

At the same time, Lucas struck at Anzio but failed to push on to the adjacent Alban Hills, possession of which would sever the German line of communications and force Germany to withdraw from southern Italy. Unfortunately, Clark had failed to convey his intent to Lucas, who in turn failed to display aggressive leadership. Clark believed that the establishment of the beachhead would suffice to weaken the German line, but he was mistaken. Instead of withdrawing, the Germans counterattacked with greater ferocity than at Salerno. Again, Clark contemplated withdrawal and relieved the VI Corps commander, this time replacing Lucas with Maj. Gen. Lucian K. Truscott Jr., who had distinguished himself in Sicily.

For several months, Fifth Army attempted to join with Truscott's besieged corps. During this time Clark experienced further disappointment. Halted for weeks before the Benedictine abbey atop Monte Cassino, Clark's troops suffered increasing casualties in an effort to penetrate the Gustav Line. What Clark needed most was a victory, but the Germans were in no mood to accommodate. Finally, Fifth Army, reinforced by the British Eighth Army, surged forward in a combined Fifteenth Army Group attack on May 11, 1944. German defenses collapsed, but Clark again failed to destroy the German force. Having advanced sixty miles in fourteen days, Fifth Army eventually joined with Truscott on May 25.

With his entire army once again intact, Clark abandoned British Gen. Alexander's instructions to cut Highway 6 and destroy the retreating German army. Instead, he directed the majority of his force toward Rome in an effort to capture the first Axis capital to fall into Allied hands. In a highly publicized ceremony, Clark led Fifth Army into the Italian capital on June 5. The Germans had long since escaped, but Clark had his moment of glory.

The capture of Rome was Clark's greatest triumph, but it was hardly his last. As the Allied armies surged north, Clark assumed command of Fifteenth Army Group in late November. At the same time, Alexander, promoted to field marshal, replaced Field Marshal Sir Henry M. Wilson as Supreme Allied Commander of the Mediterranean Theater of operations.

Clark's promotion, noted his biographer, was partly the result of Winston Churchill's esteem and admiration for Clark since 1942. Promotion to full general followed on March 10.

Clark did not disappoint Churchill. Under its new commanding general Fifteenth Army Group renewed its offensive as soon as the spring rains stopped, and sufficient infantry replacements arrived to fill Fifth Army's depleted ranks. In mid-spring, Bologna and the Po River Valley were in Clark's hands. On May 2, one day after Clark's forty-ninth birthday, German plenipotentiaries in Italy signed the instruments of unconditional surrender. Three days later, elements of the US Fifth and Seventh Armies joined hands at the Brenner Pass near Innsbruck. The war in the Mediterranean Theater was over. For Clark it was the moment of ultimate triumph. A lieutenant colonel in 1941, he was now a full general and, after Eisenhower, Bradley, and Patton, the most visible and highly acclaimed American general in the European Theater.

Though Clark had played a leading role in the Allied victory over Italy, his leadership remained controversial. His order to attack across the Rapido River, his relief of two corps commanders, his bombing of Monte Cassino, and his opting to seize Rome and stage a victory parade rather than trap the retreating Germans left questions concerning his tactical and operational acumen. Nor was he as successful as Eisenhower in mastering the art of coalition command. Moreover, Clark's paranoia about a British conspiracy to deny him and his Fifth Army their due marked him as a begrudging Allied commander at best. Yet it was Clark who stamped the indelible imprint of his personality on the Italian campaign. To Eisenhower, the "clever, shrewd and capable" Clark ranked fifth on his merit list of senior commanders.

Unlike Bradley and Clark, Jacob L. Devers never enjoyed a close personal relationship with the Supreme Commander. Yet his contributions to victory were on a par with his more famous contemporaries. Born in York, Pennsylvania, in 1887 Devers graduated from the US Military Academy in 1909, the same class that produced George S. Patton Jr., Robert L. Eichelberger, and William H. Simpson. For the next thirty years, Devers served in a variety of field artillery assignments and on the staff and faculty of the US Military Academy. From June 1939 to July 1940, he was chief of staff of the Panama Canal Department. In the autumn of 1940, Devers took command of Fort Bragg, North Carolina, and the Ninth Infantry Division. He oversaw an intensive training program for draftees and National Guard troops, as well as an extensive building program as the army expanded on the eve of America's entry into the war. His most notable assignment before combat in World War II was as chief of the armored force at Fort Knox, Kentucky, where he was instrumental in the mobilization and training of the force that proved so decisive in ground combat in Africa and Europe. Under Devers's dynamic leadership, the armored force expanded from four to twelve armored divisions in twenty months.

In May 1943, Devers, having been promoted to lieutenant general, assumed command of the European Theater of Operations, where he represented the United States in planning the cross-channel attack and where he supervised the buildup of the US Army in the British Isles. In this capacity Devers ran afoul of Eisenhower over the allocation of aircraft in support of Eisenhower's Mediterranean operations. When Bradley arrived in England the following September, Devers became largely superfluous. It was just as well because Bradley, already designated to play a prominent role in the forthcoming invasion, found Devers "overly garrulous, egotistical, shallow and much too inclined to rush off half-cocked." Patton echoed Bradley's sentiments in early February, stating that Devers was ".22 caliber." Eisenhower agreed, preferring combat-tested officers "accustomed to his views of combat" to Devers, who had yet to meet the rigors of combat. With the greatest challenge of his career before him, Eisenhower preferred members of the Mediterranean clique that had performed so well in North Africa and Sicily for the invasion of northwest Europe. Not surprisingly, Devers received a new assignment as soon as Eisenhower arrived in the United Kingdom to command the Allied Expeditionary Force.

Transferred to the Mediterranean, Devers served as deputy supreme Allied commander of the Mediterranean Theater of operations under Wilson. Devers's principal responsibility was to plan for Operation Anvil (also known as Dragoon), the invasion of southern France. In July 1944, with Anvil only a month away, Eisenhower wrote Marshall to express his support for Devers and to extinguish any rumors that Marshall might have heard concerning Eisenhower's reservations about Devers as commander of the operation. Eisenhower informed his chief that he had nothing personally against Devers and those positive reports he had heard from the theater tended to eliminate the "uneasy feeling" he once held with respect to Devers.

Anvil began on August 15, 1944, with Alexander Patch's Seventh Army wading ashore against light opposition. On September 15, by agreement between Eisenhower and Wilson, French and American forces that had participated in the invasion passed to Supreme Headquarters, Allied Expeditionary Force (SHAEF) control and were placed under Sixth Army Group, which became operational on that date under the command of Devers. Devers's command consisted of Patch's Seventh Army and the First French Army commanded by Gen. Jean-Marie de Lattre de Tassigny. In the ensuing campaign, Devers commanded Sixth Army Group with characteristic vigor, but stiff German resistance in the Vosges Mountain region, coupled with a long logistical tail, impeded his advance. A shortage of infantry replacements also prevented Devers from fulfilling his promise to sweep the enemy west of the Rhine. Though he had reached the Rhine ahead of schedule, Devers found himself the object of obvious displeasure at SHAEF. Nor was the Supreme Commander pleased that the Germans still held a deep pocket west of the Rhine in the vicinity of Colmar.

Once the Germans launched their offensive in the Ardennes on December 16, 1944, Devers halted his own offensive and relieved Bradley west of the Moselle River to facilitate Bradley's attack of the southern shoulder of the bulge. With his own front exceeding three hundred kilometers, Devers awaited an inevitable counterattack that Operation Ultra intercepts foretold would strike between January 1 and 3, 1945. Code-named Nordwind, the German assault began near midnight on New Year's Eve. Disdaining Eisenhower's suggestions to abandon Strasbourg and the surrounding territory to shorten and strengthen his line, Devers prepared a forward defense. It was almost the final straw for the Supreme Commander.

Exasperated with his Sixth Army Group commander, Eisenhower ordered SHAEF Chief of Staff Lt. Gen. Walter B. Smith to "call up Devers and tell him he is not doing what he was told." Though Devers halted and eventually crushed the German attack, he earned what historian Russell Weigley termed the "unwonted coolness" of the Supreme Commander for the remainder of the war. Part of the problem lay in the fact that Devers had not earned his combat spurs before being elevated to army group command. Nothing was further from the truth, but the existence of the Colmar pocket remained a burr under Eisenhower's saddle for which he blamed Devers. Consequently, the relationship between Eisenhower and Devers deteriorated considerably, but Eisenhower, ever conscious that Devers was Marshall's man, never seriously considered relieving him once the war entered its final stage.

January found Sixth Army Group once again attacking to clean up the Colmar salient. Led primarily by Lattre de Tassigny's army, Devers finally eliminated the pocket, at a cost of eighteen thousand casualties. In the process the southern army group destroyed seven of the eight German divisional formations. Despite the victory, Devers remained banished from Eisenhower's inner circle. The Supreme Commander informed Marshall in mid-January that he was not yet ready to recommend Devers for promotion to four-star rank, even though Devers was already an army group commander.

Eisenhower noted that the Sixth Army Group commander had not inspired the trust and confidence that was so necessary to continued success. Damning him with faint praise, Eisenhower characterized Devers as "enthusiastic, but often inaccurate in statements and evaluations; loyal and energetic." Marshall obviously disagreed, promoting Devers to general on March 8, 1945, ahead of Bradley, Patton, and Clark.

The remainder of the war added luster to Devers's star. He crossed the Rhine on March 27 and drove rapidly to the south and southeast. His specific orders were to protect Bradley's right flanks and to advance to meet the Russians in the Danube valley.

By May 6, 1945, his forward units had captured Munich, reached the Brenner Pass and crossed the Austrian frontier. That same day, Devers received the unconditional surrender of German Army Group G, which comprised all German forces in Austria—nearly 1 million men. Among the prisoners were Hermann Göring, Albert Kesselring, and (Karl R.) Gerd von Rundstedt. It was a climactic finish for the "outsider" who had served the Supreme Commander and his nation so well.

Bradley, Clark, and Devers played a significant role in the ultimate defeat of Germany. Elevated to a command position for which they had no training or experience, each overcame initial obstacles and performed reasonably well. Part of their difficulties, noted historian Charles B.

MacDonald, was that the American military experience provided no clearly prescribed guidelines for the conduct of an army group command.

Except for the final stages of World War I, where Pershing had established that command for himself, American commanders had never operated at a level higher than army level. At this new level of command, the army group headquarters in essence was a glorified corps command, but without directly assigned troops and with an additional logistical function.

How the army groups organized their respective headquarters was largely a function of the individual commanders. In meeting that challenge, Bradley, Clark, and Devers became indispensable to victory.

"World War II's Army Group Commanders: Travails and Triumphs" was originally published in *ARMY Magazine* (January 1997).

35

Marshall's Mavericks

Colorful Commanders Handpicked to Lead Army in World War II

At the height of World War II, Army Chief of Staff Gen. George C. Marshall addressed the difficulty of selecting competent combat leaders before their employment in active operations. "The most important factor of all," Marshall said, "is character, which involves integrity, unselfish and devoted purpose, a sturdiness of bearing when everything goes wrong and all are critical, and a willingness to sacrifice self in the interest of the common good."

Three unorthodox commanders in World War II personified Marshall's selection criteria. Despite their caustic personalities and rather strong vocabularies, Gens. Joseph W. Stilwell, George S. Patton Jr. and Maj. Gen. Terry de la Mesa Allen more than justified Marshall's confidence to lead American soldiers in battle. In the early stages of the war, Marshall assigned each to critical leadership roles. The army chief seemed unimpressed by the prejudices against this trio of commanders in certain quarters, maintaining that such prejudices attach frequently to persons of strong personality.

Joseph Warren Stilwell was destined to be a soldier, albeit over his father's objections. Graduating from West Point in 1904, Stilwell served as the US Fourth Corps intelligence officer and helped plan the Saint-Mihiel Offensive in World War I. Awarded the Distinguished Service Medal for his service in France, he found his true calling in China, where he served three tours before World War II, one of them as a battalion commander in Marshall's regiment in the early 1920s.

Marshall, himself an "old China hand," assumed the post of assistant commandant of the US Army Infantry School at Fort Benning, Georgia, in 1927. There Marshall strove to revamp instruction and technique. Heading the Tactical Section at Fort Benning in 1930 was Lt. Col. Stilwell. Marshall had sought him out and held the position as chief of the Tactical Section open for a year until Stilwell became available for reassignment. Stilwell did not disappoint.

What attracted him to Marshall was the future army chief of staff's penchant for nonconformity. In the words of Marshall's foremost biographer, Forrest C. Pogue, Stilwell was "intense, intolerant, energetic, sparing neither himself nor those who worked for him. A rebel by instinct, Stilwell chafed against any and all authority, mocked at those in command, and walked the razor's edge of insubordination." Nevertheless, Stilwell was a brilliant soldier, an excellent instructor and a superb trainer of ground troops.

After Stilwell left the Infantry School, he returned to China, where he served as the military attaché at the US Legation in Beijing. So highly did Marshall prize Stilwell for his candor and tactical expertise that Stilwell became the second colonel to receive stars once Marshall became army chief of staff.

Once the United States entered the war, the American military mission changed significantly. Chiang Kai-shek, now commander in chief of the China Theater, requested a senior commander of at least lieutenant general rank to serve as his chief of staff. In Marshall's eyes, Stilwell was the most qualified officer to meet Chiang's criteria.

Stilwell would have preferred a European command, but he told the chief of staff, "I'll go where I'm sent." That type of unselfish service endeared Stilwell to Marshall, and the army chief became "a more determined partisan of that general's cause than that of any other officer in the war," Pogue wrote.

Another one of Marshall's favorite officers was George S. Patton Jr. Patton, a friend of Secretary of War Henry L. Stimson and Marshall since World War I, cultivated his relationship with the new army chief of staff in 1939. Two years later, Maj. Gen. Patton commanded the Second Armored Division at Fort Benning. In the Louisiana–Texas maneuvers of September

1941, Patton stole the show with his slashing attacks against the opposing army.

In a sense, Patton and Marshall were polar opposites. In contrast to Marshall's reserved demeanor and careful judgments, Patton's flamboyance and profanity were known army wide.

Marshall remembered his own wife saying to Patton, when Patton was a colonel, "George, you mustn't talk like that. You say these outrageous things and then you look at me to see if I'm going to smile . . . and a general cannot talk in any such wild way." Marshall hardly condoned Patton's profanity, but he knew his wife had hit the nail on the head.

Marshall could overlook Patton's character flaws because the army chief recognized that even though Patton was fifty-six years old by the time of Pearl Harbor, he was the epitome of vigor and leadership. According to Pogue, Patton's love of violence, his needless profanity and obscenity, and his gaudy showmanship were serious defects in a commander. Yet Marshall tolerated Patton's behavior because he saw Patton as a skilled professional who developed a natural talent for fighting and the ability to motivate soldiers to go beyond what they believed themselves capable of doing in battle.

Along with Stilwell, Marshall ensured that Patton received his general's star on October 2, 1940. Six months later, Patton received his second star and was assigned as commander of the Second Armored Division. His performance at the US Army GHQ Maneuvers of 1941 added to Patton's fame and justified Marshall's support. At the army chief of staff's recommendation, Patton received a corps-level command of I Armored Corps a month following the Japanese attack on Pearl Harbor.

In early 1942, Marshall assigned Patton to command the Desert Training Center, California. There, Patton never lost sight of his true objective—preparing his men for combat. His time at the training center was short-lived because Marshall had something more urgent for Patton. At British Prime Minister Winston Churchill's urging, US President Franklin D. Roosevelt approved the invasion of North Africa for November 1942. Code-named Operation Torch, the invasion under the command of Gen. Dwight D. Eisenhower consisted of three principal landings. The Western Task Force was to land on the western coast of Africa under Patton's command.

Three months later, following the disaster at Kasserine Pass in Tunisia in February 1943, Patton received command of II Corps. One week later, Congress approved Patton's promotion to lieutenant general. Though he commanded American troops in combat for less than three years, Patton emerged as the finest operational commander of the European war. None of it would have been possible had it not been for Marshall's unwavering support of his recalcitrant commander. More than once, Marshall saved Patton from himself, once in Sicily following the infamous slapping incidents, when Patton slapped two soldiers, and again in England before the Normandy invasion when Patton delivered indiscreet remarks about the Soviet Union. In the end, Patton's talent for dashing attacks outweighed his demerits.

To journalist Ernie Pyle, Maj. Gen. Terry de la Mesa Allen was one of his favorite people. That is partly because Allen "didn't give a damn for hell or high water; partly because he was more colorful than most; and partly because he was the only general outside the Air Forces I could call by his first name," Pyle wrote. Allen was cut from the same bolt of cloth as Patton.

As a major in 1931, Allen enrolled in the advanced course at the Infantry School. Arriving at Fort Benning, Allen accepted a position as cavalry instructor at the school where Marshall was assistant commandant. Aware that Allen prided himself as a champion polo player, Marshall quizzed Allen about whether he intended to work or to play polo while he was in Georgia. The irascible Allen informed him that he hoped to do both.

During his year at Fort Benning, Allen impressed Marshall with his understanding of operations, strategy, and tactics. From then on, the mercurial Allen had a strong supporter. On Allen's graduation from the advanced course, Marshall rated him as "superior" in physical activity, endurance, tact, judgment, leadership initiative and "force in carrying out with energy and resolution what is believed reasonable, right or duty."

Six years later, Allen, then stationed at Fort Riley, Kansas, sent Marshall a copy of the US Army Cavalry School's text that he had written—*Methods of Combat for Cavalry*—that included instructional matter on the execution of combat missions. Marshall commented that Allen's pedagogical methods were identical to those Marshall sponsored during his tenure as assistant commandant.

From that day forward, Marshall demonstrated a strong attachment to Allen. Allen's fondness for fighting may have made him enemies in peacetime, but friends in battle. One of those friends happened to be the future army chief of staff. Marshall promoted Allen from lieutenant colonel to brigadier general in October 1940 ahead of nine hundred men on the promotion list. Allen's friend Patton congratulated his fellow cavalryman: "The ARMY HAS CERTAINLY GONE TO HELL when both of us are made" (meaning promoted).

Accelerated promotion to general officer resulted in recriminations from previous peers, but Marshall stood by his man. A year later, Marshall wrote, Allen "can do anything with men and officers, though unprepossessing in appearance and apparently casual in manner."

By May 1942, Allen was commander of the Thirty-Sixth Infantry Division at Camp Blanding, Florida, when he received notice that Marshall had assigned him command of the First Infantry Division at Fort Benning. Allen commanded the "Fighting First" in North Africa and Sicily, but II Corps commander Maj. Gen. Omar N. Bradley relieved him of command for "weariness" at the conclusion of the Sicilian campaign. The real reason was Bradley's disdain for the free-spirited Allen. In Bradley's opinion, Allen was too undisciplined in spirit, and he was not a team player.

Was Allen's relief justified? It depends on who you ask. Brought back to the United States, Allen received a chance at redemption when Marshall assigned him command of the 104th "Timberwolf" Infantry Division, which he led with high distinction for the remainder of the European war.

Warriors at Heart

In a letter to Maj. Gen. Roy D. Keehn in June 1942, Marshall wrote that highly efficient and energetic leadership is essential to success. In a radio broadcast to cadets and alumni of the US Military Academy on March 13, 1943, Marshall amplified his sentiments when he stated, "Our success in this war now depends on leadership. . . . Given adequate leadership, the victory is certain."

What leadership traits did Stilwell, Patton, and Allen possess that Marshall admired? The common denominators were colorful speech "that no writer could fully capture . . . on paper, because [their] talk was so wonderfully profane it couldn't be put down in black and white," Pyle wrote about Allen, but it could well apply to all three. More times than not, the trio also demonstrated they were devoid of tact. Similarly, all three commanders cultivated close relationships with Marshall throughout their respective careers.

What mattered most to the army chief of staff, however, was that Stilwell, Patton, and Allen were natural fighters and commanders who skillfully trained, motivated, and led soldiers in battle. Throughout his own career, Marshall demonstrated a genuine fondness for rough-and-ready fighters. Marshall enjoyed the company of "swashbuckling" commanders who led from the front lines. Stilwell, Patton, and Allen proved to be warriors at heart. Now, many years after World War II, the army, as well as the nation, remain in their debt.

"Marshall's Mavericks: Colorful Commanders Handpicked to Lead Army in World War II" was originally published in *ARMY Magazine* (April 2019).

36

Class Action

West Point's 1909 Graduates Pivotal to Prosecuting World War II

Since the founding of the US Military Academy at West Point, New York, in 1802, each class has bequeathed an exemplary legacy of selfless service to the nation. Perhaps the most heralded graduating class is the West Point Class of 1915 that produced Dwight Eisenhower, Omar Bradley, and another fifty future general officers. Few classes can match the achievements of "The Class the Stars Fell on," but the West Point Class of 1909 remains distinctive in its own right.

Among the newly commissioned graduates who received their diplomas from Secretary of War Jacob Dickinson on June 11, 1909, were future general officers Jacob Devers, George Patton Jr., Robert L. Eichelberger, and William Simpson. In his own unique way, each officer embraced the Allied cause and was instrumental to victory in World War II. History has been kinder to some than others.

On graduating from the Military Academy, "Jake" Devers entered field artillery. A gifted artilleryman and administrator, Devers did not serve overseas during World War I. Receiving his first star in 1940, Devers served as chief of the armored force from 1941 to 1943. In that post, he advocated for the formation of an all-armored corps that would employ enormous firepower on future battlefields.

With Army Chief of Staff Gen. George Marshall as his patron, Devers became commander of US forces in Europe in 1943. His place in history might have been more storied had he not antagonized Eisenhower, the future commander of Operation Overlord (the code name for the invasion of northwest Europe). During the early part of Devers's tenure commanding US forces in Europe, while Eisenhower commanded Allied forces in the Mediterranean Theater, Devers alienated Eisenhower when he refused to release bomber squadrons from England to Eisenhower's theater.

When Eisenhower assumed his role as Supreme Commander Allied Expeditionary Force in February 1944, Devers and Eisenhower traded places, with Devers serving as the American theater commander in the Mediterranean. Not wishing to lose his most experienced corps commander in theater, Devers again irritated Eisenhower when he refused Eisenhower's request to release Maj. Gen. Lucian Truscott Jr. to be one of Eisenhower's Overlord corps commanders.

In August 1944, Marshall selected Devers to command Operation Anvil, later Dragoon, the invasion of southern France. Devers performed superbly in that role, and on September 15, he activated Sixth Army Group in central France. Sixth Army Group then became operational under Eisenhower's direct command. Eisenhower positioned Devers's command on the right flank of the Allied advance toward Germany.

When Marshall asked for Eisenhower's assessment of his general officers in 1945, Eisenhower rated Devers twenty-fourth out of thirty-eight generals. Devers was "enthusiastic, but often inaccurate in statements and evaluations . . . loyal and energetic," Eisenhower stated, adding the caveat that Devers "has not, so far, produced among the seniors of the American organization here that feeling of trust and confidence that is so necessary to continued success."

Of the future generals from the Class of 1909, Patton was destined to become the shining star of his graduating class. Selecting cavalry as his branch, Patton established an enviable record as aide to Brig. Gen. John Pershing during the punitive expedition to Mexico in 1916 and became the first officer assigned to the newly established tank corps in the American Expeditionary Forces in France. Patton led his tankers with conspicuous gallantry in the battle of Saint-Mihiel, France, and in the Meuse–Argonne Offensive in France, where he received the Distinguished Service Cross.

Following the Armistice of November 11, 1918, Patton returned to his basic branch of cavalry. During the interwar period, Patton served in a variety of command and staff assignments. In July 1940, Patton was transferred to command armored forces at Fort Benning, Georgia, now known as Fort Moore. Promotions to brigadier general and major general quickly followed. By January 15, 1942, Patton commanded I Armored Corps.

Patton's record in World War II was astonishing. He commanded the Western Task Force during Operation Torch in November 1942, rehabilitated II Corps in Tunisia, led US Seventh Army to victory in Sicily in the summer of 1943, led Third US Army in its spectacular dash across France and the drive to the Rhine River in Germany, and relieved the beleaguered 101st Airborne division at Bastogne, Belgium. For Patton, World War II was a glorious experience.

Small wonder that Eisenhower rated Patton first among his army-level commanders. Patton was a "dashing fighter, shrewd, and courageous," Eisenhower dictated. In a personal cable to Patton, Eisenhower informed his Third Army that he "made [his] Army a fighting force that is not excelled in effectiveness by any other of equal size in the world." By then a household name, Patton earned four stars in April 1945 and led the American advance into Czechoslovakia by war's end. Patton's untimely death on December 21, 1945, due to injuries sustained in an automobile accident, catapulted him to legendary status.

Lt. Gen. Simpson emerged from the war as perhaps the most forgotten American field army commander of the Western Front. Commanding US Ninth Army throughout operations from Brittany in western France to the Elbe River in Germany between September 5, 1944, and V-E Day, Simpson established a credible record of combat excellence.

Unlike Lt. Gen. Courtney Hodges's First US Army and Patton's Third Army, which remained under Bradley's Twelfth Army Group, Ninth Army came under operational control of British Field Marshal Bernard Law Montgomery during the Battle of the Bulge in mid-December 1944. Simpson remained under Montgomery's command until the envelopment of the Ruhr Pocket in Germany on April 4, 1945. As a result, Simpson never received the accolades afforded to Bradley's other army commanders.

In retrospect, Simpson was far more suited to work with Montgomery than the temperamental Hodges or the outspoken Patton. More than any of Bradley's commanders, Simpson immediately recognized the thrust of the initial German Ardennes Offensive in December 1944. Massing the full weight of Ninth Army's power to bolster the northern shoulder of the enemy penetration in Belgium, Simpson proved indispensable in blunting the German offensive in the Ardennes.

To Simpson's chagrin, Ninth Army remained under Montgomery's command until the final month of the war. Then, under Bradley's direct command in April 1945, Simpson's Ninth Army spearheaded the American advance to Berlin before Eisenhower and Bradley diverted it to meet the Russians on the Elbe River.

Eisenhower rated Simpson a "clear thinker, [and an] energetic, balanced" fighter. Though Eisenhower remained more comfortable with the Mediterranean clique with which he had served since 1942, the Supreme Commander later revised his assessment of Simpson, ranking him nearly equal with Hodges and Patton. In his postwar memoirs, Eisenhower lauded Simpson's performance as Ninth Army commander, stating, "If Simpson ever made a mistake as an Army commander, it never came to my attention." Eisenhower's remarks seemed a fitting epitaph to one of the America's most unheralded army commanders.

Graduating sixty-eighth in his class at West Point, Eichelberger branched into infantry and soon found himself serving in Panama and along the Mexican border. He then participated in the Siberian Expedition of 1918 to 1920 under Maj. Gen. William Graves. In Russia, Eichelberger received both the Distinguished Service Cross and the Distinguished Service Medal. More important, he gained insight into the Japanese military mind—observations that afforded him the opportunity to understand his opponent two decades later.

Service as the secretary of the general staff under army chiefs of staff Gens. Douglas MacArthur and Malin Craig led to Eichelberger's appointment as superintendent of West Point. When the United States entered World War II in December 1941, Eichelberger requested a combat assignment. Marshall soon selected Eichelberger as commanding general of the Seventy-Seventh Infantry Division and promoted him to major general.

When MacArthur, now chief of the Southwest Pacific Area, requested an officer to command a corps on the island of New Guinea in 1942, Marshall appointed Eichelberger and dispatched him to the Pacific. On November 30, MacArthur summoned Eichelberger and gave him succinct orders to capture Buna on New Guinea's northern coast. "Bob, I want you to take Buna, or not come back alive," MacArthur said. MacArthur continued, "I'll release your name for newspaper publication [if you are successful]."

Following weeks of intense fighting around Buna, organized Japanese resistance ceased on January 22, 1943. Eichelberger had performed a miracle and had restored the fighting spirit of the American forces. Over the course of the war, Eichelberger conducted fifty-five successful amphibious assaults. Twice more the "Big Chief," Eichelberger's nickname for MacArthur, summoned his "fireman" to extinguish additional fires, first at Hollandia, Dutch New Guinea, in April 1944 and Biak, a coral island three hundred miles west of Hollandia, from May to August, then in the final conquest of Luzon, the Philippines, from January to May 1945.

Though he commanded Eighth Army for slightly more than a year, few commanders could match Eichelberger's combat record at corps and army levels. At the war's conclusion, even MacArthur begrudgingly admitted, "No Army of the war has achieved greater glory than the Eighth."

Other notable graduates of the Long Gray Line in 1909 were future Lt. Gens. John C. H. Lee and Delos Emmons. Promoted to lieutenant general in February 1944, Lee commanded the Communications Zone in the European Theater. Army Chief of Staff Marshall assigned Emmons as commanding general of the Hawaiian Department, where he served for two years. Emmons later commanded the Western Defense Command at the Presidio, San Francisco, and eventually headed the Alaskan Department from June 1944 to June 1946.

In the final analysis, the West Point Class of 1909 produced one army group commander and three army-level commanding generalss "Many of their experiences as they gained appointment to the Military Academy, survived its rigors, and then carried on through eight years of service before World War I, would have a familiar ring to their World War II contemporaries," military historian Edward Coffman wrote in his 2004 book, *The Regulars: The American Army, 1898–1941*. Though overshadowed by the Class of 1915, West Point graduates of 1909 contributed mightily to Allied victory in the century's most deadly conflict.

"Class Action: West Point's 1909 Graduates Pivotal to Prosecuting World War II" was originally published in *ARMY Magazine* (February 2024).

37

"So That They Can Understand"

World War II Correspondents Informed the Homefront

To military historian Stephen Ambrose, the American press corps covering the European Theater in World War II—whether for the wire services, individual newspapers or magazines, radio, or the GI's paper *Stars and Stripes*—did an outstanding job in conveying news from the battlefront to the American public. Army Chief of Staff Gen. George Marshall concurred, noting in a 1957 interview with historian Forrest Pogue that in an army of a democracy, publications such as *Stars and Stripes* and *Yank* were "pretty near a necessity" as correspondents provided a "voice of the enlisted man." Over the course of the war, the news media employed a formidable array of correspondents to educate America.

Foremost of the war correspondents whose stories unfolded in print was a hundred-pound Indiana Hoosier named Ernie Pyle. By the end of World War II, he emerged as the country's most beloved war correspondent. Pyle's legacy endured long after his untimely death—he was the victim of Japanese machine-gun fire on the island of le Shima in April 1945. When the Library of America in 1995 published a two-volume anthology of the best of the World War II reporting, twenty-six of Pyle's dispatches from the battlefront were highlighted.

Writing six times a week from North Africa, Sicily, Italy, France, and the Pacific, Pyle educated Americans as he described the circumstances of "the mud-rain-frost-and-wind boys" engaged in combat. Biographer James Tobin wrote that Pyle was "America's eyewitness to the twentieth century's supreme ordeal." Author Rick Atkinson proclaimed in his 2007 book, *The Day of Battle: The War in Sicily and Italy, 1943–1944*, that Pyle's dispatch from Italy describing the death of beloved army Capt. Henry Waskow was "perhaps the finest expository passage of World War II."

Augmenting Pyle's dispatches from the front were Walter Cronkite, Drew Middleton, Andy Rooney, Martha Gellhorn, W. C. Heinz, and a host of other intrepid reporters. Most Americans remember Cronkite as a CBS television news anchor, but during World War II, he earned his stripes as a reporter covering the air war.

Writing for the United Press, Cronkite accompanied a B-17 Flying Fortress bomber crew over Germany; covered the invasion of Normandy, France; and covered Operation Market Garden in the Netherlands and the Battle of the Bulge in Belgium; and provided a firsthand account of the Nuremberg war trials. Drew Middleton of the Associated Press and the *New York Times* was well established by the onset of the war. His generation was perhaps the last to grow up in an America where the professional soldier or sailor was something of a rarity. In his 1973 book, *Where Has Last July Gone: Memoirs*, Middleton wrote of the opportunity to cover the greatest military drama of the twentieth century. For the remainder of his life, Middletown sought to exorcise war's demons, but he could never forget what he had witnessed in the European Theater.

Grim Vision

Sgt. Andy Rooney wrote more than two hundred articles for *Stars and Stripes*. Rooney was an avowed pacifist and comfortably reported on the air war, but what he witnessed in Normandy became his grimmest vision of combat. "Walking the same road a day or so after a tank had passed through, I would often come upon the gruesome sight of the whole halves of four or five men, and four or five halves of what had been men, mashed into the dirt and mud by the grinding tracks of a ten-ton tank," Rooney wrote in his 1995 memoir, *My War*.

Gellhorn was a celebrity in her own right as the wife of Ernest Hemingway. An ardent admirer of the Eighty-Second Airborne Division, Gellhorn followed the division across Europe. Writing for Collier's, Gellhorn took up the division's cause "like a suffragette" when she discovered the War Department had scheduled the Eighty-Second for disbandment following the war, according to author and division veteran

Guy LoFaro in his 2011 book, *The Sword of St. Michael: The 82nd Airborne Division in World War II*. In early November 1945, the War Department reversed its decision and substituted the 101st Airborne Division for the Eighty-Second for deactivation.

Credentialed by *The New York Sun*, Heinz reported on the war from the Normandy invasion to the junction of Allied armies on the Elbe River in Germany in April 1945. Heinz's most stirring dispatches outlined the intense fighting along the Verlautenheide Ridge outside Aachen, the first German city to be occupied by the US Army. There, Heinz spent his time with a forward company from the Sixteenth Infantry Regiment, First Infantry Division. That "one lousy little old G Company," as commander Capt. Joseph Dawson called it, "stopped the three best divisions the Germans had to offer." By October 17, 1944, the gates of Aachen were shut for good, Heinz reported.

Other correspondents conveyed the horrors of war to the American public using a different medium: radio. Live radio reporting of an in-progress war was in its infancy in 1940. Radio soon altered the way Americans received, understood, and responded to news in real time.

Foremost of the broadcast journalists was CBS's Edward Murrow, who captured the nation's attention with his dramatic description of the Blitz from the rooftops of London. Describing Great Britain's finest hour to his American audience, Murrow pioneered the concepts of nightly news roundups and live "you are there" broadcasts.

Murrow's first live rooftop broadcast occurred on September 21, 1940. "I'm standing on a rooftop looking out over London," Murrow said. "Off to my left still, I can see just that red snap of the anti-aircraft fire. . . . I think probably in a minute we shall have the sound of guns in the immediate vicinity." Assembling a renowned group of CBS journalists known as the "Murrow Boys," Murrow acquired the services of Charles Collingwood, Howard Smith, Winston Burdett, Richard Hottelet, and Eric Sevareid.

Three sensational events during the war seemed to captivate the majority of wartime correspondents in the European Theater: D-Day, the liberation of Paris, and the US Army's discovery of Nazi concentration camps.

After accompanying an American bomber crew on a flight over the Normandy beaches on D-Day, Cronkite wrote the lead story for the United Press. Don Whitehead of the Associated Press, Jack "Beaver" Thompson of the *Chicago Tribune* and photographer Robert Capa witnessed the carnage that greeted the First Infantry Division on Omaha Beach.

As soon as Capa's landing craft grounded ashore on the most heavily contested zone of the beach, he removed his camera from its waterproof oilskin and shot some of the most iconic photographs of the war in the European Theater.

Less than three months later, the Allies liberated the French capital on August 25, 1944. The hysteria from the Parisian populace astounded even the most resolute reporters, including Pyle. The veteran journalist felt "totally incapable of reporting" the arrival of the Allies in Paris. "A good many of us feel we have failed to present adequately what was the loveliest, brightest story of our time. It may be that this was because we have been so unused, for so long, to anything bright," Pyle reported.

Rooney also observed Paris's liberation. In Rooney's estimation, the following day, August 26, was even more dramatic: That was the day the leader of the Free French and future French president Charles de Gaulle arrived in Paris. De Gaulle staged a parade from the Arc de Triomphe down the broad expanse of the Champs-Elysees to the Place de la Concorde.

From his perspective, Rooney estimated that nearly everyone in Paris watched the parade and the triumphant return of de Gaulle. "De Gaulle was perfect. [He] may have been egotistical and pompous, but egotists can be great, too, and he was great," Rooney wrote in *My War*.

In contrast to the task of relaying the euphoria surrounding the liberation of Paris lay the duty to describe what had been transpiring in Germany during the war. No reporter could have envisioned the abject horror of the Nazi concentration camps that were exposed once the Allies entered Germany.

On April 11, 1945, two experienced newsmen—Thompson and Hal Boyle of the Associated Press—encountered Rooney in Weimar, Germany. Thompson and Boyle had just returned from a camp called Buchenwald. So outraged by what they had observed, they offered Rooney what they believed would be the story of the war. Rooney declined the invitation, knowing he could not write so important a story without seeing the camp. Eventually, Thompson and Boyle sat down and wrote, and as the pages came off their typewriters, they handed them to Rooney. The next day, Rooney decided to visit Buchenwald to verify the story. There, he stared in embarrassed silence, thinking about the previous doubts he originally held. To Rooney, Buchenwald represented the worst of everything in all the Nazi extermination camps. The dead and dying were still everywhere. For the first time in his life, Rooney reflected that "any peace is not better than any war," he recalled in *My War*.

Murrow traveled to Buchenwald a few days later. As with Thompson, Boyle, and Rooney, he feared that no one could believe what he had seen. On his CBS radio program, Murrow concluded, "I pray you to believe what I have said about Buchenwald. For most of it I have no words. . . . If I have offended you by this rather mild account of Buchenwald, I'm not in the least sorry."

Press coverage of the European Theater was far from perfect, and yet the frontline reporters made an invaluable contribution to the war effort. Not only did the correspondents raise the morale of the American troops, but they also educated the men and women on the home front. The most successful print correspondents provided the public with the stories of what the Allied high command and GIs were doing. The vast majority of the broadcast journalists were event oriented. That was why Murrow's evening roundup of news was so revolutionary.

With few exceptions, the cadre of war correspondents was successful in informing America about what their sons and daughters were doing on the battlefront. In the words of reporter Middleton in *Where Has Last July Gone?* "I did my best to tell my countrymen what was happening." Pyle did Middleton one better in explaining his motives on the eve of the invasion of Okinawa, Japan, as he turned his attention to the soldiers preparing for the invasion: "In writing about tomorrow and the days that will follow, I'll try to give the folks at home an honest picture of what happens—so that they can understand enough to give you the credit you deserve." The American public demanded nothing less.

"So That They Can Understand: World War II Correspondents Informed the Homefront" was originally published in *ARMY Magazine* (December 2022).

38

Ernie's Heroes—Correspondent Loved Frontline Troops

They Loved Him Back

In the seventy-plus years since his death on Le Shima, Okinawa, on April 18, 1945, Ernest Taylor Pyle remains this country's most celebrated war correspondent. To the American GI (government/general issue), he was simply "Ernie," a fellow soldier who shared their hardships and misery. What so endeared Ernie Pyle to the American public was his ability to communicate what the GIs and the high command were doing in the Mediterranean, European, and Pacific Theaters. Eleanor Roosevelt read Pyle's dispatches on a regular basis, as did millions of American parents anxious to hear about their sons on the front lines.

Long before he became a war correspondent, Pyle had written more than 2 million words as a roving reporter during the Great Depression. World War II presented Pyle with his great opportunity, as well as with his deliverance from economic turmoil. Writing for the Scripps Howard chain of newspapers, Pyle covered World War II the way the individual fighting man fought it. Seldom did he write about the "big picture." That was the war of "brass hats." Pyle's world was that of the individual combatant.

Pyle was born August 3, 1900, on a farm outside Dana, Indiana. He entered Indiana University in 1919, but he departed the university his senior year to take a general-reporting job at the *La Porte* (IN) *Herald.* Shortly thereafter, Pyle joined Scripps-Howard's *Washington* (DC) *Daily News*, and in 1944 earned a Pulitzer Prize. Shortly after World War II commenced, Pyle traveled to England to report on the Battle of Britain and later on the soldiers destined to participate in Operation Torch, the invasion of North Africa.

In his superb *Liberation Trilogy* of books, Pulitzer Prize–winning author Rick Atkinson describes Pyle's introduction to the ground war: "A redhead in a knit cap, slender as a thread at 100 pounds and given to drink and melancholy, showed up with a typewriter to educate America."

As did most soldiers on the front line, Pyle greatly admired cartoonist Sgt. Bill Mauldin of Mountain Park, New Mexico. Mauldin served in the Forty-Fifth Division, a unit that witnessed its fair share of fighting and one whose losses had been heavy. Mauldin's central cartoon characters were Willie and Joe, "two soldiers, unshaven, unwashed, unsmiling." Pyle concurred with *Stars and Stripes* editor Capt. Bob Neville, who identified Mauldin as "the outstanding cartoonist of the war." Willie and Joe were cartoon characters; Pyle's soldiers had real names and faces.

Throughout his career, Pyle demonstrated his obsession with soldiers' names and addresses to acquaint his readers with the nearly anonymous aspects of war and its most debilitating features. Pyle reminded his readers that the infantryman's world could never be known to those enjoying the comforts of stateside living. In one of Pyle's dispatches from Tunisia, readers came to understand that "war coarsens most people. Men live rough and talk rough, and if they didn't toughen up inside, they simply wouldn't be able to take it." But if the men and women back home could see the infantry soldiers just once, just for an instant, the public would know that "no matter how hard people worked back home, they were not keeping pace with these infantrymen."

And who were these soldiers? Who were Ernie Pyle's heroes? One was then–Lt. Gen. Omar Bradley, commanding II Corps in Sicily and Twelfth Army Group in northwest Europe. Bradley was initially wary of newsmen. "I'd feel better off without all that publicity," Bradley wrote. Bradley's aide, Maj. Chet Hansen of Elizabeth, New Jersey, urged Bradley to reconsider because there were a "quarter-million fathers, mothers, wives and what-have-you in the United States, all of them worrying about the men under Bradley's command and the officer who was most responsible for their safety." Hansen convinced Bradley that the American public deserved an answer. "And believe me, General, Pyle is just the bird to give them a good one."

In *Brave Men*, Pyle wrote that he accompanied Bradley for three days and "at times I was so engulfed in stars I thought I must be a comet." To Pyle, Bradley appeared more like a schoolteacher than a soldier, but "Brad" commanded the admiration of the soldiers under his command. Shortly thereafter, Pyle returned to his beat because his "friends would accuse him of selling out to the brass."

Another senior commander who fascinated Pyle was then–Lt. Gen. Mark Clark, Fifth Army commanding general. Pyle found Clark congenial and straightforward and was impressed with Clark's honesty. In Naples, Pyle renewed his friendship with Lt. Gen. Ira Eaker, head of Mediterranean Allied Air Forces. Eaker and Pyle had known each other for fifteen years. Eaker frequently amused his guests by saying, "I knew Ernie when he wasn't anybody."

On the eve of the Normandy invasion, Pyle "went gallivantin' around with lieutenant generals again." This time it was Jimmy Doolittle, "who was still the same magnificent guy with three stars on his shoulder that he had been with a captain's bars." Pyle described Doolittle "as one of the most engaging human beings I ever ran across. He talked with animation, his voice was clear and keen, and it carried a sense of quick and right decision."

Hobnobbing with the brass, however, was not Pyle's war. He preferred the junior officers, the noncommissioned officers (NCOs), and the frontline troops. One stood out. In what became his most heralded column, "The Death of Captain Waskow," Pyle described the Battle of San Pietro near the base of Monte Cassino, Italy. Capt. Henry T. Waskow of Belton, Texas, was a company commander in the Thirty-Sixth Division. "Never have I crossed the trail of any man as beloved as Capt. Henry T. Waskow," Pyle wrote. "After my father, he came next," a sergeant told Pyle. "He always looked after us," another soldier said. "He'd go to bat for us every time."

Pyle sat at the foot of a mule trail the night his men brought Waskow's body down. "Dead men had been coming down the mountain all evening, lashed onto the backs of mules." Pyle described the scene when the soldiers untied the corpses and laid them along a stone wall. "This one is Captain Waskow," one of the men said quietly. Pyle stood by, observing the impact on the rifle company. "The men in the road seemed reluctant to leave," Pyle wrote. "They stood around, and gradually one by one, I could sense them moving close to Capt. Waskow's body. Not so much to look, I think, as to say something in finality to him, and to themselves."

Following the Battle of San Pietro, Pyle moved to the Air Corps, which he found colorless and anticlimactic. "Knowing my weakness for the foot soldier," he returned to the infantry. To Pyle, the "dogface soldier" was the true hero of the war. Out of one frontline company of around two hundrd men in the Thirty-Fourth Division, Pyle discovered there were usually fewer than a dozen men who had initially shipped overseas with the division. In another company, only eight men remained. In one battalion, none of the original officers were left by the time Pyle departed Italy in 1944.

Not surprisingly, Pyle felt most at home with "the infantry soldier—the God-damned infantry, as they liked to call themselves." The infantry soldier did not wear stars, but they were "just guys from Broadway and Main Street." Pyle loved the infantry because "they are the underdogs. They are the mud, rain, frost, and wind boys. They enjoyed no comforts, and they even learned to live without the necessities. And in the end, they were the guys that wars cannot be won without."

Pyle went on, "Their life consisted wholly and solely of war. . . . They survived because the fates were kind to them, certainly—but also because they had become hard and immensely wise in animal-like ways of self-preservation. None of them liked war. They all wanted to go home."

D-Day plus one found Pyle on Omaha Beach. Two months later, Pyle accompanied French troops as they reentered Paris on August 25, 1944, "the loveliest story of our time." Pyle wrote his last column on the European war on September 5 under an apple tree in a lovely green orchard in France. By that time, Pyle had had enough and decided to go home for a rest. "I've been immersed in it too long. My spirit is wobbly, and my mind is confused. The hurt has finally become too great. . . . If I heard one more shot or saw one more dead man, I would go off my nut."

Pyle's respite from combat was short-lived. His editors asked him to cover the Pacific Theater, and Pyle acquiesced. In "Back Again," Pyle wrote, "Anybody who has been in war and wants to go back is a plain damn fool in my book." Asked why he returned to a combat theater, Pyle replied, "I owe it to these guys."

The Pacific war, however, was a different war, a war of aircraft carriers, a war of vast distances, a war in which the enemy was "looked upon as something inhuman and squirmy—like some people feel about cockroaches or mice." Pyle met his fate during the Okinawa campaign. He had promised not to make any more landings. He kept his promise, arriving at Ie Shima one day after the initial landing. Spending the night in a soldier's dugout, Pyle set out with four soldiers to find the command post bunker of the 305th Regiment of the Seventy-Seventh Division. Japanese soldiers fired on the jeep and Pyle took cover in a ditch. Raising his head, he was instantly killed when a bullet pierced his left temple.

Pyle was buried in a soldier's wooden coffin, but his remains were reinterred in 1949 in the National Memorial Cemetery of the Pacific in the Punchbowl near Honolulu. There he remains, along with the men about whom he wrote. Bill Mauldin echoed what millions of Americans felt on hearing that Ernie Pyle died. "The only difference between Ernie's death and the death of any other good guy is that the other guy is mourned by his company. Ernie is mourned by his army," Mauldin said. It seemed a fitting epitaph.

"Ernie's Heroes—Correspondent Loved Frontline Troops: They Loved Him Back" was originally published in *ARMY Magazine* (June 2017).

39

"Ties of Great Strength"

Infantry Soldiers Forge Unique Kinship in Battle

THE WORD "INFANTRY" IS DEFINED BY THE *MERRIAM-WEBSTER DICTIONARY* as "soldiers trained, armed, and equipped to fight on foot." This is a modest definition for soldiers who, since time immemorial, have fought as the vanguard of the military power of their respective national entities.

In his landmark 1997 book, *The World Within War: America's Combat Experience in World War II*, author Gerald Linderman notes that in numerous theaters, army infantrymen and Marine riflemen constituted 14 percent of American troops overseas while suffering 70 percent of the casualties. Since World War II, 4 percent of the total uniformed force—the infantry squad—has suffered almost 90 percent of US military combat deaths, according to a 2018 Association of the US Army (AUSA) Spotlight paper called "Regaining Tactical Overmatch; The Close Combat Lethality Task Force," by retired Col. Daniel Roper. Roper is AUSA's director of National Security Studies.

This disproportionate discrepancy of casualties among combat soldiers leads to a fellowship among infantry soldiers that is unlike those from other branches. While virtually all branches of service experience the rigors of combat, the intimacy of life in infantry battalions is unique. Examining infantry combat among frontline units of World War II reveals how the sacred bond is fostered and why it endures.

Ernie Pyle, America's most famous war correspondent of World War II, described life in infantry companies in a newspaper column headlined "The Fabulous Infantry." As inspiration for his column, Pyle, a veteran combat correspondent of North Africa and Sicily, accompanied the Thirty-Fourth Infantry Division to Italy. By the winter of 1943–1944 when Pyle joined it, the Thirty-Fourth Division had been away from home two years.

As part of his assignment, Pyle spent a week with an infantry company commanded by Lt. John Sheehy. Sheehy's company was typical of infantry units in World War II. The lives of these battle-tested warriors consisted wholly and solely of war, wrote Pyle, "for they were and always had been front-line infantrymen." Each had survived "because the fates were kind to them, certainly—but they had become hard and immensely wise in animal-like ways of self-preservation." As replacements filled the depleted ranks of Sheehy's company, they coalesced around this small cadre of battle-hardened veterans.

Sheehy informed Pyle that each veteran comprised everything a military man would want in a soldier. After a few days, Sheehy introduced Pyle to his personal hero, a platoon sergeant named Frank "Buc" Eversole, cowboy from Twin Falls, Idaho. Eversole had been at the front for more than a year and was one of the company's "old-timers." In Pyle's words, "War was old to him, and he had become almost the master of it, a senior parent in the institution of death."

Pyle asked Eversole about the burdens of sending men into combat. "I know it ain't my fault that they get killed," Eversole replied, "and I do the best I can for them. But I've got so I feel like it's me killin' them instead of a German. I've got so I feel like a murderer. I hate to look at them when the new ones come in."

Pyle was deeply affected by his observation of—and admiration for—Sheehy's company. Before he departed the unit, he summarized the tenacity of these men's bonds to one another this way: "The ties that grow between men who live savagely together, relentlessly communing with Death, are ties of great strength. There is a sense of fidelity to each other in a little corps of men who have endured so long, and whose hope in the end can be so small."

Baptism of fire is an infantryman's sacrament. Two junior officers, Capt. Joe Dawson of the First Infantry Division and First Lt. Dick Winters of the 101st Airborne Division, were baptized as company commanders on D-Day. Their accounts of the experience reinforce Pyle's observations of the intimacy that exists withing the infantry community.

Dawson's command—Company G, Second Battalion, Sixteenth Infantry Regiment, First Infantry Division—had served in the Mediterranean Theater, but D-Day was the first time its men had been under Dawson's command. Like Pyle, Dawson was a veteran of North Africa and Sicily, but he had never led soldiers in combat. Landing at Omaha Beach in Normandy, France, Dawson was reported the first company commander to penetrate enemy lines on the bluffs overlooking "Bloody Omaha."

Shortly after D-Day, Dawson reflected on what Company G had accomplished, writing, "Amid the apple trees of this bit of France, with the symphony of war encompassing me, I have found peace of heart and soul never before attained in all my life. For here, I am with the bravest, finest, grandest bunch of men that God ever breathed life into. Before it's all over, you will know this is true and that this company is my life."

Several miles west of Omaha Beach, First Lt. Winters assumed command of Company E[asy], 506th Parachute Infantry Regiment, when its company commander was killed. Gathering twelve paratroopers from his dispersed company near Brecourt Manor on the outskirts of Sainte-Marie-du-Mont, Winters's team destroyed four German artillery guns firing on Utah Beach. Outnumbered four-to-one, it dispatched the battery in thirty minutes.

Years later, Winters became the subject of Stephen Ambrose's 1992 book, *Band of Brothers: E Company, 506th Regiment, 101st Airborne Division from Normandy to Hitler's Eagle's Nest.* I had the opportunity to interview Winters on multiple occasions. Though Winters was promoted to battalion command, his paratroopers in Easy Company remained dearest to his heart. Winters said, "Easy Company were the best men I have ever known. The result of sharing all the stress throughout training and combat has created a bond between the men that will last forever. I don't think I ever left Company E. As I reflect on my life since the war, I can honestly say that it has been a lifetime search for men like those I knew in Easy Company."

Numerous real-time dispatches from the front, along with retrospective narratives from soldier memoirs, evidence the cohesion within frontline infantry units. Comradeship, to paraphrase Linderman, was an agreement between soldiers that they would, in the service of self-preservation assist one another to survive battle.

So strong was company identity that wounded infantrymen frequently refused to be evacuated from the front lines. Many who were initially treated for their wounds hastily returned to their respective commands rather than be reassigned once they recovered.

Dawson, for example, went absent without official leave (AWOL) from the evacuation station after D-Day to return to Company G. And when Eversole's company commander ordered him off the line for five days near Monte Cassino, Italy, Eversole informed Pyle, "I feel like a deserter. This is the first battle I've missed that this battalion has been in. I sure do hope they have good luck."

On Verlautenheide Ridge outside of Aachen, Germany, in mid-October 1944, war correspondent Bill Heinz visited Dawson and his company in the heat of the battle. After a few days, Heinz got the beleaguered company commander to talk, asking him why he had selected two Pennsylvania soldiers—Sergeant William Cuff and Private First Class James Mullen—and offered them a six-day furlough in Paris. The next morning Cuff and Mullen's platoon leader arrived at Dawson's command post and informed the commander, "Captain, Cuff and Mullen say they don't want to go to Paris." "All right," Dawson replied, "Get two other guys—if you can."

The commander next informed Heinz that he had men who had been wounded in mid-September and had returned because they were concerned for their buddies if Company G remained on the ridge. "Then," Dawson continued, "somehow they get out of these hospitals and the first thing I know they show up again here, and they're grinning from ear to ear."

Why? Left unsaid was the camaraderie that existed among the fighting men of Dawson's company, closeness that compelled soldiers to repeatedly risk their lives for their buddies on the front line.

During the Battle of the Bulge, Sgt. Joe Toye of the 101st Airborne Division returned to the line after being wounded several times prior to the division entering Bastogne, Belgium. Two days later, he suffered his fourth wound and lost a leg.

"No one wanted to leave his buddies in Easy Company," Winters said. "There are few positions in the Army that provide greater joy and sorrow because it is a privilege to be associated with soldiers in their success and gut-wrenching when the gods of war snuff them away."

"'Ties of Great Strength': Infantry Soldiers Forge Unique Kinship in Battle" was originally published in *ARMY Magazine* (November 2023).

40

The Big Red One Loses Its Commander

As the campaign in Sicily drew to a close in August 1943, the US Army's heralded First Infantry Division lost its commander when II Corps commander Lt. Gen. Omar N. Bradley relieved Maj. Gen. Terry de la Mesa Allen from command of the Big Red One. Assistant division commander Brig. Gen. Theodore Roosevelt Jr. was out, too. Bradley's decisions, fully supported by Seventh Army commander LTG George S. Patton Jr. at the end of a highly successful campaign that brought new glory to the First Division, remain controversial years after the fall of Messina.

If the First Division had performed so valiantly in North Africa and Sicily under Allen's command, why were Allen and Roosevelt relieved? As Allen's story demonstrates, battlefield success alone is not always enough to outweigh other factors once a senior commander has lost confidence in a subordinate officer's ability to exercise command.

Protégé of General Marshall

As with many officers who received initial favor as the United States prepared for war, Allen enjoyed a long history with Army Chief of Staff Gen. George C. Marshall. The men served together at Fort Benning, Georgia, the traditional "Home of the Infantry." According to Marshall's principal biographer, Forrest C. Pogue Jr., the army chief of staff had frequently shown a fondness for rough-and-ready fighters like Patton, Adm. William (Bull) Halsey Jr., and Allen. As a young captain, Allen had produced a paper at Fort Benning that then–Lt. Col. Marshall liked, and Allen picked a day to show his dash and gumption when the "old man" was watching. After that, Allen could do little wrong in Marshall's eyes.

Allen's Success in North Africa

When the First Division became one of the commands designated for overseas deployment in 1942, Marshall, who had served in the division in World War I, appointed Allen commanding general as a sign of favor and selected Roosevelt as deputy commander. Thus began the "Terry-Teddy era" of the First Division. Allen proved an inspired choice as he led the division to new glory in both North Africa and Sicily. As part of Operation Torch on November 8, 1942, Allen and the Big Red One captured Oran, Algeria, after a brief fight. By mid-January 1943, the division deployed to Tunisia for the inevitable clash with Field Marshal Erwin Rommel's Afrika Korps. Under Allen's command, the First Division was in the forefront as the American Army picked itself up after the drubbing at Kasserine Pass and began to develop the fighting skills necessary to face the Germans.

Following the Battle of El Guettar in March and April, Patton issued II Corps General Orders 25, which praised the soldiers of II Corps and Allen's First Division for conspicuous gallantry in battle. Patton also sent a personal letter of commendation to Allen, praising him and his men, who "never faltered," were "undeterred by cold, lack of sleep, and by continued losses" conquered in "relentless battle," and whose "valorous exploits have brought undying fame [and] added new imperishable laurels to the proud record of the United States Army."

Trouble Beneath the Surface

In spite of Allen's impressive combat achievements, his commanding officers believed there were serious deficiencies in the way he led his division. Bradley had noted his initial reservations with the Allen–Roosevelt team when he arrived in theater in North Africa to serve as Gen. Dwight D. Eisenhower's "eyes and ears" in February 1943, before he assumed command of II Corps. "Both [Allen and Roosevelt] had the same weakness: utter disregard for the discipline, everywhere evident in their cocky division," Bradley wrote. "It was clear that the division needed firm discipline and intensive training. I was not certain that Allen or Roosevelt had the inner toughness to impose the discipline and training or the willingness to take orders from and play on the same team with higher command." From then on, Allen was a marked man.

Immediately after the victory in Tunisia, Bradley, now commanding II Corps, wrote that an "inexplicable rumor spread like wildfire that those divisions that had fought in Tunisia had 'done their share' and would be returned to the States. For them, 'the war was over.'" The "rebellion" was centered primarily in Allen's First Division and in Maj. Gen. Lucian K. Truscott Jr.'s Third Division. Whereas Truscott took proper disciplinary and leadership measures, according to Bradley, Allen let the situation get completely out of hand. After Big Red One soldiers assaulted rear area troops in Oran, touching off widespread rioting, Eisenhower became so furious that he ordered Bradley to expel the First Division from the city. Bradley considered "the second battle of Oran" inexcusable and further evidence that the First Division's chain of command needed an overhaul. Bradley wrote, "Terry Allen was not fit to command, and I was determined to remove him and Teddy Roosevelt from the division." The Big Red One, despite its combat record, "was piratical at heart."

Yet Patton at the time had no intention of replacing Allen, whom he admired as a pure fighter. Though Patton felt that Allen's division lacked discipline, the Big Red One was "good in the fight." When the Seventh Army commander heard that Eisenhower was contemplating recommending Allen to command a corps in the United States, Patton requested Allen's retention in command "at least until the initial phase of the operation is consummated" because of the "critical nature" of the invasion and Allen's "experience as a combat leader."

Despite Patton's outward support of Allen, he began taking a harder look at him as planning for Operation Husky, the invasion of Sicily, intensified. On June 5, about one month before the amphibious landings on Sicily, Patton recorded in his diary that Allen "thinks that the 1st Division is the only unit in the show."

Regarding Roosevelt, Patton wrote, "The 1st Division is back on its feet and so is Terry. Teddy [Roosevelt] is a problem, but I think [he] should have the 1st Division when Allen goes. He will need a strong No. 2 as he is weak on discipline but a brave and fairly good fighter." Three weeks later, Patton remarked that Roosevelt was "weak on discipline and training but a fine battle leader. . . . There are too few." The press concurred. "Ted

Roosevelt is perhaps the only man I've ever met who was born to combat," wrote veteran war correspondent Quentin Reynolds. And so, when the First Division hit the beach in Sicily, Allen and Roosevelt were still in command.

The First Division landed at Gela on July 10, 1943. The day following the amphibious assault, a heavy German counterattack by the Hermann Goering Division almost penetrated Allen's front, but with inspired leadership, Allen and Roosevelt were able to hold off the enemy. By midafternoon on July 11, the front stabilized, but the fighting had been fierce. Patton ordered an immediate attack. As the division moved into Sicily's interior, both Bradley and Patton began to express great displeasure at the pace of the advance. Up one hill and down another, the Big Red One fought three weeks of continuous fighting in mountainous terrain; Allen stood on the outskirts of Troina in Sicily's central mountains.

Allen hoped that, with luck, the Germans would continue their retreat to Messina, and Bradley's headquarters confirmed his expectation in its latest intelligence estimate. On July 29, Allen's intelligence officer agreed, "Germans are very tired, little ammo, many casualties, morale low." In addition, II Corps reported, "Indications are Troina lightly held." The major problem was that both the corps and the division intelligence estimates were wrong. The Germans were skillfully trading space for time—time for senior commanders to extricate most of their forces to the Italian mainland. Bradley had already notified Allen that he intended to replace the First Division on the line with the Ninth Division, but Allen reminded his officers of "our moral obligation to capture Troina before being relieved."

Despite the intelligence estimates, Troina proved a tough nut to crack. The battle consumed the first six days of August. "Hills were won and lost, won again and lost again," Pulitzer Prize–winning author Rick Atkinson writes in *The Day of Battle: The War in Sicily and Italy, 1943–1944*, "Valor alone would not capture Troina, and Allen ordered a full-scale assault." The First Division did not so much capture Troina as the Germans voluntarily withdrew on August 5 and 6. The Germans suffered sixteen hundred casualties, but they were confident that they had impeded the American advance for a week. Allen's casualties were severe as well, totaling five hundred soldiers. Eisenhower's personal representative, Maj. Gen. John P.

Lucas, said, "Troina was the toughest battle Americans have fought since World War I, and there were very few in that war which were its equal."

Within days, the American casualty toll became higher and three telegrams from Bradley's headquarters arrived at Allen's command post. The first two relieved Allen as commanding general of the First Division and Roosevelt as assistant commander. The third announced Allen's successor, Maj. Gen. Clarence R. Huebner, a "Fighting First" veteran who had commanded a regiment in World War I.

More than seventy years after Allen's relief from command, Bradley's true intentions remain obscure. Allen had proven a pugnacious fighter in both North Africa and Sicily, but Bradley resented Allen's weakness as a disciplinarian and his inability to consider himself a team player. The same characteristics that Bradley found so abhorrent in Patton's leadership style were identical to those he now found in Allen. As II Corps commander, Bradley could do nothing with Patton, his boss in Seventh Army, but he could address his differences with Allen.

Since North Africa, Bradley considered Allen "temperamental, disdainful" and "too full of self-pity and pride." Sicily did nothing to change Bradley's mind. In his posthumously published autobiography, *A General's Life*, Bradley noted, "Under Allen, the 1st Division had become increasingly temperamental, disdainful of both regulations and senior commands. It thought itself exempted from the need for discipline by virtue of its months on the line. And it believed itself to be the only division carrying its fair share of the war." Bradley continued, "He [Allen] attempted to operate much as he had in the past, as an undisciplined, independent army, unresponsive to my wishes—or in some cases, orders."

Following the capture of Troina, Bradley informed Eisenhower that the First Division was "battle weary, I suspect that it is more Terry [Allen] and Ted [Roosevelt] than it is the division as a whole." Seemingly lost to Bradley was the fact that the Big Red One had been in continuous contact for the better part of one month. In any event, the telegrams announcing the decision to relieve Allen and Roosevelt went out.

Patton supported Bradley in his decision to relieve Allen, not because he believed that the action was justified, but because he felt obligated to support one of his corps commanders who presented him with a command issue that demanded his immediate action. Still, Patton's actions are more difficult to decipher than Bradley's. Patton and Allen were longtime friends from the cavalry days, and Patton had been especially pleased by Allen's handling of the First Division in the fighting in North Africa and at Gela, even though the commanders frequently were at odds over tactics. According to Patton biographer Carlo D'Este, Patton always seemed to overreact when he and Allen came into contact. Despite their friendship "it was inevitable that these two charismatic and iron-willed men would clash."

In spite of their previous relationship, Patton, like Bradley, was appalled at the lack of discipline in the Big Red One and often criticized what he considered Allen's slow pace of advance in both North Africa and Sicily. Patton resorted to any means to urge his subordinate commanders to accelerate their attacks, including profanity and humiliation. In this regard, Allen was not the exception, but the rule. During the campaign in Sicily, Third Division commander Maj. Gen. Truscott also endured Patton's wrath on more than one occasion over a series of amphibious operations that Patton ordered so he could beat Gen. Bernard L. Montgomery to Messina. Patton admired Truscott as much as he did Allen.

Patton never established a reputation for relieving subordinate commanders. Then why did he support Bradley? Perhaps because Patton and Bradley were cognizant that Maj. Gen. Huebner, whom they both admired, was now available for reassignment. During World War I, Huebner served in the Big Red One and was widely known as an iron disciplinarian as well as a superb combat officer.

Patton made some effort to ameliorate Bradley's decision. When informed that Bradley intended to relieve Allen in the middle of the campaign, Patton suggested that Bradley delay the announcement of both Allen's and Roosevelt's reliefs until after the First Division was relieved by the Ninth Division. Patton then attempted to soften the blow by ensuring the relief was "without prejudice." Bradley reluctantly acquiesced.

To his credit, Bradley assumed full accountability for Allen's relief. In *A General's Life*, Bradley stated categorically, "Responsibility for the relief of Terry Allen was mine and mine alone. Patton merely concurred."

The relief came as a severe blow to Allen and Roosevelt, but, to their credit, both officers continued to serve the country and the army with honor and courage. Brig. Gen. Clift Andrus, Allen's chief of artillery, recalled, "Terry read the thing [order relieving him from command], said nothing for a while, and then burst into tears like a high-strung schoolgirl. It came as a terrible shock." True soldier that he was, Allen accepted his fate and returned to the United States for reassignment. He returned to Europe in the fall of 1944 in command of the 104th Division and led it in combat with brilliance and distinction.

Roosevelt was equally distraught. Bidding farewell to the Twenty-Sixth Infantry that he had commanded in World War I, he wept. Never one to mince words, Roosevelt wrote Bradley, "Brad, we get along a helluva lot better with the Krauts up front than we do with your people back here in the rear." Eisenhower attempted to soften the blow by appointing Roosevelt liaison officer to the French forces in Fifth Army. Later, as a supernumerary general officer in the Fourth Division, Roosevelt, who was Fifty-Five at the time, would land in Normandy along the leading assault waves. For conspicuous gallantry under fire at Utah Beach, Roosevelt was posthumously awarded the Medal of Honor. Bradley next selected Roosevelt as commander of the troubled Ninetieth Division, but Roosevelt suffered a fatal heart attack before assuming command.

The View from History

Bradley later claimed that he had no alternative but to relieve Allen. In his initial autobiography, *A Soldier's Story*, Bradley wrote that he decided to separate Allen from the First Division "to save Allen both from himself and from his brilliant record and to save the division from the heady effects of too much success. . . . Only in this way could I hope to preserve the extraordinary value of that division's experience in the Mediterranean war, an experience that would be of incalculable value in the Normandy attack."

It does seem clear that even had Patton not concurred, Allen's days in Bradley's command were numbered. As the senior American land commander for Operation Overlord, with no one to answer to except Eisenhower, Bradley most certainly would never have permitted Allen to command the invasion force that struck Omaha Beach. The evidence, however, does not support Bradley's timeline. Bradley had made his decision long before the First Division attacked Troina, and though he later wrote Allen an extraordinarily laudatory efficiency report in which he extolled Allen for his well-planned, well-executed attacks that had obtained decisive results, Bradley later claimed that Allen had "flubbed badly" at Troina. As in the past, "the whole division had assumed Allen's cavalier attitude. I personally took over the tactical planning."

Not surprisingly, Bradley's actions did not sit well with the rank and file of the division who had fought with Allen and Roosevelt from Oran through Tunisia and then from Gela to Troina. Capt. Joe Dawson, who served as Roosevelt's aide in North Africa and later as a regimental liaison officer in Sicily, captured the sentiment of the individual GI when he wrote on August 6, "Terry [Allen] left tonight, and with him went a record unequaled by any general officer in the divisions of the US Army. We've been through a lot, and we all feel keenly sad about his going, though it is to a higher post of duty. I should like to be with him." Dawson added, "It is a mark of great credit to him that we have always delivered in the pinches and have lived up to our creed, 'No mission too difficult; no sacrifice too great.'"

In the final analysis, relief of a subordinate commander is always a prerogative of a senior commander. Was Allen's relief justified? Allen, then and now, has many supporters who think not. Biographer Gerald Astor refuted all of Bradley's allegations of combat fatigue and lack of discipline in *Terrible Terry Allen: Combat General of World War II—The Life of an American Soldier*; so did H. Paul Jeffers in his biography of Roosevelt, *Theodore Roosevelt Jr.: The Life of a War Hero*. Both biographers, however, remarked that Allen and Roosevelt were rugged individualists who often found themselves in conflict with senior headquarters.

Warranted or not, from Bradley's perspective, Allen's relief was long overdue. As II Corps commander, Bradley exercised his authority to take whatever action necessary to improve the readiness of his command. Having lost confidence in Allen's ability to command, subordinate himself to the corps's mission, and participate willingly as part of a combination, Bradley took the only action he felt he could. In his mind, both Terry Allen and Teddy Roosevelt "had sinned by loving the division too much." Putting sentiment aside, even with many years' hindsight, it is difficult to say Bradley was wrong.

"The Big Red One Loses Its Commander" was originally published in *ARMY Magazine* (November 2013).

41

Heroism Outlasts Prejudice

The Saga of Vernon J. Baker

Aside from those who saw a three-minute segment honoring living Medal of Honor recipients on *NBC Nightly News*, there are probably few Americans familiar with the wartime exploits of First Lt. Vernon J. Baker, who distinguished himself by extraordinary heroism at Castle Aghinolfi in Italy's northern Apennine Mountains during World War II. Denied the nation's highest military honor because of the army's refusal to award Black soldiers the Medal of Honor, Baker eventually became one of only seven Black World War II soldiers to receive the coveted medal when President Bill Clinton recognized the achievements of all Black service members in a White House ceremony in 1997.

Vernon J. Baker was the unlikeliest of heroes. Orphaned at four, he was raised by his grandparents in Cheyenne, Wyoming. The first time he walked into the recruiting office, a sergeant sitting behind the desk informed him, "We don't have any quotas for you people." Undeterred, Baker swallowed his pride and later returned to the recruiting office, where a different recruiter processed his enlistment. Within weeks, Baker arrived at Camp Wolters, Texas, in the summer of 1941. Because he was one of the few soldiers in his company who could read and write, Baker was assigned to company headquarters.

By the time the Japanese attacked Pearl Harbor later that year, Baker was serving as the company supply sergeant. Because of his meritorious service, his regimental commander informed Baker that he was "volunteering" for Officer Candidate School (OCS) to fill the growing need for a cadre of Black officers to command the rapidly expanding military force. Baker served in a segregated platoon in a White company, OCS Class 148. As did his fellow Black candidates, Baker lived in a separate barracks, isolated from his White classmates except when he attended class.

Baker performed well, earning a commission as a second lieutenant and was posted to Arizona as a platoon leader in Dog Company, Twenty-Fifth Infantry Regiment. Later this unit evolved into Company C, 370th Infantry Regiment, when the Ninety-Second Infantry (Buffalo) Division was reactivated. Maj. Gen. Edward M. Almond, a Virginian, was assigned command of the all-Black division. It was commanded above platoon level by White officers who themselves considered such assignments as professionally demeaning.

Following corps field exercises outside Camp Polk, Louisiana, Almond announced that the Buffalo Division would join the Fifth US Army in the Mediterranean Theater of Operations. The announcement came none too soon because by mid-1944, the need for infantry replacements had increased tremendously as casualties had taken an excessive toll on the units serving in the forward battle areas. Consequently, the Ninety-Second Infantry Division deployed to Italy in July with Baker's 370th Infantry Regimental Combat Team in the lead. Transshipping at Oran, the regiment arrived at Naples shortly thereafter.

In preparing for combat, Baker studied past missions and every manual he could find. For weeks, the platoon trained in an extinct volcano crater outside Naples. It was there that Baker got to know the platoon, and the platoon gradually took stock of its commander. Baker later recalled that if anything, "he got too close" to the men, acting as their mother and father, reading their letters to them and generally doing everything for them in order to develop the type of teamwork that he knew was essential for survival. Initially, the men were somewhat skeptical and suspicious of his paternal leadership style, but after the second patrol, in which they suffered a few casualties, the platoon coalesced around its leader. After months of constant patrolling, Baker had matured as a dynamic combat leader in the intense crucible of war. In October 1944, Baker suffered a wound that confined him to a field hospital through December.

Returning to his unit, Baker found himself the senior officer in the company until Capt. John F. Runyon and two additional White officers arrived in late March 1945 to occupy the senior leadership positions. In early April, Baker received word that the company was preparing for a "big push" to seize enemy defenses confronting the division. Reverting to weapons platoon leader just as he learned that Charlie Company would lead the next attack on Castle Aghinolfi, Baker again prepared his men for combat.

Baker's weapons platoon consisted of two mortar squads and two machine-gun squads, all of which were understrength. The objective was a small castle that sat atop a hill, anchoring one leg of what the Italian partisans called the "Triangle of Death." Used primarily as an artillery observation post, the castle dominated the coastal highway on the western end of the Gothic Line. The defensive line followed a natural barrier of rugged terrain that stretched across the Italian peninsula. Three previous attacks had met with unmitigated disaster. Now the First Battalion would get its turn, moving along similar routes as the preceding attacks. The assault was scheduled to begin before dawn on April 5. Fully 70 percent of Baker's men were replacements with little or no combat experience.

Awakened at 3:00 a.m., Baker discarded his combat helmet and his utilities and donned his dress uniform and his customary wool helmet liner. The day foreshadowed death, and if Baker was going to die, he "wanted to go up sharp." Wrapping two bandoliers of ammunition around his waist, he next attached four grenades to the pockets of his Eisenhower jacket. Baker remembered that he was lucky "to have 96 rifle rounds to take into battle." Next, he grabbed his M1 rifle and instinctively rechecked it thoroughly.

Baker was ready for battle, but he was without the services of his senior noncommissioned officer. The preceding evening, his platoon sergeant reported that he was going to the dispensary; hence he would be unavailable to join his platoon on the attack. Disgusted with the sergeant's cowardice, Baker dismissed him and told him to get the hell out of the platoon area. There would be no room for cowards on the upcoming attack.

Following an artillery preparation of fifteen minutes, Baker's company crossed the line of departure at 5:00 a.m. on April 5 to seize the high ground around Castle Aghinolfi. Baker's weapons platoon followed the Second Platoon, which was close on the heels of the Third Platoon, three-fourths of the way up the hill. Single file, rock to rock, Baker's men followed with .30-caliber light machine guns, sixty-millimeter mortars, and ammunition.

Initially, Charlie Company encountered little opposition as Baker advanced at the head of his platoon toward its objective. Castle Aghinolfi stood approximately two miles from the 370th Infantry Regiment's starting point. Moving more rapidly than the remainder of the company, Baker and about twenty-five men reached the south side of a draw, some 250 yards from the castle, within two hours. In reconnoitering for a suitable position to set up a machine gun, Baker observed two cylindrical objects pointing out of a slit in a mount at the edge of a hill. Crawling up and under the opening, he stuck his M1 into the slit and emptied the clip, killing the observation post's two occupants. Moving to another position in the same area, Baker stumbled on a well-camouflaged machine-gun nest, the crew of which was eating breakfast. He promptly shot and killed both soldiers.

After Capt. Runyon joined the group, a German soldier appeared from the draw and hurled a grenade, which failed to explode. Baker was not exactly sure what happened next, but three things occurred simultaneously: The grenade landed five feet from him, bounced, but did not explode; Baker squeezed off two shots, slamming the German man in the back; and Runyon disappeared. Borrowing a Thompson submachine gun from one of his squad leaders, Baker then proceeded into the draw alone. There he blasted open the concealed entrance of a second dugout with a hand grenade, shot one German soldier who emerged after the explosion, tossed another grenade into the dugout and entered, firing his submachine gun and killing two more Germans.

Leaving the dugout, Baker then returned to the summit of the hill, where he joined Runyon. There, the company commander informed Baker that in his absence the other men had been engaged in a hand-grenade battle. Meanwhile, the enemy began to "zero in" on the American position with heavy mortars, inflicting heavy casualties among the group of twenty-five soldiers around the two officers. The mortar position could not be located at the beginning of the barrage, but as the firing continued, one soldier, glancing up into the air, happened to see what appeared to be a flock of birds. The "birds" were actually a barrage of mortar shells that had just been fired from a position behind a demolished house on the adjacent hill.

Explosions followed in rapid succession, killing three of Baker's men and wounding three others. Directing his forward observer to call for artillery support, Baker discovered that his regiment refused to fire because they could not believe that American forces were so close to the castle. After a heated discussion, the regiment finally fired the support and temporarily quieted the German mortars. By then, Baker had suffered an inordinate number of casualties.

The Americans did not have long to wait before the Germans launched another counterattack at 2:30 p.m. As Baker directed the defense, he searched in vain for his company commander. Finally, one of his soldiers informed him that Runyon was in a stone house in an olive grove at the edge of the battlefield. Using the scant brush for concealment, Baker sprinted for the building. There he found Runyon sitting on the dirt floor, knees pulled up to his chest, arms wrapped around his legs. Just then another barrage fell on the company, and it completely unnerved Runyon. Directing Baker to cover his withdrawal and fighting to make his shaking voice sound flat and controlled, Runyon ordered, "Look, Baker, I'm going for reinforcements."

"All right, Captain. We'll be here when you get back," Baker replied, knowing he would never see any reinforcements and not sure why his company commander was deserting his men for a job that any noncommissioned officer could do.

What happened next distinguished Baker as an exceptional combat soldier. With Runyon gone, he quickly collected the dog tags from his fallen soldiers and prepared for the inevitable German counterattack. An hour and a half after the initial request for reinforcements, another mortar barrage fell in the area, followed by an attack by approximately a platoon of enemy soldiers disguised as medics and litter-bearers. Approaching to within fifty meters of Baker's command post under the protection of a Red Cross, the enemy dropped their disguise, took a machine gun from the litter, and prepared to assault the remnants of the beleaguered American platoon.

Baker's men immediately returned fire, routing the attacking force and leaving their dead and wounded on the southern slope of the battalion objective. By this time, Baker's effective strength totaled eight men, including the artillery forward observer. Down to a few clips per man and with no hope of reinforcements, Baker reluctantly ordered a withdrawal. It was the toughest decision he made, recalling that "my men wanted to stay, but I wanted to ensure some of them stayed alive." Baker covered their withdrawal himself, killing one of four enemy soldiers who ventured to get a clearer picture of the front. The remaining Germans fled to the opposite side of the hill.

Waiting a few minutes to see whether any more of the enemy appeared, Baker then moved out and joined the survivors. Nearing a demolished house, Baker's survivors were spotted by an enemy mortar crew and immediately brought under indirect fire by a barrage of light mortars. One of his men was wounded, bringing the number in his party to seven. As Baker and his men moved forward another three hundred yards, a sniper shot and killed the only medic with the platoon, decreasing their number to six.

Reaching the crest of a hill, Baker heard the explosions from two more grenades and discovered two additional machine-gun nests that the Americans had bypassed on their ascent to the castle. Directing one of his soldiers to cover him, Baker crawled to the positions and destroyed each with white phosphorus grenades, thus clearing the way for his small party to safely evacuate their casualties to the battalion aid station. Totally exhausted from the day's ordeal, Baker turned, lowered himself to the side of the road and vomited. He had been in intense combat for twelve consecutive hours. In all, Baker personally accounted for nine dead enemy soldiers and the elimination of three machine-gun positions, an observation post, and a dugout.

Unfortunately, Baker's tumultuous day was far from over. Standard operating procedures dictated that Baker deliver the dog tags from his fallen comrades to headquarters. Exhaustion again crept in, and Baker fell asleep en route to the regimental commander. Ordinarily, a commander would give the tags to the intelligence officer, but instead Baker encountered Col. Raymond G. Sherman, the regimental commander. Unlike his battalion commander, Sherman had not earned the respect of the Black officers and men in the 370th Infantry. He would later characterize the Black troops as unreliable and prone to cowardice under fire.

Directing the intelligence officer to give Baker a helmet, Sherman continued, "Now that you're in uniform, lieutenant, I've got other news for you. The 473rd Infantry Regiment is taking over the advance to the castle tomorrow. They need somebody who knows the terrain. You're volunteering to lead them."

As ordered, Baker met a company commander from the 473rd Infantry Regiment, one of the White organizations assigned to the Buffalo Division in the recent reorganization. Briefing the commander, Baker retraced his steps along the path he had taken the previous day. Dead American and German soldiers littered the field. As Baker relived the thumping of mortar shells, the rat-a-tat-tat of machine-gun fire and the dying cries of his men, not a single round was fired in anger as the Americans reached the deserted castle. Only the remnants of a heroic struggle remained. A few days later, Baker discovered that Runyon had recommended him for the Distinguished Service Cross.

Baker's shooting war ended the day his platoon fought the Germans to a standstill outside Castle Aghinolfi. Again, he was glad of it—too many lives lost, too much suffering, too much death. As with most soldiers who experienced the intensity of combat, he was haunted by the memories of the fight at Castle Aghinolfi. Even today, he sees dead men on a hill and hears the screams of the wounded. He made it back alive, but nineteen of his men remained on the hill.

Three months after the battle, Baker received the Distinguished Service Cross in a ceremony on the Fourth of July in Viareggio. It proved to be his last encounter with both Capt. Runyon and Gen. Almond in Italy. Fifth Army commander Gen. Lucian Truscott presided. To Baker's chagrin, Runyon joined him on the reviewing stand. Both Almond and Runyon received awards of their own: Almond, oak leaf clusters on his Silver Star; Runyon, the Silver Star. True to form, Almond and Runyon assumed the positions of honor to the right of Baker, even though tradition dictated that the soldier receiving the highest award stand on the right of the line.

With the war over, Vernon Baker remained in Italy on occupation duty until February 1947. Taking six months leave, he reverted to enlisted status as master sergeant as his commission expired and the army demobilized its wartime force. The next day, he appeared at the recruiting station and embarked on a new career as an army photographer. Assigned to Fort Bragg, North Carolina, with the Eighty-Second Airborne Division, Baker volunteered for combat duty with the Eleventh Airborne Division in order to regain his commission. He made his last jump at age forty-eight, but never returned to combat. Baker soldiered on, rising to command an all-White company in 1951 when his unit was finally desegregated.

Following the Korean War, Baker returned to the Signal Corps and photography. Without a college degree, he again relinquished his commission. Baker served an additional thirteen years at Fort Ord, California, and was first sergeant of a training company. Transferred to Germany, Baker again encountered racism as the army coped with the socioeconomic problems of the Vietnam era. Rampant drug use compounded the disciplinary problems. For Baker it was enough. On August 31, 1968, he retired from the army, having completed nearly three decades of distinguished service.

Jump ahead twenty-nine years as President Clinton presented Baker the Medal of Honor in a White House ceremony. Former chairman of the Joint Chiefs of Staff Gen. Colin Powell, US Army retired, hailed Baker as an inspirational hero who helped pave the way for Powell to become the nation's top military officer. Baker accepted the award on behalf of the 1.2 million Black Americans who served in World War II. Recalling his fallen comrades, Baker noted, "We've all been vindicated. Those that are not here with me, thank you, fellas, well done. I'll always remember you."

To this day, Baker uncomfortably wears his hero's mantle. He is more at home in the Idaho wilderness than he is receiving public accolades that accompanied receipt of the nation's highest tribute for military heroism, but his deeds at Castle Aghinolfi, coupled with subsequent decades of selfless service, serve as quiet inspiration to future generations and as a star testimony that heroism outlasts prejudice.

"Heroism Outlasts Prejudice: The Saga of Vernon J. Baker" was originally published in *ARMY Magazine* (February 2008).

42

Patton Pains Eisenhower

Generals Were Old Friends but Parted Ways

GENS. DWIGHT EISENHOWER AND GEORGE PATTON JR. EMERGED FROM World War II as the most recognizable American heroes from the European Theater. Eisenhower, as Supreme Commander of Allied forces, led the invasions of North Africa, Sicily, Italy, and Western Europe. Patton, as commanding general of II Corps in Africa, Seventh US Army in Sicily and Third US Army in northwest Europe, led his armies to victory and proved to be the most successful operational commander in the Allied war effort.

Though Patton's martial achievements during the European war were considerable—some would argue spectacular—no American commander frustrated, exasperated, and embarrassed Eisenhower more than Patton. Because he so valued Patton's ruthless drive in exploitation and pursuit, Eisenhower repeatedly shielded his subordinate when the fighting demanded the consummate warrior that Patton always envisioned himself to be. More than once, Eisenhower rescued Patton when critics called for Patton's head on a platter. The two officers were opposite in temperament, Eisenhower was warm, self-effacing, and garrulous; Patton proved profane, self-promoting, and eccentric.

Eisenhower's and Patton's association dated from 1919, when both officers were stationed at Camp Meade, Maryland. Eisenhower, five years younger than Patton, served as the junior partner in the interwar army. World War II reversed their roles once Army Chief of Staff Gen.

George Marshall nominated Eisenhower to command the European and Mediterranean Theaters in 1942.

Three incidents during World War II nearly derailed Patton's chance to command American soldiers in what Patton biographer Martin Blumenson termed Patton's "greatest adventure, his greatest success, and—Patton was sure of it—the fulfillment of his destiny." How could a general, so steeped in history, jeopardize his opportunity to achieve martial immortality? What led to the deterioration of the friendship between these two dynamic commanders?

Despite Patton's achievements in Sicily in July through August 1943—Eisenhower informed Marshall that Patton's operations of Seventh Army were "going to be classed as a model of swift conquest by future classes in the War College in Leavenworth," Kansas—Patton's campaign was marred by disconcerting reports that while visiting field hospitals, he slapped two soldiers recovering from battle fatigue.

Several correspondents investigated the stories, found them to be accurate and refrained from publishing them until they conferred with Eisenhower. Eisenhower promised to investigate the allegations, and he informed the reporters that he would take appropriate action. The reporters agreed to withhold the story. Eisenhower expressed "extreme displeasure" with his Seventh Army commander and ordered Patton to make "proper amends" to the soldiers involved and to his whole army. Yet Eisenhower did not administer an official reprimand. Eisenhower later wrote to Marshall that "George Patton continues to exhibit some of those unfortunate personal traits of which you and I have always known and which during this campaign caused me some most uncomfortable days."

More uncomfortable days followed when reporter Drew Pearson revealed the slapping incidents during a radio broadcast. A member of Congress asked that Secretary of War Henry Stimson verify the reports. Stimson, Patton's longstanding friend, reported to the Senate Committee on Military Affairs that Eisenhower had weighed Patton's "indefensible indiscretion" against his outstanding service in combat and had determined that the country could not afford to lose Patton for the battles still to come, Blumenson wrote in his 1974 book, *The Patton Papers, 1940–1945*.

Stimson later confirmed that keeping Patton in command of his army was a public relations disaster but militarily sound. Eisenhower concurred, but he wrote Marshall that he would never advance Patton beyond army-level command. Consequently, it would be Lt. Gen. Omar Bradley, not Lt. Gen. Patton, who would command the American ground troops destined to land in Normandy, France, on D-Day. As for Patton, Eisenhower lobbied Marshall for Patton to command one of the follow-on American armies once the Normandy lodging was secured.

Patton arrived in the United Kingdom on January 26, 1944. Since Eisenhower wanted to ensure his hard-driving commander would be available for Operation Overlord, the code name of the planned invasion of northwest Europe, Eisenhower assigned Patton to command Third Army. However, Patton soon found himself in Eisenhower's doghouse once again, two months before the invasion. Patton's presence in England was being kept secret as part of the huge deception plan code-named Fortitude. Capitalizing on Patton's well-earned reputation as Eisenhower's most offensive-minded commander, Allied commanders sought to convince the Germans that Patton would lead a fictitious army group scheduled to assault the Pas-de-Calais region of northern France.

As the Allies prepared for D-Day, the British imposed censorship throughout the UK. On April 25, 1944, Patton attended the opening of a British Welcome Club in Knutsford, England, hosted by the Women's Voluntary Service and the British Legion. Patton initially declined to speak at the event, stating his presence in England had to remain a secret, but he felt obliged to attend the welcoming, provided that neither photographers nor reporters would be present.

No sooner had Patton arrived at Knutsford than several photographers snapped his photo. As Patton went upstairs to the meeting, he was asked to offer a few remarks. Caught off guard, Patton delivered what he thought was an innocuous address in which he is said to have stated, "Undoubtedly it is our destiny to rule the world—the Americans, the British, and of course the Russians." Although he had said his welcoming would be off the record, Patton's remarks soon appeared in British and American newspapers.

Eisenhower was livid. Not only had Patton embarrassed the War Department, to say nothing of President Franklin Roosevelt's administration, but he also violated Eisenhower's repeated warnings to avoid the press. Under ordinary circumstances, the affair might have blown over, but on the heels of the slapping incidents, Patton knew he had overstepped his bounds. Once again, Eisenhower summoned Patton to his headquarters and delivered a sharp rebuke. Patton's critics, both in Congress and among the press, demanded Patton's removal from command. Marshall deferred to Eisenhower.

Eisenhower kept Patton in England for the upcoming invasion, but Eisenhower wrote to Marshall, "Frankly I am exceedingly weary of his habit of getting everybody into hot water through the immature character of his public actions and statements . . . the fact remains that he simply does not keep his mouth shut."

Patton's Third Army was activated in France on August 1, 1944, nearly two months after D-Day. Patton's mercurial drive across Normandy and this counteroffensive that relieved the Americans at Bastogne, Belgium, during the Battle of the Bulge more than validated Eisenhower's confidence in Patton as an army commander. On March 22, 1945, Patton led Third Army across the Rhine River in force and entered Germany.

At the very moment of Patton's historic achievement of bridging the Rhine, another episode threatened his career. Intelligence reports had indicated that Patton's son-in-law, Lt. Col. John Waters, was captured in Tunisia in February 1943 and was being held in a prisoner-of-war camp near Hammelburg, Germany. On March 25, Patton ordered an expeditionary force to rescue Waters and other Allied officers. At no time did Patton reveal to subordinate commanders that his kinsman was one of the captives.

The armored column that Patton dispatched under the command of Capt. Abraham Baum was undersized for the task, and the intelligence reports had not been verified. Baum's three hundred–man force reached the prisoner compound on March 27 and liberated the captives. Baum had anticipated finding three hundred US prisoners. Instead, he found 1,500, and he did not have sufficient transportation to return all the prisoners to American lines. By the next morning, German reinforcements arrived and obliterated Baum's entire force. Every vehicle was lost and virtually every man was killed, wounded, or captured.

When Patton finally heard the news of the failed mission, he attempted to evade responsibility, blaming both the division and the corps commanders for sending an undersized force. Moreover, he claimed the raid was merely a feint to disguise Third Army's actual movement northward. According to Pulitzer Prize–winning author Rick Atkinson in his 2013 book, *The Guns at Last Light: The War in Western Europe, 1944–1945*, "Patton had abused his authority, issuing reckless, impulsive orders to indulge his personal interests."

Eisenhower characterized the Hammelburg expedition as another of "Patton's latest crackpot actions." What bothered Eisenhower more than anything was that Patton had imposed censorship on the movement. Eisenhower informed Marshall that "Patton is a problem child, but he is a great fighting leader in pursuit and exploitation." With the European war nearly over and on the verge of Allied victory, there was little attempt by Eisenhower to corral Patton.

When Germany surrendered unconditionally on May 7, 1945, Patton contemplated that he had lost his usefulness when Eisenhower made him military governor of Bavaria in conjunction with his Third Army command. Eisenhower reiterated to Patton that the firm policy of the Supreme Headquarters Allied Expeditionary Force was to uproot the entire Nazi organization despite local administrative inefficiency. Eisenhower said, "Victory is not complete until we have eliminated from positions of responsibility . . . every active adherent to the Nazi party."

Personally opposed to Eisenhower's policy of denazification, Patton was no longer in sync with his commander's stated policies. It was simply a matter of time before Patton self-destructed, and this time, Eisenhower refused to shield his finest operational commander. When Patton expressed his personal views to reporters that denazification was similar to a Democratic–Republican election scrap, the die was cast.

Eisenhower immediately summoned Patton to his headquarters in Frankfurt, Germany, to account for his stewardship as miliary governor of Bavaria. Even though Eisenhower and Patton had been close friends for a quarter of a century, and Eisenhower claimed "almost a proprietary interest in [Patton] because of the stand he had taken in several instances" during the war, according to a March 26, 1945, cable, the Supreme Allied

Commander relieved Patton from command of his beloved Third Army on October 7, 1945.

To compensate for Patton's relief of command, Eisenhower assigned him to command Fifteenth US Army, which had the principal task of compiling the lessons of the Western European campaign. It was a bitter end to Patton's storied career. Patton died on December 21, 1945, as a result of an embolism caused by a vehicular accident in Germany on December 9.

Eisenhower and Patton played pivotal roles in winning the European war. Whatever difficulties Patton caused Eisenhower, nothing had diminished the Supreme Allied Commander's faith in Patton's ability to mount and sustain a combat offensive. Small wonder that Eisenhower rated Patton as his most indispensable army-level commander.

"Patton Pains Eisenhower: Generals Were Old Friends but Parted Ways" was originally published in *ARMY Magazine* (February 2023).

43

The Pacific War

The US Army's Forgotten Theater of World War II

An iconic photograph of the American flag raised during the Battle of Iwo Jima, taken by Joe Rosenthal on February 23, 1945, remains the most visible symbol of the Pacific Theater in World War II. Observing the raising of the flag from the deck of an assault vessel, Secretary of the Navy James V. Forrestal turned to US Marine Corps Gen. Holland M. Smith and said, "The raising of that flag on Suribachi means a Marine Corps for the next 500 years." Ironically, the historic victory at Iwo Jima also contributed to the eclipse of the enormous contribution made by the US Army to the ultimate victory over Imperial Japan.

Over the course of the war, the army deployed three field armies and twenty-one divisions in the Pacific Theater, excluding the units serving in the China–Burma–India Theater. Most of these forces had arrived before large-scale operations commenced in the Mediterranean and European Theaters. Moreover, the army actually conducted far more amphibious landings in the Pacific than its sister service, the Marine Corps.

Casualty lists reflected the severity of extended operations. From December 1941 through August 1945, the army suffered 41,592 killed or missing in action and 145,706 wounded. Added to this total must be the Army Air Forces, which sustained 15,694 killed in action from 24,230 total casualties. Army losses in the theater were significantly higher—though not proportionally—than those suffered by the Marines, and yet the army's role in winning the war against the Japanese has been largely forgotten amid the carnage of the Pacific war. Why is this so?

Five major factors have contributed to the diminution of the army's perceived role in the war that raged across the Pacific from 1941 to 1945: a "Europe-first" grand strategy directed by President Franklin Roosevelt; the maritime nature of the oceanic theater of operations; the cult of personality; unbalanced press coverage; and the savagery and racial tone of the combat in the war against Japan. These factors, combined with the barren and inhospitable battle sites in the Pacific and the difficulty of access for modern visitors and veterans, have tended to detract from the American public's comprehension of the scope of combat in the Pacific and the instrumental contribution of the army to ultimate victory.

Long before the Japanese launched the surprise attack against Pearl Harbor, Roosevelt had determined that in a global war against the totalitarian states of Japan and Germany, Germany posed a far greater threat to the United States's existence. On November 12, 1940, Admiral Harold R. Stark, chief of naval operations, addressed a communication to Secretary of the Navy Frank Knox. Now remembered as the Plan Dog memorandum, Stark argued for an Atlantic-first strategy, promoted its acceptability to the army and encouraged close coordination with the British. Within months, the president endorsed Plan Dog with slight modifications, and the document became the cornerstone of American military-political strategic thought during the war.

In Roosevelt's mind, the survival of Great Britain in the war against Hitler's Germany was tied to American vital interests. Not surprisingly, Roosevelt recognized this special relationship with Great Britain by initiating a secret correspondence with then–first lord of the admiralty Winston Churchill as soon as the European war began. By the spring of 1941, the American president approved the Destroyers for Bases Agreement and laid the foundation for material support to Great Britain in the form of the Lend-Lease Act.

After the attack on Pearl Harbor, Churchill hurried to Washington to confer with Roosevelt to ensure that the Europe-first strategy remained intact. The resulting Arcadia Conference in late December reaffirmed that "notwithstanding the entry of Japan into the war, our view remains that Germany is still the prime enemy, and her defeat is the key to victory. Once Germany is defeated, the collapse of Italy and the defeat of Japan must follow."

The American public demanded immediate retaliation against Japan, and although Roosevelt maintained a Europe-first strategy throughout the war, comparable numbers of army units deployed to the Pacific in order to stem the Japanese offensive. Once military bases were established in Great Britain to prepare for the cross–English Channel attack, however, the preponderance of the army's effort was dedicated to the European war. Until that time, the total number of American service members dedicated to the Pacific—including ground, naval and air forces—was roughly equal to those who deployed to the European Theater.

Though the Navy dedicated roughly 70 percent of its resources and the entire Marine Corps to the Pacific, only 37 percent of the army and Army Air Forces saw wartime service across the broad expanse of the Pacific Ocean and its adjacent waters. Not surprisingly, army historians have tended to concentrate on the crusade in Europe, where the army played the principal role in defeating Hitler, thus leaving the Pacific to the Marines and the Navy.

The maritime nature of the theater also proved instrumental in understanding why the army did not focus as much on Pacific operations in the postwar analysis of its own contribution to winning World War II. The Pacific constituted a shared theater with the Marine Corps, with the Marines playing the prominent role in ground operations across the Central Pacific. The army worked closely with the Marines in the latter stages of the Guadalcanal campaign and thereafter played a more critical role throughout Gen. Douglas A. MacArthur's Southwest Pacific Area (SWPA) as MacArthur sought to return to the Philippines.

Until the campaigns to seize the Philippines (October 1944–1945) and capture Okinawa (April–June 1945), the topography precluded the deployment of corps and army-size units for the most part. Moreover, the small and fragmented scale of combat—and the unfamiliarity of the geography vis-à-vis Europe, with its continuous and easily comprehended flow of plans and operation—made it difficult to identify senior commanders since much of the combat centered at small unit levels to follow operations. In contrast to Europe, senior commanders such as LTG Robert L. Eichelberger and Lt. Gen. Walter Krueger, both army-level commanders, became more involved in tactical operations than their European counterparts.

In 1943, Eichelberger, the future commander of Eighth US Army, characterized the fighting in the Pacific using a weary army phrase: "Hurry up and wait." In the Southwest Pacific, Eichelberger stated that the American Army often hurried up and waited for many months. Famed war correspondent Ernie Pyle wrote, "One admiral said that directing this [Pacific] war was like watching a slow-motion picture. You plan something for months, then finally the great day came when you launch your plans, and then it is days or weeks before the attack happens, because it takes that long to get there."

Just as the dispersed nature of the fighting precluded name recognition of senior commanders, so did the cult of personality as personified by MacArthur, the senior army commander in the Pacific. In assigning Eichelberger to command I Corps during the bitter fighting at Buna in November 1942, MacArthur directed him to "take Buna or not come back alive. . . . If you capture Buna . . . I'll release your name for newspaper publication." Publicity may have motivated MacArthur, but public acclaim meant nothing to Eichelberger. In his own reminiscences of World War II titled *Our Jungle War to Tokyo*, Eichelberger remarked that he "never understood the public relations policy that either he [MacArthur] or his immediate assistants established." Ill-advised announcements that only "mopping up" operations remained, and that MacArthur himself had achieved victory after victory long before the fighting ceased, amazed Eichelberger.

All communiques from MacArthur's headquarters credited him with the victories. Unlike Gen. Dwight D. Eisenhower, who eschewed public recognition and directed Pyle to "discover Gen. Omar Bradley" to offset Gen. George S. Patton Jr.'s penchant for attracting all the publicity, his personal correspondence with his wife, which he later published as *Dear Miss Em*, Eichelberger frequently referred to MacArthur as "Sarah Bernhardt," a French stage and film actress of the early twentieth century. Army Chief of Staff Gen. George C. Marshall concurred with Eichelberger's assessment and is rumored to have informed MacArthur that the SWPA commander did not have a staff but rather a "court."

In general, the press in World War II did a credible job covering the war, but the best-known and most read correspondents deployed to Europe instead of the Pacific, including Pyle, Ernest Hemingway, Walter Cronkite, Edward R. Murrow, and W. C. Heinz. While some correspondents, such as Hemingway, followed MacArthur's pattern and centered their stories on themselves instead of the common soldier, others—like Pyle—did not see war that way. Historian Stephen Ambrose asserts that this is why Pyle's wartime dispatches are read years after World War II and Hemingway's are not.

The focus of the press on army operations in Europe, of course, helped create the impression that the army was not as actively engaged in the Pacific. Press coverage focused on the dramatic naval battles in the early part of the war, the heroic Marine defense of Wake Island, and the amphibious invasions of Guadalcanal, Tarawa, and Iwo Jima. While President Harry Truman, a World War I army veteran, did not use the most diplomatic language when he complained about the Marines' "publicity machine," it is a fact that in contrast to the army, the Marine Corps has frequently succeeded in maximizing public awareness of its heroic exploits.

This success has the undesired effect of diminishing the contribution of the other services in the public eye. Pyle, who did not reach the Pacific until the spring of 1945, contrasted his new theater to the European Theater. "Covering this Pacific war is, for me, like learning to live in a new city. The methods of war, attitude toward it, the homesickness, distances, climate—everything was different from what we had known in the European war. . . . I suspect it would take months to get adjusted," he wrote. Unfortunately, Pyle never had time to adjust. He was killed accompanying the Army's Seventy-Seventh Infantry Division during the Battle of le Shima on April 18, 1945.

Aboard a ship destined for the invasion of Okinawa, Pyle had identified another reason why the army focused on the European Theater vis-à-vis the Pacific Theater. "In Europe," Pyle noted, "we felt that our enemies, horrible and deadly as they were, were still people. But out here, I've already gathered the feeling that the Japanese are looked upon as something not human . . . the way some people feel about cockroaches or mice."

Not surprisingly, then, the memoirs written by veterans of the Pacific war have a decidedly different tone from those of Europe. The HBO miniseries *The Pacific* provides a stark contrast to HBO's previously released *Band of Brothers*, based on the veterans of Easy Company, 506th Parachute Infantry Regiment. *The Pacific* relied heavily on E. B. Sledge's *With the Old Breed* and Robert Leckie's *Helmet for My Pillow*. Both authors depict the Japanese as ruthless combatants with little regard for American prisoners or their own wounded.

According to Gerald F. Linderman in *The World within War: America's Combat Experience in World War II*, "The inexplicability of Japanese behavior in tandem with the conviction of the enemy's singular cruelty led to another verdict: that the Japanese lacked all humanity." In short, no rules complicated American soldiers' encounters with the enemy and no respect inhibited action against them. Newsreels of the Bataan Death March and photographs of execution-style murders of noncombatants fueled soldiers' hatred of their foe. "The Pacific conflict," Linderman noted, "had reduced itself to war's fundamentals: killing and dying."

Fighting the Japanese led to unrestrained war against an implacable enemy. E. B. Sledge, a Marine who fought at Peleliu and Okinawa, summed up the attitudes of both soldiers and marines when he wrote, "It was so savage. We were savages. We had all become hardened. We were out there, human beings, the most highly developed form of life on earth, fighting each other like wild animals." Such memories were difficult to ignore and not pleasant to remember.

Collectively, the army contributed mightily to victory over the Japanese empire in the world's greatest conflict—and American soldiers' deeds and heroism deserve recognition. Serving in the army became a badge of distinction for the soldiers who served in the Pacific Theater. Trying to capture the bond that linked the soldiers, marines, sailors, and airmen who battled the Japanese, Col. Paul Tibbets, the Army Air Forces pilot who dropped the atomic bomb on Hiroshima, Japan, stated why those years meant so much to the army's Pacific warriors: "It was the one time in their lives that they were absolutely proud of what they were doing, and they were absolutely proud of their friends and what they were doing. It's a relationship of man to man. . . . And you go on, and the war is over, and you become the person you will be for the rest of your life. But inside of you, the time when you were men among men will never go away."

Through the impenetrable jungles of New Guinea and the Philippines, over the fissured surface of Okinawa, and across the broad expanse of the Pacific, American soldiers made a significant contribution to the Allied victory. Because of their achievement, their deeds should not be forgotten.

"The Pacific War: Forgotten Theater" was originally published in *ARMY Magazine* (April 2013).

44
Will the Real MacArthur Please Wade Ashore?

It has been eighty years since Gen. Douglas MacArthur presided over the Japanese surrender in Tokyo Bay. Despite the considerable passage of time, the narrative surrounding MacArthur's contributions to Allied victory in the Pacific remains as it was in 1945: conflicted. Pulitzer Prize–winning journalist and author David Halberstam characterizes MacArthur as "narcissist, brilliant, talented, petulant, manipulative, and given to remarkable mood swings." At the same time, he opines that MacArthur was the most brilliant strategist in the American Army and a fearless warrior in battle. Another MacArthur biographer, D. Clayton James, alludes to the dichotomies by observing that no other figure in American military history has been the simultaneous subject of as much adulation and condemnation.

Wherein Lies the Truth? Who Was the Real MacArthur?

MacArthur's contemporaries, such as Gens. Dwight Eisenhower and George Marshall, viewed the Pacific general as imperious, aloof, and grandiose. Marshall, in particular, regarded MacArthur as a political opportunist and overrated commander. But, as army chief of staff, he understood President Franklin Roosevelt's support of MacArthur as a needed symbol of Allied resistance to the Japanese. So, it was Marshall who carefully drafted MacArthur's Medal of Honor citation for his defense of the Philippines in 1942—ensuring nothing would be noted about the troops he left in a perilous position while escaping Corregidor Island (at Roosevelt's behest) in the early stages of the war.

Marshall also never said an adverse word about MacArthur in front of the army general staff, though he later described MacArthur as "very difficult—very, very difficult at times—particularly when he was on a political procedure basis." For his part, Eisenhower worked for MacArthur seven years before World War II, first as an aide to Army Chief of Staff MacArthur and then as a senior adviser to MacArthur in the Philippines from 1935 to 1939. One might expect a close relationship between the future theater commanders, given the proximity of their offices; in fact, the opposite was true. Their personalities and approaches to command were not conducive to a bond. As MacArthur biographer William Manchester summarized, "Ike asked to be liked, and he was; MacArthur demanded that he be revered, and he wasn't."

Foremost of those who portray MacArthur as an ineffective theater commander is author Eric Larrabee, who offers that MacArthur sometimes gave the impression of having wandered into World War II by mistake. What was MacArthur's contribution to the war? Not much, really, Larrabee states: MacArthur mishandled the defense of the Philippine Islands; he allowed the Far Eastern Air Force to be destroyed on the ground at Clark Field; he was slow to advance up the northern coast of New Guinea; and he was a late and somewhat resistant convert to the strategy of leapfrogging against Japanese-occupied islands.

Historian and author John McManus echoes Larrabee's assessment of MacArthur in the opening stages of the Pacific war. McManus states that MacArthur's transition into a wartime mentality was not swift and chastises the Southwest Pacific Area chief's views as "myopic and self-interested."

Historians Williamson Murray and Allan Millett also are critical of MacArthur's campaign to liberate the Philippines. Rather than focusing on the destruction of Japanese forces on Luzon, Murray and Millett state, MacArthur focused more on the capture of Manila, the political and cultural heart of the Philippines. Prodding his commanders to capture the Filipino capital by his birthday (January 26, 1945), MacArthur underestimated the Japanese strength on Luzon. The subsequent battle of Manila proved one of the costlier victories of American arms in the Pacific.

MacArthur's field commanders, Gens. Robert Eichelberger and Walter Krueger, also disparaged their chief. Eichelberger, who commanded Eighth US Army, developed a healthy dislike of MacArthur, who he felt had denied him his place in history. Frequently confiding his frustrations in letters to his wife, Eichelberger wrote, "We have difficulty in following the satellites of MacArthur, for like those of Jupiter, we cannot see the moons on account of the brilliance of the planet [MacArthur]."

Commanding Alamo Force and eventually Sixth US Army, Krueger disapproved of his chief's operational plan once American forces landed on Luzon on January 9, 1945. While MacArthur viewed Krueger's operations as too slow and methodical, Krueger refused to be bullied into a faster pace. Krueger's conclusion? The capture of Manila for MacArthur's birthday was insufficient reason to risk a corps in a premature advance on the Philippine capital.

In defense of MacArthur is Manchester, who writes that MacArthur "was the most gifted man-at-arms this nation has produced." Still, Manchester notes, there is something disturbing about MacArthur's "thespianism." "What Douglas MacArthur believed in most was Douglas MacArthur," Manchester states.

A more recent biographer, Geoffrey Perret, claims that to understand MacArthur, one must understand Thomas Carlyle's dictum that history is created by the actions of great men. MacArthur's only goal in life was to be numbered among the great. "History is merely the sum of their biographies," MacArthur once told Philippine Commonwealth President Manuel Quezon. To be honored as a great man became the central obsession of MacArthur's life.

Was MacArthur the greatest soldier in American history as Manchester claims? Not according to Perret. MacArthur was too difficult a subordinate to be an entirely successful commander. He created more headaches for his superiors, such as Roosevelt and Marshall, than a commander should, especially in time of war. At his best, Perret states, MacArthur was "probably the second-greatest soldier in American history, second only to Ulysses Grant."

British historian John Keegan views MacArthur's advance to the Philippines as his crowning achievement as a strategist. MacArthur was not interested in liberating New Guinea for its own sake, but merely as a base of sufficient position to enable him to reach the Philippine archipelago. The ensuing campaign demonstrated lessons learned in joint operations.

Fortunately, MacArthur was well served by air and naval commanders Gen. George Kenney and Rear Adm. Thomas Kincaid. As long as they understood MacArthur's quest for speed, MacArthur allowed considerable flexibility to his subordinate commanders. Kenney and Kinkaid proved resourceful when MacArthur waded ashore at Leyte in the Philippines on October 20, 1944. Senior foreign officers also applauded MacArthur's campaigns from New Guinea to the Philippines and on to Tokyo. Field Marshal Viscount Alanbrooke, chief of Britain's Imperial General Staff and his country's senior soldier, wrote in his diary that MacArthur "outshone Marshall, Eisenhower, and all the other American and British generals including [Bernard Law] Montgomery."

War theorist B. H. Liddell Hart concurred: "MacArthur was supreme among the generals. His combination of strong personality, strategic grasp, tactical skill, operative mobility, and vision put him in a class above other allied commanders in any theater."

In the final analysis, biographer James is close to the mark when he posits that MacArthur in World War II alternated and acted with strategic moves with brilliance and boldness on some occasions yet displayed inexplicable hesitancy at other times. James says MacArthur was indeed a battle captain of inherent contradictions—personally brave to a fault but unwilling to share the limelight with subordinate commanders. Like Eisenhower, MacArthur was a late Victorian, a nineteenth-century figure, with the same prejudices and nationalistic tendencies of most Americans born near the outset of the twentieth century.

MacArthur's concept to defend the Philippines at the beaches certainly does not compel admiration, nor does his failure to stockpile provisions for defense of the Bataan Peninsula. His refusal to credit and give recognition to his subordinate commanders was inexcusable. MacArthur's ego proved both his greatest strength and his greatest weakness. Moreover, subsequent campaigns in the Philippines following the capture of Luzon did little to contribute to the destruction of Japan's ability to continue waging war.

Yet there remains little doubt that MacArthur provided the United States with its first hero on a national stage during the war. His campaign in the Southwest Pacific Area over thousands of miles, amid seemingly insurmountable logistical difficulties and against a determined enemy, is one of the great successes of American and Allied arms in World War II. MacArthur not only devised the strategy of the Southwest Pacific Area but also ensured support from senior American political and military leaders to accept his strategy.

Over the course of the war, MacArthur oversaw eighty-seven amphibious landings, all of them successful, severing Japanese lines of communication and supplies, and isolating enemy garrisons. Though island-hopping may not have been his original idea, he executed the Southwest Pacific campaign with boldness and dexterity. MacArthur's crowning achievement was the reconquest of the Philippine Islands, a fulfillment of a promise he made to the Filipino people in March 1942. And it was MacArthur, then Supreme Commander for the Allied Powers, who accepted the unconditional surrender of Japan on September 2, 1945, aboard the battleship *Missouri.*

It was MacArthur's finest hour.

"Will the Real MacArthur Please Wade Ashore" was originally published in *ARMY Magazine* (July 2020).

45

What Free Men Will Do

Seventy-Five Years on, Lessons from D-Day for Today's Army

More than seventy-five years ago, the Allies stormed the Normandy beaches to confront Nazi totalitarianism and liberate Europe. D-Day, June 6, 1944, was a watershed event in World War II and arguably the defining moment of the twentieth century in the West. To paraphrase Supreme Allied Commander Gen. Dwight D. Eisenhower: American soldiers, in conjunction with America's allies, came for one purpose only, not to gain anything for themselves, not to fulfill any ambitions that the United States had for conquest, but to preserve freedom—systems of self-government in the world . . . to make sure that Hitler could not destroy freedom in the world. It just shows what free men will do rather than be slaves.

By any standard, D-Day was the most complex and daring military operation in the history of Western warfare. By the time the full moon rose above the blood-stained French beaches, nearly 156,000 Allied soldiers had been deposited on the Continent. It was the beginning of the end of Nazi Germany. But why is D-Day relevant to today's American Army? What lessons can our fighting force derive from what Eisenhower termed "the Great Crusade"?

First, the coalition that launched Operation Overlord was the most successful joint/combined operation in modern warfare. From the start, the United States depended on other nations—the Western coalition and the Soviet Union—to defeat Nazi Germany. Eisenhower clearly understood that victory depended on the cooperation of powerful allies. Consequently, he appointed British officers as his principal subordinates to oversee all land, air, and naval commanders. The United States could never have attempted the amphibious landings alone, to say nothing of the airborne operations that were heavily dependent on British ships and aircraft.

In a similar manner, Eisenhower's relationships—and frequent disagreements—with British Field Marshal Bernard Law Montgomery (Eisenhower's land forces commander), British Prime Minister Winston Churchill and French Gen. Charles de Gaulle were contentious at best. Relationships with American commanders such as Lt. Gens. Omar N. Bradley and George S. Patton Jr., albeit not as confrontational as with Montgomery, tasked Eisenhower's patience as well. It was Eisenhower's ability to lay aside his own ego for the greater good of the Western coalition that made D-Day so successful.

The tension-filled political climate in the months preceding D-Day directly correlates to the current fragility of the NATO alliance, where there exists a perception of a loss of confidence in the United States's commitment to European defense. The Western coalition was founded in 1941 on mutual respect in addition to the threat of a common adversary. Three-quarters of a century since World War II, current political and military leaders should be reminded that America's warfighting capabilities are enhanced not only by a system of alliances but also through respect for its partners in the international community.

Rick Atkinson, the Pulitzer Prize–winning author of *The Guns at Last Light: The War in Western Europe, 1944–1945*, opines that if D-Day proved anything, it's that American soldiers need not look far to know what they are fighting for. The grave markers in the American cemetery at Colleville-sur-Mer, France, remain stark reminders that the United States must confront totalitarianism in order to safeguard freedom for those who are unable to do so themselves.

Andy Rooney, the late *Stars and Stripes* reporter who later gained fame as a folksy commentator on CBS's *60 Minutes*, echoed Atkinson. Rooney wrote, "Even if you don't know anyone who died, the heart knows something the brain does not—and you weep. If you think the world is selfish and rotten, go to the cemetery at Colleville overlooking Omaha Beach. See what one group of men did for another on D-Day, June 6, 1944."

Fifty years after the Normandy invasion, a group of West Point cadets toured the battlefield. On visiting the Normandy American Cemetery and Memorial, one cadet said, "At times one has a tendency to forget the intense commitment and feelings that go into soldiering, but this is a place that brings you back and reminds you what being a soldier is all about." Another said, "Leading from the front became ingrained in my mind after studying Brig. Gen. Teddy Roosevelt Jr. on Utah Beach and Lt. Col. James Rudder at Pointe du Hoc." Leadership by example, the spirit of "Follow me!" carried the day.

D-Day's success rested on the ingenuity and flexibility of small-unit leaders to close with and destroy the enemy. Like today's fighting force, D-Day demonstrated the value of mission-type orders and a clear understanding of the concept of "commander's intent." First Sgt. "Bud" Lomell and Capt. Joe Dawson were but two of hundreds of officers and NCOs who remained focused on and accomplished their respective unit missions when they encountered unexpected obstacles.

Over the course of "the Longest Day," Lomell personally destroyed the German artillery battery at Pointe du Hoc, a mission that Bradley, the First Army commander, labeled the most dangerous mission on D-Day. That morning, Lomell scaled the one-hundred-foot cliffs at Pointe du Hoc. When he reached the summit, Lomell and his Rangers discovered that the gun emplacements were vacant. Knowing his primary mission was to destroy the 155-millimeter enemy battery, Lomell led a two-man patrol inland and discovered the enemy battery set up in textbook battery position and prepared to fire on Utah Beach. Lomell quickly gathered several thermite grenades and started destroying the traversing and elevation mechanisms of each gun, which would render the battery inoperable.

Three miles east of Pointe du Hoc, Dawson, of the First Infantry Division's Sixteenth Infantry Regiment, was reportedly the first company commander to lead his company to the top of the bluffs overlooking Omaha Beach. Landing in the second wave, Dawson later noted that "utter chaos reigned because the Germans controlled the field of fire completely. Most of the first wave lay dead or dying." Unfazed by the chaos he witnessed, Dawson collected the survivors and proceeded to the base of the bluffs.

Knowing his battalion's mission was to secure Colleville, Dawson led a squad to the crest of the bluff, dispatching two enemy machine-gun emplacements in the process. He was first to crack the German defenses.

Lomell and Dawson were typical of the small-unit leaders who spearheaded the invasion. Along with their airborne counterparts, these valiant warriors personified Eisenhower's adage that before the battle is joined, plans are everything. Once the battle is joined, however, plans go out the window. These lessons mirror the challenges the US Army faces today in the unconventional warfare prevalent in the Middle East

D-Day also reminds today's army that immersion in war requires medical treatment to combat the effects of posttraumatic stress disorder (PTSD). One of the principal lessons of D-Day is that war does not end when the combatants sign the documents of surrender or an armistice, or when soldiers depart the battlefront.

PTSD is a mental health condition that develops in some people who have experienced or witnessed a terrifying event. Omaha Beach was such an event. For the soldiers of the Twenty-Ninth Infantry Division who stormed Omaha Beach, the assault was their initial taste of combat. But even the veteran First Infantry Division was appalled at the losses incurred by the first two waves that landed at H-Hour. Company A, 116th Regiment, Twenty-Ninth Division, the so-called Bedford Boys, suffered 90 percent killed, wounded, or missing, including nineteen from the town of Bedford, Virginia, alone.

According to historian Stephen E. Ambrose, as many as 25 percent of battle casualties were uninjured physically but were shaking or stunned, unable to hear or talk. Medics and doctors treated the men suffering from "battle fatigue" as close to the front lines as possible. Ninety of every hundred men diagnosed as exhaustion cases in the European Theater were restored to some form of duty, usually on the line.

Ernie Pyle, America's foremost war correspondent, captured the impact of the initial assault along the Normandy coast and the subsequent fighting in the hedgerow country. "There are days when you see things so horrible that you wonder what it is that can make this war worthwhile," he wrote. The American Army was still eight months from seeing the answer to Pyle's question when the Western Allies entered Germany. Later Pyle wrote, "All of us together will have to learn how to reassemble our broken world into a pattern so firm and so fair that another great war cannot soon be possible. To tell the simple truth, most of us over in France don't pretend to know the right answer. All we can do is fumble and try once more—try out of the memory of our anguish—and be as tolerant with each other as we can."

By the time the sun set on June 6, 1944, the Allies had secured a successful lodgment in Normandy. They had landed nearly 156,000 men onto French soil by aircraft and ship—75,215 across the beaches in the British or Commonwealth zone, 57,500 in the American zone, and 23,000 paratroopers and glider-borne infantry. Allied casualties on D-Day totaled more than ten thousand men. The number of German casualties is unknown, but from that day, the Third Reich had less than a year to survive.

To those who survived D-Day, the end of the Longest Day provided a brief respite before the next day's engagements. Private Felix Branham was a member of Company K, 116th Infantry, the regiment that took the heaviest casualties of the Allied regiments on D-Day. "I have gone through lots of tragedies since D-Day," he said, "but to me, D-Day will live with me till the day I die. It was the longest, most miserable, horrible day that I or anyone else ever went through." Sergeant John Ellery, Sixteenth Regiment, recalled, "My contribution to the heroic tradition of the United States Army might have been the smallest achievement in the history of courage, but at least, for a time, I had walked in the company of very brave men."

Maj. Dick Winters of the 101st Airborne Division, one of Eisenhower's company commanders who received a Distinguished Service Cross for his actions at Brecourt Manor near Sainte-Marie-du-Mont, later reflected on the sacrifices of the soldiers of D-Day and addressed American soldiers, past and present. Winters said, "Wars do not make men great, but sometimes war brings out the greatness in good men." It seems a fitting epitaph and a lesson for today's army.

"What Free Men Will Do: Seventy-Five Years On, Lessons from D-Day for Today's Army" was originally published in *ARMY Magazine* (May 2019).

46

The GI Generation

Valor Was Common Throughout the Ranks

As the country commemorated the seventy-fifth anniversary of V-E Day, May 8, 1945, we looked no further than Army Chief of Staff Gen. George Marshall's first cable to General of the Army Dwight Eisenhower following Nazi Germany's unconditional surrender on May 7, 1945: "You have made history, great history for the good of all mankind." Though Marshall was expressing his gratitude to the Supreme Commander of the Allied Expeditionary Force, he was also expressing his admiration to the US Army as part of that force.

Of all the warriors who battled the Nazi regime from 1941 to 1945, only a few remain. According to author Rick Atkinson, by 2036, US government demographers estimate that fewer than four hundred World War II veterans will remain alive. We always remember the Eisenhowers, the Bradleys, and the Pattons, but what about the men and women who shouldered the principal burden of combat, or directly supported them? Do they not deserve special recognition?

Among the soldiers who served in Eisenhower's Allied Expeditionary Force were Capt. Joe Dawson, First Sgt. Leonard "Bud" Lomell, First Lt. Lyle Bouck Jr., and Women's Army Auxiliary Corps Lt. Col. Charity Adams. This quartet of warriors is representative of the US Army that came of age in the Great Depression, then helped destroy Nazi tyranny in the twentieth century's greatest conflict.

Dawson was a thirty-one-year-old company commander in the fabled First Infantry Division. The son of a Baptist preacher, Dawson, commanding Company G, Sixteenth Infantry Regiment, landed in the second wave on Omaha Beach on D-Day. Under constant fire, Dawson was the first company commander to penetrate the German defenses on the bluffs overlooking "Bloody Omaha." Later, the First Infantry Division pursued the German Army across France and Belgium.

As the Big Red One entered Germany, Dawson's company repelled three enemy attacks of battalion strength at Eilendorf, Germany, as the First Infantry Division attacked Aachen, the first major German city to fall into American hands. Dawson's unit suffered 112 casualties of 136 men on Eilendorf Ridge outside Aachen, but as he proclaimed to a reporter, "We took this ridge, and we're holding it. We died right here, because they'll never be another G Company like this one. Never." Dawson held Eilendorf Ridge until relieved, and fifty years after D-Day, it was Dawson who introduced then-president Bill Clinton during D-Day commemorative ceremonies in Normandy, France.

Lomell, acting platoon leader in the Second Ranger Battalion, landed at the base of Pointe du Hoc. Wounded as soon as he disembarked the landing craft, Lomell scaled the cliffs and led a two-man reconnaissance patrol that discovered the German artillery guns that were prepared to fire on the amphibious forces at Utah Beach. Lomell successfully destroyed the guns as well as the ammunition supply.

On December 7, 1944, he and his Rangers secured Hill 400 near the Hurtgen Forest along the border between Belgium and Germany. Conspicuously leading from the front when his commanding officer was wounded, Lomell directed the successful defense of the strategic hilltop in the face of repeated enemy counterattacks. Severely wounded, Lomell was discharged from the army at the end of the war. Taking advantage of the GI Bill following the war, Lomell graduated from law school and later built what he said was the largest legal practice in Ocean County, New Jersey. Until he died in March 2011, Lomell welcomed Rangers to his home in Toms River, New Jersey.

The Battle of the Bulge was the largest battle ever fought by the US Army in terms of number of troops involved. When the Germans launched the Ardennes Offensive on December 16, 1944, Bouck and his Intelligence and Reconnaissance (I&R) Platoon of the 394th Infantry Regiment, Ninety-Ninth Infantry Division, blocked the way. Ordered to hold their position at Lanzerath, Belgium, at all costs, Bouck and his outmatched platoon repelled several enemy assaults before they were eventually captured. The platoon's heroic stand disrupted the German timetable for an entire day. Bouck spent the remainder of the war in a prisoner of war camp before he was liberated by American forces. Seldom has such a handful of men been able to make such a valuable contribution in a single day.

Through the efforts of military historian John Eisenhower, Bouck and the I&R Platoon were formally recognized in 1981 when they were awarded four Distinguished Service Crosses, five Silver Stars, and nine Bronze Star medals with "V" devices, making it World War II's most decorated platoon for a single engagement. On January 15, 1981, President Jimmy Carter approved a Presidential Unit Citation for "extraordinary heroism" for the platoon. It had indeed measured up.

Adams chose a different path to greatness. As an African American officer, she holds the distinction of being not only the first female officer in the Women's Army Auxiliary Corps (WAAC), later the Women's Army Corps (WAC), but also the commanding officer of the first battalion of African American women to serve overseas in World War II. The barriers of sex and race were, and sometimes still are, difficult to overcome. It is ironic, historian Stephen Ambrose says, that the army fought the greatest racist in history with a segregated army.

A graduate of Wilberforce University, Ohio, Adams joined the WAAC on July 13, 1942, and completed her training on August 29. Commissioned as a second lieutenant on graduation, Adams remained at the training center at Fort Des Moines, Iowa, until 1944. In December 1944, the major was chosen to be the commanding officer of the first African American battalion to serve in the European Theater. In March 1945, Adams assumed command of the 6888th Central Postal Directory Battalion. Adams's battalion was responsible for the distribution and redirection of mail to US personnel in the European Theater.

Adams commanded the battalion until autumn 1945. Returning stateside, Adams received her promotion to lieutenant colonel effective December 26, 1945, and was relieved from active duty at the end of March 1946. She had reached the highest rank possible in the WAC, as by law, in 1945, there could be only one full colonel, and that rank was held by the WAC director. By any standard of excellence, Adams was a trailblazer for women who served in the military during World War II. Her story remains a testament to one woman's courage to overcome institutional prejudices.

The US Army's contribution to Allied victory in Europe was unparalleled in military history. Americans provided more than two-thirds of Eisenhower's ninety-one divisions and half the Allies' 28,000 combat aircraft. But it was to the individual soldier that Eisenhower paid homage when he spoke at London's Guildhall on June 12, 1945: "Humility must always be the portion of any man who receives acclaim earned in blood of his followers and sacrifices of his friends."

And what was the cost? Casualties among the Western Allies from D-Day through V-E Day exceeded three-quarters of a million, of whom at least 165,000 were dead. Added were 10,000 naval losses, half of whom died, and 62,000 air casualties, half of whom were dead. American soldiers bore the brunt for the Western armies in the climactic final year preceding V-E Day: the 587,000 US casualties in Western Europe included 135,000 dead, almost half the United States total worldwide. Thirteen US divisions in Europe suffered at least 100 percent casualties. Five more divisions exceeded 200 percent.

Small wonder that Gen. Omar Bradley said at the conclusion of the European war, "We know more about war than we know about peace, more about killing than we know about living." War correspondent Ernie Pyle said, "The end of the war will be a gigantic relief, but it cannot be a matter of hilarity for most of us. . . . It would seem sacrilegious to sing and dance when the great day comes while there are so many who can never sing or dance again."

In his coauthored memoir of the war, *G Company's War: Two Personal Accounts of the Campaigns in Europe, 1944–1945*, Staff Sgt. Bruce Egger reflects on his experience as an infantry soldier. "We were miserable and cold and exhausted most of the time. . . . But we were young and strong then, possessed by the marvelous resilience of youth. . . . Not a man among us would want to go through it again, but we are all proud of having been so severely tested and found adequate." Eisenhower concurred: "To them, and to those who bear the wounds of battle, we, their comrades in arms, render most grateful and humble tribute."

Ambrose, whose work popularized the GI experience in the European Theater, gets the final word. At the core, Ambrose writes, "The American citizen soldiers knew the difference between right and wrong, and they didn't want to live in a world in which wrong prevailed. So, they fought, and won, and we, all of us, living and yet to be born, must be forever profoundly grateful."

"The GI Generation: Valor Was Common Throughout the Ranks" was originally published in *ARMY Magazine* (May 2020).

47

Gavin—"Soul of the Airborne"

Young World War II General Commanded Troops' Respect

Few generals in World War II personified the warrior ethos more than then–Maj. Gen. James Maurice Gavin, commanding general of the Eighty-Second Airborne Division from August 1944 until the end of the conflict in Europe. At thirty-seven years old, Gavin not only became the youngest major general in the US Army during the war but also was the youngest division commander since the Civil War. In battle, he exhibited the finest attributes of a combat leader.

Gavin was hardly born to be a soldier. The adopted son of a Pennsylvania coal miner, Gavin drifted through early life. On his seventeenth birthday, Gavin ran away from home and enlisted in the army in April 1924. Matriculating to West Point the following year, he graduated in the middle of his class in 1929. Having been orphaned at a tender age, Gavin may not have known who his birth parents were, but he later wrote that West Point served as his "Spartan mother." It was at West Point that Gavin developed his character and found his soul.

When Gavin assumed command of the Eighty-Second Airborne Division in August 1944, he inherited a division that had earned its combat laurels in North Africa, Sicily, Italy, and Normandy, France. Under Gavin's dynamic leadership, the division would fulfill its destiny as one of the US Army's premier fighting divisions. Yet the legend of "Jumpin' Jim" Gavin remains sacrosanct among the paratroopers of the Eighty-Second Airborne Division in today's force. Over eighty years after the conclusion of the European war, why does Gavin's legacy endure?

Gavin's first decade of commissioned service was unremarkable at best. Like many officers, he was immersed in institutionalized professional education and army protocol that characterized the interwar period. But on the eve of the US entry into World War II, Gavin was stationed at the US Military Academy at West Point, New York, where he served as a faculty member in the Department of Tactics.

At West Point, Gavin became enamored with airborne warfare and the common threads of mobility and deep penetration. To his delight, his request to attend the Airborne School at Fort Benning, Georgia, was belatedly approved, and Gavin earned his jump wings in August 1941.

"The whole concept of vertical envelopment was an exciting one," he declared, offering a "new dimension of tactics" that could revolutionize warfare. Gavin's drive and ideas surrounding airborne warfare brought him to the attention of Brig. Gen. William Lee, the officer shepherding the nascent airborne force. When Lee formed the Provisional Parachute Group, he appointed Gavin as the group's training and doctrine officer. In that role, Maj. Gavin wrote *Tactics and Techniques of Air-Borne Troops*, which was later published as *Army Field Manual 31–30*.

Due to his experience as a trainer and conceptual thinker, Gavin became the natural choice to command one of the parachute regiments when it was activated in July 1942, taking over the 505th Parachute Infantry Regiment (PIR). According to journalist and author Clay Blair Jr., the 505th may well have been one of the best-trained and most highly motivated regiments the army had ever fielded. "God, they were tough!" an Eighty-Second Airborne Division staffer later recalled. "Every man a clone of the [commanding officer], Gavin." Doc Eaton, a division chief of staff, said Gavin's regiment reminded him of "a pack of jackals."

In early 1932, Gavin and the 505th joined the Eighty-Second Airborne Division, commanded by Maj. Gen. Matthew Ridgway. When Ridgway reorganized the division for combat, he personally selected the 505th to replace one of his glider regiments. Already familiar with Gavin's reputation, Ridgway welcomed him to the Eighty-Second Airborne Division and later wrote that Gavin is "one of the finest battle leaders, and one of the most brilliant thinkers, the Army has produced."

With the cessation of hostilities in North Africa in May 1943, Ridgway chose Gavin's regiment to spearhead Operation Husky, the invasion of

Sicily. On July 9, 1943, the 505th Parachute Infantry Regiment conducted the first regimental night drop in American history. Scattered across southern Sicily, the regiment's mission was to protect Seventh US Army's landings at Gela and Scoglitti beaches. Assembling his dispersed paratroopers, Gavin quickly organized a spirited defense of Biazza Ridge north of the Scoglitti beachhead and warded off repeated attacks from the German Hermann Goering Division. For his extraordinary heroism under fire, Gavin received the Distinguished Service Cross (DSC).

Once the Sicilian campaign was concluded in August 1943, Ridgway designated Gavin airborne task force commander for the upcoming invasion of the Italian mainland. Lt. Gen. Mark Clark's Fifth US Army landed at the Gulf of Salerno south of Naples on September 9 but immediately ran into trouble due to intense German resistance. Within four days of landing, Clark requested that Ridgway order "one of your infantry regimental combat teams drop today within our defended beach-head." At the head of the 505th Parachute Infantry Regiment, Gavin conducted his second combat jump on September 14 and helped rescue the beleaguered assault force. Col. Reuben Tucker's 504th Parachute Infantry Regiment had jumped the preceding evening. Together, the airborne regiments strengthened Clark's beachhead and, in subsequent days, helped liberate Naples.

On October 10, 1943, Ridgway pinned a brigadier general's star on Gavin and officially named him assistant division commander. Shortly thereafter, Gavin was detailed to go to England as an airborne adviser for Operation Overlord, the invasion of northwest France. Gavin confided in his diary, "I may be fortunate enough to get the division although I will certainly be rather young." Gavin was thirty-six. On D-Day, June 6, 1944, Gavin followed his personal creed, "Leaders jump first, eat last." First out the door from his aircraft, Gavin landed west of Sainte-Mère-Église, the key objective of the division located behind Utah Beach.

As the commander of Task Force A, consisting of the 505th, 507th, and 508th Parachute Infantry Regiments, Gavin established his command post near the La Fière Bridge over the Merderet River. For his frontline leadership on June 9 during the defense of La Fière and the subsequent seizure of the causeway over the Merderet, Gavin received the Bronze Oak Leaf Cluster, denoting his second Distinguished Service Cross award.

Some of the most severe combat in the European Theater transpired in the month following the D-Day invasion. When the Eighty-Second Airborne Division was officially relieved of combat duties on July 8, 1944, its record may well have been the most remarkable of any division in army history. The cost was frightful, totaling about 46 percent of the division committed to Normandy. Not surprisingly, once Ridgway was elevated to corps command, Gavin assumed command of the Eighty-Second Airborne Division. He was thirty-seven years old. Soon after, Gavin was promoted to major general.

If D-Day became "the stuff of instant legend," as Blair put it, September 20, 1944, marked a day unprecedented in the division's combat history. Each of Gavin's three regiments fought a critical battle in its own area and emerged victorious against heavy odds as part of Operation Market Garden in Holland. But the most brilliant and spectacular battle of all played out when the 504th Parachute Infantry Regiment crossed Holland's Waal River. Led by Maj. Julian Cook, the assault crossing earned the praise of British Lt. Gen. Frederick Browning, who stated, "I have never seen a more gallant action.'' Browning, commander of the British I Airborne Corps and deputy chief of the First Allied Airborne Army, was charged with the execution of Operation Market Garden.

When Germany launched its winter offensive in Belgium on December 16, 1944, Gavin served as acting XVIII Corps commander while Ridgway was on leave in England. It was Gavin who decided where the two airborne divisions would go. He immediately dispatched the 101st to Bastogne, while his Eighty-Second would hold the northern shoulder of the "bulge."

While the 101st achieved renown for its heroic defense of Bastogne, the Eighty-Second Airborne blunted the main thrust of the Ardennes Offensive along the northern rim of the penetration.

In 1945, the Eighty-Second was held in strategic reserve until American soldiers crossed the Elbe River in Germany. They met the Russians there on May 5. In the interim, Gavin personally received the surrender of Gen. Kurt von Tippelskirch, commander of the German Twenty-First Army Group, totaling more than 150,000 soldiers. Thus ended Gavin's combat odyssey.

By V-E Day, Gavin had led the division in the invasion of Holland, the Battle of the Bulge and the assault into Germany, all within his first ten months of command. In recognition of its achievement, the War Department selected the Eighty-Second Airborne Division as the Honor Guard Company in Soviet-occupied Berlin. Gavin's paratroopers next represented the US Army in the Victory Parade in New York City in January 1946. It was a fitting triumph for one of the most heralded divisions in American history.

What, then, was the secret of Gavin's success as a combat commander? And what lessons from his battlefield exploits are most relevant for today's leaders? Author Guy LoFaro states that Gavin was that rare commander who was not only respected but also worshipped by his troopers. He possessed "the 'inward eye' that allows a great captain to make a 'sound decision in the midst of action,'" LoFaro wrote, quoting military theorist Carl von Clausewitz.

Throughout the war, Gavin adhered to a phrase he took from Voltaire: "That calm courage in the midst of tumult, that serenity of a soul in danger, which is the greatest gift of nature for command." What most endeared soldiers to Gavin was his command presence in the thickest of action. From Sicily to the Italian mainland, to Normandy, and on to Holland and the Belgian Ardennes, Gavin led from the front, constantly exposing himself to enemy fire. In the process, he emerged from the war as the quintessential frontline commander. His behavior in the line of duty earned the paratroopers' deep respect; his raw courage and aggressive spirit inspired them in action. Stephen Ambrose, the dean of D-Day historians, states that Gavin was the most beloved division commander in the European Theater. A plaque at the base of the Iron Mike statue overlooking the Merderet River in Normandy best summarizes the adulation Gavin's paratroopers held for their commander: "General Gavin never sent his men anywhere. He always led them. He is the soul of the Airborne."

But it was planning and preparation, violent execution and frontline leadership, that provided the winning formula by which Gavin led the Eighty-Second Airborne Division as it marched into history.

"Gavin: 'Soul of the Airborne': Young World War II General Commanded Troops' Respect" was originally published in *ARMY Magazine* (March 2022).

48

All-American Lieutenants

The Eighty-Second Airborne in Normandy

Few divisions in World War II possess a more heralded combat history than the Eighty-Second Airborne. Under command of Maj. Gen. Matthew Ridgway and later, Maj. Gen. James Gavin, the division contained soldiers of exceptional quality. Nicknamed the All-Americans because its members initially came from all the states, its mission on D-Day was to seize, clear, and secure the general area around Sainte-Mère-Église, France, and then to be prepared to advance to the west on corps orders. Sainte-Mère-Église was a typical Norman town that became a critical military objective because six major roads in the Cotentin Peninsula went through it. Whichever combatant held the town would control access to the avenues of approach to and from Utah Beach.

The strength of the Eighty-Second Airborne Division lay in the junior officers and noncommissioned officers (NCOs) who carried the war to the enemy. During the opening hours of D-Day—June 6, 1944—three All-American lieutenants personified the fighting spirit of Ridgway's paratroopers and made a significant contribution to the Allied success. Their names were John Dolan, Turner Turnbull, and Waverly Wray. Collectively, they personified Ridgway's emphasis on frontline leadership, which Ridgway defined as "the art of imposing one's will upon others in such a manner as to command their implicit obedience, their utmost confidence, their profound respect, and their wholehearted cooperation."

Of the three lieutenants, the first to see action was John Dolan, commanding Company A, First Battalion, 505th Parachute Infantry Regiment (PIR). The 505th PIR was the only parachute regiment to land on D-Day that had combat experience. Dolan was an experienced warrior and a harsh trainer. The specific objective of his company was to seize and defend the bridge crossing the Merderet River on the road that ran from Sainte-Mère-Église, with the purpose of preventing the movement of German troops to the Utah beachhead.

Fortunately, Company A landed in good order on the outskirts of town. As Dolan later recalled, "We hit our drop zone right on the nose, because within 20 minutes to one-half hour, I knew our exact location." Not surprisingly, Dolan encountered the usual problems of organization in the dark, but a half-hour before dawn, Company A departed the drop zone with about 90 percent of the men accounted for. He then moved toward La Fière bridge. In the confusion of the night, Dolan lost contact with his lead platoon, but undaunted, he pressed on to the objective.

Approximately seven hundred yards from the bridge, Dolan came across a dirt road with a wide field beyond it. Deploying his scouts, Dolan maneuvered one of his platoons just as the German defenders opened fire, killing one of his platoon leaders. After eliminating the enemy squad, Dolan continued toward the bridge, where he encountered intense German fire that pinned him down for about an hour. Shortly after daybreak, Dolan and paratroopers from the adjacent 508th Parachute Infantry Regiment (PIR) occupied the manor house adjacent to the bridge.

With his primary mission complete, Dolan deployed the remainder of his company just east of the Merderet River. To the front of his position was a marsh at least one thousand yards wide at its narrowest point. Dolan had just deployed his three bazooka teams when the enemy attacked with three tanks. Dolan later explained, "To this day, I'll never be able to explain why all . . . of them were not killed. They fired and reloaded with the precision of well-oiled machinery. . . . I don't think that either crew wasted a shot." The combat remained intense, and when his battalion commander was killed by artillery fire, Dolan took command of the battalion until Gavin replaced him.

Aside from continued mortar and artillery fire, La Fière witnessed no more combat on D-Day. By day's end, however, seventeen of Dolan's men had been killed in action and about three times that number had been wounded. Nevertheless, he held the bridge. As Gavin contemplated pulling Dolan's company from the line, Dolan refused to leave without direct orders. He told one of his platoons, "Stay where you are. I don't know a better place than this to die." Such was the spirit of the American paratroopers on D-Day.

Just as Dolan was fighting for his life at the bridge at La Fière, Turner Turnbull encountered his rendezvous with destiny at Neuville-au-Plain, a small hamlet about two kilometers northwest of Sainte-Mère-Église that sat astride the major north–south road that led to Cherbourg at the tip of the Cotentin Peninsula. Securing Neuville-au-Plain was the mission of Lt. Col. Ben Vandervoort, commander of the Second Battalion, 505th PIR. As he redirected his battalion to Sainte-Mère-Église, Vandervoort dispatched one platoon north to outpost the area around Neuville-au-Plain, which originally was to have been held by Vandervoort's battalion, and to block any German reinforcements arriving from the direction of Cherbourg.

Vandervoort selected Turnbull of Company D for the critical mission of securing Neuville-au-Plain while he maneuvered the remainder of the battalion to Sainte-Mère-Église. An experienced combat leader, Turnbull hastened north to Neuville-au-Plain and deployed his platoon on a rise about forty yards north of the village. His fields of fire extended six hundred yards to the front and gave him perfect observation of the road from which he anticipated that the Germans would launch their attack. No sooner had Turnbull placed his platoon in position than Vandervoort arrived with a fifty-seven-millimeter antitank gun to bolster the defense.

The enemy to Turnbull's front was a reinforced battalion that had been alerted to move toward Sainte-Mère-Église earlier in the morning. The enemy now found its way blocked by a determined platoon of American paratroopers commanded by a seasoned combat veteran. Turnbull was gratified when Vandervoort directed his battalion reserve to come to his aid. By this time, he had already sustained sixteen casualties, including six dead. The combat continued unabated through the afternoon. By dusk, Turnbull had endured several additional attacks, and his platoon was down to twenty-three men.

Turnbull contemplated his options, and after discussion with several paratroopers, he decided to withdraw to Sainte-Mère-Église. Due to the excessive casualties, he realized that he would be forced to abandon his dead and severely wounded paratroopers. Three soldiers volunteered to stay and fight while the platoon medic administered to the wounded. Having made his decision, Turnbull then led his remaining men to safety in Sainte-Mère-Église. Just before sunset, the Germans occupied Neuville-au-Plain. Forty-three men of Company D had gone to Neuville-au-Plain that morning; only sixteen came out with Turnbull at dusk.

In his post-battle report, Vandervoort was extremely proud of Turnbull and the Third Platoon of Company D for delaying two battalions for more than four hours, calling it "a small-unit performance that has seldom been equaled." The next day, an enemy mortar burst killed Turnbull outside the village that he fought so hard to save. Though seemingly inconsequential in the overall scheme of combat on D-Day, Turnbull's spirited defense of Neuville-au-Plain bought precious time for Ridgway to coordinate the all-round defense of Sainte-Mère-Église, preventing the Germans from attacking the town from both north and south. Like Dolan's defense of La Fière, Turnbull played a critical role in holding Sainte-Mère-Église, the town both Ridgway and Gavin considered vital to the Eighty-Second Airborne's mission.

As dawn broke on June 7, the beleaguered paratroopers at Sainte-Mère-Église awaited another attack from the Germans. Since the principal threat to Sainte-Mère-Église was developing north of the village, Vandervoort focused his efforts in that direction. On the northwest side of the town, Vandervoort's Company D, the same company to which Turnbull belonged, decided to take matters into their own hands.

Waverly Wray, Company D's executive officer, was sure that the German counterattack was imminent. Wray prided himself as a hunter and a crack shot. He once boasted that he never missed a shot that he didn't mean to. He was in his early twenties, extremely physically fit, and mentally alert. One observer noted that Wray possessed the "combat 'sixth sense' of the true warrior—an indefinable intuition, which warns of danger before it appears."

Wray began June 7 by supporting Company D's defense against a determined attack by two reinforced German battalions. The fighting was ferocious. When an enemy machine gun was inflicting a number of casualties, Wray crawled in front of his lines, destroyed the position with grenades and killed the surviving members of the crew with rifle fire. He then occupied the position and remained in close contact with the enemy until he saw a German officer running toward another machine-gun emplacement. Wray shot and killed the officer and then crawled toward the second emplacement, still under direct fire. He destroyed the crew with hand grenades and rifle fire and returned to his platoon.

Wray's one-man counterattack killed fifteen enemy soldiers. After resupplying his men, Wray reported to Vandervoort and explained the situation confronting Company D. Vandervoort ordered Wray to return to company headquarters and launch a spoiling attack. Wray prepared D Company for the assault and conveyed Vandervoort's orders to his wounded commander. Wray then decided to conduct a personal reconnaissance in order to determine the size of the enemy force and to formulate a plan of attack. Armed with his M1, a .45-caliber semiautomatic pistol, a .38 revolver, and as many hand grenades as he could carry, Wray crawled along the hedgerows, venturing beyond Sainte-Mère-Église.

Eventually, he heard several German soldiers talking on the other side of the hedgerow. Stepping up and looking over the earthen embankment, he saw eight Germans in a sunken lane gathered around a radio. Unbeknownst to Wray, he had stumbled into the battalion command group of the First Battalion, 1058th Grenadier Regiment, just as they were preparing to attack the Americans.

Without hesitation, Wray burst from the hedgerow and demanded that the Germans surrender. Seven officers instinctively raised their hands, but the eighth reached for his pistol. Wray shot the man instantly. At the same time, two enemy soldiers in a slit trench about one hundred yards away fired at Wray. One bullet tore off part of his right ear.

Historian Stephen Ambrose described what happened next. Ignoring the return fire, "Wray dropped to his knee and began shooting the other seven officers, one at a time, as they attempted to run away. When he had used up his clip, Wray jumped into a ditch, put another clip into his M-1, and dropped the German soldiers with the *Schmeissers* with one shot each."

Watching Wray as he completed his reconnaissance, one soldier noticed, "The bullet had struck his steel helmet almost dead center at the front rim. A quarter of an inch lower and it would certainly have gone into his forehead. Instead, the bullet was deflected and struck the hinge of his chin strap and clipped a piece of Lieutenant Wray's ear, leaving his face, neck, shoulder, and part of his uniform covered with blood." Returning to company headquarters, Wray collected more grenades and led his men in a counterattack. After finding the German battalion deployed in a sunken lane bordering one of the hedgerows, Wray positioned the platoon's sixty-millimeter mortar and a .30-caliber machine gun to fire down the lane into the enemy's left flank. Now leaderless because of Wray's heroics, the Germans fled northward. By midmorning, the German counterattack was halted and Sainte-Mère-Église was secure.

The next day, Wray and Vandervoort returned to the spot where Wray had killed the German officers. On examining the corpses, Vandervoort noted that Wray had killed each officer with a single shot in the head. Looking at Wray's field jacket and his ear, he remarked, "They've been getting kind of close to you, haven't they, Waverly?"

Wray replied, "Not as close as I've been getting to them, Suh!" Company D's First Sgt. John Rabig overheard the exchange and turned to Vandervoort and said, "Colonel, aren't you glad Waverly's on our side?" About three months later, Wray was killed in action near Nijmegen, Holland, while covering his company's movement to the rear. As Wray raised his head over a railroad track embankment, a German sniper killed him with a single shot in the middle of his head. "The last I saw of him," one trooper remembered, "he was headed for the Germans with a grenade in one hand and a tommy gun in the other."

Before the Normandy campaign was over, the Eighty-Second Airborne Division paid a frightful cost among its junior officers. According to military historian Guy A. LoFaro, 71 percent of the Eighty-Second's Infantry first lieutenants and 65 percent of its infantry second lieutenants became casualties. Of Dolan, Turnbull, and Wray, only Dolan survived the war. Historian S. L. A. Marshall best captured the fighting spirit of the Eighty-Second Airborne Division on D-Day: "Veterans who fought at Sainte-Mère-Église recall it as an affair of blood and iron, filled with shock, suspense, and crisis amid the constant threat of being overrun. [The town] was won and held in a series of small alley brawls, and wreaths of laurel cannot make them larger."

As the nation commemorated the seventieth anniversary of D-Day, we cherished the memory of All-American Lts. John Dolan, Turner Turnbull, and Waverly Wray, along with a host of junior warriors who spearheaded the invasion and liberated Europe.

"All-American Lieutenants: The Eighty-Second Airborne in Normandy" was originally published in *ARMY Magazine* (June 2014).

49

Fall from Grace

The Parallel Careers of General of the Army Douglas MacArthur and Major General George B. McClellan

Since its founding in 1775, the US Army has fielded a formidable array of warriors led by distinguished commanders. Few of these leaders have proved as controversial as Maj. Gen. George B. McClellan and General of the Army Douglas MacArthur. Though both had considerable military talent and achieved enormous popular support in their time, MacArthur and McClellan are remembered today more for their challenges to civilian authority and their removal from command than for their military prowess. Through their extremely rapid rise to the pinnacle of the military profession, these remarkable commanders also exemplify the limitations of unrivaled egotism and insatiable ambition. History loves comparisons, and McClellan and MacArthur provide abundant parallels.

Both men established enviable records at the US Military Academy at West Point. McClellan graduated second in the class of 1846, while MacArthur graduated first in the class of 1903. As junior officers, both men established reputations for courage under fire: McClellan in the Mexican–American War of 1846–1848 and MacArthur in the Vera Cruz expedition of 1914. Fifteen years following graduation from West Point, both achieved general officer rank as they burst on the national scene and captured the public imagination.

The excessive vanity that characterized both future commanders was evident early on while they were cadets at West Point. At the US Military Academy, his peers elected McClellan president of the Dialectic Society, the intellectual cream of West Point's upperclassmen. As he approached graduation, McClellan felt that his overall achievements entitled him to first place in the class of 1846. He wound up second to Cadet Charles S. Stewart, and McClellan did not accept his runner-up status gracefully. "I must confess that I have malice enough to want to show them that if I did not graduate head of my class, I can nevertheless do something," he wrote his family. True to his word, McClellan would command nineteen of his classmates in the Army of the Potomac.

MacArthur mirrored McClellan's defense of his presumed rights and easily wounded egotism. MacArthur missed several of the weekly tests in mathematics during his second year due to illness. When he was informed that he would have to take a special examination with the "goats" of the class to avoid failing the course, Cadet MacArthur went directly to the instructor and demanded his name be removed from the list due to his superior standing on the tests he had already taken. Told that his stance was challenging a direct order, MacArthur informed the officer, "I will not take the test." The next morning, an orderly arrived at MacArthur's room and informed him that his name had been removed from the list. The instructor had backed off his demand, not as much due to MacArthur's insistence as to the instructor's desire not to alienate MacArthur's father, Maj. Gen. Arthur MacArthur Jr., who was expected momentarily on a well-publicized visit to see his son.

The similarities between McClellan and MacArthur are even more apparent when considering the public adulation that accompanied their rise to fame. As he took command of the defenses of Washington in the summer of 1861, McClellan wrote, "I find myself in a new & strange position here—President, Cabinet, Genl Scott & all deferring to me—by some strange operation of magic I seem to have become the power of the land." Dubbed the Young Napoleon by the press and Little Mac by his soldiers—McClellan was only thirty-four years old when Lincoln conferred on him the title of general in chief of all Union armies—McClellan assuaged Lincoln's fears that "this vast increase in responsibilities . . . will entail a vast labor upon you" by assuring him, "I can do it all"—and then did nothing.

MacArthur, too, savored the adulation that greeted his "escape" from the Philippines in March 1942, just after President Franklin Roosevelt directed his transfer to Australia so that MacArthur could eventually play an integral role in leading the Allies to victory against the Japanese in World War II. Though Roosevelt was not personally fond of his Far Eastern general, he released a public statement that said, "Every man and woman in the United States admires with me General MacArthur's determination to fight to the finish with his men in the Philippines." He added, however, that "all important decisions must be made with a view toward the successful termination of the war," so that is why, Roosevelt explained, "every American, if faced individually with the question as to where General MacArthur could best serve his country, could come to only one answer."

At the urging of Army Chief of Staff Gen. George C. Marshall, Congress then bestowed the Medal of Honor on MacArthur for his heroic defense of the Bataan Peninsula. George Gallup's American Institute of Public Opinion discovered in a poll in early May that MacArthur had suddenly emerged as one of the top five men considered by the people as "presidential material for 1944." Not surprisingly, MacArthur bathed in the limelight and ensured that he remained on center stage by monopolizing all the press releases emanating from his headquarters in Australia.

MacArthur was showered with the praise he so earnestly coveted following his pledge, "I shall return!" (to the Philippines). In the aftermath of his arrival in Australia, a reporter with *The New York Times* announced that thirteen babies born in the city between March 1 and April 8 were given the first and middle names of Douglas MacArthur. Shortly thereafter, the Newspaper Guild of New York voted to award him its most prestigious honor, the Column One, Page One Plaque.

Neither McClellan nor MacArthur worked well with civilian authority, and, in particular, neither respected the prerogatives or the problems of the presidents they served. Embroiled in a bitter civil war, all Lincoln wanted was a field commander who was not afraid to engage the enemy—a general who would fight and use the superior resources of the North to grind down the Confederacy. The enemy army—not Richmond—must be your objective, the president emphatically stated to every commander of the Army of the Potomac.

Speed in engaging the Confederate Army was also essential in Lincoln's estimation. "It is of great importance you should move as soon as possible," the president informed Maj. Gen. Ambrose E. Burnside, a

McClellan favorite, on December 26, 1861. "Consumption of time is killing us."

Although Lincoln's call for action would become a familiar refrain, the commanders he appointed often dallied and wasted the best months for campaigning, and no commander tried the president's patience with the slow pace of combat more than McClellan. Supremely convinced of his martial prowess, Commander McClellan would move against the enemy only when he felt conditions warranted it.

Dissatisfied with McClellan's unwillingness to attack Confederate forces entrenched at Manassas Junction astride the battlefield of Bull Run, Lincoln took an extraordinary step at the end of January 1862 and issued Special War Order No. 1, directing the Army of the Potomac to move against the enemy on or before February 22. Again, McClellan vacillated, prompting another presidential visit to encourage his advance. By the time McClellan finally moved his army to the base of the James River–York River peninsula in the spring of 1862, Lincoln was already questioning his indispensability.

Six months later, in the aftermath of Confederate Gen. Robert E. Lee's failed invasion of Maryland, Lincoln paid a final visit to McClellan's headquarters to urge him to cross the Potomac and attack the enemy. After several additional weeks of inaction, McClellan transmitted a report about his lame and sore-tongued horses to the War Department to justify his slow pursuit of Lee. Lincoln exploded: "Will you pardon me for asking what the horses of your army have done since the Battle of Antietam that fatigues anything?"

McClellan finally crossed the Potomac into Virginia, but by then Lee's Army of Northern Virginia was firmly entrenched in the northern Virginia countryside. For Lincoln, Lee's escape proved the final straw. In a private conversation with Francis Preston Blair, Lincoln said he had "tried long enough to bore with an auger too dull to take hold. I said I would remove him if he let Lee's army get away from him, and I must do so. He has got the 'slows,' Mr. Blair."

Lincoln's lack of confidence in McClellan mirrored Little Mac's disdain for the president. McClellan was astonished when Lincoln issued his preliminary emancipation proclamation on September 22, 1862, in the immediate aftermath of the Union victory at Antietam. Two days later

Lincoln suspended the privilege of habeas corpus and specified military trial for anyone charged with discouraging enlistments and militia drafts or with any "disloyal practice" of giving aid and comfort to the enemy.

Lincoln's pronouncements ran counter to McClellan's own political philosophy. In a July 1862 letter written to the president, McClellan had already expressed his firm opposition to emancipation and had even warned that the army might "disintegrate" if the war became a fight for abolition as opposed to a fight for union. On September 17, following the Battle of Antietam, the general was fast to voice his opposition to the administration's path. McClellan professed to his wife that he would never fight for the "accursed doctrine . . . of a servile insurrection," writing that "it is too infamous."

On September 26, just four days after Lincoln issued the proclamation, McClellan wrote William Aspinwall, a wealthy and influential Democratic Party leader. He told Aspinwall that he wanted to know how Northern governors viewed the president's proclamations "inaugurating servile war, emancipating the slaves, and at one stroke of the pen changing our free institutions into despotism." McClellan would continue to cultivate the favor of high-ranking Democrats throughout the war, and in 1864, he accepted the Democratic nomination for the presidency.

As did McClellan, MacArthur demonstrated little respect for his commander in chief. While serving as army chief of staff in 1932, MacArthur faced the dilemma of confronting the Bonus Army that began descending on Washington in late May. The unemployed "army" of World War I veterans sought early payment of pledged bonuses to offset joblessness and financial insecurity. By the end of June, the ranks of the so-called Bonus Expeditionary Forces (BEF) had swollen to more than twenty thousand. The situation had become a political embarrassment to President Herbert Hoover. On July 28, the situation erupted, prompting Secretary of War Patrick Hurley to call on MacArthur to take appropriate action to "maintain law and order in the District [of Columbia]."

MacArthur donned his military uniform—senior officers on duty in the War Department usually wore civilian attire while in Washington—and accompanied the troops against the bonus marchers, "not with a view of commanding the troops, but to be on hand as things progressed, so that he could issue necessary instructions on the ground," according to

D. Clayton James in *The Years of MacArthur, Volume I: 1880–1941.* To avoid the impression that the US Army was abridging free speech, President Hoover directed Hurley to order MacArthur not to pursue the BEF across the Anacostia River, where the billets of the Bonus Army were located. According to Maj. Dwight D. Eisenhower, serving as MacArthur's aide, the chief of staff ignored the presidential order. "In neither instance," wrote Eisenhower, "did General MacArthur hear these instructions. He said he was too busy and did not want either himself or his staff bothered by people coming down and pretending to bring orders."

Two decades later, commanding troops in the Korean War, MacArthur again followed McClellan's path by rejecting the decisions of his civilian leadership. MacArthur simply refused to acquiesce to President Harry Truman's strategy to fight a limited war. In MacArthur's eyes, success required total military victory. While Truman and Secretary of State Dean Acheson sought viable alternatives, MacArthur proposed an "annihilation or evacuation" scenario once the People's Republic of China entered the conflict. Despite MacArthur's insistence that the war be expanded into Manchuria, Truman felt strongly that a negotiated settlement was a legitimate substitute for military victory. MacArthur's blatant refusal to accept these evolving war aims made his subsequent relief from command unavoidable.

Like the frustrated McClellan, MacArthur was in frequent contact with political opponents of the current administration. Just as McClellan had solicited support from the Democratic opposition to President Lincoln, MacArthur courted the support of Truman detractors, freely criticizing administration policy in communiqués to Republican Party House members. Long considered the darling of the Republican Party, he was frequently mentioned as a possible presidential candidate in 1944 and 1948.

The Error of Their Ways

While McClellan and MacArthur actively opposed the policies of their civilian leaders, both commanders committed serious military errors, making it politically feasible for their respective commanders in chief to relieve them from command. Because he frequently overestimated the strength of Lee's army, McClellan squandered the chance of a crushing victory at Antietam, throwing away one of the best opportunities any general had in the Civil War to achieve a Napoleonic-style victory. His subsequent delay in pursuing Lee into Virginia finally caused Lincoln to lose patience.

MacArthur also mistook the size of the enemy, but whereas McClellan consistently overestimated the size of his foe, MacArthur underestimated the size of his enemy. As Chinese Communist forces prepared to attack United Nations forces as they approached the Yalu River in October 1950, MacArthur assured the president in their only face-to-face meeting on Wake Island on October 15 that there was little chance of Chinese intervention. "Only fifty to sixty thousand could be gotten across the Yalu River. They have no air force. . . . If the Chinese tried to get down to Pyongyang, there would be the greatest slaughter." Weeks later, the initial reports of Chinese intervention were received, but MacArthur summarily dismissed the reports even though battlefield commanders confirmed the presence of significant numbers of Chinese troops. The result of MacArthur's refusal to face reality was a bloody repulse at Unsan and the Chosin Reservoir in North Korea and a prolonged retreat of the United Nations armies south of the Thirty-Eighth Parallel.

Neither general accepted accountability for his respective military defeats. Harboring a disdain for the nation's political leadership, McClellan and MacArthur ignored their own misjudgments and accused their civilian authorities of snatching defeat from the jaws of victory.

As McClellan's Army of the Potomac advanced up the Virginia Peninsula toward Richmond in May 1862, McClellan wrote, "When I see the hand of God guarding one so weak as myself, I can almost think myself a chosen instrument to carry out his schemes," and later, "I know that God may even now deem best to crush all the high hopes of the nation and this army—I will do the best I can to insure success and will do my best to be contented with whatever result God sees fit to terminate our efforts."

By the time he reached the outskirts of the enemy capital, however, McClellan was already predicting disaster. Infuriated that Lincoln held back Maj. Gen. Irvin McDowell's corps to defend Washington, DC, in the aftermath of Stonewall Jackson's Valley Campaign of 1862, McClellan cabled, "I will do all that a general can do with the splendid Army I have the honor to command and if it is destroyed by overwhelming numbers . . . the responsibility cannot be thrown on my shoulders—it must rest where it belongs." After Gaines's Mill on June 27, McClellan wrote, "If I save this

Army now, I tell you plainly that I owe no thanks to you [Secretary of War Edwin M. Stanton] or any other persons in Washington—you have done your best to sacrifice this Army." Small wonder why Lincoln and Stanton found McClellan so irritating.

MacArthur also sought to escape accountability when his military fortunes were reversed by the enemy's action. Before the Chinese Communists entered the war in the late autumn of 1950, MacArthur ordered the bridges across the Yalu River, over which armies of Chinese Communists might cross to reinforce the North Korean forces, to be immediately bombed to sever lines of communication between Manchuria and North Korea. An immediate dispatch from Secretary of Defense George C. Marshall countermanded MacArthur's order and directed him "to postpone all bombing of targets within five miles of the Manchurian border." MacArthur informed his chief of staff, "For the first time in military history, a commander has been denied the use of his military power to safeguard the lives of his soldiers and safety of his army." If he were forced to withdraw, MacArthur had found his scapegoat.

In retrospect, the most striking similarity between McClellan and MacArthur is that both commanders were summarily relieved of their commands. In the aftermath of the Seven Days' Battles, McClellan predicted that the Lincoln administration would force him to resign. If they did, McClellan wrote, they would "begin to reap the whirlwind that they have sown." He wrote his wife, Ellen, on July 27, 1862, "I am confident that he [Lincoln] would relieve me tomorrow if he dared do so. His cowardice alone prevents it. I can never regard him with other feelings than those of thorough contempt—for his mind, heart, and morality."

Such blatant insubordination, albeit in private correspondence, coupled with his well-publicized refusal to bring the president into his confidence and his unwillingness to address the enemy, merited McClellan's immediate relief. Why Lincoln did not relieve McClellan earlier than he did was quite clear. Despite McClellan's failure before Richmond, Lincoln needed the popular commander at the point of the country's greatest crisis after Second Manassas. When Lee invaded Maryland in September 1862, the president felt compelled to restore McClellan to command even though he had serious misgivings. When Benjamin Wade, the chairman of the Joint Committee on the Conduct of the War, denounced McClellan's reappointment and demanded that anyone but McClellan should be put in command, Lincoln responded, "Wade, anybody will do for you, but not for me. I must have somebody." Lincoln thus gave McClellan one more chance to redeem his reputation, but McClellan failed to meet Lincoln's expectation. Then and only then, Lincoln relieved McClellan of command of the Army of the Potomac and sent him to New Jersey to await orders that never arrived.

Once relieved, McClellan could only say, "They have made a great mistake—alas for my poor country—I know in my innermost heart she never had a truer servant . . . I do not see any great blunders—but no one can judge of himself." Naturally he found blame elsewhere: "We have tried to do what was right—if we have failed it was not our fault."

MacArthur's stubborn unwillingness to accept Truman's war aims—and execute military strategy consistent with it—lay at the heart of his command failure. In addition, his defeatist-sounding communiqués in the aftermath of Chinese intervention (and resulting battle failures in North Korea) did nothing to increase his prestige among the highest-level decision-makers in the Truman administration. The final straw in MacArthur's dismissal was his penchant for public chatter: Against direct orders to clear public pronouncements with the administration, MacArthur repeatedly released press statements that interfered with potential truce negotiations.

MacArthur's criticism of President Truman following his abrupt relief from command paralleled that of McClellan. In his memoirs, MacArthur noted that Truman's nerves were at the breaking point—"not only his nerves, but what was far more menacing in the Chief Executive of a country at war—his nerve." What rankled MacArthur most was the manner in which he was notified after the press had already leaked the news. "No office boy, no charwoman, no servant of any sort would have been dismissed with such callous disregard for the ordinary decencies," he later wrote. "No slightest opportunity was given me to explain my position, to answer allegations or objections, to present my future concepts and plans," MacArthur recalled in his postwar reminiscences.

Given their refusal to acknowledge civilian control of the military, it seems remarkable that McClellan and MacArthur harbored presidential ambitions of their own. McClellan ran against Lincoln in the presidential race of 1864 and was soundly defeated. He retired from active military service and subsequently served as governor of New Jersey for a single three-year term. He was only fifty-eight years old when, on October 29, 1885, he died from complications following a severe attack of angina pectoris. His death, announced just three months after the nation's greatest military hero, Ulysses S. Grant, had passed away, attracted national attention and appeared on the front page of every major newspaper across the country.

Following his relief from duty as military commander, MacArthur returned to the United States to a hero's welcome and gave a historic address to Congress. His luster began to dim, however, after congressional hearings disclosed some of the complexities faced by the administration in the Far East. His advocates hoped that MacArthur's keynote address at the Republican Convention in Chicago would propel him to his party's nomination for president in 1952. The nomination fell instead to Dwight D. Eisenhower. "The best clerk I ever had," MacArthur allegedly remarked once Ike entered the White House. Other than a highly publicized address to the Corps of Cadets at West Point in May 1962 on the occasion of his receipt of the Sylvanus Thayer Award, MacArthur faded into obscurity. He spent his last decade in an elaborate suite in the Towers of the Waldorf Astoria in New York City. On April 5, 1964, he died of biliary cirrhosis. Not surprisingly, he planned every detail of his funeral. MacArthur lies today in the magnificent MacArthur Memorial in Norfolk, Virginia.

Despite the similarities between McClellan and MacArthur, there were important differences as well. MacArthur's career spanned half a century, including service in two world wars and the Korean conflict. Over the course of the Great War, he was repeatedly cited for heroism by his senior officers. The recipient of two Distinguished Service Crosses, the Distinguished Service Medal, seven Silver Stars, and two Croix de Guerre medals, MacArthur emerged from World War I as the most highly decorated officer in the American Expeditionary Forces. On his own elevation to corps-level command, Maj. Gen. Charles T. Menoher said of his former chief of staff, "MacArthur is the bloodiest fighting man in this army." Command of the Southwest Pacific Theater in World War II and of the United Nations command during the initial months of the Korean War only added to MacArthur's laurels.

No biographer, no matter how pro-McClellan, ever mistook McClellan for a fighting general. McClellan's rise to fame was far more meteoric than even MacArthur's. In contrast to MacArthur's sterling battlefield record, McClellan's star shone brightly for a scant eighteen months before he fell into disfavor with the Lincoln administration. In many ways, Little Mac was a victim of his initial success against mediocre opposition. Battling Lee and the Army of Northern Virginia proved a far more daunting task than fighting his initial opponents in Western Virginia in 1861. What is most revealing in McClellan's case is how rapidly he fell from grace following his arrival in the nation's capital in July. What the public and Lincoln demanded was action, and McClellan's refusal to act decisively weakened his position as general in chief from the outset.

McClellan never comprehended that to defeat the enemy, he would have to witness the loss of a portion of the very army that he had so skillfully created. Every observer noted that McClellan proved an adept trainer of troops. What his generals recognized was something the public could not possibly know: Their favorite general lost confidence once the battle was joined. There is little doubt that McClellan's true genius lay in organization, not in tactics. Both before Richmond and along the banks of Antietam Creek, McClellan designed elaborate plans, but then he abandoned them as soon as his army contacted the enemy. According to Stephen Sears, McClellan's foremost biographer, Little Mac had "lost his inner composure and with it the courage to command under the press of combat."

Loss of confidence was almost never a problem for MacArthur. In the summer of 1950, when the military fortunes of the United Nations seemed at their nadir, MacArthur conceived and, later in September, boldly executed a turning movement deep into the North Korean rear at Inchon. The plan to invade Inchon was MacArthur's military masterpiece and gave him the opportunity to force his will on the unconvinced Joint Chiefs of Staff. Most opposed to MacArthur's plan were Army Chief of Staff J. Lawton Collins and Chief of Naval Operations Forrest P. Sherman, but he was confident that, in spite of the odds, Inchon would succeed.

Inchon, of course, succeeded and further convinced MacArthur that he had a better grasp of strategy than Washington bureaucrats, whose fear of failure was greater than their drive for success. Said MacArthur biographer

Geoffrey Perret, "The most fitting conclusion to MacArthur's life would have been to die a soldier's death in the waters off Inchon at the height of his glory with his legend not simply intact but magnified beyond even his florid imaginings."

Simply stated, MacArthur believed in the hard hand of war. McClellan did not. Schooled in the Napoleonic art of war, which sought a single, decisive battle of annihilation, McClellan failed to recognize that he could achieve exactly that when he trapped Lee's army at Sharpsburg, Maryland, on September 17, 1862. Badly bruised, Lee's army remained intact when a single push, using readily available reserves, would have destroyed it and might have ended the war in one bold stroke similar to MacArthur's success at Inchon eighty-eight years later. Unlike MacArthur, however, McClellan could not order himself to make the attack, and thus Lee's battered army escaped to Virginia to fight another day.

In contrast, MacArthur's proposal to establish a nuclear belt five miles on each side of the Yalu River risked a nuclear war that the Truman administration wisely wished to avoid. In the bitter fighting in Manila and later in Seoul, MacArthur demonstrated his willingness to wage total war, regardless of collateral damage. Such escalation of potential casualties would have found no place in McClellan's heart.

So where does this analysis leave us? McClellan and MacArthur were certainly the military heroes of their days. Both commanders viewed themselves as preeminent military strategists. Both demonstrated admirable military attributes and were greatly admired by their troops. Yet both McClellan and MacArthur overstepped their bounds by crossing the invisible line that separated civil–military control of the armed forces.

In summing up his services to MacArthur in both Washington and the Philippines, Gen. Eisenhower could just as easily have been describing McClellan when he stated emphatically, "Most of the senior officers I had known always drew a clean-cut line between the military and the political. Off duty, among themselves and close civilian friends, they might explosively denounce everything they thought was wrong with Washington . . . and propose their own cure for its evils. On duty, nothing could induce them to cross the line they, and old Army tradition, had established. But if General MacArthur [and for purposes of comparison, General McClellan as well] ever recognized the existence of that line, he usually chose to ignore it."

Leave it to Ike to place things into perspective.

"Fall from Grace: The Parallel Careers of General of the Army Douglas MacArthur and Major General George B. McClellan" was originally published in *ARMY Magazine* (November 2019).

50

Tarnished Legacies

Disgraced Generals Viewed Through Lens of History

Throughout history, several prominent US Army officers have encountered censure and condemnation for alleged command failures. The list includes Maj. Gen. George McClellan, Confederate Lt. Gen. James Longstreet, Lt. Col. George Armstrong Custer, and Gen. Douglas MacArthur, with the addition of a host of junior officers in every conflict the army has fought.

Two twentieth-century commanders, Lt. Gen. Walter Short and Gen. William Westmoreland, endured charges of either dereliction of duty or failure to develop effective strategies to vanquish their respective adversaries. Are such criticisms justified?

Lt. Gen. Walter Campbell Short commanded the Hawaiian Department of the US Army when the Japanese launched the surprise attack on the US Pacific Fleet at Pearl Harbor. A gifted staff officer and trainer, Short earned the Distinguished Service Medal for his work in the development of machine-gun tactics and training in World War I. During the interwar period, Short's career was characterized by steady advancement and attendance in the army's professional education system. Before America's entry into World War II, Short commanded the First Infantry Division, then the Fourth Army Corps during the War Department's maneuvers in 1940.

Army Chief of Staff Gen. George Marshall promoted Short to the temporary rank of lieutenant general and assigned him to command the Army's Hawaiian Department in February 1941. In selecting Short, Marshall picked an officer with an excellent record for training troops.

Most important, Short had done a superb job as assistant commandant at Fort Benning, Georgia, the job Marshall himself once held. As commander of the Hawaiian Department, Short was responsible for the ground defense of the Hawaiian Islands and was jointly responsible with the US Navy for the islands' aerial defense. Marshall expressed the urgency of the post in a cable to Short in which he stated, "The fullest protection for the Fleet is a major consideration for us, there can be little question about that."

Between his assumption of command until the Japanese attack on December 7, 1941, Short worked diligently with his naval counterpart, Adm. Husband Kimmel, to defend Hawaii. His reports to Marshall frequently stressed his preoccupation with the possibility of surprise from the air: As tensions escalated between the United States and Japan, the War Department on November 27, 1941, issued a warning to Short that "hostile action [is] possible at any moment." Though the United States desired that Japan commit the first overt act, "This policy should not be construed as restricting you to a course of action that might jeopardize your defense."

According to Marshall biographer Forrest Pogue, Short reacted to the message with amazing speed. "Believing that subversive activities by Japanese inhabitants of Oahu constituted his major problem," Pogue wrote in *George C. Marshall: Ordeal and Hope, 1939–1942*, Short ordered his planes be lined up wingtip to wingtip as dictated by Alert No. 1. This arrangement constituted Short's primary defense against sabotage. In retrospect, that was a fatal error, as the lack of dispersion at Wheeler and Hickam Airfields made the aircraft more vulnerable to air attack.

The execution of the surprise attack needs no retelling here. Since the navy had been hardest hit, President Franklin Roosevelt sent Secretary of the Navy Frank Knox to make a preliminary investigation. Knox's report evolved into a presidential commission headed by Associate Supreme Court Justice Owen Roberts. The Roberts Commission reported its findings in January 1942, stating that "in the light of the warnings [issued before the attack] and directions to take appropriate action . . . it was a dereliction of duty on the part of each of them [Short and Kimmel] not to consult and confer with the other respecting the meaning and intent of the warnings, and the appropriate measures of defense required by the imminence of hostilities."

When the findings of the Roberts Commission were made public, Short submitted his resignation. Marshall recommended to Secretary of War Henry Stimson that he accept Short's retirement, and "do this quietly without any publicity at the moment." On February 28, 1942, Short retired at a reduced two-star rank.

Should Short have been relieved from command from the Hawaiian Department? Were Short and Kimmel convenient scapegoats for what occurred on December 7, 1941? If so, they were certainly not alone with respect to culpability. Both the War Department and the Roosevelt administration must bear a portion of the blame for the Pearl Harbor disaster. That said, all commanders bear the ultimate responsibility for what their commands do and fail to do.

A quarter-century following the attack on Pearl Harbor, Gen. William Childs Westmoreland encountered criticism for subscribing to a "flawed strategy" of attrition in the context of limited war. Now, many years following his death, Westmoreland is best remembered, and sometimes vilified, for the four years from 1964 to 1968 when he commanded US combat forces in Vietnam, and he is inevitably linked with America's ignominious defeat in Southeast Asia.

Westmoreland was a South Carolina native who fought in three wars, answered to four presidents, and rose to the rank of four-star general. In June 1964, Westmoreland assumed command of the US Military Assistance Command, Vietnam (MACV) from Gen. Paul Harkins. Having served as Harkins's deputy, Westmoreland immediately warned against further American escalation until US leaders were assured that the South Vietnamese government was "established on [a] reasonably firm political, military, and psychological base."

Westmoreland's detractors, then and now—and there are many—characterize the new MACV commander as a political general who failed to comprehend the intricacies of war in the limited age. Some allege that Westmoreland's reliance on search and destroy operations ignored the pacification effort and resulted in excessive American casualties in a war of attrition that America could not hope to win, given the will of the North Vietnamese government to pay an exorbitant price to achieve military victory. In his 2011 biography of the MACV commander, Lewis Sorley goes so far as to claim that Westmoreland was "the general who lost Vietnam."

In fact, that is the title of Sorley's book: *Westmoreland: The General Who Lost Vietnam*.

Historian Gregory Daddis presents an opposing view, noting that Westmoreland was not "wedded to a narrow, conventional concept of warfare." Moreover, retired Col. Paul Miles, who served as Westmoreland's aide during the general's tenure as army chief of staff, in 2013 stated that Westmoreland's "appreciation of the rationale for limited war did not mean that he considered the strategy of gradualism pursued by the Lyndon Johnson administration as altogether ideal. Rather, he believed that even a limited war could be fought in a more forceful manner."

Westmoreland dedicated an entire chapter of his memoirs to the evolution of strategy during his tenure as MACV commander. From the outset, Westmoreland envisioned his strategy in three phases. In the first phase, American combat troops would be used at first to protect developing logistical bases, although some might be committed periodically as "fire brigades" whenever the enemy's big units posed a threat. In the second phase, American troops would gain the initiative, penetrate and, whenever possible, eliminate the enemy's base camps and sanctuaries. In the third and final phase, American troops would "move into sustained ground combat and mop up the last of the main forces and guerrillas."

Important complements of Westmoreland's strategy were always supporting the pacification effort and equipping and training the Army of the Republic of Vietnam (ARVN). By the time Westmoreland's strategy reached its final phase, he fully expected the South Vietnamese government would assume control of the countryside and the ARVN would be prepared to assume full responsibility for Vietnamization.

Did Westmoreland consider alternate strategies? In *A Soldier Reports*, the MACV commander states emphatically that he did. Options that he considered were providing territorial security through South Vietnam and eliminating the enemy's base areas, accelerating the bombing of North Vietnam, raiding enemy border sanctuaries in Laos and Cambodia, and launching amphibious and airmobile operations north of the demilitarized zone. And given the heavy losses inflicted on the North Vietnamese and the Viet Cong during the Tet Offensive, Westmoreland proposed escalating the American commitment.

Would Westmoreland's alternative strategy have been successful? Given the political climate at the time and the willingness of North Vietnam to pay any price in human casualties, perhaps not. The fact remains that Westmoreland constantly reassessed the strategy and was quite cognizant of the political ramifications of his military strategy. In retrospect, Westmoreland developed a comprehensive military strategy that was consistent with Johnson's political goals.

Westmoreland did not lose Vietnam any more than President Harry Truman lost China in 1949 when Mao Zedong proclaimed the People's Republic of China. In his seminal work, *America's Longest War: The United States and Vietnam, 1950–1975*, historian George Herring posits that "the war could not have been won in any meaningful sense or at a moral or material price Americans would—or should—have been willing to pay."

There is an adage, famously uttered by President John Kennedy in 1961, that victory has a hundred fathers and defeat is an orphan. Hindsight always makes the circumstances and the outcomes look clearer than observers at the time viewed them. As World War II and Vietnam fade from our collective consciousness, few will remember Short's and Westmoreland's military achievements.

Given the time lapse from their respective conflicts, will these commanders be remembered only by their perceived failures? What makes the answer imponderable is that even successful soldiers, with few exceptions, are generally soon forgotten. Rather than recalling Short and Westmoreland with scorn, remember that both commanders served honorably as highly qualified professional soldiers who performed their duties to the best of their abilities. Given the extraordinary challenges under which they operated, perhaps Short and Westmoreland deserve our gratitude rather than our indifference.

"Tarnished Legacies: Disgraced Generals Viewed Through Lens of History" was originally published in *ARMY Magazine* (December 2020).

51

A Commander's Pride

World War II Pioneer Led Postal Battalion

After more than two centuries of distinguished service by women in the military, the future of female soldiers in today's army seems assured. Leadership positions in every branch of the service are no longer restricted by gender or race. Nominated by President George W. Bush, Gen. Ann Dunwoody became the nation's first female four-star officer in 2008. Other female leaders quickly followed.

What is sometimes lost in military annals is the story of how this transition to a fully integrated force occurred. In his 1997 history of the US Army in the European Theater, *Citizen Soldiers: The US Army from the Normandy Beaches to the Bulge to the Surrender of Germany, June 7, 1944–May 7, 1945*, author Stephen Ambrose says, "The world's greatest democracy fought the world's greatest racist with a segregated Army." Women in the service, particularly African American female soldiers, were often subjected to ridicule and disrespect.

One officer who shattered stereotypes and fought prejudice was Lt. Col. Charity Adams, who commanded the only all-female African American battalion deployed overseas during World War II. This trailblazer not only bequeathed a legacy of exemplary service to the nation but also paved the way for future generations of female soldiers to break the glass ceiling to reach the highest echelons of command.

Born on December 5, 1918, one of Adams's first memories was of a large Ku Klux Klan parade outside the parsonage that housed her minister father and family in Columbia, South Carolina. Following her graduation from Booker T. Washington High School, Adams matriculated to Ohio's Wilberforce University, one of the nation's premier historically Black colleges. Returning to her hometown after graduation, she taught junior high school students in mathematics and general science.

After four years of teaching, Adams applied for membership in the Women's Army Auxiliary Corps (WAAC). The corps was created in the spring of 1942 as part of a US military expansion effort in the midst of World War II. On July 13, 1942, Adams reported to Fort Hayes, Ohio, and was sworn into the WAAC. Officer training took place at Fort Des Moines, Iowa. The segregated Third Platoon, First Company at the first WAAC Training Center, consisted of thirty-nine women. Following six weeks of intense training, Adams and her classmates were commissioned third officers (comparable to second lieutenants in the US Army) on August 29, 1942.

By the summer of 1943, the ranks of the WAAC had risen to sixty thousand women. That same summer, Congress passed a bill granting army women full military status. President Franklin Roosevelt signed the bill into law on July 1, and the Women's Army Corps (WAC) was born.

At that point, Adams was serving as a company commander at Fort Des Moines. On September 20, 1943, she was promoted to major, making her the highest-ranking Black female officer at the training center. Adams was scheduled to attend the Army's Command and General Staff School at Fort Leavenworth, Kansas, in 1945, but instead was ordered to Fort Oglethorpe, Georgia, where the army's overseas training center was located. There, she joined the first unit of African American WACs preparing to deploy overseas. Due to her elevated rank, Adams was directed to prepare herself for extended service overseas. Adams and Capt. Abbie Noel Campbell arrived in London on January 28, 1945, where Brig. Gen. Benjamin Davis Sr., the army's first African American general, welcomed them to the European Theater.

In London, Adams discovered that she had been assigned as the commanding officer of a Central Postal Directory Battalion for the theater. Campbell served as Adams's executive officer. They arrived in the immediate aftermath of the Battle of the Bulge, along with the battalion soldiers they would lead in replacing male troops who were being sent to the front lines.

By February 3, 1945, the initial contingent of the 6888th Central Postal Directory Battalion, nicknamed the "Six Triple Eight," sailed across the Atlantic aboard the *Ile de France*. Adams met her soldiers in Glasgow, Scotland, and billeted her battalion in Birmingham, England. The second contingent of the 6888th arrived in Glasgow on April 1. All in all, the Six Triple Eight consisted of 817 enlisted personnel and thirty-one officers.

On March 21, 1945, Adams issued General Order No. 1, formally assuming command of the 6888th Central Postal Directory. The battalion was responsible for the redirection of mail to US personnel in the European Theater. Warehouses in Birmingham were overflowing with six months' worth of delinquent mail. The Six Triple Eight's motto soon became "No mail, low morale." The battalion quickly broke all records for redirecting mail, averaging more than sixty-five thousand pieces of mail per eight-hour shift and clearing the six-month backlog in three months.

Shortly after Germany's surrender on May 7, 1945, the 6888th moved from Birmingham to Rouen, France, and eventually to Paris. There, they performed in the same exemplary manner that characterized their service in England. With the end of the war, the number of personnel in the Six Triple Eight dwindled as soldiers rotated home. In March 1946, Adams requested to be released from the European Theater and from active duty, and to return to the United States. Before her discharge, Adams's promotion to lieutenant colonel became effective on December 26, 1945.

Throughout her life, Adams remained extremely proud of the Six Triple Eight. "My feeling of personal achievement was only a minute part of my pride in the unit," Adams said in 1998. "The women of the 6888th had ventured into a service area where they were not really wanted; they had assumed jobs that had normally been assigned to men; and they had been and were performing in a valiant and praiseworthy manner."

Adams never seriously considered making the army a career. By law, she had reached the pinnacle of rank within the WAC because full colonel was authorized only for the WAC director. With discharge in hand effective March 26, 1946, Adams returned to Ohio State University, where she once had been enrolled as a graduate student. On graduating with a master's degree, Adams joined the Veterans Administration in Cleveland as a registration officer. Later, she served as dean of Student Personnel Services at Tennessee A&I College, then accepted a similar post at Georgia State College.

In 1949, Adams married Stanley Earley, a medical student studying in Zurich. She and her husband returned to the United States three years later. Adams dedicated the remainder of her life to educational pursuits, community service, and being a spokesperson for women's rights and civil rights.

In 1989, Adams's memoir was published. In *One Woman's Army: A Black Officer Remembers the WAC*, she wrote, "In another generation young black women who join the military will have scant record of their predecessors who fought on the two fronts of discrimination—segregation and reluctant acceptance by males." Left unsaid was her concern that the contributions of all women who served in the Allied cause during World War II would be forgotten. It took nearly three generations before Adams's fears were eased.

On November 30, 2018, the 6888th Central Postal Directory Battalion Monument was dedicated at the Buffalo Soldier Commemorative Area at Fort Leavenworth, Kansas. The monument is topped by a bust of Adams with the inscription, "There is no pleasure in achievement if it is not shared." Two and a half months later, Secretary of the Army Mark Esper awarded the 6888th Battalion the Meritorious Service Commendation for meritorious service during military operations. Accolades continued.

Signed into law by President Joe Biden on March 14, 2022, the 6888th Central Postal Directory Battalion received the Congressional Gold Medal. And two decades following Adams's death on January 13, 2002, the federal Naming Commission, congressionally tasked with recommending new names for military bases that honor Confederate leaders, endorsed changing the name of Fort Lee, Virginia, to Fort Gregg-Adams to honor two groundbreaking Black officers—Adams and Lt. Gen. Arthur Gregg—for their distinguished service.

I had the privilege of meeting Adams at her home in Dayton, Ohio, in the autumn of 1998. For two hours, she patiently answered my inquiries concerning her role and that of the WAC. Did she consider herself a pioneer? "Not really," she replied. "You don't know you're making history when it's happening. I just wanted to do my job." And for how she wanted to be remembered, "I want my troops to remember me as a person who never forgot any of them," she said. "Most of the general public do not understand and do not believe these women played such an important part in the war."

And that is how I remember Adams, an indefatigable patriot who took pride in commanding her battalion. In performing their duties in a "valiant and praiseworthy manner, surviving racial prejudice and discrimination with dignity, the Six Triple Eight proved proud American soldiers, and had every right to be," she said.

"A Commander's Pride: World War II Pioneer Led Postal Battalion" was originally published in *ARMY Magazine* (January 2023).

52

First Hispanic Four-Star Exemplified Warrior Spirit

In the annals of American military history, Gen. Richard Cavazos occupies a singular place. A two-time recipient of the Distinguished Service Cross, Cavazos became the first Hispanic officer to reach four-star rank in the US Army in 1982. One of the most highly decorated soldiers of the Korean and Vietnam Wars, Cavazos led by example and instilled confidence in future generations of American soldiers. In today's army, his legacy serves as a shining example of the warrior spirit. What made Cavazos unique was the importance he attached to a commander's role as a trainer and a mentor for army leaders. Nearly nine years after Cavazos's death in October 2017, it is time to reassess this legendary officer's contribution to the modern force.

Born on January 31, 1929, the second son of a Texas cowhand at the King Ranch in Texas, Cavazos received his commission as second lieutenant of infantry in 1951 from the Texas Technological University Reserve Officer Training Corps (ROTC). On graduation, Cavazos attended the Infantry Officer Basic Course at Fort Benning, Georgia, and volunteered for a combat assignment in the Republic of Korea.

Deploying to Korea in the autumn of 1952, Cavazos joined the Sixty-Fifth Infantry Regiment, "The Borinqueneers," a regiment assigned to the Third Infantry Division. Before it had been reorganized prior to Cavazos's arrival, the Borinqueneers were part of the Puerto Rico National Guard and had compiled a distinguished combat record. According to one observer, Cavazos "was a natural leader, as drawn to soldiers as they were to him."

On the night of February 25, 1953, a large Chinese force attacked Cavazos's company. The company repelled the enemy assault and inflicted numerous casualties. By the light of a flare, Cavazos observed a wounded enemy soldier in front of his position. Receiving permission from his company commander, Cavazos led a patrol to secure the fallen soldier. With complete disregard for his personal safety, Cavazos continued alone through intense enemy fire to capture and return with the enemy soldier. For his action, Cavazos received his first Silver Star.

Four months later, on June 14, Cavazos, now commanding Company E, led his unit in a series of company-sized raids in the vicinity of Sagimak, each time inflicting numerous casualties on the enemy. His extraordinary heroism in connection with these raids resulted in the award of the Distinguished Service Cross (DSC), his second award for valor in four months.

The Distinguished Service Cross citation reads in part, "When the United Nations element was ordered to withdraw, Lieutenant Cavazos remained alone on the enemy outpost to search the area for missing men. Exposed to heavy hostile fire, Lieutenant Cavazos located five men who had been wounded in the action. He evacuated them, one at a time, to a point on the reverse slope of the hill from which they could be removed to the safety of the friendly lines." Not until then did Cavazos stop to have his own wounds treated.

By the time the Vietnam War was in full swing, Cavazos had become commander of the First Battalion, Eighteenth Infantry Regiment, in the First Infantry Division, the fabled Big Red One. Lt. Col. Cavazos distinguished himself by exceptionally valorous actions on October 30, 1967, while, as battalion commander, he led his unit on a search and destroy operation in a large rubber plantation near Loe Ninh, close to the Cambodian border.

When one of Cavazos's companies was making a reconnaissance, it suddenly began receiving heavy fire from a Viet Cong battalion in well-entrenched positions on the slope of a hill. Cavazos immediately led his remaining companies forward and engaged the enemy forces. Constantly exposed to hostile fire and shrapnel from exploding grenades, Cavazos moved among his troops, directing a counterattack.

As the Viet Cong broke contact and fled to fortified positions on the hillside, Cavazos called for airstrikes and artillery fire on the crest and forward slopes of the hill in order to cut off the insurgents' line of retreat. "When the fighting reached such close quarters that supporting fire could no longer be used, [Cavazos] completely disregarded his own safety and personally led a determined assault on the enemy positions. The assault was carried out with such force and aggressiveness that the Viet Cong were overrun and fled their trenches." For his brilliant leadership in the face of grave danger at Loe Ninh, Cavazos received the Distinguished Service Cross with first oak leaf cluster.

What made Cavazos special, according to Dr. Jim Oenbrink, battalion surgeon in the First Battalion, Eighteenth Infantry Regiment, "was his commander's sixth sense. Lt. Col. Cavazos always anticipated what the enemy was going to do and what needed to be done to throw him off-balance. Our commander was immune to fear. We all knew we were safe with him." To Maj. James Tucker, Cavazos's operations officer, his commander was simply "the Boss." Arriving in Vietnam in 1967, Tucker pondered how he would react in combat. "Pure luck placed me with the best battalion commander who ever served in Vietnam. Cavazos was, all rolled together, teacher, mentor, ass-chewer, and best friend."

The Boss taught Tucker and his officers that no matter what the nature of the conflict, artillery must be the predominant supporting fire. "I am alive today," Tucker said, "because he taught me to keep our soldiers safe and let the artillery do the killing." The Boss's use of artillery became legendary in the Big Red One. Tucker would serve under Cavazos again as a battalion commander when Cavazos commanded the Second Brigade, First Infantry Division, at Fort Riley, Kansas. Serving with and working for Col. Cavazos was just as rewarding at Fort Riley as it had been in Vietnam. Tucker attributed his commander's success to "Cavazos's incredible qualities of intelligence, judgment, character, and his amazing capacity for hard work. I love him as much as anyone can love another human being."

"When I joined the First Infantry Division in September 1971, I reported to then–Col. Cavazos for my initial assignment. The commander directed me to sit down and outlined what he expected from his junior officers. "This is the age of the cynic and the skeptic," Cavazos began. "You will be second-guessed throughout your career by seniors and subordinates alike. Just take care of your soldiers, because they are the nation's most valuable assets."

Then, quoting Rudyard Kipling, a favorite pastime for the colonel, Cavazos continued: "If you can meet with Triumph and Disaster / And treat those two impostors just the same; / If you can talk with crowds and keep your virtue, / Or walk with Kings—not lose the common touch," you will be a successful platoon leader.

The colonel gave me a choice: "I will assign you to an experienced battalion commander or to the toughest warrior I have ever met." I opted for the latter. Cavazos smiled and said, "You are now a platoon leader in my old battalion, the First Battalion, Eighteenth Infantry, commanded by my old operations officer, Lt. Col. Jim Tucker. Let Tucker take care of the battalion; you take care of your platoon."

Five years later, Cavazos became the first Hispanic officer to reach the rank of brigadier general. Clearly destined for a higher station, Cavazos next commanded the Ninth Infantry Division, III Corps, and ultimately, the US Army Forces Command in 1982. He was the first officer of Hispanic descent to hold four-star rank in the US Army before his retirement in 1984.

As Forces Command commanding general, Cavazos was an ardent supporter of the National Training Center at Fort Irwin, California. His involvement in the development of the Battle Command Training Program enormously influenced the army's warfighting capabilities. Cavazos's emphasis on leadership development inspired a generation of combat leaders, including Gens. H. Norman Schwarzkopf and Colin Powell. Schwarzkopf served as a brigade commander under Cavazos in the Ninth Infantry Division. In his autobiography, *It Doesn't Take a Hero*, Schwarzkopf wrote, "Cavazos was a great commander of troops. He was superb at rallying the men . . . I'd also never met a better trainer." What Schwarzkopf most respected was Cavazos's emphasis on taking care of his soldiers. Those lessons proved instrumental in Schwarzkopf's personal success during Operations Desert Shield and Desert Storm.

Powell, too, owed a debt of gratitude to Cavazos's inspired tutelage. As Forces Command commander, Cavazos was impressed with Powell's candor and blunt talk on an inspection tour that Cavazos conducted. Powell later credited Cavazos for rescuing his career from oblivion by positively influencing the senior reviewer of one of his efficiency reports. When Cavazos talked about what it meant to be a soldier, to offer one's life in the service of our country, Powell said, "He could bring grown men to tears."

Never recognized as a traditional product of the army's officer commissioning or school system, Cavazos was never beholden to traditional ways. His innovative thinking and his leadership as a combat officer in two wars serve as sterling examples that soldiers thrive on good leadership. His emphasis on solid training, soldier welfare and leadership development remain as relevant today as they were during Cavazos's distinguished career.

"First Hispanic Four-Star Exemplified Warrior Spirit" was originally published in *ARMY Magazine* (September 2020).

53

Intuitive Commanders

Successful Leaders Like Patton and Moore Anticipate Enemy Intentions

In his treatise on war, Prussian military theorist Carl von Clausewitz defined a commander's intuition, what he termed *coup d'oeil*, as a critical component of military genius. *Coup d'oeil* refers to the quick recognition of a truth that the mind would ordinarily miss or would perceive only after long study and reflection.

On the battlefield, intuitive commanders possess a distinctive advantage over their adversaries, as they can more readily decipher an opponent's intentions and decisions. Since war is the province of chance and uncertainty, intuition, combined with experience and expertise, facilitates a field commander's ability to sense how a battle or maneuver is unfolding, how the overall engagement is evolving, and when to seize the strategic moment of importance, even in the absence of critical information. Two American warriors, Gen. George Patton Jr. and Lt. Col. Harold "Hal" Moore, personify the value of intuitive command in warfare.

Patton epitomized the offensive spirit and was arguably the finest operational commander fielded by the US Army in World War II. In the aftermath of the Sicilian Campaign in which Patton commanded Seventh US Army, Gen. Dwight Eisenhower, then Supreme Commander, Allied Forces Headquarters, cabled Army Chief of Staff Gen. George Marshall that Patton had "conducted a campaign where the brilliant successes must be attributed directly to his energy, determination, and unflagging aggressiveness."

Yet Patton's fame as a combat commander rests not so much on what he did in North Africa and Sicily as much as on his command of Third US Army in the campaign in northwest Europe. Third Army's breakout across France in August 1944 and the relief of Bastogne, Belgium, that December was brilliantly orchestrated and executed against a determined enemy. Not surprisingly, Patton's adversaries rated him as the most dangerous enemy they faced in the final year of the European war. A review of his final campaign in Normandy, France, explains why.

On August 1, 1944, Third Army became operational in France with Patton as its commanding officer. Four days earlier, Patton had assumed control of VIII Corps following the success of Operation Cobra in the hedgerow battles of Normandy. By August 1, Patton closed in on Avranches, the gateway to the Brittany peninsula. Breaking through enemy lines, Patton directed only his VIII Corps toward Brest. Astutely anticipating that the decisive battles of the European campaign would be fought to the east, Patton ordered the bulk of Third Army toward the Seine River.

In two weeks, he advanced farther than any army in history in what he termed "probably the fastest and biggest pursuit in history." In his diary, dated August 21, Patton recorded that "we have at this time, the greatest chance to win the war ever presented. . . . [W]e can be in Germany in ten days. . . . It is such a sure thing that I fear these blind moles don't see it."

Patton's predictions to terminate the war proved overly optimistic. Nevertheless, he had attacked so rapidly that the German high command could not react quickly enough to halt Third Army's advance. Eventually, it was logistical problems, not enemy resistance, that stalled Patton's progress. Finally resupplied by late autumn, the Allies approached the Rhine River, the final natural obstacle before invading the German homeland. Adolf Hitler, however, had other plans.

On December 16, 1944, Hitler launched a massive counteroffensive in the Ardennes region that pushed a salient into Lt. Gen. Courtney Hodges's First US Army's front. When informed of the German breakthrough, Patton immediately prepared a number of contingencies. As soon as Gen. Omar Bradley, commander of Twelfth US Army Group, informed him of the extent of the German offensive, Patton directed his chief of staff to prepare plans to pivot Third Army ninety degrees northward and smash the southern shoulder of the "bulge." Patton's performance in what became known as the Battle of the Bulge, the largest battle ever fought by the US Army in terms of numbers of combatants and casualties, was the supreme hour of his career.

Three days after the German onslaught, Eisenhower assembled his senior commanders at his headquarters in Versailles, France, and inquired how soon anyone could attack. Patton replied that he could attack in three days with three divisions. Such a proposal was astonishing, both operationally and logistically. The Supreme Commander, Allied Expeditionary Force advised caution, but Patton stated that if he waited for additional reinforcements, the element of surprise would be sacrificed.

Again, Patton's instincts proved correct. On December 22, Third Army moved north to relieve Bastogne. Refusing to take counsel of his fears, Patton confided in his diary, "Of course [we] may be cut off, but I doubt it. . . . The speed of our movements is amazing, even to me, and must be a constant source of surprise to the Germans." Four days later, on December 26, Patton's advance elements broke through German lines and contacted the 101st Airborne Division. Bastogne was saved. In retrospect, the relief of Bastogne provided Patton his proudest professional achievement as an army commander.

Of all the American warriors in World War II, Patton stands supreme—a twentieth-century Achilles. The essence of Patton's generalship, according to biographer Martin Blumenson, revolved around his insatiable impatience to attack and his desire to overwhelm the enemy. Then his "drive and his will, as well as his sixth sense of anticipation, triggered a near-faultless implementation of what his imagination and his mastery of the art of war had projected."

Twenty years later and half a world away, a tactical commander's intuition resulted in a hard-fought victory in the first major battle of the Vietnam War between the US Army and the People's Army of Vietnam. Command of the First Battalion, Seventh Cavalry Regiment, Lt. Col. George Armstrong Custer's former regimental command, rested on Hal Moore's shoulders. A West Point graduate in 1945, Moore had compiled a distinguished war record as a company commander in the Korean War. In those desperate hilltop battles along what eventually became the demilitarized zone in the spring of 1953, Moore matured as a combat leader.

Moore and his battalion deployed to South Vietnam in 1965 and immediately commenced combat operations in the rugged Central Highlands. The First Battalion, Seventh Cavalry, was assigned to the First Cavalry Division (Airmobile). On November 14, Moore received orders to search and destroy any enemy in the vicinity of the Ia Drang-Chu Pong massif, adjacent to the Cambodian border where intelligence reports had concluded that a North Vietnamese Army regiment was located.

In the morning hours of November 14, Moore personally selected a landing zone called X-Ray at the base of the mountain. Unbeknownst to the Americans, the area also served as a logistical depot and staging area for the Sixty-Sixth and Thirty-Third North Vietnamese Army Regiments. Moore and his lead company landed at 10:48 a.m. and began clearing the landing zone. Moore's intuition led him to believe his troopers were already under direct observation by the enemy. His instincts proved prescient.

Within minutes, Moore's troopers encountered enemy fire. If the prisoner that his men captured during the initial skirmish was right, Moore's 175-man force would be outnumbered eight-to-one. In Moore's words, "My instinct told me that the enemy commander was likely to strike at our left flank, heading to the clearing." Consequently, Moore directed one of his companies to deploy in that direction as rapidly as possible and took the risk of leaving his rear unguarded from the north and east of X-Ray. Fortunately, the remainder of Moore's battalion landed by mid-afternoon, augmented by an additional company from the Second Battalion, Seventh Cavalry.

For two days, Moore held off repeated enemy assaults, due in large part to his inspired leadership and massive fire support. By trusting his instincts, Moore led his troopers to a decisive victory. North Vietnamese Army casualties totaled 834 dead by body count—which Moore reduced to 634 killed in action due to "a personal allowance for the confusion and fog of war"—with an additional 1,215 enemy estimated killed and wounded by artillery, air attacks, and aerial rocket attacks. On the American side, Moore suffered seventy-nine killed in action and 121 wounded. No men were missing. To his credit, Moore never left a single trooper unaccounted for in any engagement in which he fought.

On November 16, Moore and the First Battalion, Seventh Cavalry redeployed for rest and replenishment. Years later, Moore reflected on the battle in the Ia Drang Valley. "None of the common wisdom born of the American experience in Vietnam to date applied to the [North Vietnamese Army]. We had been locked into a savage battle of fire and maneuver, a battle for survival, which only one side would be permitted to win. A commander in battle," Moore stated, "has three means of influencing the action: Fire support, his personal presence on the battlefield, and the use of his reserve." To Moore, instincts are the product of one's "personality, education, experience, reading, training, observations, and the environment in which one lives and works. When seconds count and time is critical, instincts come into play in judgment and decision making."

So, what do Patton's and Moore's careers suggest for leaders in today's army? Both Patton and Moore were dedicated officers who impressed their superiors with their professional zeal and intellectual curiosity. Due to their intuitive nature and lifelong learning from the study of military history, they developed a "sixth sense," a gut feeling, that proved instrumental in their battlefield success. By anticipating their adversaries' next steps, Patton and Moore proactively seized the initiative and forced their opponents to react to them, vis-à-vis reacting to their enemies. Patton's and Moore's successes, at both the operational and the tactical levels, were hardly happenstance, but rather born of a lifetime of study and reflection. In the process, they bequeathed a legacy of combat excellence that serves as a model for current and future army leaders.

"Intuitive Commanders: Successful Leaders Like Patton and Moore Anticipate Enemy Intentions" was originally published in *ARMY Magazine* (August 2021).

54

Medal of Honor Recipients Beat Prejudice, the Enemy

The Medal of Honor is the most revered and highest award for military valor in action. Since the decoration's inception in 1861, for the navy, the medal has been bestowed in the name of Congress 3,530 times, including on one woman and on nineteen individuals who have received multiple awards. The standards to award the medal have evolved over time. On July 25, 1963, Congress approved guidelines and established the current criteria to recognize "conspicuous gallantry and intrepidity at the risk of one's life above and beyond the call of duty."

Secretary of War Edwin Stanton first bestowed the medal on the surviving members of a Union Army scouting detachment known as Andrews' Raiders on March 25, 1863. Private (Pvt.) Jacob Parrott holds the distinction of being the medal's initial recipient.

Though each honoree possesses a unique story and deserves the gratitude of the nation, three recipients illustrate that heroism can overcome prejudice. Private First Class (Pfc.) Desmond Doss is perhaps one of the most unlikely recipients of the Medal of Honor. Born in Lynchburg, Virginia, on February 7, 1919, Doss was raised in a strict Seventh day Adventist family. Entering the army on April 1, 1942, Doss was classified 1AO, meaning conscientious objector (CO) available for noncombatant military service, as Seventh-day Adventists are prohibited from working on the Sabbath. The army did not have a separate category for a noncombatant other than CO, so Doss became a medic with the First Battalion, 307th Infantry Regiment, Seventy-Seventh Infantry Division.

Following basic training at Fort Jackson, South Carolina, Doss's company shipped to the Pacific in mid-1944. Doss's support of his fellow soldiers on Guam and subsequently on the island of Leyte in the Philippines, Gen. Douglas MacArthur's initial landfall on the Philippine Islands, was exceptional, and he received a Bronze Star with V device.

The Seventy-Seventh Division relieved the Ninety-Sixth Infantry Division on the island of Okinawa on April 28, 1945. It was on Okinawa that Doss encountered his rendezvous with destiny. Stretching across the island was a four-hundred-foot cliff called the Maeda Escarpment. Doss's company's mission was to scale the ridge and eliminate the enemy on the reverse slope of the escarpment. The climb was exceedingly difficult, with the last thirty to forty feet nearly vertical.

On May 2, 1945, Doss reached the summit with 155 soldiers from Company B. At the top of the escarpment, Company B encountered heavy resistance. When the commander ordered his men to retreat on May 5, Doss refused to abandon his wounded comrades. Over the next five hours, Doss dragged wounded soldiers individually and lowered them over the ledge to the safety of their comrades below. All the time, he kept praying, "Lord, help me get one more."

How many soldiers had Doss rescued? Division headquarters reported 155 men went up the escarpment, and only fifty-five returned from the hill on their own. Doss modestly stated that he saved fifty men. Doss's exploits were later featured in the 2016 feature film *Hacksaw Ridge*, directed by Mel Gibson.

Doss repeated his heroics over the next two weeks before he was seriously wounded on May 21, 1945. Evacuated to the United States, newly promoted Cpl. Doss received the Medal of Honor from President Harry Truman on October 12, 1945. Doss died on March 23, 2006, and is buried in Chattanooga National Cemetery in Tennessee. Doss remains the first conscientious objector to receive the nation's highest award for valor in combat. Two decades later, Thomas Bennett and Joseph La Pointe Jr., also combat medics and conscientious objectors, followed in Doss's footsteps during the Vietnam War.

Half a world away, Second Lt. Daniel Inouye encountered a different type of prejudice than Doss. During World War II, Inouye fought two wars: one against the German army and a second against racial prejudice. In the process, Inouye demonstrated that heroism is colorblind, and courage is indifferent to racial identity.

Born in Honolulu on September 7, 1924, to a second-generation Japanese American family, seventeen-year-old Daniel witnessed the Japanese attack on Pearl Harbor. As soon as he graduated from high school in 1942, he attempted to enlist in the army, but the War Department classified Japanese Americans as "enemy aliens." Not until those restrictions were lifted the following year could Inouye enlist.

Inouye joined the 442nd Regimental Combat Team, a unit comprised almost entirely of second-generation American soldiers of Japanese ancestry but commanded by Caucasian officers. Inouye progressed rapidly through the ranks, and in 1944, the 442nd deployed to Italy where Inouye earned his combat spurs in the fighting around Rome and central Italy. Transferred to southern France to meet Germany's late-winter offensive in the Vosges Mountains, Inouye cheated death when a German round hit him in the chest just above the heart. For his valor, Inouye received a battlefield commission to second lieutenant and a Bronze Star.

Inouye's regiment returned to Italy in the spring of 1945. On April 21, Inouye led his platoon against a heavily defended ridge outside of San Terenzo. Unfazed by enemy fire, Inouye identified three enemy machine-gun positions. Crawling up a treacherous slope to within five yards of the nearest machine gun, he hurled two grenades and destroyed the enemy emplacement. He then neutralized the second position. Although seriously wounded by a sniper's bullet, Inouye engaged more enemy positions until a grenade shattered his right arm.

Refusing evacuation, Inouye continued to direct his platoon until the ridge was safely in American hands. His wounds were considered life-threatening, but he survived. Inouye remained in the army until 1947 when he was honorably discharged at the rank of captain. After the war, Inouye returned to Hawaii and earned a college education through the GI Bill. In 1959, he was one of Hawaii's first delegates to the US House of Representatives. He later served in the US Senate from 1962 to 2012, culminating in his position as president pro tempore of the Senate.

On June 21, 2000, in the name of Congress, President Bill Clinton bestowed the Medal of Honor on Inouye and nineteen other members of the 442nd Regimental Combat Team. Thirteen years later, President

Barack Obama granted Inouye a posthumous award of the Presidential Medal of Freedom. Inouye is buried in the National Memorial Cemetery of the Pacific in Honolulu.

Like Doss and Inouye, Staff Sgt. Roy Benavidez embarked on a journey from poverty and prejudice to receive the highest accolades of a grateful nation. Born on August 5, 1935, near Cuero, Texas, Benavidez's given name at birth was Raul Perez Benavidez. He changed "Raul" to "Roy" when he joined the army in 1955.

The son of a Mexican farmer and a Yaqui Indian mother, Benavidez was a high school dropout and a troubled youth until he joined the Texas National Guard in 1952. Seven years later and after multiple overseas tours, Benavidez graduated from Airborne School at Fort Bragg, North Carolina. The school transformed Benavidez's life. In his words, "Until I became Airborne, I had often allowed my temper and my insecurities to control the direction of my life." From 1959 to 1965, Benavidez served with the Eighty-Second Airborne Division, and in 1965, he deployed to the Republic of Vietnam as an adviser to a South Vietnamese infantry unit. His tenure as an adviser was short-lived after he stepped on a land mine. Evacuated to the United States, Benavidez was told he would never walk again. Benavidez proved the doctors wrong, undertaking a severe physical regimen and cramming eighteen months of healing and therapy into six months.

By 1966, he volunteered for Special Forces and received the coveted Green Beret the following year. In January 1968, Benavidez received orders to deploy to South Vietnam for his second tour. On May 2, 1968, a twelve-man Special Forces reconnaissance team was inserted by helicopters into a dense jungle to gather intelligence about confirmed large-scale enemy activity. Under heavy enemy fire, the team requested extraction. Three helicopters attempted to extract the team and were all shot down. Benavidez, who was monitoring the operation by radio, voluntarily boarded another aircraft to assist in another extraction attempt.

Unable to land at the designated pickup zone, he jumped from his aircraft and ran approximately seventy-five yards under withering small-arms fire to the crippled team. Despite multiple wounds in the abdomen and grenade fragments in his back, he repositioned the team members and directed their fire to facilitate the landing of an extraction aircraft. Despite his wounds, Benavidez gathered sensitive documents from the downed aircraft. Directing aerial and artillery fire against the enemy, Benavidez refused extraction until every surviving team member was safely aboard an aircraft.

By the time he returned to base camp, Benavidez was convinced he was dying. "My eyes were blinded. My jaws were broken. I had over thirty-seven puncture wounds. My intestines were exposed," Benavidez wrote in his book with John Craig, *Medal of Honor: One Man's Journey from Poverty and Prejudice*. For his actions on May 2, Benavidez received the Distinguished Service Cross.

Following a year of recovery, Benavidez returned to active duty. He retired as a master sergeant with a total disability in 1976 and returned to Texas. After years of bureaucratic machinations to gather pertinent information surrounding Benavidez's heroic actions in the war, President Ronald Reagan presented Benavidez with the Medal of Honor on February 24, 1981. Benavidez died in 1998 and is buried at Fort Sam Houston National Cemetery in San Antonio.

Because the Medal of Honor is presented "in the name of the Congress of the United States," it is frequently called the Congressional Medal of Honor. The terms are used interchangeably, but regardless of designation, the Medal of Honor remains the most prestigious and treasured of all decorations in the armed services. Doss, Inouye, and Benavidez are typical of the Medal of Honor recipients who have received the coveted award on behalf of their fallen comrades. May their shadows loom large and serve as a beacon to every soldier who wears the uniform of the US Army.

"Medal of Honor Recipients Beat Prejudice, the Enemy" was originally published in *ARMY Magazine* (April 2022).

55

Beyond the Ia Drang Valley

In his novel of the Battle of Thermopylae, author Steven Pressfield describes a scene in which Dionekes, a Spartan officer, prepares his men for a battle against a numerically superior army of Persians. Watching Dionekes rally and tend to his men, the narrator identifies the essential role of an officer in combat: to prevent those under his command, at all stages of battle—before, during, and after—from becoming so overcome by terror or anger that emotion usurps dominion of the mind. "To fire their valor when it flagged and rein in their fury when it threatened to take them out of hand"—that was Dionekes's job.

Two and a half millennia later, a modern Spartan displayed similar attributes of self-restraint and self-composure when Lt. Col. Harold G. (Hal) Moore led the men of the First Battalion, Seventh Cavalry into the Ia Drang Valley in the Republic of Vietnam in November 1965. Like Dionekes before him, Moore bequeathed a legacy of raw courage and inspirational leadership in war's darkest crucible. By his own admission, Moore is not a hero, but to his men and to a generation of future officers whom he addressed at the US Military Academy, he is the penultimate battle captain. When actor Mel Gibson and his entourage visited West Point in the spring of 2002 to launch the premier of his movie, *We Were Soldiers*, the greatest applause was reserved not for Gibson, but for Moore, who quietly slipped away unnoticed during the film's battle scenes. Not surprisingly, in a recent survey conducted following one of his visits, the majority of cadets identified Moore as the most inspirational officer in their cadet experience.

To a Long Gray Line accustomed to visits by the army's most distinguished leaders, why does Moore stand out? The true essence of his popularity within the Corps of Cadets is not limited to his command of American troops in the first pitched battle in the Vietnam War between the US Army and the North Vietnamese Army. Scores of commanders have conducted similar battles and achieved like success. What differentiates Moore from his fellow warriors is his message concerning preparation for battlefield leadership and his own philosophy on the conduct of a leader in battle.

The road to Hal Moore's status as a cadet icon began in the hills of Kentucky in a small town called Bardstown. Born on February 13, 1922, Moore matriculated to West Point by a circuitous path. Unable to secure an appointment before his graduation from high school, Moore left home in February 1940 and traveled to Washington, DC, where he hoped his chances to secure a congressional appointment would be enhanced. He completed high school at night and attended George Washington University in the evenings for two years. When Congress doubled the size of the corps of cadets in 1942 to meet wartime commitments, Moore finally obtained his appointment from a Georgia congressman. The entire process reinforced Moore's belief that the first person you must learn to lead is yourself. Set lofty goals and persist until you achieve them.

Never the best student in the mathematical sciences, Moore struggled, taking refuge in religious activities that further honed his character. His greatest joy in Beast Barracks was firing Expert on the M1 rifle with the top score in the company. His academic pursuits proved more difficult. In his own words, his first semester at West Point was "an academic trip from hell." Moments of quiet meditation in the Catholic chapel and long hours of study finally paid dividends. As cited in West Point's yearbook, Hal Moore graduated in 1945 under the curtailed curriculum "untouched by the machinations of the T.D. [Tactical Department] and Academic Departments."

Not surprising to anyone who knew him well, Moore selected Infantry as his branch and joined the 187th Airborne Regiment in Sendai, Japan. The summer of 1948 found First Lt. Moore at Fort Bragg, North Carolina, where he jump-tested experimental parachutes and other airborne gear. By his own calculation, he made upward of 150 jump tests over the course of the next three years. On his first test jump, however, the parachute hung on the tail of a C-46 aircraft and Moore was dragged behind the plane, at 110 miles per hour, 1,500 feet above the drop zone before he could cut it off and use his reserve. The ability to take a few seconds to think under such hazardous conditions would become a hallmark of Moore's character for the remainder of his military career. The years at Bragg also marked Moore as quiet, professional, and unfazed by challenges.

In June 1952, Moore, now a husband and father of two children, deployed to Korea. Over the course of the next fourteen months, he commanded a rifle company and heavy mortar company in the Seventeenth Infantry, Seventh Infantry Division, seeing action in the battles of attrition on Pork Chop Hill, T-Bone, Alligator Jaws, and Charlie Outpost. By now, Moore was a battle-tested commander. When the armistice was signed in July 1953, he reported to the US Military Academy to teach infantry tactics to aspiring officers. The post–Korean War army also brought Moore to the Pentagon, where he served with distinction in the Air Mobility Division in the office of the Chief of Research and Development, in the Office of the Deputy Chief of Staff for Operations and Plans.

Following graduation from the Naval War College in June 1964, Lt. Col. Moore received a by-name request from Brig. Gen. Harry W. O. Kinnard, commanding general, Eleventh Air Assault Division (Test), to serve as a battalion commander. Redesignated the First Cavalry Division (Airmobile) in July 1965, the division deployed to South Vietnam's Central Highlands in response to Lyndon Johnson's escalation of the war. It was in that capacity that Moore's First Battalion, Seventh Cavalry fought the first major pitched battle with the North Vietnamese Army (NVA) at Landing Zone X-Ray in the Ia Drang Valley in November 1965.

Moore's conduct of the battle is well chronicled in his and Joe Galloway's *We Were Soldiers Once and Young* and needs little elaboration here. Suffice it to say that the success of Moore's soldiers in repelling the attack of a well-disciplined enemy force five times their own size was the result of Moore's battlefield leadership and the indomitable spirit of his men. Moore was the first man off the lead helicopter and the last soldier to leave the battlefield three days later. Putting everything he had learned at West Point and twenty years of leadership in battle into the action, Moore inflicted more than six hundred dead on the enemy at a cost of seventy-nine killed and 121 wounded. True to his word, he brought out every one of his troopers. In fact, throughout his thirty-two-year career, Hal Moore never abandoned an American soldier on the battlefield.

Following the Ia Drang battle, Moore was promoted to command the First Cavalry Division's Third Brigade that saw action on the Bong Son Plain in January 1966. Subsequent tours of duty included service with the International Security Affairs, Office of the Secretary of Defense; commanding general of the Seventh Infantry Division in Korea, and then commanding general of Fort Ord, California. Moore ended his career as deputy chief of staff for personnel. When he retired in 1977, he became an executive vice president of the company that developed the ski area at Crested Butte, Colorado. Four years later he formed a computer software company. During retirement, Moore spent his time with his wife Julie and their family in their homes in Crested Butte, Colorado, and Auburn, Alabama.

Moore's achievements in a career spanning three decades are legendary. First in his West Point class to be promoted to one, two, and, three stars, Moore received accelerated promotions on six occasions. Recipient of the Purple Heart and seven awards for battlefield valor, including the Distinguished Service Cross, Moore never lost a man as prisoner or missing in action, which brings us back to West Point and why the Corps of Cadets holds Moore in such high esteem.

On the twenty-fifth anniversary of the fall of Saigon, Gen. Moore returned to his alma mater at the invitation of the Department of History to address the Corps of Cadets on battlefield leadership during the Battle of the Ia Drang Valley. Following a brief narration of the battle, Moore got to the main purpose of his visit: the preparation of American soldiers for combat. Cadet time is carefully regimented, but two hundred of the thousand cadets remained one hour beyond the scheduled lecture to hear the old warrior's remarks. For an additional hour, Moore captivated his audience, dividing his comments between a leader's preparations for battlefield leadership and his own philosophy on the conduct of a leader in battle.

In preparing America's sons and daughters for combat, Gen. Moore directed the cadets to read military history, particularly small unit actions. The personality of a big battle is often formed by a small unit action. During the Ia Drang Battle, for example, much of Moore's efforts were directed at rescuing an isolated platoon of one of his companies. In addition to

Steven Pressfield's *Gates of Fire*, Moore cited Stephen E. Ambrose's *Band of Brothers* and Ian Knight's books on the defense of *Rorke's Drift During the Zulu Wars of 1879*. All three books have appeared on the army chief of staff's recommended reading list.

Second, Moore urged cadets to visit historic battlefields with maps, books, and narratives from actual participants to understand the intricacies of battles and campaigns. The staff ride concept was pioneered by Capt. Arthur L. Wagner at Fort Leavenworth, Kansas, at the turn of the twentieth century and emerged as a vital component of officer professional development for more than a hundred years. Today most commanders incorporate some aspect of the staff ride in their training to enhance unit morale and to determine how and why key leaders made their decisions under hazardous conditions. Moore himself once returned from the Normandy battlefields where he contemplated the decisions by the senior Allied commanders.

Next Moore stressed the necessity of installing the will to win in one's command. He was adamant that commanders should not place any second-place trophies in the unit. "Focus on winning, being first," and the soldiers will respond more rapidly. His remarks were reminiscent of former Green Bay Packer coach Vince Lombardi who demanded a commitment to excellence and victory above all else. To Lombardi the greatest joy in life was to give one's last ounce of strength and to lie exhausted in victory.

Fourth, Moore concentrated on building unit discipline and teamwork. When he commanded Fort Ord in 1971, Moore instituted bayonet and pugil stick training, hand-to-hand combat training, confidence, and close combat courses, field marches, and rappelling to improve morale and prepare his soldiers for combat. Such combat-enhancing courses resulted in a "family of warriors," much the same as his First Battalion, Seventh Cavalry in the Ia Drang Valley. Only by installing "layer after layer after layer of personal discipline on one's troops" will units "stand tall, hang in, and stay alive when the going gets tough."

Fifth, Moore urged the cadets to prepare their commands for their own death and that of their subordinate leaders. Squad leaders must be ready to assume command of a platoon and a company.

To illustrate his point, Moore remembered on the first day of the Ia Drang fight, one of Bravo Company's platoons lost every officer and noncommissioned officer save one. Faced with overwhelming pressure from the North Vietnamese Army, Sgt. Ernie Savage, the fourth man to inherit Lt. Henry Herrick's "Lost Platoon," called indirect fire on his own position. Savage's action saved the remainder of the platoon, which had suffered nine dead and thirteen wounded in the first ninety minutes of combat. Not only must platoon leaders train squad and fire team leaders to adjust artillery and mortar fire but leaders at all levels must prepare for wounded men, yelling for "Medic" or "Mom." In battle, leaders must divorce themselves from the sounds of combat and concentrate on making clear, logical decisions.

Gen. Moore concluded his comments on preparation for battlefield leadership by reminding the cadets that mission accomplishment comes first, then care of their soldiers. The easiest part is responding to the soldiers' personal needs: food, water, mail, and information on what is going on. The more important steps are developing stressful realistic training, rigorous physical conditioning and "stern, fair and square discipline." With respect to his own battalion, Moore's precombat training inculcated the Spartan qualities of self-denial, discipline, and sacrifice into the troopers who deployed to Vietnam in 1965.

Treated right, Moore said, the least private first class (Pfc.) is capable of acts of valor and sacrifice that are breathtaking. One only has to return to the Ia Drang to confirm Moore's theory. Two cavalry troopers, Russell Adams and Bill Beck, manned an M60 machine gun and with another crew, they protected Alpha Company's left flank during the opening stages of the battle. When Adams suffered a debilitating wound, it fell to assistant gunner Beck to maintain a withering fire on the enemy, now within thirty yards of his position. Moore later recalled that when Specialist 4 Beck's company and his country needed him most, Beck rose to the occasion and answered the call.

Gen. Moore summarized his remarks on battlefield preparation by reminding the cadets to "live each of your troop duty days to the fullest." No one ever wrote a book about the joy and delights of being a staff officer, stated Moore, so "spend time with your soldiers. Talk with them. Never ever abuse them by an act of omission. They are the secret to successful command on or off the battlefield." Again, his words are reminiscent of the Spartan warrior who described his king Leonidas as a monarch "who did not command his men's loyalty through fear nor purchase it with gold, rather he earned their respect by the sweat of his own back and the pains he endured for their sake."

Turning his attention to conduct in battle, Moore next outlined four basic principles to govern ground combat. First, "Three strikes and you are not out!" A commander has two alternatives in battle. He can either contaminate his environment and his unit with his attitude and actions or inspire confidence. To inspire confidence a leader must be visible on the battlefield and must be in the battle. Moore cautioned cadets to possess and display the will to win by one's actions, one's words, one's tone of voice on the radio, and face-to-face.

Moreover, a commander must display quiet confidence and display no fear, ignoring "the noise, dust, smoke, thirst, explosions, screams of wounded, the yells, the dead lying around him." Such chaos is normal in battle, not the exception. Battle by its nature is chaotic. Good commanders strive to make battle organized chaos, rather than disorganized carnage. In la Orang, Moore's lead helicopter pilot, Maj. Bruce Crandall, remembered Moore as "always making the right decision, always fully aware of the situation."

Second, "There's always one more thing you can do to influence any situation in your favor—and after that one more thing—and after that one more thing." Taking a few seconds to separate oneself mentally from the battle, Moore repeatedly asked himself, "What am I doing that I should not be doing? And what am I not doing that I should be doing to influence the situation in my favor?" These quiet seconds of reflection allowed Moore to enter a "zone" in which opportunities rapidly crystallized. By refusing to surrender the tactical initiative to the enemy, Moore dictated the course of the battle to the best of his ability, directing arriving units to the most dangerous portions of the battlefield, often minutes before the enemy attacked.

The third principle is, "When there's nothing wrong, there is nothing wrong except there's nothing wrong!" That was exactly when a leader must be most alert. On the morning of the battle's second day, Moore noticed that things were too quiet, not even the birds were singing. Something in his gut told him that something was wrong, so he directed each company to send out patrols. Within minutes these patrols intercepted the enemy as the NVA moved into position to assault Moore's beleaguered troopers. The Americans repelled the attack, inflicting massive casualties on the enemy.

Last, Moore urged the cadets to trust their instincts. In a rapidly developing battle, one's instincts amount to an instant estimate of the situation. There is no time to conduct a detailed commander's estimate by rule book and to make a matrix of alternative courses of action. An officer's instincts are the product of education, training, reading, personality, and experience according to Moore. Leaders must act fast and impart confidence. Don't second guess decisions. Face up to the facts, deal with them, and move on to the next situation. In the Ia Drang's opening minutes, Moore's instincts told him that the enemy commander was likely to strike on his left flank, heading for the clearing that marked the landing zone. As soon as Moore's Charlie Company arrived on the landing zone, he directed them to take position on Alpha Company's left, taking the risk of leaving his own rear unguarded from the north and east. They arrived just as the NVA launched an attack.

Moore concluded his remarks by stressing the bond that exists between a commander and his soldiers. When one cadet inquired about the feeling of comrades in arms, Moore's eyes welled with tears and he said, "When your men die and you don't, you feel guilty. That's all I can say about it." Years after the Battle in the Ia Drang Valley, Moore made annual pilgrimages to the cemetery at Fort Benning, Georgia, where several of his troopers are interred, and to the Vietnam Veterans' War Memorial in Washington, DC. In the wake of the tragedy of September 11, the old commander, then in his eightieth year, paid his respects to Rick Rescorla, a former lieutenant who died in the destruction of the World Trade Center.

How was Moore received by West Point's Corps of Cadets? A random sample of unedited comments tells the story. "The most important part of Gen. Moore's lecture was the advice on how people should lead," noted one cadet. Another said, "The single most noteworthy accomplishment was being able to keep his cool and composure while on the verge of being overrun. . . . He inspired me to always remain optimistic, even when things look bad." Yet another remarked, "I was hanging on every word. It was the best lecture I have ever heard at West Point. . . . I would have stayed and listened to him all night if that were possible."

Perhaps the most touching comment came from a first-class cadet who said Moore's presentation was the "best, most down-to-earth lecture I have ever experienced. It made me feel proud becoming an officer and entering into the army as a profession. His words are inspirational, and his experiences are a model of admiration. I wish I would have gone Infantry."

How many other cadets Moore inspired to select Infantry as a branch is speculative, but the general consensus that April evening was that listening to Hal Moore made these cadets better future commanders. Listening to Moore could make one a better officer and possibly a better person.

One final observation. In the audience the night Moore addressed the Corps was *New York Times* reporter John Kifver, who asked Moore whether his comments were on the record. "All my comments are for the record," Moore replied. "Feel free to publish anything you desire." In the subsequent column that graced the front page of the *Times*, Kifver described Moore as a "courtly old warrior."

In the final analysis, Moore typified the finest attributes of the US Army's officer corps and West Point's motto of "Duty, Honor, Country." His mantra for years was "hate war, love the American warrior." As heroic and inspirational as his battlefield leadership was in countless battles in two foreign wars, however, Moore's greatest legacy remains the preparation of future officers to lead America's finest soldiers into battle. That is why he is cherished by officers and soldiers alike.

"Beyond the Ia Drang Valley" was originally published in *ARMY Magazine* (November 2002).

56

Team of Two

Moore Is Recognized for Exceptional Service

After Congress created the Naming Commission to rename army military posts that honored Confederate officers, commissioners recommended changing the name of Fort Benning, Georgia, to Fort Moore. The recommendation to honor both Lt. Gen. Harold "Hal" Moore and Julia "Julie" Compton Moore makes sense: The couple defined the role of command team long before family support groups became the norm.

In November 1965, then–Lt. Col. Moore commanded the First Battalion, Seventh Cavalry Regiment, during the first pitched battle of the Vietnam War, in the Central Highlands of South Vietnam. Moore and United Press International correspondent Joseph Galloway later described the fighting in the Ia Drang Valley in two books: *We Were Soldiers Once and Young: Ia Drang—The Battle That Changed the War in Vietnam* and *We Are Soldiers Still: A Journey Back to the Battlefields of Vietnam*. Moore's combat exploits were later featured in the 2002 movie *We Were Soldiers*, starring Mel Gibson.

Throughout her husband's career, Julie Moore established family support groups. These groups have since become common throughout the Department of Defense. And in the midst of the Ia Drang fighting, she challenged the army's impersonal practice of delivering death notices by telegram to grieving families.

Soldier's Soldier

Born in Bardstown, Kentucky, in 1922, Hal Moore was destined to be a soldier. He held a deep fascination for all things military and aspired to be an army officer from an early age. Matriculating to the US Military Academy at West Point, New York, in 1942, Moore struggled academically. He described his cadet experience as an "academic trip to Hell." In later years, Moore took great pride in graduating in the top 15 percent of the bottom 15 percent of his West Point Class of 1945.

Commissioned in the infantry, Moore found his true calling in leading soldiers. Early assignments included with the 187th Glider Infantry Regiment at Camp Crawford near Sapporo, Japan, and the Eighty-Second Airborne Division at Fort Bragg, North Carolina. Always fascinated by airborne warfare, Moore volunteered for Fort Bragg's Airborne Test Section, a special unit that was testing experimental parachutes. Over the course of his career, Moore became a master parachutist with more than three hundred jumps.

During the Korean War, Moore, by then a seasoned officer, served with distinction as a heavy mortar company commander; as the Seventeenth Infantry Regimental assistant chief of staff of operations and plans; and as Company K commander in the Seventh Infantry Division. Receiving an accelerated promotion to major, Moore returned to West Point, where he served for three years as an instructor in infantry tactics.

HEADING FOR THE HIGHLANDS

In 1964, Moore assumed command of the Second Battalion, Twenty-Third Infantry Regiment, part of the Eleventh Air Assault Division (Test) at Fort Benning. When President Lyndon Johnson announced on July 28, 1965, that he was sending the division to Vietnam, Moore's battalion was redesignated the First Battalion, Seventh Cavalry Regiment, and his division was redesignated the First Cavalry Division (Airmobile).

By late summer, the First Cavalry was stationed in South Vietnam's Central Highlands. Beginning November 14, 1965, Moore led his battalion in a fierce battle around Landing Zone X-Ray in the Ia Drang Valley. For his extraordinary heroism and gallantry in action around Landing Zone X-Ray, Moore received the Distinguished Service Cross. Following the Battle of Ia Drang, he was promoted to colonel and took command of the Third Brigade, First Cavalry Division. He led the brigade in the Bong Son campaign of 1966.

Over the remainder of his career, Moore became the first member of his West Point class to be promoted to one-star, two-star, and three-star rank.

His assignments included commander of the Seventh Infantry Division; commander of Fort Ord, California, and an army training center there; and army deputy chief of staff for personnel.

Lt. Gen. Moore retired from active service in 1977 following thirty-two years of commissioned service. His awards include the Distinguished Service Cross, Army Distinguished Service Medal, Legion of Merit with two bronze oak leaf clusters, Bronze Star (four awards, including two for valor), and multiple other medals.

Another of Moore's significant contributions to the army lay far from the battlefields of Korea and South Vietnam. He accepted invitations from the service academies military schools and commands within the US Army to speak about the principles of leadership and his combat experience. As he wrote in *We Are Soldiers Still,* I felt "an obligation to give something back to our country and our troops. . . . I owe that to this new generation of warriors just as I owe it to my fallen comrades."

In recognition of Moore's contributions to a spiring officers at West Point, the US Military Academy in 2010 instituted the Lt. Gen. Harold "Hal" G. Moore Warrior Athlete of Excellence Award. West Point presents the award to the top male and female athletes in their senior year.

Born at Fort Sill, Oklahoma, on February 10, 1929, to Col. and Mrs. Louis Compton Julie Moore's life was inextricably linked to the army. Married in 1949, Julie Moore joined her husband at Fort Bragg, and they began raising a family. She "served as the rock of our family," her husband said, and her quiet heroism during five of America's conflicts in which those she loved served in combat—World War II, Korea, Vietnam, Panama, and the First Gulf War—proved invaluable in times of crisis and helped Hal Moore build unit cohesion.

Over the course of their marriage, Hal and Julie Moore lived in nine states, two foreign countries and twenty-five different homes. At every post where they lived, Julie Moore did everything possible to assist soldiers' families. Those duties included hosting official functions, organizing childcare facilities and serving as a Red Cross volunteer in various military hospitals.

In November 1965, then the wife of a Fort Benning battalion commander whose unit had deployed to South Vietnam, Julie Moore made perhaps her greatest contribution to the army. She followed taxi drivers from house to house, trailer park to trailer park, in Columbus, Georgia, as they delivered telegrams to army wives informing them that they had lost their husbands. She personally comforted the bereaved family members and attended the funeral of every soldier lost in combat.

Along with the wife of the First Cavalry Division's commanding general, Julie Moore bombarded the Pentagon with telephone calls and letters, insisting that the army's impersonal notifications to families of fallen soldiers be changed. Within weeks, the policy was changed. An army officer and an army chaplain began to personally break the news to bereaved family members.

When one of her sons deployed to Kuwait on the eve of Operation Desert Storm in 1990, Julie Moore clearly understood a soldier's life and worried that her son might not return. Hal Moore's coauthor, Galloway, expressed astonishment that since Julie Moore had sent both her father and her husband to war, she ought to be used to combat deployments.

Julie Moore's response was swift: "Joe Galloway, you don't understand one damn thing about this. You can replace a husband, but you can never replace a son!"

I met Hal Moore on numerous occasions when he visited West Point to address my classes about combat leadership during the Vietnam War. His message to me and the Corps of Cadets was always the same: Hate war but love the American warrior.

Julie Moore extended her appreciation to me for repeatedly welcoming her husband to West Point. Following her death in 2004, I visited Moore at his home in Auburn, Alabama. Three times over the course of our interview, Moore spoke lovingly about his wife, stating, "A soldier needs his mate. My wife was every inch a soldier as I was."

Hal Moore died in 2017, two days shy of what would have been his ninety-fifth birthday. His grave marker notes that he was "devoted to faith, family and service." Galloway, Moore's friend for over a half-century delivered a powerful eulogy, stating, "Hal Moore, you changed my life. . . . I have loved you as a brother and a father. . . . You were my captain in battle."

Hal and Julie Moore lay today in the Old Post Cemetery at Fort Benning, in the arms of what Julie Moore frequently called "Holy Mother Army."

"Team of Two: Moore Is Recognized for Exceptional Service" was originally published in *Army Magazine* (March 2023)

57

America's Greatest Battle Captains

Who's Your Pick for Top of the Class?

In the nearly two and a half centuries of its existence, the US Army has fielded a formidable array of battle captains who have made their indelible imprint on the history of the United States. However, Lt. Gen. Winfield Scott, Gens. John Pershing, Douglas MacArthur, H. Norman Schwarzkopf, and a host of others are but a footnote to history in the minds of most Americans, as the memories of their achievements have faded from national consciousness. They were outstanding commanders, and their achievements thrilled the nation. Today, they are rarely mentioned other than in the pages of military histories.

But which army officer who wore stars on his shoulders deserves recognition as America's greatest battle captain? Does a general have to win all his battles to be considered a great captain? Does a commander have to achieve sustained excellence in warfare to reach exalted status?

Each of us has an opinion, but here are a few suggestions as to who holds the title of America's greatest field commander.

During the Revolutionary War era, two generals stand in the forefront of military leaders: Gen. George Washington and Maj. Gen. Nathanael Greene. Washington lost more battles than he won, but his greatest achievement was keeping the Continental Army intact through nearly eight years of war. His tactical victories at Trenton and Princeton, both in New Jersey, reinvigorated the Patriot cause in the war's darkest days. With the help of the French, Washington supervised the final victory over British Gen. Lord Charles Cornwallis at Yorktown, Virginia, on October

19, 1781, ensuring American independence. No commander in chief faced more formidable obstacles than Washington did. He is, indeed, "first in war."

With the destruction of two Continental armies in South Carolina in 1780, Washington appointed Greene commander of the American Southern Department. In short order, Greene employed the unorthodox strategy of partisan warfare to reverse the tide of American fortunes. "We fight, get beat, rise and fight again" characterized Greene's Southern campaign.

Perhaps the most successful commander in the antebellum period is Winfield Scott, the conqueror of Mexico City in the Mexican–American War of 1846–1848. Scott's campaign from Veracruz to Mexico City drew adulation from the Duke of Wellington, Europe's most distinguished soldier. The Iron Duke stated that Scott's "campaign was unsurpassed in military annals. [Scott] is the greatest living soldier."

Several of Scott's junior officers emerged from the Mexican conflict to lead armies and corps in the Civil War. Along with William Tecumseh Sherman, who did not see combat during the war with Mexico, future Gens. Robert Lee and Ulysses Grant and Lt. Gen. Thomas "Stonewall" Jackson earned reputations as adept commanders. Lee and Jackson were unmatched as tactical commanders. Jackson fell victim to friendly fire at the peak of his greatest triumph at Chancellorsville, Virginia, and Lee protracted the war for two more years before he surrendered at Appomattox, Virginia, on April 9, 1865.

Lee was, in essence, a military genius of the Napoleonic era, out of tune with the technological and industrial advances of modern warfare. The defeat at Gettysburg, Pennsylvania aside, Lee was magnificent in defeat, an American Hannibal who achieved improbable tactical success, but ultimately succumbed to overwhelming resources of a more prosperous antagonist.

No general, North or South, achieved greater martial success than Grant. Lee may have been the better tactician, but Grant proved to be the superior strategist. Once given command of all Northern armies in March 1864, Grant orchestrated the strategy that ensured Union victory over the Confederacy. Grant's premier protege, then–Maj. Gen. Sherman, complemented his strategy of indirect approach and attritional warfare at Atlanta and the subsequent March to the Sea. Both deserve accolades as two of America's most distinguished soldiers.

In the early twentieth century, John Pershing, commander in chief of the American Expeditionary Forces in World War I, remains America's most notable battle captain prior to World War II. Following the end of "the war to end all wars," Congress elevated Pershing to the rank of general of the armies of the United States as a reward for his service during that conflict.

The second global conflict produced the most recognizable commanders in US history. Gens. Dwight Eisenhower, Douglas MacArthur, and George Patton Jr. emerged from World War II in resplendent glory. Of the three commanders, MacArthur received mixed reviews from contemporary and modern military historians. MacArthur's heroic defenses of Bataan and Corregidor, both in the Philippines, galvanized a nation hungry for heroes following the disaster at Pearl Harbor. From 1943 to 1945, MacArthur successfully executed the island-hopping campaign that then liberated the Philippines. And it was General of the Army MacArthur who accepted the Japanese surrender on the deck of the battleship *Missouri* on September 2, 1945. During the Korean War, MacArthur conducted an amphibious assault at Inchon that serves as a model of sheer audacity that turned the tide of the war.

On the operational level of war, Patton stands alone. No more than two or three officers are worthy of comparison. Patton's conquest of western Sicily in 1943, the breakout from Normandy, France, and the relief of Bastogne, Belgium, in December 1944 serve as his greatest accomplishments. Patton's untimely demise as a result of an automobile accident in December 1945 propelled Third US Army to legendary status and ensured Patton's memory will never be diminished.

Among the American commanders who served with distinction in World War II, none received greater fame than Eisenhower. Before the war, Eisenhower possessed limited field experience. He commanded a training camp at Gettysburg in 1918 and an infantry battalion for a brief time in 1940. Two years later, Army Chief of Staff Gen. George Marshall propelled Eisenhower to command the Mediterranean Theater and, later, the Northwest European Theater. Eisenhower clearly understood that Allied victory would be achieved by all members of the coalition. With

Eisenhower as Supreme Allied Commander, the Allies successfully landed in France on D-Day and, later, achieved the destruction of Hitler's forces in Western Europe.

In the Cold War era, several commanders merited recognition as superb leaders in battle. When President Harry Truman relieved MacArthur of command of United Nations forces in April 1951 during the Korean War, the president replaced him with Lt. Gen. Matthew Ridgway. Ridgway had compiled a distinguished record as a division and corps commander in World War II. When he arrived in Korea in December 1950, Ridgway restored the fighting spirit of US Eighth Army, then energized the UN forces. Truman was so impressed with Ridgway that he designated Ridgway as Eisenhower's replacement as Supreme Allied Commander of NATO's military forces.

Two generals from the Vietnam War should be listed in the ranks of America's notable commanders: Gens. William Westmoreland and Creighton Abrams Jr. As commanders of Military Assistance Command, Vietnam, both officers led American forces in the most unpopular war in American history. Each achieved limited success, but their military strategies failed to achieve the political goals of two presidential administrations. In recent times, Schwarzkopf commanded coalition forces in Operation Desert Storm to expel Iraqi dictator Saddam Hussein from Kuwait in 1991. His adept employment of the principles of operational art remains a sterling example for future commanders in the post–Cold War era.

According to military historian Martin Blumenson, there is no objective way to measure generalship. Each situation in which a general officer serves is unique, and some commanders are more controversial than others. For the sake of argument, I'd like to offer my personal observations concerning those officers who have achieved legendary status as great captains.

As a coalition commander, Eisenhower stands alone. More than any commander, Eisenhower matured in the job, from North Africa to Sicily, and through the campaign in northwest Europe. Beset by political intrigue among the senior political leaders of the Grand Alliance and egotistical subordinates such as Field Marshal Bernard Law Montgomery and Patton, Eisenhower ensured the ultimate victory over Nazi Germany would be an Allied victory, not a national triumph, with British and American forces contributing an equal role.

Multiple commanders have demonstrated tactical acumen on the battlefield in the US Army's history, including Brig. Gen. Daniel Morgan, Lt. Gen. James Gavin, and Lt. Gen. Clarence Huebner. The list seems endless, but Lee occupies first place. The Battle of Gettysburg and the current political environment have diminished his status as America's premier tactician. Always outnumbered by his opponents, Lee's victories at Second Manassas (Bull Run), Virginia; Antietam, Maryland; Fredericksburg and Chancellorsville, both in Virginia; and the individual engagements of the Overland Campaign of 1864 in Virginia are unmatched by any American commander.

On the operational level, Patton reigns supreme, with Scott a distant second. When summoned by Eisenhower to restore the fighting spirit of the American Army at Kasserine Pass in Africa, Patton imbued his fighting spirit, reversing the tide of battle at Gafsa and El Guetter. The operations of Patton's newly formed US Seventh Army in Sicily were "going to be classed as a model of swift conquest by future classes in the War College and Leavenworth," Eisenhower told Army Chief of Staff Gen. George Marshall. In Normandy, Patton transformed a local breakthrough to a theater breakout. Patton's crowning achievement occurred in Belgium, where he changed Third Army's attack ninety degrees and relieved the beleaguered garrison at Bastogne. He was the indispensable army-level commander for Allied victory in Europe.

So, who serves as America's premier battle captain? That honor, in my opinion, goes to Grant. From humble origins, Grant emerged from the Civil War as the most successful general on either side. Over the course of the conflict, Grant destroyed three Confederate armies: first at Fort Donelson, Tennessee, in 1862; then at Vicksburg, Mississippi, in July 1863; and finally, the fabled Army of Northern Virginia at Appomattox, Virginia, in 1865. Grant embodied the essence of total war in the industrial era. In the process, he became not only the savior of the Union but also the US Army's greatest field commander.

"America's Greatest Battle Captains: Who's Your Pick for Top of the Class?" was originally published in *ARMY Magazine* (June 2021).

58

Women Played Roles in Army from the Start

The assimilation of women into the US Army has been a centuries-long process. The beginning can be traced back as early as 1775, when Gen. George Washington asked Congress to authorize the assignment of one civilian nurse for every ten soldier patients. Now, some 247 years later, female soldiers are fully integrated into combat units. We know the names and stories of some of those early heroines: Margaret Corbin and Deborah Sampson from the Revolutionary War; and Sally Louisa Tompkins, Dorothea Dix, Clara Barton, Mary "Mother" Bickerdyke, and Cathay Williams of the Civil War era. Many other names are lost to history.

Three women stand out when examining the evolutionary role of women in the army. Dr. Mary Walker, Beatrice Mary MacDonald, and First Lt. Annie Fox were army pioneers. Their competence, bravery in the line of duty and tremendous personal sacrifice brought visibility to the role women could play in the army they served—and changed the opportunities available to the women who followed.

Born in Oswego County, New York, in 1832, Walker graduated as the only woman in her class from Syracuse Medical College, New York, in 1855. At the outbreak of the Civil War, Walker applied for a commission as a US Army surgeon. Rejected because of gender discrimination, she ministered to casualties as a civilian doctor at the Battles of First Bull Run and Fredericksburg, both in Virginia, and Chickamauga, Georgia. Maj. Gen. George Thomas was so impressed with Walker's service near Chattanooga, Tennessee, that he appointed her as a contract assistant surgeon in the Army of the Cumberland, which Thomas commanded. In April 1864, Walker was captured by Confederate troops and imprisoned before being exchanged for a Confederate surgeon in August 1864.

Immediately on her release from captivity, Walker rejoined Maj. Gen. William Tecumseh Sherman's army outside of Atlanta, where she cared for wounded American soldiers in the battles around Georgia's capital. Despite her repeated attempts to remain in the field, the War Department transferred Walker to a women's prison hospital in Louisville, Kentucky, and later to an orphanage in Clarksville, Tennessee, where she remained until the cessation of hostilities.

Following the war, Walker lobbied for a commission due to her wartime service but was unsuccessful given her civilian status. However, both Sherman and Thomas recommended her for the Medal of Honor, and President Andrew Johnson signed the order on November 11, 1865. Walker's citation states that she "rendered valuable service to the Government, and her efforts have been earnest and untiring . . . and she has devoted herself with much patriotic zeal to the sick and wounded soldiers, both in the field and hospitals, to the detriment of her own health, and has also endured hardships as a prisoner of war."

On February 5, 1916, the War Department's Medal of Honor Review Board released its findings, rescinding the medals of 911 individuals, including Walker's. The board determined their service did not meet the criteria for the nation's highest award for military valor in action. More than a half-century later, however, the Army Board for Correction of Military Records reviewed Walker's case and recommended that her award be restored. On June 10, 1977, President Jimmy Carter signed an executive order posthumously reinstating Walker as the first and only woman to receive the nation's highest award for valor.

Two-and-a-half years after the War Department revoked Walker's Medal of Honor, army nurse Beatrice MacDonald became one of six women who received the Distinguished Service Cross during World War I. Canadian by birth, MacDonald immigrated to New York and completed her nursing training in 1905. When the Great War commenced, she volunteered for the American Ambulance Service.

Following a short stint with the American Hospital of Paris, MacDonald enlisted in the US Nurse Corps in 1917 with a unit organized by Presbyterian Hospital, now part of New York Presbyterian Hospital. On the night of August 17, 1917, a German shell exploded at a military field hospital in Belgium, severely wounding MacDonald during her shift caring for wounded Allied soldiers during the Third Battle of Ypres. After six weeks spent recovering from her injury, MacDonald returned to duty in military hospitals in France and Belgium. After the war, she served with Allied forces in occupied Germany until returning to the United States in 1919.

For her dedicated and exemplary service, MacDonald received the Distinguished Service Cross on February 17, 1919. She also received the French Croix de Guerre with Bronze Star, British Royal Red Cross (second class) and the British Military Medal. Like other World War I veterans, MacDonald had to apply for her Purple Heart after Army Chief of Staff Gen. Douglas MacArthur signed the order creating the modern Purple Heart on February 22, 1932. On January 4, 1936, MacDonald received the first Purple Heart awarded to a female soldier.

On December 7, 1941, First Lt. Annie Fox was serving as head nurse at Hickam Field's Station Hospital, Hawaii. Having enlisted in 1918, a few months before the end of World War I, Fox was a twenty-three-year veteran of the army at the time of the Japanese attack. Although she had served in the military for more than two decades, the attack on Pearl Harbor was the first time Fox had been under hostile fire.

Quickly rallying her nurses, she organized the hospital's response to the enemy assault. Over the course of the day, Fox's team applied dressings to hundreds of wounded servicemen and assisted with patient care. As head nurse, Fox participated in surgery, administered anesthesia and organized civilian medical volunteers under her immediate supervision. For her extraordinary bravery under fire, Fox was awarded the Purple Heart on September 23, 1942. She became the first US servicewoman during World War II to receive the award. Later, the Purple Heart was awarded to soldiers wounded or killed in action, but at the beginning of the war, the medal was for any "singularly meritorious act of extraordinary fidelity or essential service."

Fox's citation for the Purple Heart reads, "During the attack, Lieutenant Fox, in an exemplary manner, performed her duties as head nurse of the Station Hospital. In addition, she administered anesthesia to patients during the heaviest part of the bombardment, assisted in dressing the wounded, taught civilian volunteer nurses to make dressings, and worked ceaselessly with coolness and efficiency, and her fine example of calmness, courage, and leadership was a great benefit to the morale of all with whom she came in contact."

In 1944, a War Department review board convened and considered Fox's record. By majority rule, the board recommended that Fox receive the Bronze Star in lieu of the Purple Heart, as she had not been wounded in action. Although greatly disappointed by the board's finding, Fox continued to serve for the duration of the war, retiring from military service on December 31, 1945.

Walker, MacDonald, and Fox paved the way for women who have served the United States honorably during and since World War II. In the aftermath of Pearl Harbor, Edith Nourse Rogers, a member of Congress from Massachusetts, in May 1941, introduced the first bill to establish a women's army auxiliary. A year later, on May 14, 1942, Congress approved the creation of a Women's Army Auxiliary Corps (WAAC). Oveta Culp Hobby was appointed the first director of the WAACs.

As an auxiliary of the army, the WAAC possessed no military status. To address what she considered a gross injustice, Rogers introduced another bill in 1943 to enlist and appoint women in the US Army. President Franklin Roosevelt signed the bill on July 1, and 90 days later, the WAAC was discontinued. In its place the Women's Army Corps (WAC) came into existence. Hobby continued as director of the WAC.

Six months before women received military status, the first WAAC contingent had arrived in Algeria, North Africa. In July 1943, the first WAAC Separate Battalion arrived in England, led by Lt. Col. Mary Hallaren. Two years later, Maj. Charity Adams commanded the first and only female, all-Black battalion deployed overseas during World War II, the 6888th Central Postal Directory Battalion. Later, Hallaren was instrumental in securing passage of the Women's Armed Services Integration Act of 1948, becoming the first female commissioned officer in the Regular Army.

Other women followed the footsteps of these pioneers. In 1979, Brig. Gen. Hazel Johnson served as the first African American chief of the Army Nurse Corps. In November 2008, Gen. Ann Dunwoody became the first female four-star officer in the army. And in 2015, Maj. Gen. Nadja West served as the army's first female African American to achieve a two- and three-star rank. Later, West became the forty-fourth surgeon general of the army.

Today's soldiers owe an immense debt to the pioneers who championed gender integration of the army. The US fields a better army because of them. Their achievements should never be forgotten.

"Women Played Roles in Army from the Start" was originally published in *ARMY Magazine* (June 2022).

Acknowledgments

I CAN NEVER HOPE TO ASSIGN PROPER CREDIT TO THE MILITARY VETERans, past and present, and to the military historians who have made possible this seventh book that I have written. My entire adult life revolves around the concept of leadership. I spent thirty years of commissioned service as an infantry officer in the US Army, followed by two additional decades of corporate leadership consultant. I founded two consulting companies, Brecourt Leadership Experience Inc. and Battlefield Leadership LLC, both of which specialized in bringing corporate leaders to battlefields to examine the connections between military and corporate leaders in times of crisis and uncertainty.

Visits to these battlefields reinforced my lifelong interest in leadership at all levels, from both military and civilian perspectives. The preceding essays remind me that leaders frequently encounter similar challenges, among which are dealing with ambiguities, influencing upwardly, character-based decisions, and ensuring a leader's intent is comprehended throughout the organization two levels up and two levels down. American heroes and heroines throughout our history have risen to the challenge and answered our nation's call to arms.

I would be remiss if I did not acknowledge three superb historians who have influenced my study of leadership: Allan R. Millett, Martin Blumenson, and Stephen E. Ambrose. As a graduate student at Ohio State University from 1978 to 1980, I had the distinct honor of having Professor Millett serve as my faculty advisor. I was a junior military officer when I arrived at the university, en route to my first tour of duty as an instructor at the US Military Academy at West Point, New York. Millett immediately took me under his wing and supervised my study, always offering sage advice that allowed me to earn a doctorate in history before I returned to field duty as an army officer.

To military historian Stephen E. Ambrose, I owe an incalculable debt. I first met Ambrose on the centennial anniversary of Dwight D. Eisenhower's birth in a symposium sponsored by Gettysburg College in Gettysburg, Pennsylvania, in 1990. I was familiar with his work on D-Day and his many other publications. Over the course of the next decade, I attended many of Ambrose's symposia in New Orleans, Louisiana, and at Cantigny, Illinois. Through Ambrose, I met many veterans of World War II, particularly those who served on D-Day, June 6, 1944. And it was Ambrose who was solely responsible for Louisiana State University Press publishing my first book, *President Eisenhower and the Suez Crisis of 1956*. Years later, I paid tribute to Steven Ambrose by informing him that I had strived to imitate his writing style that I classified "conversational history." Ambrose chuckled and said that was high praise indeed, but do not feel overly grateful, because he had imitated his style from his mentor, William B. Hesseltine.

Martin Blumenson, the dean of Gen. George S. Patton biographers, was not only the editor of the two-volume *The Patton Papers* and numerous works on Patton and World War II but also a close personal friend. It was Blumenson who encouraged me to write for *ARMY magazine*, whose articles fill these pages. To my everlasting gratitude, Blumenson suggested that I focus the majority of my writing on the exploits of what commentator Tom Brokaw labeled "The Greatest Generation."

At the Association of the United States Army (AUSA) the redoubtable triumvirate of editors in chief Mary Blake French, Rick Maze, and Michelle Tan all provided constant support of my literary efforts over the past three decades. So too did managing editor Elizabeth Rathbun and Joseph Craig, the director of AUSA's Book Program. More than anyone, Joe was instrumental in getting this book published. I am also extremely grateful to Dave Reisch, senior acquisition editor of Stackpole Books. To Dave and Joe Craig, I owe an incalculable debt. Through the good offices of AUSA, I renewed my relationship with Roger Cirillo and my dear friend Kevin Hymel, both of whom supported my writings with timely photographs and suggestions to enhance the text.

I am especially grateful to friends and family who have always been available to offer recommendations and guidance: Gen. David A. Bramlett, US-retired; Lt. Gens. James Dubik and H. R. McMaster, US-retired;

retired Cols. Paul L. Miles, US, and Gregory Fontenot, US; and historians Carlo D'Este and John McManus have inspired me with their mentorship and personal writings. I owe special thanks to Morgan FitzGerald who typed the manuscript and edited the text. Thank you all for many moments of affection and tutelage. As always, I owe a special debt to my wife and soul mate, Mary, who has tolerated my prolonged absences to visit foreign and domestic battlefields and my visits to the warriors who have shaped our country's destiny with their sacrifices and service in war and peace. I offer my sincere apologies to those whom I have inadvertently omitted, but my gratitude to these unheralded leaders and friends remains paramount.

Any errors in this book are of course my responsibility, but my shortcomings should never detract from the accomplishments of the dedicated men and women listed in the text who have served our nation in peace and war. The views presented herein are also mine alone and do not represent the Department of Defense or its components, including the United States Army. Nor do they represent the Association of the US Army.

www.ingramcontent.com/pod-product-compliance
Ingram Content Group UK Ltd.
Pitfield, Milton Keynes, MK11 3LW, UK
UKHW032147120826
7880IPUK00002B/25

9 780811 778503